PASSPORT'S GU SO-AXL-074

ETHNIC

CHICAGO

A Complete Guide
to the Many Faces
& Cultures of
Chicago

RICHARD LINDBERG

PASSPORT BOOKS
a division of *NTC Publishing Group*
Lincolnwood, Illinois USA

Cover Photos

American Egg Board (Front, upper left; Back, lower)
Government of India Tourist Office (Front, upper right, lower left; Back, upper left)
Greater Milwaukee Convention and Visitors Bureau, Inc. (Back, upper right)
Korean National Tourism Corporation (Front, lower right)
New York Convention and Visitors Bureau (Front, middle right)
Terry Farmer/Illinois Department of Commerce and Community Affairs (Front, middle left)

Contents

List of Maps

Acknowledgments

I am indebted to the following people for generously sharing with me their rich insights, during these last two years of research and exploration into Chicago's ethnic treasures. Without their help this book could not have reached its successful conclusion. Helen Alexander/UHAC; Elisabeth Angele/the Goethe Institute; Maria Bappart/Lincoln Square Chamber of Commerce; Roy J. Bellavia/WSBC-AM; Tony Burroughs/the Afro-American Genealogical Society; George Cheung; Pauris Dadadahoi; Mrs. Raymond Dojinski; Jane Edwards/Mitchell Indian Museum; James Futris/the Hellenic Museum; Irene Gajecky; Marge Greenberg; John Griffin/Gaelic Park; Teri Hays/Scottish Cultural Society; Stephen Hormann; Birute Jasaitis/the Lithuanian Community; Gretchen Johnson/North Park College; Nathan Kaplan/Merry Gangsters; Frank Kilker/the Irish American Heritage Center; Gera-Lind Kolarik; Thelma Krupp; Kerstin Lane/the Swedish American Museum Center; Denise Lindberg; Roy Lundberg; Anne Lunde; Diane McKay/the Museum of Science and Industry; Pawel Migacz/the Polish Zgoda; Joan Murphy/the British Club; Timothy O'Connell; Alice Palach/CSA Fraternal Life; Rodica Perciali/the Romanian Museum; Anilkumar Pillai/the Federation of India Association; Val Ramonis/the Balzekas Museum; Fred Randazzo/the Joint Civic Community of Italian Americans; Bill Reilly/Merry Gangsters; Roberto Roque/Filipino American Council of Chicago; Michael Ross; Walter Roth/the Jewish Historical Society; Norman Scaman/Cermak Road Business Association; Dan Sharon/the Asher Library; Charlie Soo/the Asian American Small Business Association; Kathy Taylor/the Irish Fellowship Club; Adele Vacek; Faro Vitale; Anna Williams; Dee and Patrick Woodtar.

Judith Helm—in memoriam.

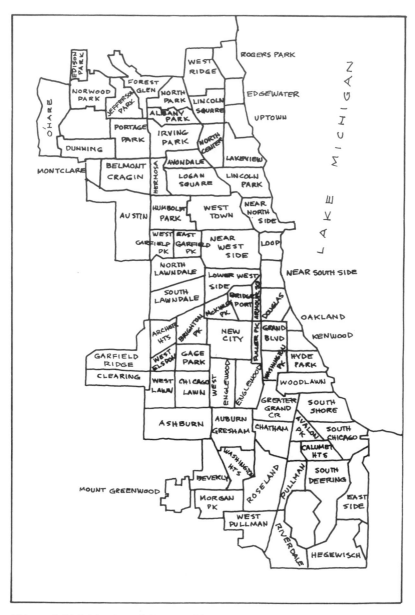

Chicago's Neighborhood Communities

Introduction

When the French *voyageur* Louis Joliet returned to Canada from his historic expedition of 1673 down the Mississippi River, he reported to the Comte de Frontenac, New France's "Fighting Governor," the many natural wonders he had observed. Joliet boldly declared that this land of the tall grass—described by the English cartographer Herman Moll as the "carriage of Chekakou"—was all that stood in the way of linking the Great Lakes to the drainage basin of the Mississippi River system. If there could be a way to successfully negotiate the "Chicago Portage," French military power could encompass the western frontier from Canada to the Gulf of Mexico. But as Robert Cavelier Sieur de La Salle was to find out later, any hope of turning the marshy swamp at the shore of Lake Michigan into a commercial trading port for France was marred by the natural barriers posed by the land and the water. The Des Plaines River could only be navigated by canoe, which thwarted any plan to bring goods into Chicago by barge. Spring flooding was another problem that canceled out Joliet's carefully laid plans. This land had many possibilities as a strategic military outpost, but for purposes of trade and commerce, the obstacles seemed almost insurmountable to the seventeenth century explorers. In the winter of 1674, Father Jacques Marquette established a campsight at the present-day intersection of Damen Avenue and the south branch of the Chicago River, but it was LaSalle who eventually succeeded in claiming the entire Mississippi Basin for the greater glory of France on April 9, 1682. He named this land "Louisiana" in honor of the French king, and a year later established Fort Saint Louis at the Starved Rock site on the Illinois River. The military outpost and French settlement was located about sixty miles west of Chicago. But France was forced to relinquish all military and political claims to this territory on February 10, 1763, by the terms of the Treaty of Paris, which put an end to the costly seven-year war with England. For many years Chicago continued to remain a desolate, marshy mudflat, inhabited exclusively by Indians.

One hundred years after Joliet completed his historic mission for de Frontenac, Jean Baptiste Point Du Sable, the mulatto son of a French merchant and a Haitian woman, became the first non-Indian resident of Chicago. He conducted regular trade with other trappers, merchants, and adventurers who found the area much to their liking. The explosive economic growth of Chicago foretold by Joliet in the seventeenth century was hastened by events taking shape in the East. The opening of the Erie Canal in 1825 linked the Atlantic seaboard states to the Great Lakes region, and for the first time shifted the westward movement of goods, services, and people northward from the Ohio River. Thus Chicago's strategic location on the Great Lakes made *it,* rather than the older, entrenched river cities of Cincinnati or St. Louis, the major western terminus of the nation. The Illinois-Michigan Canal, linking the Great Lakes and the Mississippi systems (a project completed in 1848) and a pair of railroad lines that connected the city to the eastern markets beginning in 1852, permanently secured Chicago's place as the commercial heartland of the burgeoning West. On Christmas Day of 1865, the consolidated Union Stockyards opened for business on Chicago's South Side. This project was financed by the nine railroad consortiums that regularly transported cattle, hogs, and sheep from the "cowtowns" west of the Mississippi River for slaughter in the Midwest markets.

But it was the construction of the canal that was the impetus for the arrival of the first great wave of European immigrants—the "potato famine" Irish, who came to the U.S. brimming with the expectation of good-paying jobs digging the costly new waterway. The unparalleled growth of Chicago in the middle to late nineteenth century was made possible by the hard work and industry of succeeding waves of immigrants who left their homeland for much the same reasons: political upheaval, economic deprivation, and religious and ethnic persecution at the hands of the host government. The Irish were followed by trainloads of Scandinavians, Germans, Poles, Bohemians, Greeks, Italians, Russian Jews, and smaller Eastern European groups in that imprecise order. There were few Asians and Hispanics counted in the census during this earliest period of Chicago history; their numbers rapidly accelerated after World War II, particularly during the 1960s and 1970s. The city's African-American population was small before 1900, but changing social patterns in the "Jim Crow" South and improved communications with the urban corridors of the industrial North spurred the great migration beginning around 1907.

Population statistics tell us much about the demographic and ethnic makeup of a region. In 1970, for example, the major countries of origin represented in the city census included Poland, Germany, Italy, the Soviet

Union, Sweden, and Ireland. Ten years later, African-Americans, the Spanish-speaking and Asian peoples, were shown to be the fastest growing ethnic groups in the city. These changing realities inevitably upset the political equilibrium that guided Chicago's destiny since the time of the Civil War. Blacks accounted for two-fifths of the city's population in 1980, and as a result they were able to wrest considerable power away from the white ethnics who had controlled the municipal departments and the appointment process since time immemorial. In Chicago, this concept is better understood as "clout." Racial fears predicated over real or imagined concerns about neighborhood safety, the proliferation of gangs and drugs, and a resulting decline in property values compelled the children and grandchildren of many first-generation Europeans to abandon the same inner-city neighborhoods their parents and grandparents inhabited years earlier. The dilution of European culture is evident in such diverse neighborhoods as the West Side Pilsen (formerly Czech-Bohemian, now almost entirely Mexican) community, and Lincoln Square on the North Side, where only the delicatessens, restaurants, and gift shops are left to suggest the heavy German concentration of former years.

Chicago remains, in my estimation, the most ethnic and culturally diverse of all American cities. It is a spacious city (twenty-five miles long, ten miles wide) that is spread across the flat plain in an interlocking grid pattern of streets. Because of natural and manmade barriers—railroad embankments, expressways, and the three branches of the Chicago River, extending for fifty miles across the landscape—unintended "turf" boundaries have resulted. It is possible for one group of people to live in relative seclusion from the next, even though the distance of a few hundred feet may be all that separates them. Hermetically sealed neighborhoods made it possible for the immigrants to practice their social and religious customs, read the latest news from the old country in the foreign language press, shop for imported foods at independent grocers within a block or two of their homes, and virtually live out their entire adult lives unaffected by mainstream American culture.

There is an unshakeable pride in who we are and from where we came, though most, if not all, would admit that there is no going back. Successive waves of European immigrants shaped the essential character of the city and contributed to its majestic splendor, reflected in spacious boulevards, towering skyscrapers, and a "green necklace" of parkways and forest preserves that still dot Cook County today. But they were also victimized by the relentless grind of big city life and the Darwinist social philosophy of the nineteenth century "Robber Barons" and captains of industry who held each man accountable for his own triumphs or failure. Those who live in Chicago for a period of years before returning to their places of origin to visit or resettle would very often complain that the old country was not as they remembered, and that the living standards there had changed for the worse. The frenzy to succeed within a new and highly competitive economic system, one that championed an entirely different set of values and mores, forced these European pilgrims to make a radical adjustment to the rigors of American life. By the time they returned to greet the friends and family who remained behind, their only shared experiences were nostalgia and the sentiment of the past, and the warm reassurances that can only come from kin.

In November 1924, my father, Oscar W. Lindberg, set sail from Göteborg, Sweden, aboard a lumbering transport ship called the *Drottningholm*. He carried in his valise a change of clothes, the collected works of the playwright August Strindberg, and a handbill offering useful tips about negotiating a successful transatlantic crossing. Oscar was twenty-seven, and was imbued with the fiery convictions of the embryonic Social Democratic Party, which sought to circumvent the power of the monarchists and privileged classes. He felt immense pride in having agitated for socialized medicine and other noteworthy programs to benefit the impoverished peasant classes. There were times when the king's soldiers bloodied his face during civil disturbances in Göteborg. Such things were common in Europe before and after World War I, as the royal families desperately sought to consolidate their waning power in the face of a growing "red menace."

Facing mandatory conscription, my father decided to come to the U.S. rather than serve in the hated king's army. With a mixture of pride and characteristic stubbornness born out of the conviction that he was absolutely right in standing up for principles of a higher order, Oscar made this journey to Chicago, a city he would both revile and cherish for the remainder of his life. My father entered the country illegally through Windsor, Canada, using the acronym of "Waldemar Carlson"; his own middle name and his father's first name. He settled on Wilton Avenue in the heart of the congested "Swede Town," then located near the intersection of Belmont and Clark streets on the North Side. In a messy two-flat underneath the city's rumbling elevated line, he wrote inflammatory editorials for a Swedish-language newspaper catering to the "free thinkers" in the neighborhood. They were men who swilled prohibition gin on Saturday night at the Idrott Cafe, while deserting church services at the Ebenezer Lutheran Church on Sunday mornings. Oscar and his fellow Swedes, though experienced in the building trades, were neophytes in the land of Big Business.

During the 1930s my father exchanged his bib overalls for a tie and a stickpin as he launched his formative years by constructing customized

Sears, Roebuck "catalog" bungalows up and down Belmont Avenue for other European immigrants seeking to make their way in this sometimes bewildering ethnic melting pot called Chicago. After World War II, Oscar capitalized on the suburban land boom beginning to take shape in Skokie, Morton Grove, Lincolnwood, and other points along the North Shore. Almost overnight, serene, picturesque farmlands and small suburban villages were transformed into sprawling subdivisions with schools, public parks, and interlocking expressways. Returning G.I.s who had grown up in Pilsen, Bridgeport, Lawndale, and other city neighborhoods before the war, were now ready to begin the task of child-rearing in suburbia where the houses were cheap and durable, and the backyards a lush green. Once again Chicago was a city on the move. My father organized his own construction company founded on the principles of the Swedish cooperative movement, which he had feverishly embraced in his idealistic youth. In between, he took time out to join the Masons and the Swedish fraternal and choral societies, which provided a social outlet, status among his peers, and the means of preserving a foreign culture which was just beginning to break apart in the old Andersonville neighborhood.

No longer fearing the wrath of the Swedish authorities and armed with his U.S. citizenship papers, Oscar would make three pilgrimages back to his boyhood village in Ronneby before he died, the first one in 1956. By now the famous system of "cradle to grave" socialism was in place in Sweden. The goals worth fighting for in the early twenties had been achieved long ago, and the living standards were among the highest in Europe. But Oscar was sadly disillusioned by the profound social and political changes that had taken place in his absence. Why had the strong work ethic of former years seemingly vanished with this younger generation? My father groped for the answers to unsolvable riddles, but at last returned to Chicago unable to reconcile the painful truth that he had become . . . an *American.*

It is the children of the first generation who acutely experience this cultural clash between the old world and the new. Their intention to conform within a school or neighborhood peer group often runs counter to their parent's desire for them to speak the native tongue, wear traditional clothing, intermarry, and observe the religious and social customs of the old country. There first comes a period of embarrassment and denial, but with maturity these childhood anxieties give way to something altogether different—a gradual feeling of acceptance and pride.

My own experience of growing up in an immigrant household weighed heavily on my decision to write *An Ethnic Guide To Chicago,* a book that blends the history of neighborhood settlement with contemporary cultural attractions, parades, festivals, banquets and cotillions, tours, ethnic museums, and a comprehensive dining and shopping guide. My book will spirit you away from the boutiques and stately grandeur of North Michigan Avenue into what I've always considered to be the "soul of Chicago"—the ethnic enclaves and side streets seldom previewed by conventioneers and out-of-town guests. In order to fully comprehend a great city such as this one, it is first necessary to observe the pace of life as it is being lived along the boulevards and thoroughfares; outside the bailiwick of accommodating head waiters, hotel doormen, and impolite cabbies.

We have based our criteria for inclusion in this book solely on the historic importance of each immigrant group's contribution to the city's development, its future direction, and continuing neighborhood presence. We hope that you will want to experience firsthand Chicago's unique international flavor, and discover for yourself the majesty, the strength, determination, and inner resolve that have recast Carl Sandburg's "Hog Butcher of the World" into a truly world-class city.

Irish/Scottish/English Chicago

History and Settlement

At one time, not so many years ago, virtually every policeman on the beat, street sanitation worker, and neighborhood precinct captain was a son of the "Auld Sod." The Irish dominated Chicago political and religious life for over 125 years, even though they were outnumbered by native-born Americans and German immigrants for much of the period in question.

The migratory Irish brought with them a foreign culture and a way of life that was often at odds with the Anglo-Saxon Nativists who branded them unworthy to share in the bountiful harvest of America. In time the Irish would overcome much of the ethnic prejudice and anti-Catholic phobia of the new world to take their place in the mainstream. It was a long, arduous journey, however.

From 1845 to 1847, Ireland suffered a disastrous famine that resulted from the failure of the potato crop. Nearly one-and-a-half million penniless, half-starved immigrants spilled onto U.S. shores at the ports of Boston and New York. The overwhelming majority of them were tenant farmers who had suffered under a corrupt landlord system imposed upon them by the pro-British aristocracy. The Irish immigrants disdained the farmer's life in order to become manual laborers in America's burgeoning urban centers. Those who chose not to remain in Boston or New York inevitably made their way to the Pennsylvania coal fields or the eastern canals then under construction.

The history of the Irish settlement in Chicago rightfully begins on July 4, 1836, when Dr. William B. Egan, a native of County Kerry, delivered the ground-breaking address to kick off the first phase of construction on the Illinois-Michigan Canal. The waterway was Chicago's first great civic undertaking—connecting Lake Michigan to the Illinois and Mississippi rivers. When it was completed in 1848, the canal quickly established Chicago as the most important transportation hub of the Midwest. According to Professor Lawrence McCaffrey's essay "The Irish Dimension," hundreds of anonymous Irishmen found their final resting place along the banks of the Erie and Illinois-Michigan canals. The entry of the Irish into city politics coincided with the construction of the canal. Michael Kehoe blazed new trails for his countrymen when he was elected alderman of what was then the third ward in 1846. He refused a second term in order to become a canal inspector. Kehoe gained considerable prominence when he exposed the canal "scrip" frauds, one of the early Chicago political scandals.

The earliest Irish settlement was located on the Near North Side along Market (Orleans) Street between Kinzie and Erie. This community of shanties was dubiously known as Kilgubbin, after a large estate in County Cork from which so many of the immigrants fled after being evicted by their landlords. From just a few hundred canal workers in the 1830s, the Irish population of Chicago stood at 6,096 in 1850. As the city continued to grow, thousands more poured into the city to take advantage of job opportunities in the packing houses, brickyards, construction industry, and municipal government. By 1870 there were 39,988 Irishmen in Chicago, accounting for 13.37% of the population.

The construction of the canal spurred the growth of Bridgeport, a South Side community located on the South Branch of the Chicago River. The northeastern terminus of the Illinois-Michigan Canal (Canalport) was located here, in what was once a sleepy little village outside the main city limits. The Irish settlement of Kilgubbin on the North Side was quickly dwarfed by Irish Bridgeport, as thousands of workers' "cottages" sprang up almost overnight. Before 1848 the neighborhood was known as "Hardscrabble," because disease, despair, and mortality ran high. The first Catholic parish, St. Bridget's was founded in 1850, just two years after the canal project was completed. The Irish, more than any other ethnic group, derived a sense of identity from their neighborhood parishes. The historic antagonisms between Catholic and Protestant that characterized much of Irish history since the sixteenth century were imported to U.S.

shores. Irish nationalism is an important theme interwoven into the history of Chicago.

The Fenian Brotherhood, founded in 1858 in New York, sent financial aid, weapons, and partisans to Ireland to fight the British. The Fenians gave way to the Clan-na-Gael in 1867, a secret oath-bound brotherhood composed of many prominent men in finance, industry, and government. In Chicago, the para-militaristic Clan counted among its supporters the furniture magnate John M. Smyth, ranking members of the police and fire departments, Mayor John Hopkins (1893–95), and John Finerty, a wheel horse in local politics for two decades. The Clan became an issue of concern to other ethnic groups when Dr. Patrick Cronin, a well known physician, was murdered by a rival faction in May 1889. The subsequent investigation into the disappearance of Cronin revealed the group's deep and pervasive roots in the city's infrastructure. In some cases Irish nationalism subordinated other issues of political importance to Chicagoans. The influence of the Clan-na-Gael waned, but only after years of vicious infighting that eventually discredited the movement.

Following the completion of the canal, the Irish laborers whose livelihood was tied to the seasonal nature of the work, were forced to seek alternative employment within Bridgeport. A steel mill opened at the Southeast corner of Ashland and Archer in the 1860s, followed by breweries, brickyards, and meat packing firms. In 1865 the animal slaughtering and packaging was transferred to the Union Stockyards immediately to the south. The industrial base of Bridgeport (so named because of a low-slung bridge erected across the Chicago River at Ashland Avenue in the 1840s) was cemented in 1905 when the central manufacturing district was founded on the western border.

Bridgeport is one of Chicago's oldest, most stratified neighborhoods. Its pleasant tree-lined streets are filled with modest wooden and brick two-flats, interspersed with ma-and-pa grocery stores and corner saloons. Symbolic of its ties to the Irish community, Bridgeport is the home of the Chicago White Sox—founded in 1900 by Charles Comiskey.

The "Old Roman" as he was known to friends and associates, was the son of John Comiskey, an Irish immigrant who served as alderman of the tenth ward, and was one of the most notable Chicago politicians of the Civil War period. The son far eclipsed him in popularity, and his ballpark, opened on July 1, 1910, was a monument to the Bridgeport Irish. On ground-breaking day—St. Patrick's Day 1910—a "lucky" green Irish brick was laid in place by the architect Zachary Davis. Seventy years later Bill Veeck dug the brick out of the wall and certified to a disbelieving press that this was the genuine article. There was no trace of green on the brick, however. Comiskey Park, which stood at 35th and Shields (Bill Veeck Drive) was demolished during the 1990 season to make way for a newer, more spacious ballpark across the street. It is called appropriately enough, Comiskey Park II.

In the 1890s, political satirist Finley Peter Dunne captured better than most the spirit of Bridgeport. Writing for the *Chicago Evening Post,* Dunne introduced his readers to the fictional Martin Dooley, who provided a heartfelt glimpse at Irish social customs along "Archey" (Archer) Road. Dunne also lampooned a variety of less-than-circumspect politicians, men like Alderman Johnny Powers, Democratic power broker Roger Sullivan, and the irrepressible "Bathhouse" John Coughlin. These men were representative of a generation of Irish politicians whose day has long since passed. But in their time, Coughlin, Powers, and their minions carved out an impressive power base by cultivating the "saloon vote," the liquor trade, and the denizens of the criminal underworld. Politics in the mid to late nineteenth century was the lifeblood of the Irish community. The immigrants enjoyed an edge over the Germans, Italians or Poles through their knowledge of the language and their inherent organizational skills.

The Irish were able to take advantage of a situation and to quickly fill the political vacuum created by the Anglo "blue bloods," who looked upon the jobs in the government sector be it policeman or city gas inspector, as a less-than-honorable calling in life. Consequently, the Irish were there to weld a continuing "machine," from their precincts and wards. Their tolerance of public drinking and gambling flew in the face of traditional Anglo-Puritan thinking, but were perfectly acceptable to other newly arrived Europeans who supported their elective bid. Thus, the Irish were able to control the ebb and flow of city politics for many years.

The career of John Coughlin—Chicago's most colorful, notorious boss of the 1890s and 1900s—is illustrative of the path well traveled by Irish political figures of that era. Born on Aug. 15, 1860 in "Connelly's Patch," an Irish enclave east of the Chicago River between Adams and Monroe, Coughlin helped his father tend the family grocery store on Polk Street. After the Chicago Fire swept away the store and much of the "Patch," young John was forced to strike out on his own. Recalling the event years later, Coughlin would say: "I'm glad that fire came along and burned the store. Say, if not for that bonfire I might have been a rich man's son and gone to Yale and never amounted to anything!" As a young man he went to work as a "rubber" in a Turkish bath on Clark Street. Here he laid the basis for his future career in the City Council by "rubbing elbows"—quite literally—with the city's leading political figures. With the help of some of gambler Mike McDonald's people, Coughlin was elected alderman of

Chicago's bawdy, expansive first ward, infested with bordellos, clip joints, and opium dens. Coughlin and his partner in crime, Michael "Hinky Dink" Kenna regulated vice on the principle that "Chicago ain't no Sunday School," after all. Summing up the attitudes of the press toward these two rogues, the *Chicago Herald* observed: "The average Democratic representative in the city council is a tramp, if not worse. He represents or claims to represent a political party having respectable principles and leaders of known good character and ability. He comes from twenty-five or thirty different wards, some of them widely separated, and when he reaches the city hall, whether from the west, the south, or the north division, he is in nine cases out of ten a bummer and a disreputable who can be bought and sold as hogs are bought and sold at the stockyards. Do these vicious vagabonds stand for the decency and intelligence of the Democratic Party in Chicago?"

Politically the Irish have a long history of dominating both the city council and the Chicago Archdiocese. The city has elected eight Irish mayors—some good, some bad—while nine of the twelve men to head the Catholic church since 1844 were Irish born or of Irish parentage. Between 1844 when Bishop William J. Quarter was appointed to head the church, until the death of Archbishop James Quigley in 1915, only one man, Bishop James Van de Velde (a Belgian), presided over the diocese. Van de Velde served from 1849–1854.

The Irish Democratic Machine that had its origins in the late nineteenth century was a local phenomenon that did not extend much past Cook County. The Irish generally conceded state and national office, concentrating their efforts on the local level. Since the days of "Boss" Roger Sullivan and his protege Mayor Hopkins—a Damon and Pythias of Chicago politics for nearly twenty years—a succession of ward bosses have dispensed patronage jobs to the voting constituents. After Sullivan died in 1920, George F. Brennan took over the county Democracy. He was followed by Pat Nash, Jake Arvey, and in recent years George F. Dunne, former president of the Cook County Board.

Professor McCaffrey is an outspoken critic of the city's Irish political connection, calling it "nationally irrelevant." McCaffrey decries what he sees as a lack of cultural contributions from his people, noting that: "Not all Irish-Americans became prosperous and self-confident. The drunks, sexual neurotics and political reactionaries featured in the novels of Jimmy Breslin, Joe Flaherty, Tom McHale, Pete Hamill and John Gregory Dunne had and have real-life counterparts. Failures and insecurities also fostered paranoid politics."

In the fine Chicago literary tradition of the first half of the twentieth century, Washington Parker James T. Farrell towers above the rest. In the gloomy reality of his working class hero Studs Lonigan, Farrell embodies much of what Professor McCaffrey finds objectionable about Irish life in America—racial intolerance, alcoholism, and the schisms within the nuclear family. Farrell wrote twenty-two novels and 250 short stories, but he is best remembered for the Washington Park stories—*Young Lonigan,* 1932; *The Young Manhood of Studs Lonigan,* 1934; *Judgment Day,* 1935; *A World I Never Made,* 1936; *No Star Is Lost,* 1938; *Father and Son,* 1940; *My Days of Anger,* and *The Face of Time,* 1953.

Farrell was an urban realist in the Theodore Dreiser tradition. His first and second generation Irish characters struggled to make ends meet in an unfriendly, rough, city environment populated by street corner hustlers, Apple Annies, opium junkies, and inebriates. Against this backdrop is the family unit and the church; buttressing the chaos of the streets. Farrell's Irish lived in their three story "flats" equipped with all the modern conveniences; steam heat, electricity, a fold-down ironing board, and plumbing. Social life in Washington Park centered around the St. Anselm Parish at 61st and Michigan Avenue, and the Corpus Christi Church, constructed at 49th St. and Grand Boulevard in 1915. Farrell attended services at St. Anselm's. His fictional O'Flahertys worshiped at Corpus Christi which he dubbed the Crucifixion Church.

Washington Park extends from 51st Street on the North to 63rd on the South, and from Cottage Grove (east) to Wentworth Avenue (west). The South Side community was originally settled by stockyard workers during the Civil War. Washington Park underwent a period of expansion and accelerated growth after 1869—the year the South Park Commission purchased 2,000 acres of city land which were reserved for the people. A "green necklace" of boulevards and spacious wooded parks was created for the recreation and enjoyment of all Chicagoans.

Beautiful Washington Park was the crowned jewel of the South Side, populated by succeeding waves of Germans, Irish, Poles, Jews, and blacks. Farrell's people—the Irish who made the big move up from "Hard Scrabble" to Washington Park steam heat—began arriving in the 1880s. Still more of them came after 1906, when the famous Washington Park Race Track was razed to make way for more apartment buildings. By 1910 the neighborhood was commercially developed with the business districts concentrated along Garfield Boulevard, 58th, 61st, and 63rd Streets.

The blue-collar Irish who lived beside their beloved park were a secular insulated people suspicious of the forces of social change swirling all around them. The racial dynamics of the city had everything to do with the great exodus out of the neighborhood beginning around the time of World War I. There were blacks counted in the 1880 Washington Park census, but they lived in the areas west of State Street for the most part. The "boundary line," set by the European ethnics, held until 1915 when the first few blacks ventured into apartment buildings east of State Street and south of Garfield Boulevard. In the next few years the pace of racial change accelerated, so by 1920 15% of the neighborhood residents were black. Ten years after that only 10% were *white*.

Racial tensions on the South Side simmered for many years. Irish street gangs like Ragen's Colts, Gerdon's, Our Flag, and the Hamburg Athletic Club—to which the late Mayor Richard J. Daley once belonged—fought for their turf block by block. In 1919 the collective hatreds of both races spilled over into an ugly race riot that began at the 31st Street beach when a young black lad violated the invisible dividing line. He was stoned to death as he played in the cooling Lake Michigan waters with his friends. In the days that followed much of the so-called "black belt" north of Washington Park and east of State became a veritable no-man's land.

The blacks were not to be denied. In the years that followed they displaced large segments of the indigenous Irish who fled into Hyde Park to the south, hoping that the University of Chicago campus might insulate them from the advancing black population. The more upscale members of the community drifted into the fashionable South Shore neighborhood along the Lake Michigan shoreline between 67th and 79th Streets. Here the Irish encountered Swedes, English Protestants, and wealthy Jewish people, many of whom belonged to the South Shore Country Club, fifty-five sprawling acres of lake front property at 71st Street. It was a deluxe playground for Chicago's cafe society from the moment Lawrence Huyworth of Prairie Avenue opened it in 1906.

South Shore's population doubled in the 1920s as the community absorbed the "white flight" from Washington Park and the communities to the north. Irish parishes were opened at 72nd and Merrill (St. Philip Neri), and St. Bridget's at 78th and Coles. St. Philip's opened in 1926, playing host to the International Eucharistic Congress. The church is modeled after the classic English cathedrals of old, and can seat 1,500. The splendor and opulence of St. Philip Neri attests to the affluence of South Shore's "lace-curtain" Irish in the 1920s. The pattern of racial integration finally caught up with South Shore in the 1960s, as it had in Washington Park forty years earlier. When the blacks broke down the color barriers, the Catholic Irish, the Protestants, and the Jews moved on.

The South Side is a very different place today from when Finley Peter Dunne and James T. Farrell wrote of the customs and mores of their people. But the history and culture will always remain, if only in the collective memories of the children and grandchildren who hear the stories handed down by their elders. The Irish traditions are interwoven into the fabric of the South Side, where the poorest of these immigrants raised their offspring in less than idyllic conditions in Bridgeport, Back of the Yards, Canaryville, and Brighton Park. Bound together by their faith in the church, the cause of Irish nationalism, the immigrants soon came to grips with their environment and were able to rise above the wheel of poverty and the "No Irish Wanted" stigma in a short period of time.

Today Chicago is not nearly as Irish as it was once was. According to the 1980 census, the Irish account for only 15.7% of the total population, ranking third behind the Germans (21.8%) and the blacks (20.1%). Nationwide the Chicago Irish are far down on the list of cities with 250,000 or more. Chicago ranks 45th in highest percentage of the Irish. Boston is the center of Gaelic culture with 24.9% of its people claiming Irish descent.

What has happened is that the Irish, like so many other Ethnic European groups, have abandoned the inner-city neighborhoods. In this case the South Side Irish tended to move farther south, to the Mount Greenwood community where 47.7% of the ethnic composition is Irish and nearby Ashburn and Beverly—suburbs within the city to be sure.

The times have changed. Irish politicians no longer dominate the political machinery of the city, though a second generation Daley now occupies the fifth floor of City Hall. The chief of police, the fire department, and the head of the Chicago Archdiocese, however, are non-Irish. But on March 17 each year, *everyone* in Chicago, regardless of race, creed, or color, celebrates St. Patrick's Day with the Irish. Only in Chicago can an out-of-towner catch a glimpse of a river turning green before their very eyes. It has been a tradition for many years to dye the Chicago River green, despite the chuckles of certain journalists in town, who search for ulterior motives on the part of the politicians.

Indeed, "St. Patty's Day" has been something special in Chicago ever since the early 1840s, when the Montgomery Guards, an Irish-American militia, decided to celebrate this most important of all holidays. For years various Irish organizations spnored local neighborhood pageants on March 17. The Chicago St. Patrick's Day parade of legend began on the West Side along Madison Street between Pulaski and Laramie in 1952. Four years later, newspaper reporter Dan Lydon and Reverend Thomas Byrne, pastor of old St. Patrick's Church on Adams Street in the West Loop dropped by Mayor Daley's office in city hall to suggest to "Hizzoner" that he bring the parade downtown. It was a splendid idea, in Daley's view. So, beginning in 1956 the floats, the musicians, the politicians, and the clowns (though in some years it was hard to tell them apart) marched proudly down the boulevards of the Loop beginning at State St. and

Wacker Drive and winding up at St. Patrick's—Chicago's oldest church, which had celebrated its 100th anniversary in 1854. Traditionally the kingpins of the county Democratic Party have served as grand marshals. Only two women have filled this role—"Sis" Daley, wife of the mayor, and Marge Bailey, spouse of committee chairman Stephen M. Bailey. Both women were accorded this honor in 1975, the year before Richard Daley's death.

Not to be outshined, the South Side Irish sponsored their own parade beginning in 1979 when forty children and their parents trekked up and down Washtenaw Avenue and Talman Street. Within a few years it became a full-blown extravaganza, featuring 202 different neighborhood organizations, which marched with pride down Western Avenue from 103rd to 113th Streets. The parade has come to symbolize neighborhood and family unity in a place where it all began. No matter where the Irish live now, they always come back to their roots.

North Side Culture, South Side Sports and Music

A spirited, good natured rivalry exists between the fun-loving South Side Irish and their North Side counterparts. "We're more into sports, music, and dancing here on the South Side," explains Tim McSweeney, one of the directors at Gaelic Park, which sponsors a full calendar of Irish football, folk dancing, and choral singing. It's not that the North Siders disdain frivolity. A large Irish pub has been constructed on the main level of the Irish American Heritage Center for the hundreds of St. Patrick's Day revelers that stop by. But it can be said that the volunteers who staff the center have prioritized the serious side of Irish ethnic history. When it is completed, the center will be for all Chicagoans, irrespective of their neighborhood identities.

Irish American Heritage Center, *4626 N. Knox Ave., Chicago, Ill., (312) 282-7035.* Located near the juncture of the Edens and Kennedy expressways on the city's Northwest Side, the Irish American Heritage Center occupies the former Mayfair College, an 86,000 square-foot Gothic-style structure that is slowly being transformed into a museum and showplace of Irish folk culture. The center is staffed by community volunteers whose "labor of love" is reflected in the work of the craftsmen who have donated many long hours. As you enter through the main doors on Knox Avenue, observe the lovely murals overhead in the foyer. They were painted by Ed Cox, and are based on the ninth-century Book of Kells. The slate floor installed in the spacious first-floor pub is done in a traditional architectural style common in Ireland. Ditto for the flagstone fireplace replete with hobs and cranes. It was installed by volunteer worker Kevin Moran. The second floor library and exhibit rooms are expected to open in 1992. The museum, which officially opened on October 6, 1991, with a visit from the president of Eire, Mary Robinson, houses an extraordinary collection of Belleek china. The museum spotlights the contributions of the Irish to American and Chicago history. It is not widely known, for example, that during one of the key battles of the Revolution, General George Washington used the secret password "St. Patrick."

During the year, the center sponsors a myriad of activities including concerts, fashion shows, beginning and advanced Gaelic classes, and step-dancing instruction. In October, and again in April, the Irish Heritage Players perform contemporary drama in the refurbished auditorium. The front row is reserved for the patrons and city dignitaries who have contributed substantial amounts of money or their time to make this project successful. The inscribed arm rests are a virtual "who's who" of Chicago. Mayor Richard M. Daley, for example, occupies his own reserved seat in the first row center. Membership is open to anyone who is interested in Irish American culture for $25 a year or $40 for two years. The offices are open Monday through Saturday, 9 A.M. to 4 P.M. Closed Sunday.

Irish-American Heritage Center Events

1. The Irish Heritage Players Theater Series. In April, and again in October–November the 680-seat theater at the Heritage Center is usually filled to capacity when the community players stage the finest in Irish drama. In 1991, for example, the troupe performed Sean O'Casey's *Plough and the Stars,* directed by Pat Nugent. For scheduled times and showings, call the center at (312) 282-7035. Free parking on the grounds. Handicap access. Member admission and senior citizens, $5.00. Non-members, $6.00.

2. Commemorative Easter Mass, sponsored by the St. Patrick's Father's Group. As a result of the historic Easter Uprising on April 24, 1916, in which sixteen Irish nationalists lost their lives, Sinn Fein became the most powerful political movement in Ireland. Sinn Fein, sworn to securing a free Irish state, waged constant warfare against the British

government until January 15, 1922. The anniversary of the pivotal 1916 uprising is marked in religious ceremony and a short program at the Heritage Center on Easter Sunday. Coffee, tea, and soda bread are served afterwards.

Regularly Scheduled Weekday Events

Mondays: Music Workshops, 7 P.M., call (312) 425-3564.

Wednesdays: Bingo in the Social Center, 6:45 P.M.
           Crafts and Needlework, Room 205, 7 P.M.
           Gaelic Classes (intermediate), third floor, 7 P.M.
           Irish Step and Folk Dancing Classes, third floor, 7 P.M.

Thursdays: Gaelic Classes (Beginning), 7 P.M.
           Irish Heritage Singers, Room 308, 7:30 P.M.

Fridays: Francis O'Neill Céilí Practice, Room 111, 8 P.M.
           Production in November. (Francis O'Neill served as chief
           of the Chicago Police Department from 1901–1905.
           In addition to being one of the most honest, forthright
           lawmen in an age known for its rascality, O'Neill
           "collected" hundreds of long-forgotten Irish folk tunes
           and catalogued them on paper and published them. Many
           of these ancient folk tunes were overheard by O'Neill as
           he wandered the back alleys and boulevards of Chicago's
           Irish neighborhoods.)

Saturdays: Scoil Baal-Tine, music lessons, 1 to 6 P.M.
           Advanced Gaelic Classes, 7 P.M.

3. Taste of Ireland Festival, held on the grounds of the IAHC in mid-September every year since 1985. The event includes an abundance of Irish entertainment, children's games, Irish folk dancing and music, cultural exhibits, recent Irish films and plenty of food for the entire family. For times and prices call the center at (312) 282-7035.

Gaelic Park, *6119 W. 147th St., Oak Forest, Ill., (708) 687-9323.* Serving the needs of Chicago's large South Side Irish contingency, Gaelic Park was founded in 1984 as a cultural, athletic and recreational facility. Local tradesmen donated their time, and building suppliers sold the materials at cost in order to ensure that the construction of the banquet hall, locker rooms, and playing fields could be built without delay. Today, the 18-acre Gaelic Park is the Chicagoland home of the Irish national pastime—hurling—and the most popular of all sports, Gaelic football. Four or five leagues from the junior and senior divisions compete here during the season. The park also provides satellite transmission of Irish football every Sunday morning during the season. The spacious meeting hall has hosted some of the biggest names in Irish entertainment over the years, including Foster and Allen, the Dubliners, Bagatelle, Mary Black, Brendan Grace, and many more. Vibrant and growing, the grand opening ceremonies marking the opening of the expanded facilities took place on March 10, 1991. In attendance were Rev. Robert L. Kealy, Chancellor for the Archdiocese of Chicago, and Gary Ansboro, Consul General of Ireland. "Gaelic Park is here to be a gathering place for the Irish and to allow Irish Americans to experience their heritage," explained President Tom Boyle. "The lounge, the games, our dances and concerts are all open to the public. We extend a warm Irish welcome to all." Located two miles west of Cicero Avenue on 147th Street. Free parking on site. For information about membership, please call (708) 687-9323.

Gaelic Park Events

1. Irish Mass and authentic Irish breakfast, held the second Sunday of every month at 10 A.M., between May and October. Breakfast includes: sausage, eggs, bacon, black pudding and soda bread. Adults: $5, senior citizens and children $3.

2. Gaelic Football. The sport has been played in America by Irish descendants since the 1920s. It is a fast-moving game utilizing a 15-ounce ball that can only be advanced if the player kicks it. Points are scored when the ball is kicked over the crossbar and between the uprights. A goal, worth three points, is awarded when the ball goes under the crossbar and into the netting between the uprights. Tinley Park (6119 W. 147th St.) is the home field for the teams comprising the Chicago Gaelic Football League. Other cities, notably New York, Los Angeles, San Francisco, Boston, Pittsburgh, Cleveland, and Detroit also host Gaelic football, but the sport enjoys a popularity here that is unique. The football games and hurling matches are staged on Sunday afternoons during the warm weather months, between May and October. Refreshments are served on the grounds, and a $3 admission is charged.

The Irish hurling and football teams are always looking for new players. For further information, please contact the teams directly at the following numbers:

Men's Division, Gaelic Football

1. St. Brendans (South Side), (312) 423-0645.

2. Celtics (South Side), (312) 581-0075.

3. Wolftones (Southwest Suburbs), (708) 361-1168.

4. John McBrides (North Side), (312) 267-9748.

5. Rovers (North Side), (312) 286-1579.

Women's Division, Gaelic Football

1. John McBrides (North Side), (312) 792-0743.

2. Erin Rovers (South Side), (312) 423-8794.

Hurling

1. Limericks (North Side), (312) 598-1095.

2. Harry Bolands (South Side), (312) 767-8720.

Step dancing, céilí dancing, and bagpipe lessons are held every night of the week in the main building at Gaelic Park. Céilí dancing consists of a number of dance routines from Ireland's principal counties, including the popular "Siege of Ennis," with eight dancers facing each other, moving across the floor in weaving, cross-over patterns. Céilí dancing classes are available to adults and children, and there is an annual competition. Step dancing, a regular feature at the various St. Patrick's Day ceremonies across the city, includes both jigs and reels in which the participants wear soft shoes. The hornpipe and treble jig, by contrast, are hard shoe dances whose sounds resonate on the hard wooden floors. During the year, folk dancing classes are generally held on Tuesdays.

Irish Fest, a four-day festival held at Gaelic Park on the Memorial Day weekend each year. Four outdoor stages with continuous entertainment featuring national and international Irish and American musicians have attracted crowds in excess of 50,000, to make this one of the most successful Irish festivals in the U.S. The merriment began in 1986, and each year virtually every inch of the 20-acre Gaelic Park has been filled to capacity. Food vendors sell an endless variety of ethnic foods and beer, with additional items from the Irish import stores in the city. Headlining the Irish Fest are such internationally known stars as the Barley Bree trio, the Clan, a Dublin rock band, and Tommie Makem and Liam Clancy. Count on seeing some down-home local talent, too. Joel Daly and the Sundowners, the Dancing Noodles, and 1960s rock singer Ronnie Rice have made appearances at the Irish Fest. Hours: Friday (Memorial Day Weekend) 4 P.M. to 11:30 P.M.; Saturday–Sunday, Noon to 11:30 P.M.; Monday, noon to 8 P.M. Admission will vary from year to year. In 1991, it was $8.00 per person, senior citizens, $5.00; children under three admitted free. Call the Gaelic Park Events Club, Inc., at (708) 598-6800.

Rose of Tralee elimination contest and dance, held in April at Gaelic Park. The Chicago Rose of Tralee competition determines who among the city's fairest colleens will represent the community in international competition in Ireland in August. The goal of the Rose of Tralee pageant is to locate the singularly unique Irish lass who is the "fairest maiden" of them all. It's quite a tall order, but the representative countries of the West send contestants every year. Young women between the ages of 18 and 25 who have never been married are eligible to join. The contest and dance take place the first week of April at Gaelic Park. Call Pat Daly at (312) 445-7946 for details.

Feis (pronounced FESH) **Competition,** second weekend in June at Gaelic Park. The Chicago Feis showcases some of the finest homegrown dance troops in Chicago at an annual competition held at Gaelic Park. The feis consists of traditional hard and soft shoe dances, including hornpipes, jigs and reels.

Annual Events and Celebrations

St. Patrick's Day Parade (Downtown). It is a grand, gala day for Chicago's Irish, who pay tribute to the patron saint of Ireland in the city's most lavish parade. But who was this celebrated figure from history, who is toasted in every pub from Bridgeport to Schaumburg on March 17? Historians believe that Patrick (389?–461? A.D.) was the son of a Roman-British government figure named Calpurnius. Tradition has it that he was born in the village of Bannavem (in what is now northern England) or possibly Kilpatrick, in Scotland. Educated in what is now France, Patrick was consecrated as bishop in 432 and assigned to Ireland by Pope Celestine to bring Christianity to the pagans. His mission was a difficult one, fraught with many perils, not the least of which was the local opposition of the Druids—pagan Celtic priests. Before he died in the Irish town of Downpatrick on March 17, the Apostle of Ireland reported the use of the shamrock as an illustration of the Trinity. Eventually the shamrock came to be regarded as the national symbol of Ireland.

Chicago's Irish have gone to great lengths to ensure that St. Patrick's achievements are not forgotten. The tradition of dyeing the Chicago River green began in the early 1960s when Stephen Bailey, parade chairman from 1958–66, seized on a novel idea. Bailey located 100 pounds of green-colored Air Force dye, and dumped it into the sluggish river. To Bailey's considerable delight the Chicago River retained its distinctive green hue for nearly a month. The outcry of the environmentalists eventually forced Bailey and his minions to change to a biodegradable dye. A peculiar local custom was born, one that was imitated in the large metropolitan areas of the U.S.

The annual rite of St. Patrick begins with the traditional early morning Mass at old St. Patrick's Church at the corner of Adams and Des Plaines. An Irish breakfast is served at 10:30 A.M. in the parish hall. Reservations for the breakfast are strongly suggested. The cost is $6–$12.50, and can be made by calling the church at (312) 782-6171. An annual event since 1956.

The parade, replete with marching bands, lavish floats, the famous Shannon Rovers, labor groups, the mayor, governor, and host of lesser lights from the Cook County Democratic and Republican parties lead an entourage that includes the queen and her court. The parade queen is chosen among the most eligible young women of Irish descent between the ages of 17 and 26. The contest is held each year in February, when a reviewing committee selects the winner from the photographs submitted.

Parade festivities kick off at noon at Dearborn Street and Wacker Drive, proceeds south down Dearborn past thousands of spectators before winding up at Van Buren Street. On St. Patrick's Day, everyone is Irish, it seems. For additional information call (312) 263-6612. *Recommended.*

The "All-Chicago Irish Dance Contest," *held on St. Patrick's Day in the West Tower Lobby of the Hyatt Regency Hotel, 151 E. Wacker Drive, Chicago, Ill., (312) 565-1234.* The hotel also offers refreshments for sale just before the parade. The main event begins at 2:30 P.M., when various dance troops compete for top prizes. The event is sponsored by the Sheila Tully School of Irish Dance, with music provided by the Johnny Gleason Band. Admission is free, but the corned beef sandwiches sell for $5 each.

South Side Irish St. Patrick's Day Parade, held on the Sunday before the holiday on Western Avenue between 103rd and 114th streets, Chicago. Deep in the heart of the 19th Ward in the neighborhood of Beverly, the South Side Irish decided to begin their own St. Patrick's Day celebration for the benefit of the children who would otherwise be unable to attend the downtown parade which is always held on the traditional holiday. The South Side parade is billed as the "largest Irish neighborhood parade outside of Dublin." Recognizing the political hay from such a large turnout, numerous politicians have forsaken the big downtown parade in order to meet and greet the Irish-American residents of Morgan Park, Beverly, Mount Greenwood, and Oak Lawn. Massachusetts Governor Michael Dukakis joined the procession along with Senator Albert Gore of Tennessee as a tune-up for the 1988 presidential sweepstakes.

The politicians are complemented by at least 70 floats, 199 marching units, and 44 bands. The Young Irish Club of Chicago, with 1,200 members in the Chicagoland area, usually have one of the most interesting floats in a parade that sometimes lasts three hours. Call (312) 238-1969 for additional information.

St. Patrick's Day Festival, *the Irish-American Heritage Center, 4626 N. Knox, Chicago, (312) 282-7035.* Continuous entertainment on five stages highlights the annual festival, which has become a Northwest Side tradition since 1986. Irish step-dancing, folk music, films, plus a special appearance by the late Mayor Richard Daley's favorite band, the Shannon Rovers, are featured in the weekend activities. Admission is $10, but only 3,500 are offered in advance, so it is wise to call well before the big day.

Gaelic Park St. Patrick's Day Festival, *6119 W. 147th Street, Oak Forest, (708) 687-9323.* Serving the South Suburban Irish community since 1979, the Gaelic Park directors sponsor a morning Mass at the meeting hall, followed by a traditional Irish breakfast of bacon, black pudding, soda bread and eggs. Following the South Side parade, the party returns to Gaelic Park with a dinner dance held that Sunday night. Continuous entertainment provided by the Gaelic Park Pipe Band, the Mullane Irish Dancers, and the Bannerman. Admission is $5.

St. Patrick's Day Concert, *Friendship Concert Hall, Kolpin and Algonquin Road, Des Plaines, (708) 255-5380.* Since 1980 the Mount Prospect Park District has sponsored an Irish folk music concert featuring bagpipe players, folk dancers, and choral groups direct from

Ireland. The concert precedes a special Irish dinner that is open to the public at the nearby Friendship Park Conservatory. Tickets for the dinner are $15 a piece, and should be purchased in advance. Call (708) 255-5380.

St. Patrick's Day Eve Concert, *the Schaumburg Prairie Center for the Arts, 201 Schaumburg Court, Schaumburg, (708) 894-3600.* The Northwest suburb of Schaumburg was originally settled by Germans, but during the St. Patrick's Day celebration, everyone wears the green. An annual folk concert featuring students from the Mayer School of Irish Dance performing their routines. Tickets are $5. Call (708) 894-3600.

"Ireland On Parade" *at the Glendora House, 10225 S. Harlem Avenue, Chicago Ridge, (708) 425-3686.* A week-long St. Patrick's Day celebration kicks off with a talent show on March 12, showcasing the finest young Irish-American talent. Step dancers, pipers, singers, and other assorted acts grace the stage. The kitchen serves up plenty of corned beef and cabbage every night of the week, culminating in the traditional St. Patrick's Day dinner, including open bar for $27.50 per person. During other times of the year the restaurant and banquet hall sponsors ballroom dancing lessons, and a regular monthly luncheon for senior citizens.

St. Patrick's Day Dinner, *Chicago Hilton and Towers, Grand Ballroom, 720 South Michigan Avenue, Chicago, Ill.* The Irish Fellowship Club, founded in 1902 to promote Irish culture and the ideals of the great city, sponsors an annual dinner featuring the very best entertainment and ballads in a convivial atmosphere. The cocktail hour begins at 6:00 P.M. with dinner at 7:30 P.M. The price of the dinner is $75. Membership in the club is open to any person of Irish birth or descent, or those who have demonstrated a knowledge and sympathy for the ideals and aspirations of the club. Annual dues are $25. Please contact Kathy Taylor at (312) 427-2926, or write to the Irish Fellowship Club at 53 W. Jackson, Chicago, Ill., 60604.

Annual Fellowship Christmas Luncheon, *Chicago Hilton and Towers, Grand Ballroom, 720 S. Michigan Ave., Chicago, Ill.* Semi-formal luncheon sponsored by the Fellowship Club on or about December 7, each year. Entertainment is provided by songstress and balladeer Cathy O'Connell. Call (312) 427-2926 for details.

Chicago Irish Fest, *Arvey Field—the South End of Grant Park—
(312) 527-9080.*   It's St Patrick's Day one more time—only without
the politicians and the blarney. The setting is Grant Park on the lake, and
three stages of continuous entertainment light up the night. Count on
seeing any number of Irish folk dancing groups, Barley Bree, the Shannon
Rovers, Tommy Makkem, and Carmel Quinn, who has appeared at Car-
negie Hall for thirty consecutive years. Irish culture area. Freckles contest. Free time-restricted phone calls to Ireland courtesy of A.T. and T.
The three-day festival takes place the second or third week in July. Hours:
Friday, 3 P.M. to 11 P.M.; Saturday–Sunday, noon to 11 P.M. Tickets are
$6.00 at the gate, or $5 in advance at most Irish import stores. Seniors
and children 6 to 12 years old, $3 at the gate. Children under 5 are
admitted free. Shuttle bus service from Soldier Field and the Monroe
Street Parking Garage available to the festival grounds.

Annual Emerald Society Dinner Dance, *second weekend in
April at the Lexington House, 7717 W. 95th St., Hickory Hills,
Ill.*   Dinner dance given by this prestigious organization of police and
law enforcement people. A special award is presented by the Emerald
Society to the "Irishman of the Year." The 1991 award winner was Illinois
State Senator Phil Rock. Admission includes cocktails and banquet. $35
per person. Call Dale Murphy at (312) 631-4710 for details.

Trinity Academy of Irish Stepdancing Fund Raiser, *mid-May,
at the Hyatt Regency O'Hare, 9300 W. Bryn Mawr, Rosemont,
(708) 246-2957.*   Annual fund raising event held to defray the costs of
the dancers who tour the U.S. and various European festivals during the
summer. The event includes a lottery drawing, cocktail reception, luncheon, and dance performances by the troop. Admission is $25 per per-
son. Interested parties should call Mary Riordan at (708) 422-6059, or
Maureen Halpin at (312) 775-8355.

St. Cajetan Irish Festival, *112th St. and Artesian Avenue.*
Church-sponsored folk festival featuring Irish musical entertainment and
dancing, food booths, carnival games, and handicraft sales. Second weekend in June. Hours: Saturday afternoon till midnight; Sunday noon to 9
P.M. Admission: $2 for adults, $1 for children. Call: (312) 238-4100 for
information.

Irish Events Outside Chicago

Milwaukee Irish Fest, *held at the Henry W. Maier Lakefront Festival Park in mid-August.* Since 1980, the Milwaukee Irish Fest has been promoted as the largest Irish cultural event of its kind in the Midwest, though the folks at Gaelic Park might take issue. There are activities for all ages, including five stages with continuous entertainment; an Irish village, which brings the wonder of old Ireland to Milwaukee; tug-of-war, rugby contests, and currach racing. The Tipperary Tea Room, which serves up an array of delightful desserts, is but one of a dozen eating establishments on the grounds. Castle McFest entertains youngsters with contests, puppet shows, theater and games. Each year the Fest spotlights a certain Irish clan. In 1991 for example, the Keanes, O'Keanes, O'Kanes, Cains, and O'Cathains enjoyed their own day in the Wisconsin sun. Tickets are available at the gate, or by contacting Milwaukee Irish Fest, Box 599, Milwaukee, WI (414) 466-6640. Admission $7 ($4 for seniors). Children under 12 are admitted free. For other Irish activities in Milwaukee, call (414) 77 IRISH, or write to the Shamrock Club, P.O. Box 08361, Milwaukee, WI 53208.

Quad Cities Irish Arts, *Quad Cities, IA, (319) 359-7800.* Reorganized with a new name, and a slate of officers, this Irish cultural group sponsors a year-round calendar of events, including a St. Patrick's Day Parade and céilí dancing classes held every Sunday from 2 to 4 P.M. at the Knights of Columbus Hall, 1111 W. 35th Street, Davenport, Iowa. General meetings of the organization are held on the first Tuesday of the month at 7 P.M. at the Rock Island Public Library.

A Guide to City and Suburban Irish Pubs

Whether your preference is Guinness stout, Paddy's whiskey, or cider on the hard side, you are sure to find the brew of your choice in any number of Irish pubs scattered across the city and suburbs. The Chicago pubs continue an old tradition that began about the time Irish workers began digging the Illinois-Michigan Canal. Despite attempts of the blue-blood reformers to close the saloons down in the 1850s and again in the 1870s when Joseph Medill was mayor, the customs endured. Traditionally the pub was a place where a man could go to warm his bones in the winter and cool his palate in the dog days of summer. Politics on the ward level were practiced in the saloon. Very often politics took place at the local polling place on election day, or at campaign headquarters, or at a job bank where the alderman or committeeman dispensed patronage as he saw fit. Sometimes the back room doubled as a gambling den, where faro, dice, and craps were played away from the watchful eye of the honest copper on the beat. If that man in blue wasn't on the square, he might be found rolling his dice with the rest of the boys. That was the Chicago of legend, when "Hinky Dink" Kenna served up the largest stein of lager east of the Mississippi. When Prohibition came, and the Dink was forced to close his Workingman's Exchange, he took one of his bottomless steins and donated it to the Chicago Historical Society, where it is on display today.

The Irish pubs are a slice of culture and blarney that is as much of Chicago as the green-colored river on St. Patty's Day. You won't find any slot machines and roulette wheels, but it's a fair bet that you'll find plenty of *crack,*—not the cocaine variety, mind you, but "crack" in the Irish sense of a good time.

City

Abbey Pub and Restaurant, *3825 N. Elston Avenue, Chicago, (312) 478-4408.*   Guiness, Harp, and Killian's on tap. Live Irish sports via satellite, and traditional folk music featured on Wednesdays and Sunday nights. Abbey Productions will convert Irish or British VCR tapes that are incompatible with U.S.-made sets for a nominal price. Call (312) 539-6000.

Remember When (Formerly Clancy's Pub and Deli, Ltd.), *1237 S. State Street, Chicago, (312) 461-9788.*   Casual downtown bar that hosts one of the city's most raucous St. Patrick's Day celebrations (in a heated tent). It's popular with off-duty Chicago police, who can appreciate the irony that Tommy Gun's Prohibition Speakeasy is located in the rear.

Kitty O'Shea's, *720 S. Michigan Avenue, in the Chicago Hilton and Towers Hotel, Chicago, (312) 922-4400.*   Authentic Irish pub named after the legendary pub in Dublin. Live music every night from 9 P.M. to 1 A.M. Very popular with tourists and conventioneers.

Emerald Isle Pub, *6686 N. Northwest Highway, Chicago, (312) 775-2848.* Northwest Side pub featuring folk and rock music, and an annual St. Patrick's Day celebration.

Tommy Nevin's Pub, *1450 Sherman, Evanston, (708) 869-0450.* Evanston used to be a dry town, but you would never know it on St. Pat's Day. A new tradition was born on March 17, 1991, when the pub hosted its first St. Patrick's Day celebration with pan-fried liver and plenty of Guinness to go 'round.

Schaller's Pump, *3714 S. Halsted, Chicago, (312) 847-9378.* Chicago's best known South Side bar and restaurant retains its Irish flavor by virtue of its location at 37th and Halsted in Bridgeport. Across the street the sachems of the 11th Ward Democratic party formulate strategy and dole out the patronage. But Schaller's is where they repair to afterward. The pump has been around for 100 years and is owned and operated by Jackie Schaller. The food is okay too, but the real attraction is the atmosphere. It's a real neighborhood kind of bar. Noisy, crowded, all Chicago.

O'Rourke's, *1625 N. Halsted, Chicago, (312) 335-1806.* Chicago's literary left bank disappeared around 1930. The city of big shoulders has never been very kind to writers, choosing instead to bestow the laurel wreaths on captains of industry, hog butchers, and boodling aldermen. In the old days—that period of awakening before Al Capone and his minions re-defined culture in Chicago—the literary lions used to gather at the Whitechapel Club in the rear of the old *Daily News* building, and at Harriet Monroe's Little Room. At various times, Floyd Dell, John T. McCutcheon, Theodore Dreiser, Sherwood Anderson and others dropped by. But the writing renaissance they helped create ended abruptly when the siren sound of the New York publishing world beckoned them to the coast. The great flowering died, and in some ways it has never returned. O'Rourkes, the Old Town Ale House, Riccardo's, and to a lesser extent Billy Goat's Tavern, became the great writer hangouts of the post-renaissance period. There have been three O'Rourkes, beginning in 1964 at the original location on Wells St. In 1966, owner Jay Kovar reopened a few blocks away on North Avenue, and remained in business until October 21, 1989, when he moved to the present location. Photographs of William Butler Yeats, Oscar Wilde, James Joyce and Brendan Behan adorn the walls, and if you're lucky you might run into Mike Royko and the rest of the *Tribune* and *Sun Times* entourage. But the times have changed. Drinking to excess is no longer kosher, so it's unlikely you'll witness drunken barroom brawls between the journalists. For all the lurid details about the Friday night fights, ask the owner. *Recommended.*

Butch McGuire's Tavern, *20 W. Division Street, Chicago, (312) 337-9080.*   The popular Rush Street bistro opened in 1961, and has long been known as one of the trendiest singles clubs in Chicago. The Hollywood film *About Last Night* (based on David Mamet's play *Sexual Perversity in Chicago*) was set at Butch McGuire's. Irish prints and photographs decorate the walls.

Harrington's Pub, *2816 N. Halsted, Chicago, (312) 248-5933.* A pub that is popular with both young professionals and newly arrived Irish immigrants who enjoy the friendly neighborhood atmosphere. The bartender Tony Griffin was born in Dublin but came to the U.S. in 1988.

Harp and Shamrock Club, *1641 W. Fullerton, Chicago, (312) 248-0123.*   The original Harp and Shamrock Club began in Canaryville, but now caters to a North Side clientele—mostly neighborhood people, Chicago police, and bagpipe players.

Coogan's Riverside Saloon, *180 N. Wacker Drive, Chicago, (312) 444-1134.*   Downtown resort that serves a traditional Irish meal of corned beef and cabbage on St. Patrick's Day.

South Side and South Suburbs

Cork and Kerry Pub, *10614 S. Western Avenue, Chicago, (312) 445-2675.*   One of several pubs located in the Beverly neighborhood of Chicago.

Dubliner Pub, *10910 S. Western Avenue, Chicago, (312) 238-0784.*   Another Irish pub on the "Western Avenue strip."

Keegan's Pub, *10618 S. Western Avenue, Chicago, (312) 233-6829.*

Innisfree Inn, *6800 W. Archer, Chicago, (312) 229-1199.*   The owner is Polish, but the patrons are Irish-born and Irish-American South Siders. You figure it out.

Robert's Roadhouse, *9090 Roberts Road, Hickory Hills, (708) 598-8181.* The South Suburbs of Chicago Ridge, Hickory Hills, and Oak Lawn are the newest ports-of-entry for young Irish immigrants seeking work in the lucrative construction industries. The building boom in the South Suburbs in the 1980s were a powerful lure, and Robert's is one of several pubs where the new arrivals can exchange information and swap stories about the homeland.

Molly Malone's, *9908 Southwest Highway, Oak Lawn, (708) 423-8200.* A great blue-collar pub serving the Irish residents of Oak Lawn and Chicago Ridge.

Fox's Pub, *9240 S. Cicero, Oak Lawn, (708) 499-2233.* Entertainment.

Fitzgerald's, *6615 Roosevelt Road, Berwyn, (708) 788-2118.* An Irish pub in Bohemian Berwyn.

Reilly's Daughter's Pub, *4010 W. 111th St., Oak Lawn, (708) 423-1188.* Open from 1 P.M. to 2 A.M., Monday through Saturday. Popular rendezvous for South Side sports fans.

Irish Theater

"Erin-Go-Bragh" Irish American Theater Company, Various theater locations across Chicago. The company performs classic and contemporary Irish drama at different times of the year. Call (312) 561-7984 for details.

Irish Heritage Players (Irish American Heritage Center). Call the center at (312) 282-7035 for dates and times.

Irish Restaurants

Irish Village, *6215 W. Diversey, Chicago, (312) 237-7555.* Chicago's most famous Irish eatery, with entertainment six nights a week. Free parking. Hours: Tuesday–Friday, 11:00–3:00 P.M. for lunch; then open for dinner from 5:00–9:00 P.M. for dinner. Tuesday through Sunday 4 P.M. to 9 P.M. Closed Monday. Credit cards accepted.

Abbey Pub and Restaurant, *3420 W. Grace, Chicago, (312) 478-4408.* Dining, sports telecasts, and a full card of entertainment acts including the Dublin City Ramblers, the Dooley Brothers, the Drovers, and the Banshees. Hours: Monday through Friday, 10 P.M. to 2 A.M.; Saturday until 3 A.M.; Sunday, 10 P.M. to 2 A.M. Credit cards accepted.

Houlihan's, *five locations: Chicago, 1207 N. Dearborn (312) 642-9647; Bloomingdale, Stratford Mall, (708) 351-2700; Oak Brook, 56 Oak Brook Center Mall, (708) 573-0220; Schaumburg, 1901 E. Golf Road, (708) 605-0002; Skokie, Old Orchard Shopping Center, (708) 674-5490.* Eclectic Irish-American pub and restaurant that caters to the Yuppie crowd. Open at noon daily. Credit cards accepted. Sunday brunch; happy hour.

Irish Import and Gift Shops

Gaelic Imports, *4736 N. Austin Avenue, Chicago, (312) 545-6515. Hours: Tuesday–Friday, 10 A.M. to 6 P.M.; Saturday, 9:30 A.M. to 5 P.M. Sundays 10 A.M. to 3 P.M. Personal checks accepted but no credit cards.* Nine years at this location, (Austin and Lawrence). Irish gifts and deli items.

Fincara Irish Imports, *1701 Central Street, Evanston, (708) 328-0665. Hours: Monday–Friday, 11 A.M. to 6 P.M.; Saturday, 10 A.M. to 5 P.M. Bank cards accepted.* Clothing, gourmet foods, jewelry, tea and jams from Ireland, Scotland, and the British Isles.

Donegal Imports, *5358 W. Devon, Chicago, (312) 792-2377. Hours: Monday, 10 A.M. to 5 P.M.; Tuesday, Wednesday and Friday, 10 A.M. to 6 P.M.; Thursday, 10 A.M. to 8 P.M.; Saturday, 10 A.M. to 5:30 P.M. All credit cards accepted.* Located in the Edgebrook neighborhood on the far Northwest Side. Gift items, sweaters, fine crystal.

Touch of Ireland and Europe, *(two locations) 4140 W. 95th St., Oaklawn, Ill., (708) 422-3473; and 140 N. LaGrange Road, LaGrange, (708) 579-3473. Hours: Monday–Friday, 10 A.M. to 5 P.M.; Thursday until 7:30 P.M.; Saturdays, 10 A.M. to 5 P.M. Credit cards accepted.* Features fine Waterford crystal, Hummel figurines, handicraft items, records, tapes, sweaters, and shirts. The LaGrange location is the larger of the two stores.

Irish Crystal, *815 E. Nerge Road, Roselle, (708) 351-3722. Hours: Tuesday through Saturday, 10 A.M. to 5 P.M.; Closed Sundays and Mondays. Bank cards accepted.* Specializing in Tyrone crystal which is comparable to Waterford, but less expensive. No jewelry items sold here.

Irish Connoisseur, *1232 Waukegan Road, Glenview, (708) 998-1988. Hours: Monday through Saturday, 9:30 A.M. to 5:30 P.M. All credit cards accepted.* Delicatessen and gift shop all in one. Irish Sausage, bacon, black and white pudding, and soda bread direct from the "auld sod." The gift section features crystal items, jewelry, books, tapes, and sweaters. On this location for five years.

Shamrock Imports, *3150 N. Laramie, Chicago, (312) 286-6866. Hours: Tuesday–Thursday, 10 A.M. to 5:30 P.M.; Friday, 10 A.M. to 8 P.M.; Saturdays, 10 A.M. to 5:30 P.M. Cash or check only.* Food, jewelry, fine china, baby items, hats and sweaters directly from Ireland.

Irish Treasure Trove, *17W424 W. 22nd St., Oakbrook Terrace, (708) 530-2522. Hours: Monday through Friday, 10 A.M. to 5:30 P.M.; Thursday until 8 P.M.; Saturday, 10 A.M. to 5 P.M.; Sundays, 12 A.M. to 4 P.M. Bank cards accepted.* Waterford crystal, elite china, records, jams, teas, and clothing items.

Irish Boutique, *434 Robert Parker Coffin Road, Long Grove, (708) 634-3540. Hours: Monday–Saturday, 10 A.M. to 5 P.M.; Sunday, 11 A.M. to 5 P.M. All credit cards accepted.* Books, gourmet foods, Waterford and Tipperary crystal, jewelry, china, and records. One of two affiliated stores in the historic village of Long Grove.

Paddy's On the Square, *428 McHenry Road, Long Grove, (708) 634-0339.* Sister store of the Irish Boutique. Two levels of merchandise, including heraldry items, woolens, hats, and records and tapes. Same hours as the Boutique. All credit cards accepted.

Shannon Imports, *5726 W. 95th Street, Oak Lawn, (708) 424-7055. Hours: Monday to Friday, 10 A.M. to 6 P.M.; Tuesdays till 8 P.M. Closed Sunday. Visa, Mastercard accepted.* Newspapers from Ireland delivered every day, gourmet foods, fine crystal, hats, caps, jewelry and souvenirs.

South Side Irish Imports, *3234 W. 111th Street, Chicago, (312) 881-8585. Hours: Monday to Friday, 10 A.M. to 5:30 P.M.; Saturday, 10 A.M. to 4 P.M.; Closed Sundays. Bank cards accepted.* China, glassware, jewelry and gift items. Located at 111th and Sawyer, one block west of Kedzie.

All Things Irish, *P.O. Box 94, Glenview, (708) 998-4510.* Importers and distributors of Irish jewelry and quality Irish merchandise. Write to them for a free catalog.

Media in Irish
Irish Radio Programming

Mary Riordan and Harry Costelloe play records, interview guests and comment on local Irish affairs on WCEV, 1450 AM, live from Gaelic Park every Sunday night from 7:05–9:00 P.M.

Colm O'Guarim, WCEV, 1450 AM, Sundays, 6:30 P.M. to 7 P.M.

Jim Daly, WPNA, 1490 AM, Saturdays, 8 A.M. to 9 A.M.

The Hagerty Family, Saturdays, 9 A.M. to 11 A.M., WPNA, 1490 AM.

Mike O'Connor, Saturdays, 11 A.M. to 1 P.M., WPNA, 1490 AM.

Martin Fahey, Saturdays, 11 A.M. to noon, WJOB, 1230 AM.

Mike Shevlin, Saturdays, 6:30 P.M. to 8 P.M., WPNA, 1490 AM.

Joe Brett, Saturdays, 8 P.M. to 9 P.M., WPNA, 1490 AM.

Maureen Looney, Wednesdays, 9 P.M. to 10 P.M., WSBC, 1240 AM.

Tom O'Malley, Saturdays, 9 P.M. to 10 P.M., WPNA, 1490 AM.

AIRN Irish Program, Tuesday evenings, 9 P.M. to 10 P.M., on WSBC, 1240 AM.

Irish TV

Cable Channel 25 in Chicago offers viewers two Irish ethnic broadcasts each week. On Monday evenings at 7 P.M., the latest news, sports, and entertainment with a local angle airs from 7 to 9 P.M. The Irish-American Journal is a regular feature on Thursday evenings from 6 to 6:30 P.M. For those without a cable hookup, these programs are regularly aired at the Abbey Pub, 3420 W. Grace Street, Chicago, (312) 478-4408.

Bridgeport: Hardscrabble
By Any Other Name

Bridgeport occupies a special place in Chicago history, not only because it continues to be the spawning ground of past and present Chicago mayors, but this community which stands on the periphery of the old Union Stockyards was home to successive waves of European immigrants. It is one of Chicago's oldest, if not most colorful, neighborhoods. During the Civil War, it was a hotbed of secessionist-Copperhead thinking. There existed an underground railroad of sorts for Confederate fugitives seeking to avoid incarceration in the nearby Union prisoner-of-war camp, Camp Douglas.

The character of Bridgeport (or Lee's Place, originally) was of course shaped by the Irish, who began arriving in 1836 to dig the Illinois and Michigan Canal, the waterway linking Chicago to the South and Southwest. They lived in meager, rotting shanties along the banks of the Chicago River, subsisting on a diet of cabbage. Since there was precious little else to eat, the South Side Irish community was derisively known for a time as "Cabbagetown." The immigrants grew the hated vegetable in a large cultivated plot of land at 30th and Halsted Streets, which is now McGuane Park. With the coming of the riverboat trade, the sea captains dubbed the area "Bridgeport," because the Ashland Avenue bridge sat so low over the river that the barges had to be unloaded in order for them to pass safely under the trestle. The heavy cargo loads had to be carried along the banks and reloaded on the other side of the bridge. The consolidation of the old South Side slaughterhouses into the Union Stockyards in 1865 brought with it increased employment opportunity for many Eastern Europeans pouring into Chicago for the first time—and despair for the area residents. The South Fork of the South Branch of the Chicago River became known as "Bubbly Creek," for this open sewer is where the stockyard workers dumped the rotting animal carcasses and offal at day's end. Very often the Germans, Irish, Poles, Italians, and Lithuanians who looked forward to their Sunday picnics were forced to cancel their outing if the wind happened to be blowing in the wrong direction. Bubbly Creek is but an unhappy memory today, though it is still possible to catch a glimpse of the site at 35th St. and the Chicago River—Bridgeport's western boundary. The stockyards closed down for good in 1971. If you want to see cattle pens, you must travel to Kansas City. All that remains on the South Side is the stone entranceway designed by Burnham and Root at Exchange Avenue and Peoria. A limestone head, carved in the likeness of "Sherman," a prize bull belonging to Burnham's father-in-law John B. Sherman (who lent his name to the stockyards), is carved over the central arch.

Sunday was their only day of rest, when the slaughterhouse workers could picnic in the city parks with their families or take in a ball game at Charley Comiskey's tiny little grandstand at 39th and Princeton (the place that served as the home of the White Sox until 1910, when spacious Comiskey Park, the "South Side Cathedral," was built four blocks north at 35th and Shields).

Bridgeport is a densely populated residential and manufacturing neighborhood. Red brick "worker cottages" and two-flats, many of them below the street level, can be found to the north and west of the new Comiskey Park. According to 1980 census figures, there were 30,923 people living in the ward, most of them white ethnics. By 1985, racial change was evident, as the Hispanic population, spilling over from Pilsen and South Lawndale, increased to 7,133 from 6,584. Blacks, who had encountered stiff resistance in their earlier efforts to purchase affordable housing in Bridgeport, began making inroads. There were only 501 African-Americans counted at this time, but the number was substantially higher than the 34 who lived in the 11th Ward in 1980. It is a secular, insulated community, where the neighbors look out for each other and tend to view outsiders with suspicion. On warm summer nights people will sit on the stoops of their buildings engaging in the kind of social interaction that has gone on in this neighborhood since the time of Finley Peter Dunne. The Maxwell Street Depot at 31st and Canal serves the best pork chop sandwiches and Polish sausages this side of Kansas City, and after a ballgame it is the place to go for a late night repast. The Maxwell Street Depot never closes.

On Wells Street and on Princeton Avenue, north of the ballpark, a passing motorist will very often be forced to weave a criss-cross pattern around double-parked, unticketed automobiles. It goes without saying that these vehicles belong to Chicago police officers, firemen, and city workers. That's real Chicago clout. That's Bridgeport.

Politics and racial polarization have characterized much of the recent history of this community. Fearful blacks do not linger in this neighborhood after dark. In a notorious incident that reflected the often brutal realities of modern urban life, two Chicago police officers picked up two black teenagers who were making their way home from Comiskey Park on August 14, 1989, and then drove them into the heart of Canaryville, where they were dropped curbside. The boys were assaulted by seven whites. Conversely, there are few white Bridgeporters who would venture into the Douglas neighborhood east of the Dan Ryan Expressway at nightfall.

Bridgeport has served as the unofficial home of the Chicago Democratic Party, long before "Hizzoner" Richard J. Daley appeared on the scene, though it can be said that the late mayor was the community's most colorful and famous resident.

Early in life, Daley was a member of the Irish branch of the Hamburg Social Athletic Club (there was a Croatian and Lithuanian faction also), a gang of roughhouse "boyos" who were not afraid to knock a few heads on behalf of the local committeeman. You came up through the ranks and paid your dues like everyone else if you wanted to get ahead. That is how politics were conducted in the old days, and no one understood this better than Daley, the father of the "bootstrap theory" of American politics. Richard J. lived in a modest bungalow on the 3500 block of Lowe Avenue his entire adult life. On Sunday mornings, Daley, his wife "Sis," and their children would stroll by the homes of their friends and neighbors as they

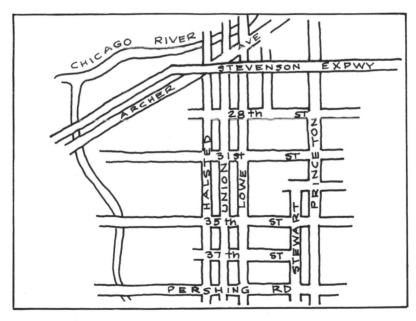

Bridgeport

made their way to the Nativity of Our Lord Church at 37th and Union for Mass. The South Side Irish are deeply rooted in their local parishes. If, for example, you strike up a conversation with a stranger on the street, he will most often ask you the name of the parish you grew up in. That will tell him all he needs to know about your circumstances.

The Daley family still maintains a residence on South Lowe, located conveniently down the block from the Deering District Police Station. The house is easily recognizable by the large American flag flapping in the breeze and by the unmarked squad car conspicuously parked in front. Within walking distance of the Daley home are the residences of former mayors Michael Bilandic (a Croatian), Martin Kennelly, and a host of lesser lights who comprised the fabled 11th Ward Democratic Machine headquartered across the street from Schaller's Pump at 37th and Halsted. "Da Mayor, Da Church, and Da White Sox"—so it goes in Bridgeport.

Prior to 1850, the canal workers living along Archer Avenue would row their small boats down the Chicago River in order to attend Mass at old St. Patrick's Cathedral, then located at Randolph and Des Plaines Ave. In 1850, St. Bridget's, the first Irish parish in the city, was established at 2928 South Archer Avenue for the benefit of the large immigrant settlement. It still serves as a house of worship, but the parishioners are no longer exclusively Irish. There are Mexicans, Poles, and Lithuanians in the congregation. Long-time residents point to the growing influx of Chinese spilling over from 22nd Street, along with the Arabs, Mexicans, and Greeks who are slowly displacing those Irish who have remained behind—out of sentiment for time-honored traditions or the feeling of identity they get from the nurturing comfort of old friends.

— Irish Soda Bread In All Colors —

Brown Soda Bread

2 cups whole wheat flour (pastry flour preferred)
1-1/2 cups of wheat bran
1 cup of unbleached white flour
1 teaspoon of baking soda
1 teaspoon of salt
1-3/4 cups of buttermilk

Pre-heat the oven to 350 degrees. Place the bran and flours in a mixing bowl. Add salt and soda, crushing lumps of soda between your fingers. Stir until combined, then add buttermilk all at once, stirring with a spoon until the mixture pulls away from the bowl. Add a splash of buttermilk if necessary. The dough should be soft but not too sticky. Turn on to floured board, flour your hands, and knead three to four times, or until the dough is smooth. Form into a rounded loaf, then make a series of one-eighth inch deep slashes to form a cross and bake 45 minutes, or until the bread sounds hollow after being thumped. Cool on the rack.

White Irish Soda Bread

4 cups unbleached white flour (pastry flour preferred)
1 teaspoon of baking soda
1 teaspoon of salt
2 cups of buttermilk

Follow the same instructions as with the brown soda bread.

Irish Dark Soda Bread

3 cups all-purpose flour
2 cups whole-wheat flour
1 tablespoon of baking powder
2 tablespoons of brown sugar
2-1/4 cups of buttermilk

Pre-heat the oven to 375 degrees. Place all of the dry ingredients in a large bowl and mix thoroughly. Pour the buttermilk into the bowl and stir with a wooden spoon until a soft dough is formed. Pour the contents of the bowl onto a plastic counter and knead it for at least one minute. Divide the dough into two portions and shape each into a round loaf, pressing the top down to flatten. Place the loaves on a large, ungreased baking sheet. Sprinkle additional flour on the top of each loaf. Allow the loaves to sit for ten minutes, then bake on the middle rack of the oven for forty minutes or until the loaves are golden brown.

Honey Walnut Oatmeal Soda Bread

1 cup rolled oats (not instant)
1-2/3 cups of buttermilk
1/3 cup of honey
2 tablespoons of unsalted butter
1-1/2 cups of whole wheat flour

1-1/2 cups of unbleached flour
2 teaspoons of baking powder
1 teaspoon of baking soda
1 cup (4 to 5 ounces) of coarsechopped walnuts

Lightly oil a large, heavy baking sheet. Sprinkle it lightly with rolled oats. Pre-heat the oven to 400 degrees. Place the oats into a large bowl and pour the buttermilk over them. Gently warm the honey and butter in a small saucepan until the butter melts. Stir them into the oats. In a large mixing bowl, combine the remaining ingredients and toss with your hands to mix. Make a well in the center of the dry ingredients, then add the liquid oat mixture. Stir from the center out until you have a soft dough. Turn it out onto a floured surface and divide in half. With floured hands, knead each half into a ball and place both on a sheet. Bake for thirty minutes until it is brown on both sides. Transfer the loaves to a rack and cool them for at least ten minutes before slicing. Store the cooled loaves in plastic bags.

Scottish Chicago

Nobody knows for sure, and the figures are not approximate, but there are probably 100,000 Chicagoans with at least a trace of Scottish blood in them. The Scots, according to Wayne Rethford, director of the Scottish Home in North Riverside, dispersed rather quickly across Cook, Lake, and DuPage Counties, and never formed their own distinctive communities as did the Italians, Germans, or Poles, for example. The English-speaking immigrants were not encumbered by language barriers, and therefore were better able to assimilate into whatever neighborhoods they chose. But their Chicago roots run very deep, and up until the 1890s, the Scots were among the ten largest European ethnic groups in the city. The majority of Scots disdained the political arena, and chose instead to pursue careers in banking and commerce.

The Illinois St. Andrew's Society was organized the night of November 30, 1845, when a group of hearty Scotsmen gathered together to celebrate in verse and song the Feast of St. Andrew, who was adopted as the patron saint of the Picts. In attendance that night was West Point cadet George McClellan, a fresh-faced nineteen-year old who happened to be passing through Chicago. McClellan, of course, went on to make a name for himself as one of the commanding generals of the Army of the Potomac during the Civil War.

An enduring city tradition was born, and for every year thereafter the oldest fraternal society in Illinois has donned the kilt every November to pay homage to the founding members, and to recall the exploits of one George Anderson. In every respect, George Anderson was the quintessential "common man." He served for a time as the postmaster at the substation located at 22nd and State Streets. But Anderson was the driving force behind the St. Andrew's Society. He helped draft the first constitution and by-laws in 1853. He secured two plots of land for his fellow Scotsmen who desired to be interred at the Rosehill Cemetery on the far North Side. At the time of his death in 1887, Anderson was the last surviving member of that historic 1845 banquet. George Anderson set the tone for all future banquets by reading aloud "Tam O'Shanter," a spirited narrative verse penned by Scotland's national poet, Robert Burns (1759–96).

Burns, a restless and dissatisfied social rebel, railed against religious orthodoxy, charming both the common folk and the literary social circles of Edinburgh, Scotland. His enduring legacy extended all the way across the Atlantic, where in 1906, a Burns Monument Society was established in Chicago. Donations were accepted from thousands of local Scots who paid for the construction of a statue to honor his memory. The Burns memorial fronts Washington Boulevard in Garfield Park, and is lovingly maintained by the Scottish Home, whose residents lay a wreath on the ground each year on the poet's birthday.

The History of the Bagpipe

Bagpipes were not invented by the Scots. Latin and Greek sculptures, dating back to 400 B.C., depict men playing the instrument, and an early reference is made to this unusual kind of music in the book of Daniel. The Scottish bagpipe dates back to about the year 100 A.D. It has filled an important role over the years. Scottish clan chiefs ordered their warriors to carry the instrument into battle as a means of psychologically terrorizing the enemy. While the bagpipe is essentially a folk instrument, its use in war dates back to the eighteenth century. It was also used for more peaceful purposes: to welcome visitors or to mourn the passing of friends or relatives. The bagpipe is also a solo instrument and each clan chieftain has always had a hereditary piper.

The highland bagpipe is a wind instrument that consists of a bag of sheepskin or elk hide from which five pipes protrude. There is a mouthpiece for inflating the bag, a single octave chanter for creating the melody and three drones, one base, and two tenors, which sound a constant two-note chord to soften the overall sound quality. The bag is covered by the tartan of the piper's family or pipe band, and the pipe major (leader of the band) will place a banner on the bass drone. The piper positions the bag under his left arm, but the drones are required to carry it over the left shoulder.

It is a melodic, but often sad music that evokes powerful feelings within the listener. In its highest form—*ceol more* (the "great music")—the piper relates a story in the mournful notes, which often requires great feeling and personal expression.

Events and Attractions

The Scottish Home, *2800 Des Plaines Ave. (28th Ave. and Des Plaines St.), North Riverside, Ill., (708) 442-7268.* The Scottish Home is the oldest non-profit corporation in Illinois, and has occupied this parcel of land since 1910, when the administrators moved from 43 Bryant Avenue (now 35th St.) on Chicago's South Side. A number of elderly Scottish people reside here under the auspices of the St. Andrews Society. A small, little known museum and Hall of Fame honoring 200 prominent local Scots is located in the "undercroft" of the home and is open to the public from 9 A.M. to 9 P.M., seven days a week. The museum is operated by the Scottish Cultural Society. The Robert Burns "corner" features original first editions and memorabilia from the poet's life. The Hall of Fame gallery, composed of 200 wall plaques, honors the notable men and women of Scottish descent in the city's history. Free admission.

Annual St. Andrews Banquet, *held on the second weekend of November, at the Chicago Hilton and Towers, 720 S. Michigan Ave., Chicago.* What began in 1845 as a small, informal dinner affair continues more than 145 years later in one of Chicago's most fashionable downtown hotels. Scottish singers, accompanied by pipe bands, provide the entertainment, and a few of the more hearty members of the society will brave the November wind-chill factor to wear the traditional kilt. Tickets can be purchased in advance for $75.00 per person, by calling (708) 442-7268. Membership in the St. Andrews Society is open to all persons of Scottish descent. Annual dues are $25.00 per person.

"Nicht Wi' Burns" ("A Night With Burns"), *Dinner and celebration on or about January 26 (the poet's birthday) at the Hilton Inn, 9333 S. Cicero Ave., Oak Lawn.* Scottish folk songs. Readings from Burns's most famous works. Pipe Bands. Native dancers.

Admission: $30.00 for adults, $10.00 for children. For additional information, call the Scottish Home at (708) 442-7268.

St. Andrew Highland Games, *held on the grounds of the Chicago College of Osteopathic Medicine, 555 31st St., Downers Grove, each year in mid-June.*   There is certainly more to Scottish culture than Robert Burns, bagpipes and folk dancing, evidenced by the Highland Games, an annual test of athletic stamina. Among the day's events is a rugby match, the 56-pound hammer throw, and sheaf and caber toss (lifting a 120-pound pole, and hurling it so that it rotates 360 degrees), by the representative Scottish clans in the U.S. In addition to these grueling feats of strength, there are the customary pipe bands, genealogy booths, a Parade of Tartans—led by Scottish deerhounds—country dancers, vendors, continuous music, food concessions, stunt kite flying exhibitions, and a fiddle workshop. The cost is $8.00 per person ($5.00 for children). The proceeds benefit the Scottish Home. Call (708) 442-SCOT for details and times. *Recommended.*

Annual Scottish Fair, *Odeum Sports and Expo Center, 1033 N. Villa Avenue, Villa Park.*   A two-day indoor festival sponsored by the Scottish Cultural Society, featuring famed local bagpipe bands including the Emerald Society and the Chicago Highlanders. During the solo bagpipe competition, over 100 local performers will compete for top prizes. A Scottish judge evaluates the contestants on technique, tuning, tempo, and musical performance. On Saturday night, the fair will host a "Ceilidh" (pronounced "kaylee"), which is a traditional Scottish sing-along led by the Canadian band Cromdale. The Scottish Fair has delighted Chicagoans since 1977. Over 10,000 people pass through the doors of the Expo Center each year. The event takes place the second weekend in October and admission is $7.00 for adults, $4.50 for seniors and children, and $18.00 for families. For information about the Scottish Fair, contact Teri Hays at (708) 629-2227.

Ethnic Society

The Scottish Cultural Society, Ltd., was formed by twelve Scottish enthusiasts in 1977 to bring the music, arts, history, and literature of the country into wide focus within the Chicagoland area. Meetings deal with a range of topics, including discussions on the life and times of famed poets and authors such as Robert Burns and Sir Walter Scott, proper highland dress, and musical entertainment. The society publishes the

Celtic Knot, a monthly newsletter sent free to the more than 500 members. To join the SCS please call (708) 629-2227, or write to P.O. Box 486, Lombard, IL, 60148-0486. A one year membership is $15 per person, or $20 for an entire family.

Restaurant, Food and Gift Shops

Duke of Perth Restaurant, *2913 N. Clark St., Chicago (312) 477-1741.* Owned by a Scotsman from Aberdeen, who specializes in Scottish gourmet foods, including shepherd's pie, Hebridean leek pie, and smoked salmon. McEwan's Export and Newcastle Brown Ale on tap. The first Saturday of the month is "Open Pipe Night" when patrons are invited to bring along their own bagpipes and perform. Open Mon.– Thurs., 11:30 A.M.–1:00 A.M.; Fridays till 2:00 A.M.; Saturday, 12:00 P.M.–2:00 A.M.; Sunday, 12:00 P.M.–1:00 A.M.

Scottish Modern, *6115 S. Archer, Summit, (708) 594-5773.* Seven thousand square feet of gift items, imported foods, jewelry, books, and Scottish clothing items, including a rich array of kilts. A tailor shop is on the premises. Open Mon.–Fri., 10:00 A.M.–6:00 P.M.; Saturday, 10:00 A.M.–5:00 P.M. Mastercard and Visa accepted.

Winston Sausage Co., *4701 W. 63rd St., Chicago, (312) 767-4353.* Specializing in Scottish meat pies, but there is also a rich assortment of imported Irish and British foods. Open 7:00 A.M.–6:00 P.M. Monday–Saturday.

International Antiques, *2907 N. Clark St., Chicago, (312) 528-4602.* Direct shipments from Scotland bimonthly. A fine line of imported furniture including hass stands, wickerwork, art deco, bric-a-brac, Victoriana, chests, bureaus. Open seven days a week 11:30 A.M.–7:00 P.M.

Rampant Lion Celtic Traders, *2004 S. 3rd St., Maywood, (312) 622-1925.* Largest selection of bagpipe recordings in the metro area. Books, jewelry, music, videos and T-shirts. Call Jack and Gayle Baker at (312) 622-1925 for hours, or send $2.00 for a catalog of merchandise.

Anglo Saxons

British Club, *meets regularly at the Latvian Community Center, 4146 N. Elston Ave., Chicago, Ill.* Membership is open to persons of English extraction, or anyone with a passing interest in the history and culture of the British Isles. The club sponsors yearly travel excursions and sightseeing tours to the United Kingdom and Ireland; holds an Annual St. George's Day Spring dance every May; offers discounts on merchandise at the various import shops around town; and publishes a newsletter for dues-paying members. Club nights are held on alternating Fridays at the Latvian center at 8:00 P.M., unless otherwise posted. A one-year membership is $20.00 per person, or $30.00 for couples. Please contact Joan Murphy at (708) 673-6335 for additional information.

The Red Lion Pub, *2446 N. Lincoln Ave., Chicago, (312) 348-2695.* Chicago's kindred spirits who fancy kidney pie, cornish pastries, and English beer meet and greet each other at the city's most famous English restaurant and pub; John Cordwell's Red Lion, across the street from the Biograph Theater, where John Dillinger was mowed down in 1934. There's no chance of that happening again. The Lincoln-Fullerton neighborhood is one of the most gentrified neighborhoods in the city, appealing to an urban mix of literary bohemians, artisans, and young professionals. But inside the Red Lion at least, the atmosphere is verrrrrry British. Hours: Monday, 4:00 P.M.–2:00 A.M.; Tuesday–Sunday, 12:00 P.M.–2:00 A.M. Credit cards accepted. *Recommended.*

British Faire, *105 W. Jefferson Ave., Naperville, (708) 717-9277.* Fine selection of British-motif sweatshirts, Scottish woolens, Staffordshire pottery, pub ornaments, and gourmet British foods. Hours: Monday–Friday, 10:30 A.M.–5:30 P.M.; Saturday, 10:00 A.M.–5:00 P.M. Closed Sunday. Credit cards taken.

Events

English Festival, *St. Lawrence Episcopal Church, 125 W. Church St., Libertyville, (708) 362-2110.* Annual festival held the third Saturday in September on church grounds. Jugglers, musicians, and clowns for the kiddies. Folk dancing and bagpipes courtesy of the Royal Scottish Dance Society, and the Morris Dancers, with music provided by a troubadour harpist, and brass quintet. Crafts and food booths. Silent auction on handmade items. Admission to the fair is free. Call (708) 362–2110 for dates and times.

Bristol Renaissance Faire (formerly King Richard's Faire), *Bristol, Wisconsin. One-quarter mile west of Interstate I-94 on State Line Road at the Illinois-Wisconsin border. Exit Russell Road, turn left and follow the signs.*   Journey back to the Renaissance and experience English Elizabethan village life in the Midwest. Each year 100 drama students are trained in Shakespearean dialogue, sword fighting, and country dance in order to authenticate the period. The Hammond-Lee Action Theatre performs three jousts a day, very often in the sweltering August humidity of Wisconsin. This is live, interactive outdoor theater at its best, combining history, culture, and medieval fun. Court jesters, pan handlers, and a delightful group calling itself the "Flaming Idiots" entertains at every turn in the road. The village merchants sell traditional foods from the Elizabethan period, and assorted souvenirs. The Bristol Renaissance Faire is open on Saturdays and Sundays in August from 10:00 A.M.–7:00 P.M.. Admission: $10.95 per person, children 5–12, $5.50, and youngsters under five are admitted free. Please contact the Bristol Renaissance Faire at 12420 128th St., Kenosha, Wis., or call (708) 395-7773; (414) 396-4320; or Ticketmaster at (708) 395-7773. *Recommended.*

Oz Park Medieval Faire, *Intersection of Webster, Lincoln Ave., and Larrabee Sts., Oz Park, Chicago, Ill.*   A gala old English pageant sponsored by the Lincoln Park Chamber of Commerce the first weekend in August. Call (312) 880-5200. For another slice of Renaissance life, the Lincoln Park Chamber of Commerce sponsors its own medieval fair, featuring 200 volunteers in authentic period costumes, puppet shows for the kids, and Shakespearean performances. It is an annual event that has expanded in size and scope since its inception in 1985. Donations requested.

Medieval Times Dinner & Tournament, *2001 Roselle Road, Schaumburg, (708) 843-3900, or 1-800-544-2001.*   The Count and Countess of Perelada welcome you to their home . . . an 11th Century English castle that looms over the Northwest Suburban landscape. The exterior of this imposing fortress is modeled after one built in Spain during the 11th century. Step back with them to the year 1093 . . . when gallant jousters, and knights defended the realm. Dine on roasted chicken, dragon ribs, and herb-basted potatoes served on pewter plates as you watch the

Andalusian horses gallop about the 1,400-seat arena. Up above, a trained falcon swoops in a figure eight pattern as you digest the remainder of your four-course meal. The evening concludes with fight-to-the-death jousting tournament, and a battle for the sword of Charlemagne. Historical fact counts for little here. It's the skills of the horsemen, the wonderfully choreographed stage combat, and the food dishes that count. Medieval Times is one of Chicago's newest and most exciting attractions, with a dinner and show every night except Monday and Tuesday. Open year-round. The one-price admission ($28–$34 for adults, $20–$24 for children) includes dinner, show, beverages, and tax (cash bar service available). For information and reservations, call 1-800-544-2001. For groups of fifteen or more call (708) 882-0555.

King's Manor Medieval Dinner Theatre, *2122 W. Lawrence Ave., Chicago, (312) 275-8400.*   Contemporary plays set during the Middle Ages. The food is served to you without silverware. This is after all, the Middle Ages. Twice each month the ensemble cast presents "Murder at the Manor," a classic mystery. Guests are asked to show up a half-hour before the show, which begins at 7:30 P.M., Wednesday–Thursday, Fridays at 8:00 P.M.; Saturdays, 6:00 P.M. & 10:00 P.M.; and Sundays at 7:00 P.M. Dinner and theater prices range from $23.50 to $26.50 per person. Please call ahead for reservations.

German Chicago

══════ History and Settlement ══════

"Discontent here is a German plant from Berlin and Leipzig!" snorted
crusty old Micheal Schaak, Police Inspector assigned to the "Nord Seid"
in the mid 1880s. Schaak, himself a native of the Grand Duchy of
Luxembourg, expressed the prejudicial attitudes of many Chicagoans
toward the much-maligned German immigrant during the hectic days and
months following the 1886 Haymarket Riot. The belief that these people
were here to foment revolution and unrest persisted through the labor
troubles of the mid- to late-nineteenth century, and through two world
wars. These factors contributed, according to Rudolf A. Hofmeister, to
the decision by many Chicagoans to deny their "German background,
refusing to indicate that they were born in Germany, or born of German
parents who had emigrated from Germany." Only in recent years have
historians looked past the "Beer, Bundist, and Gemütlichkeit" stereotypes
to rediscover the cultural contributions of these people in the total Chicago
experience.

Chicago's original German settler—Heinrich Rothenfeld—arrived in
the city in 1825, a dozen years before the city charter was granted.
Rothenfeld settled in Dunkley's Grove, now the village of Addison in the
west suburbs. He was joined by Johann Wellmacher in 1830, and
Matthias Meyer who came here from Frankfort-on-the-Main in 1831.
Meyer opened one of the first bakery shops in the city. When Chicago

was incorporated in 1837, there were eighteen registered voters of German extraction. In the city election held that year, Clemens S. Stose, a German blacksmith was elected alderman. On March 10, 1842, a German school was opened in the Dutch settlement known as "New Buffalo" on the Near North Side between Chicago and North Avenues. It was the first Germanic settlement in the city, but it did not remain homogeneous for long. In the 1850s large numbers of Swedes and Irish began populating the area. The Germans pushed further north to the "Old Town" neighborhood bounded by Division, LaSalle, Armitage, and Halsted streets. The area thrived, especially after the great fire of 1871 when improvements in public transportation provided the immigrants with easy, affordable access to the industrial corridor along the Chicago River and the famous breweries so closely associated with the German experience in Chicago.

William Haas and Konrad Sulzer—instrumental in Chicago's early development—opened the first brewery in 1836, churning out 600 barrels of foamy a year. Sulzer went into partnership with future mayor William B. Ogden. Bavarian-born Mattias Best was the second brewmaster of note; founding his business on the South Side at 14th Street and Indiana. Eight years later, Adolph P. Mueller established a small brewery on the corner of State and Randolph--Chicago's famous *Bierstube*--where the foamy suds were manufactured and sold in the shadow of the court house, which stood across the street. By 1856 the nine German breweries were churning out 16,270 barrels a year.

The Bavarians, Prussians, and the neighboring Irish who lived in close proximity on the North Side greatly alarmed the temperance advocates who feared that Chicago was about to become a beer-soaked den of iniquity. The "Nativists," a loose coalition of teetotalers, Anglo-Saxons, anti-Irish, and anti-German Catholic haters, found a sympathetic ally in the person of Dr. Levi Boone, elected mayor in 1855. In his inaugural address Boone outlined his promise to proscribe the liquor trade entirely, but the city council favored a compromise measure. Instead the saloon licensing fee rose to $300. Within days of the passage of the objectionable ordinance, the small untrained city police began to enforce the equally unpopular Sunday closing law. Such an affront to long-standing German traditions galvanized public opinion against the city administration. Some of the brewers, led by Valentin Blatz, attempted to thwart Boone and his minions by draping windows and constructing a secret side-door entrance. Those less inclined to cloak and dagger tactics decided to take a stand against the " Know Nothings."

On April 20, 1855, an angry mob of tradesmen, whose only gripe was against the prohibitionists, stormed the courthouse. "The Dutch are crossing the bridge!" The hue and cry went up. The Germans and the Irish were met at gunpoint by the police and local militias. The "Lager Beer Riot" was on. It was a short, bloody skirmish that was over within minutes. Sixty rioters were herded into the Bridewell. There was only one casualty: an immigrant cobbler named Peter Martin, who was shot in the back by the sheriff after fleeing from the police. Martin had shot and wounded a police officer named George Hunt. Despite the sizeable number of Irish on the Chicago police force at this time, it is interesting to note that a German immigrant, Casper Lauer, who was born in France, was the first officer to fall in the line of duty. He was stabbed to death in September, 1854, by a criminal offender. On October 29, 1990, his name was inscribed on the Illinios Police Memorial in Springfield, Illinois.

The Know Nothings claimed a victory but their movement was thoroughly discredited and was over as quickly as it had begun. The prohibition law, which the coalition attempted to ram down the throats of the legislature, was rejected by the popular referendum in June. The Germans earned the right to enjoy their "continental" Sundays, but the oppression did not end with the Lager Beer Riot. During the labor troubles of 1877, a detachment of police battered down the doors of the West Side Turner Hall at Roosevelt and Halsted in search of Communist "agitators" and followers of the German "apostles of anarchy," Johann Most and August Reinsdorf. On May 11, 1878, Reinsdorf fired several shots at King William of Prussia, but he missed the mark.

A peaceable assembly of German workingmen were clubbed and fired upon in a flagrant abuse of police power that was typical of those paranoic times, when foreign speaking people often were perceived to be violent revolutionaries. The incident was recounted years later by Governor John Peter Altgeld when he pardoned the imprisoned Haymarket men. The Germans who gathered at the Turner Hall of Chicago for the most part were not anarchists or bomb throwers as the police chose to believe, but disciples of Friedrich L. Jahn (1778–1852), the father of the *"Turnvereine."*

In 1804 Jahn, a physical education teacher, believed that the moral fiber of his nation was intrinsically tied to healthy minds and robust bodies. The gymnastics and paramilitaristic regimens of Jahn's Turnvereine won many converts among the German youth. Friedrich Jahn, however, was imprisoned and many of his adherents were driven out of the country. The first Chicago Turnverein was founded in 1852 by two outstanding German educators named Karl Follen and Karl Beck who arrived in the U.S. twenty-eight years earlier. The impact of this German socio-athletic society they introduced to Chicago was profound. Two days after President Abraham Lincoln issued his call to arms on April 15, 1861,

105 members of the Chicago Turnverein organized the Turner Cadets and volunteered for duty in the Union Army. The 82nd and 24th Illinois Regiments, comprised of German-born Americans and commanded by Colonel Friedrich Hecker, served with distinction during the war. In 1866, a year after the Civil War ended, a proposal to integrate physical education classes into the public school curriculum was unanimously adopted by the city board. But it would take another twenty years before the schools finally implemented the plan. In that year—1886—the board hired eight "Turners" to teach gymnastics to Chicago's students. The German community paid tribute to the visionary Friedrich Jahn in 1907, when a grammar school bearing his name opened in the Lincoln Park and Belmont community on the North Side.

It was the generation known as the "48ers" that left the greatest imprint on Chicago's history. Because of the political, social, and economic upheaval in Hessen, Baden, and Würtemberg, and the subsequent dissolution of the Frankfurt Parliament in 1849, Germans poured into Chicago in record numbers. Within a few years the Germans were second only to the Irish as the most dominant ethnic group in the city. They found employment in the packing houses adjacent to the Union Stockyards along 43rd and 47th Streets on the South Side. A number of the earlier arrivals helped build the Illinois-Michigan Canal. Still others found employment in the building trades, manufacturing, and public service. The Germans were prominent in the city police and fire departments. To reach a happy compromise between the Irish and German constituencies at election time, the mayor often found it necessary to guide the appointment process along these ethnic lines. By 1900, it was customary for the police chief to be Irish and his deputy superintendent German.

The "48ers" were a revolutionary people, to the chagrin of their more conservative countrymen who had arrived several years earlier, and had assimilated into the culture. Among the political exiles arriving in Chicago during this period was Lorenz Brentano (1813–91) who had been condemned to death in Baden for his involvement in the Liberty Party. Brentano settled in Chicago in 1859. Taking an active interest in civic affairs, he served as president of the Chicago School Board from 1863–68, then later as a member of the Illinois General Assembly and the Forty-fifth Congress. During this time he owned and managed the principal German language newspaper in the city, the *Staatszeitung*.

Those less inclined to political activism settled quietly along North Avenue in the "Old Town" Neighborhood—known in later years as the "German Broadway." Community life centered around St. Michael's Church, constructed in 1866 at Eugenie and Cleveland Streets through money donated by Michael Diversey (1810–69), prominent German brewer and Sixth Ward alderman. In his lifetime, Diversey founded three churches: St. Peter and St. Joseph in 1846 and, of course, St. Michael's, which became the largest German parish in the city by 1892. To preserve the folk traditions of the distant homeland, the German settlers founded numerous fraternal societies, singing clubs, and social organizations. Among the earliest were the St. Peter Verein founded in 1847 by Catholic parishioners on the South Side, and the Männergesangverein (Male Singing Club) in 1850. The Frier Sänger Bund staged popular choral performances at the Deutsches Haus (German Hall) built at Grand and Wells Avenue in 1856. It was a focal point of the Old Town neighborhood until it was swept away in the Chicago Fire of 1871.

During that tragic conflagration which tested the fortitude of all Chicagoans, an ethnic German single-handedly saved the city waterworks from destruction, and thereby preserved an important civic landmark on Michigan Avenue. Frank Trautman arrived in New York in 1825, where he worked as an engineer on the first ocean-going steamboat for Ran and Company. Soon afterward he settled in Chicago, and for thirty years he was the chief engineer for the city waterworks. When flames threatened to consume the pumping station on October 8, 1871, Trautman and his assistants covered it with woolen blankets and discarded sails from Lake Michigan vessels. Keeping the covers soaked in lake water, they saved the station from certain destruction and just two days later, Trautman was able to restore the water supply to the beleaguered city.

By the 1930s—the heyday of the European fraternal societies in Chicago—it was estimated that there were 452 such organizations. The Germania Club, founded in 1865 was the most influential in terms of its size and prestige. The founding members sang at the bier of the martyred President Abraham Lincoln when the funeral cortege passed through Chicago in 1865. The club later moved to its spacious headquarters at 1536 North Clark Street in 1889, east of Old Town. Through these doors passed generations of Chicago Germans, many of them prominent in government, the arts, and finance. William DeVry, founder of the DeVry Institute of Technology, served as president from 1961 to 1963. The composer Richard Strauss, Professor Albert Einstein, and German Chancellor Konrad Adenauer were a few of the many visiting dignitaries to partake of the Germania Club's hospitality.

Old Town remained a homogenous German community until the 1910s when a number of Hungarians and Eastern Europeans began to settle along North Avenue. To the north of Old Town the village of Lakeview, sparsely settled in the 1840s and 1850s became the next major hub of

German settlement. Lakeview was annexed to the city of Chicago on June 29, 1889. It was named after a lovely, old fashioned country inn opened in 1854 by James Rees at Grace Street and the lake front.

Konrad Sulzer was Lakeview's first resident, building his 100-acre farm on land formerly inhabited by Sac, Algonquin, and Pottawattami Indians. One of the principal east-west arteries, Montrose Avenue, was originally known as Sulzer Road. The spacious Sulzer Regional Library at Lincoln and Sunnyside is named in honor of the early German pioneer and is considered to be one of the finest branch libraries in the city of Chicago.

In 1881, 72 German families living in Lakeview petitioned the parish of St. Michael's for a church of their own. Cut off and isolated from city life by virtue of their proximity to the "country," the devout Bavarian settlers found it difficult to attend services at St. Michael's on a regular basis. In 1882 the Reverend Joseph Essing resolved the problem when he secured five acres of prime farmland bounded by Wellington, Southport, Oakdale, and Greenview. St. Alphonsus, constructed in 1882 with a towering Gothic ediface, brought to mind the ancient German legend "Higher Than the Church," first told by Hillern.

An impoverished German woodcarver, anxious to win the hand of the mayor's daughter is told that he must build an altar higher than the local church before he could marry the fair beauty. The enterprising young woodcarver achieved the impossible by building an altar whose spire was bent forward. Thus the altar is actually taller than the church itself. The story ends happily with the marriage of the couple amid great rejoicing. The church of St. Alphonsus and the first German school, constructed on the same site, solidified the Lakeview community. Many of the other German churches were founded between 1881 and 1900, when the tide of immigration reached its crest. Of the forty-eight predominantly German houses of worship built between 1872 and 1892, twenty were Lutheran, fifteen Catholic, six Methodist, three Baptist, three Congregational, and one Presbyterian.

What made Lakeview particularly attractive to the ethnic Germans was the tolerant attitude toward social drinking by village officials. The beer gardens flourished in "Chicagoburg" thanks to the Saloon Keeper's Society, organized to "protect and demand their common interests by all lawful means and measures." The building boom in Lakeview between 1885 and 1894, along with improvements in public transportation, encouraged settlement of the north and west sections from the more crowded enclaves to the south and along the lakeshore. Reflecting the growing importance of this up-and-coming neighborhood, the Lakeview Town

Hall was built in 1872 at Halsted and Addison Streets. Today, the 23rd Police District Station or Town Hall occupies the site. The community reached residential maturity between the years of 1910 and 1920 when the population swelled from 60,535 to 96,482. The Germans and Swedes dominated the cultural life of the community in the early years, but those of Hungarian, Polish, and Italian extraction pushed into the southern pockets of Lakeview near the industrial corridor to the southwest.

The coming of World War I presented new hardships for Chicago's burgeoning German community. Torn between their loyalty for their adopted land, and their nationalistic inclinations, the Germans came under sharp attack, especially after the fresh news of German atrocities galvanized public opinion against the Kaiser and his armies. The war, according to Professor Melvin Holli of the University of Illinois, "damaged German ethnic, linguistic, and cultural institutions beyond repair." Sizeable amounts of money were expended by German propagandists in the U.S. to sway the neutrality of Americans—with little success. The Germania Club of Chicago attempted to raise ten million marks for the German chapter of the Red Cross, but did themselves a disservice by declaring that the conflict was a "war of the Teutonic race against the Slavic . . . whether the civilization of western Europe or the barbarism of Russia is to prevail." On August 5, 1914, just a few days after the war broke out on the continent, 5,000 Germans, whipped up into a nationalistic frenzy, marched through the Loop waving flags and banners and singing songs. A stirring torchlight rally was held in Grant Park, in which the speakers exhorted the crowd to support the cause through their hearts and checkbooks. Never before had the city witnessed such a public showing for a foreign government. No other immigrant group was so well organized or financed as the Germans. The Chicago Irish were greater in number, but divided among lace-curtain factions and Clan-na-Gael revolutionaries.

The U.S. entered the war on behalf of the Allies in April 1917, which effectively eliminated German *Kultur* in Chicago. Many fraternal societies dropped their teutonic-sounding names. The Germania Männerchor, for example, became the Chicago "Lincoln Club" on May 9, 1918. When the war came many Germans were arrested and held for seditious activities. German language instruction in the Chicago public schools was temporarily suspended, while many of the immigrants "Americanized" their names, partially out of embarrassment, more likely out of fear of reprisals from other groups.

German Day, a cultural celebration and political rally held each year since June 15, 1893, when 30,000 people showed up to express their Teutonic pride, was suspended in deference to the war effort.

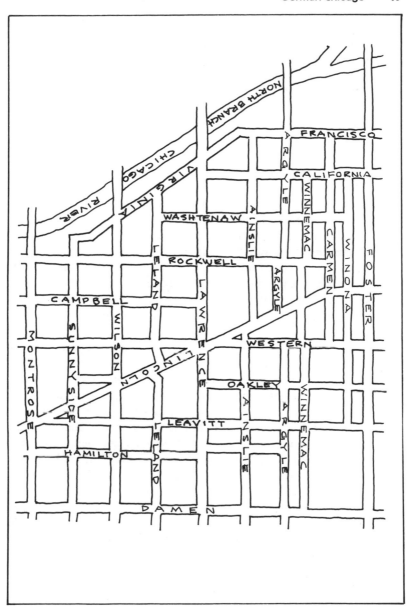

Lincoln Square

In the City Council, Alderman John Haderlein went so far as to propose a change of name for Goethe Street, to Nutwood Street. At the same time the Theodore Thomas Orchestra became the Chicago Symphony. The two world wars undermined the German community. During World War II, anti-German sentiment was such that hotheads in the community demanded that the beautiful statue of Johan Wolfgang von Goethe, designed by Hermann Hahn, and erected at Stockton Drive in Lincoln Park in 1914, be melted down and made into a bomb. Despite these prevailing attitudes, the tide of German immigration into the city continued.

Completion of the Ravenswood elevated line directly west of Lakeview in 1907 opened up the communities of Bowmanville, Ravenswood, Winnemac, and Summerdale (now known as Lincoln Square) to settlement. Three flats, small apartment buildings, and beautiful brick homes constructed along the North Branch of the Chicago River at the western edge of Lincoln Square sprang up almost overnight. Between 1920 and 1930 the Lincoln Square exploded in population growth from 27,990 to 46,419. Lincoln Avenue, once a twisting Indian trail leading to the Green Bay and Fox River portages, became the principal business district, retaining a distinctive German flavor north of Lawrence Avenue. According to 1980 census data, 22 percent of Lincoln Square's 45,954 residents were German. Sizeable Greek, Asian, and Hispanic presences are now changing the complexion of the neighborhood.

The Germans, like so many other ethnic European groups have relinquished their city neighborhoods to the newcomers from Southeast Asia and Latin America. The migration to the suburbs actually began in the 1840s, when a group of German immigrants settled the "Harlem" community (renamed Forest Park). In 1885 the Altenheim (Senior Citizens) Home was founded in this western suburb, whose political history in many ways was *defined* by the Germans. Nineteen of the first twenty-one mayors of Forest Park were of German descent, which by comparison to Chicago's highly partisan political system, tends to dwarf the accomplishments of the Irish in this regard. Chicagoans of German descent comprise 14.5 percent of Forest Park's ethnic composition, and 9.5 percent of the entire suburban population base in Cook and the surrounding collar counties. They are the largest ethnic group residing in the suburbs today, and have transplanted their Turner Halls, social clubs, and choral societies to River Grove, Elmhurst, Waukegan, Aurora, Bartlett, and Buffalo Grove.

Until recently, the German American National Congress (D.A.N.K.), with over sixty regional chapters in the U.S., was headquartered in Mount Prospect, Illinois. However, the organization has returned to the Lincoln Square neighborhood to continue the task of bringing together Americans of German descent so that they may gain a full understanding of their ancestry and heritage. The decision on the part of the D.A.N.K. executive board to return to the old neighborhood suggests a reverse pattern of settlement, a 1980s urban phenomenon likely to continue into the next decade, as thousands of suburbanites rediscover the pleasures of the city.

From the city's earliest days the Germans have left their imprimatur upon Chicago's diverse ethnic culture. The sons and daughters of Deutschland have left behind a legacy of hard work and resourcefulness and a tenacious, unswerving pride in its institutions.

Getting There: The Lincoln Avenue CTA bus (number 11) begins at Congress and Wells in the West Loop and connects downtown with Lincoln Square on the North Side. By car from the Loop, take north-bound Lake Shore Drive to the Lawrence Avenue exit and proceed west, until you reach Western Avenue. Parking can be a problem at times. The solution is to park your car on one of the adjacent side streets off Lawrence Avenue.

German Cultural Center

Goethe Institute of Chicago, *401 N. Michigan Ave., Chicago.* The newly renovated Goethe Institute in Pioneer Court sponsors a diverse program in the arts and humanities, while fostering cooperation between the German government and the people of Chicago. Founded in 1951, and sponsored in part by the Federal Republic of Germany, this nonprofit organization operates 149 branch libraries in sixty-eight nations. The Goethe Institute of Chicago has been at this location since 1978, and the collection includes a wide selection of magazines and newspapers imported from Germany, as well as video cassettes, slides, and music tapes that are available for rental. The institute offers beginning, intermediate, and advanced German language courses, and sponsors regularly scheduled musical concerts, contemporary German cinema, and lectures in the second floor auditorium. Traveling art and ceramic exhibitions are held on the ground level. Admission and rental of audio-visual equipment, including VCR tapes are free with a library card. For further information, contact Elisabeth Angele, librarian, at (312) 329-0074. The lending library is open Tuesday–Wednesday, 11:00 A.M.–6:00 P.M.; Thursday, 12:30 A.M.–8:00 P.M.; Friday, 11:00 A.M.–6:00 P.M.; Saturday, 10:00 A.M.–3:00 P.M. Closed Mondays.

Regularly Scheduled Special Events

Chicago International Art Exposition, *held at McCormick Place, Donnelley International Hall, 411 E. 23rd Street and the Lakefront,* beginning the second weekend in May and continuing for five days, featuring the work of artists and craftsmen from around the world. The Art Expo is a premier cultural event that has been sponsored every year since 1979 by John Wilson's Lakeside Group. The show affords Chicagoans a rare opportunity to browse and (and buy) the work of some of the world's most celebrated painters and sculptors of this generation, including Andy Warhol, Willem de Kooning, Claes Oldenburg, Ed Paschke, and the controvrsial Robert Maplethorpe. Hours: 12:00 P.M.–8:00 P.M., Friday–Monday, 12:00 P.M.–6:00 P.M.,Tuesday. Admission: $12. Students and senior citizens, $7.00. A two-day ticket is available for $20; a five-day pass, for $45. Shuttle busses running approximately every twenty minutes are available on Michigan Avenue. Call the Lakeside Group at (312) 787-6858 for information about special exhibits.

Though it is not directly affiliated with the Exposition, the Goethe Institute sponsors a breakfast reception, and visual display of artwork by contemporary artists from the Federal Republic of Germany in the library during the weekend of the exhibition. Members of the staff are available to answer questions. The admission is free. Contact the institute office at (312) 329-0915 for times.

Christmas Open House, held at the Goethe Institute, the first or second Saturday in December from 10:00 A.M. to 5:00 P.M. Used book sale. Complimentary food and drink, and a prize drawing in the afternoon.

Dutch Museum and Archive Repository

Dutch Heritage Center, *at Trinity Christian College, 6601 W. College Drive, Palos Heights, Ill., (708) 597-3000.* Dutch settlers began arriving in Chicago and the South Suburbs in the 1840s. By 1900—the peak year of the Dutch immigration into the city—there were some 20,000 of them who had arrived from the Netherlands. Many were poor truck farmers who tended their lands in close proximity to one another until they were forced to yield to the developers who planned towns, roads, and commercial businesses. A smaller enclave was located on the Near West side, in the vicinity of Ashland Ave. and 14th St. The history of the Dutch settlement in Englewood, Roseland, Lansing, South Holland and Palos Heights is preserved in this little-known research center located on the second floor of the Jenny Huizinga Library (opening in the Fall of 1991) at Trinity Christian College. Curator Henrick Sliekers has accumulated a fine collection of manuscripts, Dutch books, art work and historical artifacts donated by the descendants of the original settlers. Old church documents left behind are helpful tools in conducting genealogical research, and can be accessed at the library. The Heritage Center is open 8 A.M. to 4:30 P.M., Monday through Friday.

Ethnic Society: The German American National Congress

Founded in 1959, D.A.N.K. brings together Americans of German ancestry interested in preserving the culture and language in the U.S. With sixty active chapters, D.A.N.K. serves the needs of 52 million Germans, the single largest European ethnic group in the country today. Local chapters are free to sponsor whatever activities are of interest to the community, including parades, folk festivals, and German language classes. The society publishes a monthly newspaper printed in both English and German. Membership is open to individuals who are wholly, or in part of German ancestry. The annual dues are $25 for couples, and $15 for single persons. Please contact the German American National Congress at 4740 N. Western Ave., Chicago, Ill., 60625, or call (312) 275-1100.

Annual Events, and Celebrations

Annual Von Steuben Day Parade, held on the Saturday closest to the birthdate of Friedrich Wilhelm Freiherr von Steuben (b. Sept. 17, 1730). In the darkest days of the War for Independence, the Continental Congress sought ways to reverse the ominous tide of British military advances. Through the intervention of Benjamin Franklin and Silas Deane, General George Washington was prevailed upon to enlist the support of Baron (Freiherr) Von Steuben, who had previously been attached to the general staff of Frederick II. At the invitation of the beleaguered Washington, the Prussian aristocrat arrived in America in December, 1777, to train the Continental forces at their winter encampment at Valley Forge, Pennsylvania. Von Steuben whipped the troops into shape, and was rewarded with a field commission as major general, and later participated in the siege of Yorktown. Since 1966, the German societies in Chicago have sponsored an annual Von Steuben Parade, with over 200 floats, bands, the Vienna Waltz Group, German American Singers, and marchers garbed in traditional military regalia. It is, perhaps, Chicago's least publicized and poorly attended ethnic parade. The newspapers and television stations give it little attention, and consequently the number of people who turn out each year is comparatively small. In 1990 the Mexican Independence Day parade was scheduled to follow close behind. The Hispanic community, which had lined up early on the sidewalks waving their colorful green and white flags, did not know what the city was up to when the German marching bands and choral societies passed in review. The Von Steuben Parade is truly a "labor of love" for Karl Laschet, who organizes the event every year on behalf of the German-American community. The parade is paid for every year through private subscription. Despite the city's apparent indifference, the colorful pageant continues, often under less than ideal circumstances. The German parade kicks off at 11:30 A.M. at Wacker Drive, and goes down Dearborn St., before winding up at Congress Parkway and Wacker Drive. Call: Karl Laschet at (312) 478-7915 for details.

German-American Fest, held in conjunction with the Von Steuben Day Parade, for three days in mid-September, at Leland St., between Lincoln and Western Avenues. Dancing, singing, and German foods, prepared at several of the area restaurants in two large fest tents. The talents of such German organizations as the Schwaebischer Singing Society and the Rheinischer Verein are on display in this annual celebration of German culture. Sponsored by the Lincoln Square Chamber of Commerce. Call (312) 728-3890 for times and dates. *Recommended.*

German-American Day, *The Sunday on or about October 6, at St. Benedict's Church, 2215 W. Irving Park Road, Chicago, (312) 588-6484.* Since the arrival of the first German settler on the U.S. shores, October 6, 1683, the number of immigrants and their offspring has grown to an estimated 52 million. In 1987 President Ronald Reagan proclaimed October 6 "German-American Day," to honor the accomplishments and contributions of this ethnic European immigrant group. St. Benedict's, one of the oldest German parishes in the city, sponsors an hour-long church service, with music supplied by the German choral groups, and guest speakers, which may include the mayor of Chicago, the vice consul of Germany and other visiting dignitaries. No food or drink is served on the church grounds, but afterward it is customary to repair to one of the many excellent German restaurants in the area for a light repast.

German-American Children's Concerts. Three annual performances: (1) Mother's Day, at the Irish-American Cultural Center, 4626 N. Knox Ave., Chicago, (2) Christmas Concert, held the second week of December at the Irish-American Center, and (3) Christmas Around the World Festival, at the Museum of Science and Industry, throughout the month of December at 57th St. and Lake Shore Drive, Chicago. Sixty-two children comprise this choral group that sings traditional and contemporary songs in German and English. For information about the children's chorus, please call Ruth Schuebel at (312) 477-7732 for dates and prices. The Children's Chorus is an adjunct of the German-American Singers of Chicago, and is one of eighteen singing societies under the auspices of the Combined German-American Choruses, an umbrella group organized several years ago and directed by Rudi Dick (312) 763-1883. The adult choral societies come from all over the Midwest, and perform regularly at folk festivals, religious services, and the big downtown Von Steuben Parade. On the first Sunday of each month, one of the adult choral groups will sing religious hymns at the St. Alphonsus German-language Mass, held at 9:30 A.M. at 1429 W. Wellington Ave., Chicago. Call (312) 525-0709 for details.

Wicker Park Housewalk, two-hour walking tour generally held the last Saturday in May, by the Chicago Architectural Foundation, 330 S. Dearborn St., Chicago. Listed in the National Register of Historic Places, the Wicker Park neighborhood is one of the city's few remaining nineteenth century treasures. The community was given its name by philanthropists John and Charles Wicker who donated the land to the city 1870, and then capitalized on the real estate boom that followed. German immigrants poured into this area in the 1880s, and left their mark long after the Poles and Serbs became the dominant group in the community. The 1300, 1400, and 1500 blocks of Hoyne St. was once known as "Beer Row," for the many Queen Anne, and Second Empire style homes, owned by prosperous German merchants. The Schlitz house, which stood on the corner of Hoyne and Pierce, was owned by the Milwaukee brewing family until it was torn down in the 1920s to make way for an apartment complex. Hoyne Street was the first paved artery in the district, and many fine Victorian mansions, including the Waixel-Borgmeir House (1521) still stand. Adolph Borgmeir was a German craftsman who designed many of the fine furniture pieces sold by the A.P. Johnson Company. Wicker

Park, once the home to Nelson Algren, who defined the essential character of the neighborhood in his gritty prose *Chicago: City On the Make,* is today a gentrified, rehabbed artist and Yuppie colony that is still worth a visit. The Architectural Foundation tour meets at Damen (2000 West) and LeMoyne (1500 North). The walking tour, with commentary by CAF volunteers, is $5.00 per person. CAF members are admitted free. For dates and times, please call (312) 922-3431.

Wicker Park Greening Festival, *Damen and Schiller Sts., Chicago.* Two-day music, food, auto show, house tour, arts and crafts, and ethnic festival sponsored by the Old Wicker Park Committee, at 1608 N. Milwaukee Ave., Chicago, (312) 342-1966. A tour of ten historic homes, including one of Nelson Algren's dwellings, is included in the $10 admission price ($8.00 if paid in advance). The event is held the second or third weekend in August.

Fahrrad-Tour Von Schaumburg. A six-mile guided bike tour of Schaumburg's historic neighborhoods, with a special emphasis on the community's German heritage. The event kicks off from the Blackwell School, 345 N. Walnut Lane, Schaumburg, the first Sunday in June at noon time. Admission is free, but participants are encouraged to register in advance by calling the Schaumburg Park District at (708) 490-7015.

Altenheim Home Annual Picnic, *7824 Madison St., Forest Park (708) 366-2206.* Oompah bands, German brats, beer, and a bake sale highlight the annual picnic and food fest in the Western Suburbs—a yearly tradition that dates back more than sixty years. Local dignitaries are always in attendance, and they might even partake in the dancing and bingo games, but don't count on it. There are pony rides for children, a dog show, and prize raffles. All proceeds benefit the Altenheim Home, a not-for-profit nursing home for the elderly. The picnic takes place the first Sunday in August on the Altenheim grounds from 11:00 A.M.–7:00 P.M. Tickets are $2.00 per person; $1.00 for seniors and children under twelve; $5.00 for families.

Art Gallery

Gallery Vienna, *750 N. Orleans, Chicago, (312) 951-0300.* Specializing in Viennese antique furniture from the Austrian Jugendstil period (1890s–1930s), as well as the work of artists from the Secession period, including Josef Hoffmann, Otto Wagner, Adolf Loos, Robert Oerley, and Gustav Siegal. Hours: Monday through Saturday, 11 A.M to 5 P.M.

Oktoberfest Celebrations

Oktoberfest is a time-honored custom in Munich, dating back to October 12, 1812, when the Bavarian king, Ludwig I, celebrated his marriage to Therese Sachsen Hildburghausen by sponsoring a great horse race outside the city. It was a festive occasion with much pomp and revelry. And with the passing of each year they marked the anniversary by holding a festival in what came to be known as "Therese's Field." Nowadays the Munich Oktoberfest begins the next to the last Saturday in September and continues until the first Sunday in October, luring tourists from all over the world.

Oktoberfest is nothing more than singing, dancing, and eating. Quantity is the operable word when you talk about beer drinking and food consumption. To ensure that King Ludwig's special day receives its due, city and suburban restaurateurs in conjunction with local officials sponsor annual Oktoberfest celebrations to promote *Gemütlichkeit* within us all.

Berghoff Oktoberfest, *17 W. Adams St., Chicago, (312) 427-3170.* Three-day street festival held the second weekend in September, outside the restaurant between State and Dearborn streets. Chicken sandwiches, bratwurst, apple strudel, and the famous Berghoff beer are available for purchase. The scheduled entertainment is provided by any number of German bands, including Alpiners, the Red Castle Band direct from Heidelberg, and the Jan Wagner Bavarian Band, and is free. This festival began in 1985. Call the restaurant for times and dates.

Schaumburg Oktoberfest, *at the Schaumburg Marriot Hotel, 50 N. Martingale Road, Schaumburg, (708) 240-0100.* Bet you didn't know that Schaumburg, Illinois and Schaumburg, Germany, are sister cities. They are, and the special relationship between the two communities is celebrated each year in the parking lot of the hotel, where the Schaumburg Park District opens up a large beer tent on the grounds, the first or second Sunday in October. A German band performs. Handicrafts are sold inside the tent, and the children can ride ponies or roller coasters. For further information, contact the Schaumburg Park District at (708) 980-2115.

Tinley Park Oktoberfest, *174th St. and Oak Park Ave, Tinley Park, (708) 532-1733.* This annual event has become so big in recent years, that the village has its own special hotline to call for information. Four large tents serving food and featuring traditional German music highlight the weekend festivities in this south suburb with its large German concentration. The Oktoberfest is held the last weekend in September.

Villa Park Oktoberfest, *Lions Field Park, 320 E. Wildwood St., Villa Park, (708) 834-8525.* Held the last weekend in September. Flea market, German food, children's games, and handicrafts. Entertainment provided by German bands. Free parking and admission.

Batavia Oktoberfest, *held along Wilson St. (Rts. 25 and 31) and the river, in downtown Batavia the third weekend in October.* In addition to the usual sampling of German foods, the Batavia Chamber of Commerce sponsors an "herbal harvest," an antique panorama with fresh produce, fruits, and collectibles for sale by sidewalk vendors. The event runs for four days, Thursday to Sunday. For further information contact Trudy MacLaren at (708) 879-6825. The Batavia VFW Post sponsors an Oktoberfest dinner dance the first week of October at the VFW Post on Highway 25. For ticket prices and times, call Donna Whipple at (708) 879-6848.

Forest Park Oktoberfest, *at the Naval Reserve Grounds on Roosevelt Road, four blocks west of Harlem Ave., the second weekend in September.* The Forest Park fest is one of the largest in the Chicago suburban area, and has been held annually for over thirty years. The bratwurst, saurbraten, kraut, and dark rolls are served by members of the Harlem Mannerchor, one of the many adult German choral societies in the city. The event is sponsored in part by Oktoberfest Inc., and runs for three days. Call (708) 366-2543 for details.

Forest Grove Athletic Club, Oktoberfest, *1760 N. Hicks Road, Palatine, (708) 991-4646.* A yearly fund raising event for the athletic club, featuring Bavarian slap dancing, food, raffles, a German folk band and arm wrestling contests. It is a one day event held in mid-October. Tickets are $12.50 per person.

Lambs Farm Oktoberfest, *Interstate 94 and Route 176 in Libertyville.* A beer garden, oompah bands, live entertainment and German food compliment the many attractions to be found at the Lamb's Farm, including a golf course driving range, ice cream parlor, petting zoo for the kiddies, and Country Inn Restaurant. Admission to the grounds is always free. Call the hotline at (708) 362-6774 for a pre-recorded schedule of events, or (708) 362- 5050.

Hans' Bavarian Lodge, Oktoberfest, *931 N. Milwaukee Ave., Wheeling, (708) 537-4141.* The Oktoberfest celebration at Hans' Bavarian Lodge is a yearly tradition that has gone on since 1957. A large tent erected on the grounds can seat 2,500 people, who in any given year, are entertained by such musical groups as Big Twist and the Mellow Fellows, and Epic, a traditional German band that plays waltzes and polkas. The Oktoberfest is held every Friday and Saturday in October. Admission is usually $8.00 per person.

Edelweiss Restaurant, Oktoberfest, *7650 W. Irving Park Road, Norridge, (708) 452-6040.* A four-person band plays German folk songs while diners feast on pork shanks, bratwurst, and other belt-busting goodies. Friday through Sundays in September.

Bavarian Fest, *at the Oak Brook Hills Hotel and Conference Center, 3500 Midwest Road, Oak Brook, Ill., (708) 850-5555.* Three day, two night weekend package that includes Saturday breakfast and Sunday brunch, wine tasting, Bavarian cocktail reception, beer gardens, oompah bands under an outdoor tent, and polka dance parties from afternoon to evening. Every weekend from mid-September through mid-October.

Oktoberfest Weekend, *at the Indian Lakes Resort, 250 W. Schick, Bloomingdale, (708) 529-0200.* Three-day two night weekend package that includes deluxe accommodations, German cooking demonstrations by the hotel's master chefs, entertainment provided by the Oktoberfest Band, with two dinners and a Sunday brunch. Held every weekend from mid-October through mid-November. Total price is $299.00 per couple.

Milwaukee Events

German Fest, *at the Henry W. Maier Festival Park, the last week-end in July.* The spacious fairgrounds on the scenic Milwaukee Lakefront feature some of the best German entertainment in the Midwest, including bands and yodelers from Europe, Bavarian slap dancing, a glockenspiel performance, and various other acts that perform on the Pabst stage. The German Fest Parade, with over seventy units, travels through the park throughout the afternoon on Saturday. A book store sells maps, cards, cooking manuals, videos and postcards. The Mardi Gras exhibit features German porcelain, musical instruments, stuffed animals and one-of-a-kind German and Austrian style gifts and souvenirs. Ecumenical church services are conducted on the grounds Sunday morning at 10:30 A.M., and models show off the latest styles in German clothing on the main stage both Saturday and Sunday. The real attraction of German Fest is of course the food. Don't forget to try the "spanferkel" (young pig), which is roasted over an enormous spit. Other German food delights for sale include rollbraten, potato pancakes, schnitzel, dumplings, and strudel. Advance $5.00 admission tickets can be purchased through the German Fest office at 8229 W. Capitol Drive, Milwaukee, WI 53222, or by calling (414) 464-9444. The $6.00 gate price does not include a raffle ticket. Hours: noon to midnight, Friday–Sunday, last weekend in July.

Bavarian Volkfest, *the third weekend in June, at Old Heidelberg Park, behind the Bavarian Inn, 700 W. Lexington Blvd., Glendale, WI 53217. (Take I-43 to Silver Spring Drive, East cut-off. Turn right on Port Washington Road, then two blocks to Lexington and turn right.)* Bavarian dancers and brass bands highlight a two-day German festival sponsored by the United German Societies of Milwaukee, a non-profit cultural association dedicated to the preservation of the traditions, music, and dance of old Bavaria. The societies own and operate a beautiful, spacious complex on the northern edge of Milwaukee, which includes the Bavarian Inn, Old Heidelberg Park, a soccer field, and parking area. Delicious Bavarian food, including spanferkel, chicken, rollbraten, and homemade cakes, are served to the public, which is encouraged to show up in German folk dress. On Sunday, there is a children's parade with a band, balloons, and refreshments. The park opens at 5:00 P.M. on Saturday, and 1:00 P.M. on Sunday. Admission: $1.00. Children under sixteen, free. Call (414) 462-9147 for details.

Oktoberfest at Old Heidelberg Park, *700 W. Lexington Blvd., Glendale, Wisconsin, the first three weekends in September following Labor Day.* According to park officials, the United German Societies Oktoberfest is the oldest and most authentic of its kind in the Midwest. The main festivities take place on the "Bavarian Fest Garten,"—an Alpine-style pavilion equipped with weather curtains on the open sides. The picnic tables and benches can seat up to 2,000 under one roof. Continuous entertainment from 5:00 P.M. Saturday and 2:00 P.M. on Sunday includes old time German brass bands, "Schulplattler" folk dancing, yodeling, comedy, and sing alongs in which everyone is invited to participate. On the first Sunday of Oktoberfest, the Muenchner Kindl," (Oktoberfest Queen) is selected. The candidates for this event are unmarried young women representing the five German clubs in the Milwaukee area. There is plenty of German food and Milwaukee's most famous beverage (domestic and imported) is on tap. Admission is $1.00 per person, and children under sixteen are admitted free of charge. Hotel and motel accommodations can be found nearby. The Northport Inn and the Exel Inn are located one block east. Within one mile south are the Budgetel, Hilton Inn, and the North Shore Inn Motel. A Midway Motor Lodge is approximately one mile north. All are located along N. Port Washington Road. Advance reservations are strongly recommended. For further information, call (414) 462-9147.

Milwaukee Restaurants

Mader's, *1037 N. 3rd St., Milwaukee, (414) 271-3377.* In the most German of all Midwestern cities, you can find a number of fine ethnic restaurants. We recommend two in particular. For old world dining, Mader's and Karl Ratzsch's can't be beat. Mader's, the better known of the two, features a Sunday Viennese brunch. They specialize in Rheinscher sauerbraten, wienerschnitzel, and roast pork shank. Background music. German decor. Antiques and beer steins. Hours: Monday–Saturday, 11:30 A.M–9:00 P.M.; Sunday, 10:30 A.M.–9:00 P.M. Credit cards accepted.

Karl Ratzsch's, *320 E. Mason St., Milwaukee, (414) 276-2720.* After touring the 37-room Frederick Pabst Mansion, (2000 W. Wisconsin Ave, Milwaukee (414) 931-0808) the former home of the German brewmaster who made Milwaukee famous, we suggest a dinner visit to Karl Ratzsch's, where the roast goose shank is top drawer, and the string ensemble performs from 6:30 P.M. to 10:00 P.M. Monday–Saturday, and Sundays from 5:30 P.M. to 9:30 P.M. Be sure to see the collection of rare steins, and German-Austrian glassware. Other hours: Monday, 4:30 P.M.–10:30 P.M.; Tuesday–Thursday, 11:30 A.M.–10:30 P.M.; Friday and Saturday until 11:30 P.M. Family-owned since 1904. Credit cards accepted.

The Lincoln Square Mall: Chicago's ═══ Last Surviving Germantown ═══

The history of Lincoln Square dates back to three settlements, that were founded in the second half of the nineteenth century; Bowmanville (1850), Summerdale (1855), and Ravenswood (1869). These three adjoining neighborhoods were annexed to Chicago in 1889. In 1925, small segments from each of these neighborhoods were partitioned off in order to form Lincoln Square, a bustling retail, and residential community originally settled by German immigrants.

Through the efforts of the local Chamber of Commerce, the Lincoln Avenue business strip (at Western Ave.) was closed to two-way automobile traffic in 1978, and converted into a shopping mall and outdoor plaza which is a popular meeting spot for many of the long-time German and Greek residents who have chosen to remain in the city close to their parishes (St. Demetrios serves the Greek community; St. Matthias, built in 1887 at 2310 W. Ainslie, at Claremont, is a German church). Symbolic of the continuing Teutonic presence in this North Side enclave is the fifteen-foot Baroque-style lantern, which was donated to the Chamber of Commerce by the city of Hamburg in Germany. The lantern is made of heavy black cast iron with brass ornamentation and is located in back of the Abraham Lincoln statue at the intersection of Lincoln, Lawrence, and Western. Scenes from the picturesque German countryside are depicted on an expansive 96′ × 30′ wall mural at 4662 N. Lincoln Avenue. The "concrete canvas" is the work of Lothar Sanchez-Speer, a native of Stuttgart, Germany. The artist helped recruit eight to fifteen talented high school students to help him complete the project, sponsored by the City at Work program and the German Day Association. The mural, showing a medieval battle fortress and a quaint farming village, was dedicated during German Day festivities in 1991. Sanchez-Speer and his partner Fred Montano believe that the outdoor painting will affirm the longtime German ties to the community. If the response is encouraging, similar ethnic scenes important to the multinational groups residing in the city may soon appear in other Chicago neighborhoods. The mural is a good place to begin your shopping and dining tour of old Germantown on Lincoln Avenue—affectionately known as "Sauerkraut Boulevard."

Shopping and Dining in the Lincoln Square Mall

Delicatessen Meyer, *4750 N. Lincoln Ave., Chicago, (312) 561-3377.* Imported German and Swiss chocolates, baked goods, beer, toiletries, colognes, and ceramics. Sausages made on the premises in this old fashioned German deli. Hours: 9:00 A.M.–9:00 P.M., Monday–Saturday. Sundays, 10:00 A.M.–5:00 P.M. Checks accepted, but no credit cards.

Inge's Delicatessen, *4724 N. Lincoln Ave., Chicago, (312) 561-8386.* Twenty-nine years at this location. Imported French, German, Austrian, Croatian, Danish, and Dutch gourmet foods, including beer steins, cosmetics, and homemade sausages. Hours: Monday–Friday, 9:00 A.M.–6:00 P.M.; Sunday, 12:00 P.M.–5:00 P.M.

Max Van Dermeer Gallery, *4738 N. Lincoln Ave., Chicago, (312) 728-2211.* A real European flavor in this eclectic European gift emporium specializing in German and Hungarian art pieces, antique jewelry, and Dresden porcelain. L.L. Harris, resident gemologist and appraiser is available by appointment. Hours: Monday–Saturday, 10:00 A.M.–5:00 P.M.

Merz Apothecary, *4716 N. Lincoln Ave., Chicago, (312) 989-0900.* A delightfully quaint pharmacy that was formerly located in the 2900 block of Lincoln Ave., from 1875 until 1982. The owners have recreated the look and feel of an old fashioned ma-and-pa nineteenth-century retail store, with dark wood paneling on the walls and glass display cases on either side. Imported soaps, cosmetics, and medicines from Germany, England, Spain, New Zealand and Ireland. Hours: Monday–Saturday, 9:00 A.M.–6:00 P.M. *Recommended.*

Finishing Touches of Europe, *4714 N. Lincoln Ave., Chicago, (312) 784-0034.* Women's clothing and jewelry imported from Germany and greater Europe. A year and a half at this location. Hours:

Monday, 10:00 A.M.–8:00 P.M.; Tuesday–Wednesday, 10:00 A.M.– 6:30 P.M.; Thursday, 10:00 A.M.–8:00 P.M.; Friday, 10:00 A.M.–7:30 P.M.; Sunday, 12:00 P.M.–6:00 P.M.

Schmid Imports, *4606 N. Lincoln Ave., Chicago, Ill., (312) 561-2871.* Gift items and souvenirs from Germany, including figurines, Nutcracker and Smokeman dolls, pewter plates, music cassettes, decorated beer steins, greeting cards and magazines. Hours: Tuesday–Friday, 10:00 A.M.–6:00 P.M.; Saturday, 9:00 A.M.–5:00 P.M.; Closed Sunday and Monday. Accepts all credit cards.

Small Fry, *4756 N. Lincoln Ave., Chicago, (312) 784-0506.* The Graham family has owned this specialty clothing store continuously since 1949. Bavarian costumes, German and Austrian Lederhosen, Trachten, and knit goods for the "small fry." Hours: Monday, Thursday, Friday, 9:00 A.M.–8:00 P.M.; Tuesday, Wednesday, Saturday, 9:00 A.M.–6:00 P.M.; Sunday, 9:00 A.M.–5:00 P.M.

Helga's Dolls, *4624 N. Lincoln Ave., Chicago, (312) 769-0822.* Leading importer of modern collectible dolls (no antiques) from Germany, Italy, Spain, and France. The store in itself is a doll museum and well worth a visit. Hours: Saturdays, 12:00 P.M.– 6:00 P.M.; Sundays, 10:00 A.M.–4:00 P.M.; Monday, 12:00 P.M.–6:00 P.M. Other hours by appointment.

Kuhn's Delicatessen and Liquors, *3051-53 N. Lincoln Ave., Chicago, (312) 525-9019. Two other locations: 749 W. Golf Road, Des Plaines, Ill., (708) 640-0222; 1165 S. Waukegan Road, Northbrook, Ill., (708) 272-4197.* Established in 1929, Kuhn's is the largest and best known of Chicago's delicatessens, specializing in imported European foods and beverages. Lincoln Avenue hours: Monday–Saturday, 9:30 A.M.–7:00 P.M.; Sunday, 9:30 A.M.–6:00 P.M.

Lincoln Market, *4661 N. Lincoln Ave., Chicago, (312) 561-4570.* The meat shop and delicatessen is well known all over Chicago, because the beerwurst and sausages are prepared in-house by master European butchers. German meats and food products from Poland, Hungary, and Yugoslavia. Hours: Monday–Friday 9:00 A.M.– 6:00 P.M.; Saturdays, 8:00 A.M.–5:00 P.M.

Enisa's Pastry Shop and Café, *4701-03 N. Lincoln Ave., Chicago, (312) 271-7017.*   Bakery in the front, with a dining area in the rear. The cakes, imported truffles, and tortes are sweet, gooey, and loaded with calories. Better stay away if you're on a diet. Hours: Sunday–Monday, 9:00 A.M.–10:00 P.M.

Juergen's North Star Bakery, *4545 N. Lincoln Ave., Chicago, (312) 561-9858.*   Homemade bread and cookies, but no fancy pastries. Hours: Tuesday–Friday, 8:00 A.M.–3:00 P.M.; Saturday, 8:00 A.M.–1:00 P.M. No credit cards.

Restaurants

Chicago Brau Haus, *4732 N. Lincoln Ave., Chicago, (312) 784-4444.*   Traditional German restaurant with entertainment and dancing nightly. The music is provided by a three-piece German band and accordion player. In August, the restaurant hosts a Summerfest with special low prices. On the weekend of the Von Steuben Parade, the Brau Haus sponsors its own German Fest celebration in the rear parking lot. April is "Bockbierfest" time, with entertainment and dancing nightly by the Brauhaus Band and Max Wagner on the accordion. Hours: Monday–Friday, 11:00 A.M.– 2:00 A.M.; till three on Saturday, and 11:30 A.M.–2:00 A.M. on Sunday. Closed Tuesdays. Special lunch menu.

Huettenbar, *4721 N. Lincoln Ave., Chicago, (312) 561-2507.* A neighborhood tavern known for its *Gemütlichkeit*. The Huettenbar was formerly affiliated with the Brau Haus across the street, but the owner went off on his own a few years ago. Musical entertainment on Tuesday nights. Open seven days a week till the wee hours of the morning.

Heidelberger Fass, *4300 N. Lincoln Ave., Chicago, (312) 478-2486.*   Southern German cooking. Background music, but no regularly scheduled entertainment. Hours: Monday–Friday, 11:30 A.M.–10:00 P.M. (Luncheon served from 11:30 A.M.–4:00 P.M.); Saturday, 11:30 A.M.–10:00 P.M.; Sunday, 12:00 P.M.–10:00 P.M. Credit cards accepted.

Von Stuke's Hofbrau, *4128 N. Lincoln Ave., Chicago, (312) 525-4906.* Bavarian beer garden in the rear seats forty people, and is a popular gathering spot during the Oktoberfest. It's also where the Beer

Society of America meets each month. That ought to tell you something. Hours: Tuesday–Saturday, and Sunday, 11:00 A.M.–11:00 P.M. Closed Monday. Free parking. Credit cards accepted.

Hogen's Restaurant, *4560 N. Lincoln Ave., Chicago, Ill., (312) 334-9406.* Located at the corner of Wilson Ave. and Lincoln. Music from the 1950s and 1960s on Friday and Saturday nights. Monday–Friday, 11:00 A.M.–2:00 P.M.; Saturday till 3:00 A.M.; Sunday, 11:00 A.M.–2:00 P.M. The kitchen closes at ten. Credit cards accepted.

Shopping and Dining, Outlying Areas

Restaurants

The Berghoff, *17 W. Adams St., Chicago, (312) 427-3170, and 436 W. Ontario, (312) 266-7771.* Old Herman Berghoff left his home in Dortmund, Germany, in 1887, and began brewing his unique blend of beer in Ft. Wayne, Ind. In 1893, Herman introduced his special Pilsner to Chicagoans at the World's Columbian Exposition. Nowadays, the Huber Brewing Company of Monroe, Wisconsin, manufactures the beer that made the Berghoff Restaurant famous from the time it opened its doors on Adams St. in 1898. The sauerbraten, schnitzel, and seafood dishes are house specialties. The Berghoff is a real Chicago institution. Hours: Monday–Thursday, 11:00 A.M.–9:30 P.M.; Friday–Saturday, 11:00 A.M.–10:00 P.M.; Closed Sundays. *Recommended.*

Resi's Bierstube, *2034 W. Irving Park Road, Chicago, (312) 472-1749.* Austrian and German food you can enjoy in a quaint beer garden during the warm weather. Owners Herbert and Ingaborg Stover stock sixty bottled beers and eight on tap. Hours: Monday–Saturday, 2:00 P.M.–2:00 A.M.; closed on Sundays. No credit cards.

Zum Deutschen Eck, *2924 Southport, Chicago, (312) 525-8121.* A classic German restaurant that evokes the nineteenth-century tradition of beer gardens, *Gemütlichkeit*, and "continental Sundays." Located across the street from the St. Alphonsus parish in the heart of Lakeview, the restaurant is popular with the opera aficionados who regularly attend performances of the Chicago Opera Company at the Athenaeum Theatre inside one of the church buildings. A five-piece "oompah" band performs on Friday, Saturdays, and Sundays. Be sure to join the sing along. Hours: Sunday–Thursday, 11:30 A.M.–10:00 P.M.; Friday and Saturdays till midnight. Credit cards accepted.

Christi's German Inn, *45 W. Slade, Palatine, Ill., (708) 991-1040.* Specializing in Bavarian dishes. Hours: Tuesday–Saturday, 7:00 A.M.–10:00 P.M.; Sunday, 8:00 A.M.–10:00 P.M. Credit cards accepted.

Fritzel's Country Inn, *900 Ravinia Terrace, Lake Zurich, Ill., (708) 540-8844.* Formerly known as the Alpine Inn in Glenview, but now with a new name and location. Owner Bob Tshurtz serves a pleasing menu of German, Swiss, and Hungarian foods. Occasional entertainment, and Oktoberfest the last two weekends of September. Hours: Tuesday–Friday, 11:30 A.M.–4:00 P.M. for lunch, and 4:00 P.M.–10:00 P.M. for dinner. Saturdays, 4:00 p.m.–10:00 p.m.; Sundays, noon–9:00 P.M. Bank cards accepted.

Hans's Bavarian Lodge, *931 Milwaukee, Ave., Wheeling, Ill., (708) 537-4141.* Owner Jane Berghoff's, late husband owned the Adams Street eatery in downtown Chicago for many years. For the past thirteen years, she has operated Hans's Bavarian Lodge which is down the street from Wheeling's famous "Restaurant Row" which includes Bob Chinn's Crab House, and Le Francais, arguably one of the most expensive (but highly rated) dining establishments in the country. Imported bottled beers, delightful German rathskeller, and a bacon salad dressing that is out of this world. On Fridays, a piano and zither player entertain patrons. Saturdays and Sundays feature live accordion music. Hours: Tuesday–Friday, 11:30 A.M.– 10:00 P.M.; Thursday, 11:30 A.M.–11:00 P.M.; Saturdays, 4:00 P.M.–11:00 P.M.; Sunday, 12:00 P.M.–9:00 P.M.

Heidelberg Restaurant, *122 S. York Road, Elmhurst, Ill., (708) 530-5115.* Food dishes from all over Germany. An accordion player performs on Fridays and Saturdays in the basement "Rathskeller." A special menu is offered during the Oktoberfest season. German Delicatessen on the first floor. Hours: Monday–Wednesday, 11:00 A.M.–4:00 P.M.; Thursday–Saturday, 11:00 A.M.– 10:00 P.M.

Edelweiss Restaurant, *7650 Irving Park Road, Norridge, Ill.,* *(708) 452-6040.* German and continental cuisine. German bands and dancing, Friday–Sunday 5:00 P.M.–7:00 P.M. Other hours: Tuesday–Sunday, 11:00 A.M.–10:30 P.M. Credit cards accepted.

Golden Ox, *1578 N. Clybourn Ave., Chicago, (312) 664-0780.* Located near the intersection of North Avenue, which at the turn of the century was known as the "German Broadway," which was anchored by the Sieben Brewery at 1470 Larrabee and the Oscar Mayer Sausage Company on Sedgwick. Both firms provided jobs to the thousands of German immigrants who once lived in this neighborhood. Nowadays, the Golden Ox is one of the last vestiges of those former times. The restaurant specializes in Bavarian food including dumplings, spatzle, and cherry, and plum strudel. Delicious. Hours Monday–Saturday, 11:00 A.M.–11:00 P.M.; Sunday, 3:00 P.M.–9:00 P.M.

Schulien's, *2100 W. Irving Park Road, Chicago, (312) 478-2100.* An old world restaurant and saloon in Lakeview. After 6:00 P.M., professional magicians will sit down at your table and perform magic tricks. Hours: Monday–Friday, 11:30 A.M.–4:00 P.M. for lunch, and 4:00 P.M.–11:00 P.M. for dinner. Saturday–Sunday, 4:00 P.M.–12:00 A.M. Credit cards accepted.

Mirabell, *3454 W. Addison St., Chicago, (312) 463-1962.* Small, but charming Austrian-German restaurant with friendly waiters and a wide variety of dishes, which the owners proudly claim to be among the best in the city. Background German music. Hours: Tuesday–Thursday, 11:30 A.M.–10:00 P.M.; Friday and Saturday, till 11:00 P.M. Closed Mondays.

Karl Laschet's Inn, *2119 W. Irving Park Road, Chicago, (312) 478-7915.* The imported German wheat beer is served on tap. We don't know of too many places in the city that make the same claim. The tavern owner, Karl Laschet, oversees the Von Steuben Parade activities every year. Open seven days a week till 2:00 A.M.

German-American Restaurant & Lounge, *642 N. Clark St., Chicago, (312) 642-3244.* Thirty six years at this location. Modest little restaurant located just north of the Loop. Owned by the Hans Kief family. A variety of German foods are served. Catering. Hours:

Monday–Saturday, 11:00 A.M.–10:00 P.M.; Closed Sunday. Lunch served from 11:00 A.M.–3:00 P.M.

Gift Shops, Bakeries, Delis, and Coffee Houses

European Import Corner, *2315 W. Leland Ave., Chicago, (312) 561-8281.* German beer steins, china, crystal, cuckoo clocks, magazines and periodicals. Hours: Monday–Friday, 9:00 A.M.– 6:00 P.M. (Monday & Thursday till seven); Saturday–Sunday, 11:00 A.M.–4:00 P.M. No credit cards taken.

Austrian Station, *3502 N. Elston Ave., Chicago, (312) 583-8288.* Imported German crystal, beer steins, Hummel figurines, wood carvings, and clothing. Hours: Monday–Saturday, 10:00 A.M.– 4:00 P.M.; closed Sunday. Accepts credit cards.

European Imports, *7900 N. Milwaukee Ave., Niles, Ill., (708) 967-5253.* Collectible dolls, crystal, and imported gift items from Germany, Italy, and Spain. Hours: Monday–Friday, 10:00 A.M.–5:00 P.M.; Sunday, 12:00 P.M.–5:00 P.M. Credit cards accepted.

La Grand Tour, *3229 N. Clark St., Chicago, (312) 929-1836.* Chicago's headquarters for the latest published books direct from Europe. The store features hardcover and paperbound books from Germany, France, Spain, Italy, Portugal and Russia. A wide selection of language learning books, travel guidebooks, and music cassettes. Hours: Monday–Saturday, 10:00 A.M.–10:00 P.M.; Sunday, 11:00 A.M.–7:00 P.M.

Alpine Meat Market, *4030 N. Cicero Ave., Chicago, (312) 725-2121.* Located one block north of "Six Corners," (where Irving Park Road, Milwaukee Ave., and Cicero join) the delicatessen features Swiss, Austrian, and German foods. The Marzipan candy bars may be cheaper here than anywhere else in Chicago. Hours: Monday–Thursday, 8:30 A.M.–5:30 P.M.; Friday, 8:30 A.M.–7:00 P.M.; Saturday, 8:30 A.M.–5:00 P.M.

Black Forest Delicatessen, *8840 Waukegan Road, Morton Grove, Ill., (708) 965-3113.* Thirty-five years at this location. Imported deli items, and chocolates from Germany, Austria, and Switzerland. Fresh meats cut daily. Homemade sausages. Hours: Tuesday,

Thursday, Friday, 9:30 A.M.–6:00 P.M.; Saturday, 9:00 A.M.–5:00 P.M.; Sunday, 10:00 A.M.–3:00 P.M. Closed Monday.

Continental Delikatessen and Imports, *10 S. Evergreen, Plaza Shopping Center, Arlington Heights, Ill., (708) 259-9544.* German, Swedish, and Norwegian food imports. Pastries, candies, tea, and chocolates. Homemade salads on premises. Hours: Monday, 11:00 A.M.–7:00P.M.; Tuesday–Friday, 9:00 A.M.–7:00 P.M.; Saturday, 8:00 A.M.–6:00 P.M. Closed Sunday.

Olga's Delikatessen, *3209 W. Irving Park Road, Chicago, (312) 539-8038.* German imports, candy, and assorted foods. Hours: Monday–Saturday, 9:00 A.M.–7:00 P.M.; Sunday, 10:00 A.M.–5:00 P.M. No credit cards accepted.

Vienna Pastry Shop, *5411 W. Addison St., Chicago, (312) 685-4166.* Specializing in fine German pastries. Owned by Gerhard and Hedwig Kaes. Hours: Tuesday–Saturday, 6:00A.M.– 6:00 P.M.; Sundays, 7:00 A.M.–11:00 A.M. No credit cards or personal checks.

Lutz Conditorei Cafe, *2458 W. Montrose Ave., Chicago, (312) 478-7785.* Bakery in the front selling German and French pastries. Café in the rear. Hours: Tuesday–Sunday, 10:00 A.M.–10:00 P.M. Closed Monday.

Kaffee Haus 1800, (Coffee House 1800), *1800 Sherman Ave., Evanston, Ill., (708) 492-3450.* A quaint European restaurant and coffee house with a pleasing menu of German and continental foods. Hours: Monday–Friday, 9:00 A.M.–9:00P.M.; Saturday, 9:00A.M.–11:00 P.M.; Sunday, 11:00A.M.–8:00 P.M. Credit cards accepted.

Where to Purchase German Language Films

International Historic Films, *3533 S. Archer, Chicago, Ill., 60609, (312) 927-2900.* This Chicago-based mail-order firm will send you a free catalog listing hundreds of classic movies and documentaries from Germany, Russia, France, and Spain that are available for purchase. Prices range from $19.95 to $39.95. Included in their collection are a number of rare World War II era films from Germany including "Munchausen," and "Titanic," both from 1943. Many of the documentaries and films in the inventory contain sub-titles.

Swedish and Norwegian Chicago

History and Settlement

"And because the young farmer couldn't continue creation where God had left off, he must be satisfied with his seven acres and all the stones wherever he looked; broken stones, stones in piles, stone fences, stone above ground, stone in the ground, stone, stone, stone. King Oskar had ascended the kingdom of Sweden and Norway. Karl Oskar had become king in a stone kingdom . . ."

—Vilhelm Moberg, *The Emigrants*

The land was cruel and uncompromising. Tall trees blocked the sun. The stones imbedded in the lush soil broke the blade of many a good plow. Those peasant farmers of Småland, Sweden, tilled their land and paid the fealty to king and country believing that this was God's will. And then the first news of America reached them in the form of handbills and pamphlets. The circulars told of rich, fertile farmland and the great industrial city on the prairie—Chicago.

The emigrants saved their riksdalers and dreamed of the day they would board the boat in the port of Göteborg to begin the perilous journey to America. Olaf Gottfrid Lange, who was born in the port city of Göteborg in 1811 came to the U.S. as a sailor on board an American brig in 1824. Lange established permanent residence in September 18, 1838, and earned his keep by working as a druggist's assistant. As more Scandinavians began arriving in Chicago, Lange conducted English language classes inside the old blockhouse of Fort Dearborn. Word of mouth played an important role in bringing rural Swedes to Chicago. Gustav Flack, a contemporary of Lange who operated a small store near the Clark Street ferry landing in 1843, sent home glowing reports about the burgeoning metropolis growing up around the fort. Flack encouraged many of his countrymen to emigrate, and within a few short years they had founded a colony north of the Chicago River in the area bounded by Wells Street, Division Street, Chicago Avenue and LaSalle Street. Community life centered around the St. Ansgarius Episcopal Church, built in 1851. It was known as the "Jenny Lind church," because the famous Swedish songbird donated $1,000 to finance its construction.

The Larssons, Janssons, Karlstroms, and eighty other Swedes survived the deadly cholera epidemic of 1849 to prosper in the building trades as carpenters, welders, and skilled artisans. Polycarpus von Schneidau was probably the best known among the Swedes who populated frontier Chicago. In 1848 he was appointed superintendent of construction of the first railroad to run out of Chicago—the Chicago and Galena Railroad. In later years, such distinguished Swedish architects as Henry Ericsson and Andrew Lanquist helped pioneer skyscraper construction in Chicago. Lanquist designed the People's Gas, Light and Coke Co. in Chicago, and the U.S. Steel Headquarters in Gary, Indiana.

The Scandinavian Union (*Skandinaviska Sallskadet*) and the Svea Society were organized to foster cultural and ethnic unity, threatened by the melting pot called Chicago. Other organizations soon followed.

The Swedish Club, organized in 1869, was the vortex of social and intellectual life in the city. Its restaurant and club room at 1258 North LaSalle Street was a favorite gathering spot for the city's most prominent citizens of Scandinavian descent. Carl Sandburg told many engaging stories about Abraham Lincoln and his own experiences as a crime reporter for the *Chicago Daily News* over drinks at the Swedish Club. Years later, Police Superintendent Orlando W. Wilson shared the comradery and fellowship with Chicago's Swedes—an irony, one would think, given the fact that the chief was of Norwegian descent. During the heyday of Swedish immigration, there were numerous fraternal and choral societies scattered around Chicago, including the Svithiod Singing Club, organized in June 1882. It was natural for the European ethnic groups like the Swedes to find social identity and companionship in the churches where their native tongue was spoken and the hymns of the old country were sung. But the need for fellowship in a nonreligious setting was strong, especially among the socialist-thinking libertarians who preferred to adjourn to the local "sample room" after the lodge business was conducted. The Svithiod Singing Club promoted social drinking in Chicago to be sure, but its members also participated in the unveiling of the Carl von Linne monument in Lincoln Park in 1891. (Linne was a noted Swedish botanist renowned for his classification of plants and flowers), and for its sponsorship of numerous charitable and philanthropic causes.

By 1871 the homogeneous community in this teeming "river ward" began to break up. Their improved economic position and the arrival of the Italians and other groups to the area hastened their departure.

A number of them relocated to the Belmont-Sheffield neighborhood, but this was only a temporary move. The new "Swede Town"—one that would survive to the present day—sprang up near the corner of Clark and Foster avenues on the far north side. The neighborhood was sparsely populated at the time. A tiny red-brick schoolhouse, an Evangelical Lutheran Church and several itinerant farmers comprised what was then a distant suburb of Chicago.

This dramatic move outward from the city-center was an attempt by the Swedes to preserve their native identity, yet forge a uniquely American community that was relatively isolated from the urban sprawl of Chicago. Swedish historians cannot agree which of the two Andersons residing in this area at the time lent their name to the community. The Reverend Paul Anderson arrived in Chicago in 1843. He served as pastor of the Lutheran church, which by 1854, had changed its name to the Swedish Immanuel Church of Chicago. Rev. Anderson resided in the vibrant, breathing heart of Anderson*ville* at Clark and Foster. He was a Norwegian.

The proud Swedes would argue that it was John Anderson, a highway commissioner and farmer who tilled an acre of land west of Clark Street, who gave his name to the village. Perhaps the controversy could be resolved by renaming Andersonville, *Petersonville,* or *Nelsonville.*

Following the Civil War, Swedes began taking a more active role in city affairs. The original plan for Lincoln Park (once the city fathers completed the task of relocating the city cemetery further north, to Irving and Clark) was submitted by a Swedish landscape gardener named Sven Nelson, who received his training in the old country on an estate that belonged to the royal family.

Pehr Samuel Petersson (1830–1903) arrived in Chicago in 1854 to open a small nursery northwest of Swede Town. When the Chicago Fire reduced the city to cinders and ash, Petersson went to work planting trees and shrubbery along the ruined boulevards and side streets. It was estimated that he planted 60% of the city's foliage by 1901. Petersson founded Rosehill Cemetery and planted the trees at the 1893 World's Fair. As it turned out, they named a major east-west street after him, though the spelling was all wrong.

The Andersonville neighborhood experienced peak growth between 1890 and 1930 when 20-24 percent was made up of foreign-born Swedes. Across the city in 1927 there were 125,000 people of Swedish birth or descent. It was the high-tide of the Scandinavian immigration. A tremendous pride was experienced in the community when the bronze bust of philosopher, scientist, and theologian Emanuel Swedenborg was unveiled before thousands of cheering Swedes in Lincoln Park on June 29, 1924, and when Crown Prince Gustavus Adolphus and Crown Prince William visited Chicago that same month. The sixty-one Swedish churches that flourished in Chicago sponsored the traditional herring breakfast every Sunday. From the earliest times, the Swedes had fished the briny depths of the Baltic Sea in order to augment their food supply. The herring was carefully salted down in barrels before being served with boiled potatoes, sour cream, and cold beer. The Chicago herring breakfast, held in dozens of smokey church basements and fraternal meeting halls around the city lasted only as long as there was a first generation presence to sustain it. Like the polka traditions in the Polish community, the Swedish herring breakfast is a throwback to a vanished nineteenth and early twentieth century culture that is virtually nonexistent in modern-day Europe.

After 1930 the tide of Swedish immigration to Chicago slowed dramatically. New ethnic groups began moving into Andersonville, supplanting long-time residents who either passed away or abandoned the community altogether. As years passed, the neighborhood showed signs of benign neglect. Some thought was given to dropping the name of Andersonville entirely in favor or promoting cultural diversity among all the immigrant groups residing in the vicinity of Clark and Foster.

However, the North Clark Street Business Men's Association and the long-time residents of the neighborhood favored preserving the status quo. Andersonville was rededicated on October 17, 1964, a day of celebration for Chicago Swedes. Mayor Richard Daley and Governor Otto Kerner were on hand to cut the ribbon and extol the virtues of the Scandinavians who had called this neighborhood home for nearly eighty years. The bellringer tradition, now a quarter-century old, began that day. At 10:00 A.M. Dominick Lalumia marched up and down Clark Street, forlornly ringing a brass bell. Those who were unfamiliar with Swedish ways didn't quite know what to make of it, but it symbolized a rebirth of the community. The shopkeepers emerged from their stores to sweep the sidewalk. The hue and cry had been sounded. Andersonville was back in business. Today the bellringer makes his weekly rounds on Saturday morning at 10:30. He is often accompanied by Swedes in colorful folk costumes: Lucias, Vikings, Maypole dancers and Lapplanders. Regardless of their ethnic identity, each store has its own special corn-broom, handpainted in blue and yellow. It can be summed up in one word: pride. Välkommen to Andersonville.

What to See in Andersonville

The Swedish American Museum, *5211 N. Clark St. Chicago, Ill. 60640. (312) 728-8111.* Hours: Tuesday–Friday 11 A.M.–4 P.M. Saturday, 11 A.M.–3 P.M. Closed Sundays. Kersten B. Lane, Executive Director. Admission $1.00. Members free. Begin your visit of Andersonville here, midway between Foster and Winona Avenues, on the east side of Clark Street. From its modest beginnings in a tiny storefront on Clark Street in 1976, the Swedish American Cultural Museum today occupies a 24,000 square foot gallery that is rich in history and folklore. The center provides space for permanent and traveling exhibitions, and various outreach programs for senior citizens, children, and the handicapped. Swedish language instruction, special concerts, "Svensk Gammaldans" (Swedish dance lessons), and guest speakers are scheduled by Ms. Lane during the calendar year. Call for additional details.

The new expanded center was dedicated April 19, 1988, by his Majesty Carl XVI Gustaf, King of Sweden, who journeyed to the U.S. to celebrate the 350th anniversary of the founding of the first permanent Swedish settlement in America. *Recommended.*

Ebenezer Lutheran Church, *1650 W. Foster Ave. Chicago, Ill. 60640. 312/561-8496.* Sunday services: 7:30 A.M. and 11:00 A.M. Mondays and Thursdays 7:30 P.M. Paul Koch, pastor. A block and a half west of the museum stands Chicago's "Swedish Cathedral." The original Ebenezer Lutheran Church dates back to 1892. The present structure fronting busy Foster Avenue near Ashland was constructed in 1904 and dedicated eight years later. Generations of Swedish-Lutheran families attended church here. The community has changed in the intervening years, but the church still pays homage to its roots by conducting Christmas Day services in Swedish. The annual Lucia Festival is coordinated by Ebenezer the second week of December each year. Processions of beautiful girls adorned in floor-length white gowns with a crown of flickering candles participate in the traditional religious observance.

Architecture

For years Andersonville and Edgewater were neighborhoods of single-dwelling homes. By the 1920s the trend was toward the construction of two-flats and high-rise apartment buildings to accommodate a growing, shifting population escaping the inner city. The village-in-the-country concept was forever lost as the community became one of the most densely populated areas in all of Chicago.

As you leave the Clark Street business district and walk east down Berwyn to Wayne, you find yourself in the Lakewood-Balmoral neighborhood. The essential character of the community begins to emerge. Two-story walkups, courtyard apartment buildings coexisting with the spacious single-family bungalows, illustrate the tremendous changes that engulfed this area in the first quarter of the twentieth century. Several fine examples of early 1900s architecture survive in spite of the building boom that for the most part deprived Andersonville of its rural charm.

An example of the famous Prairie style of architecture can be found at 5347 N. Lakewood Avenue near Balmoral, three blocks east of Clark Street. A Queen Anne built by John Lewis Cochrane in 1893 survives at 5426 Lakewood. Cochrane was a real-estate developer, who like Louis Sullivan, made no little plans. He purchased large tracts of land between Foster and Bryn Mawr and sold his Edgewater homes for prices ranging from $5,100 to $12,000. "No two alike," he promised.

At 1430 W. Berwyn Avenue stands the Andersonville "Castle," a large, rambling Gothic-Romanesque graystone home built for a prosperous Swedish family in 1904. An Italian garden complete with fountain is one of the charming features of this old landmark.

North of Andersonville at 1500 W. Elmdale, stands the Immanuel Lutheran Church, whose congregation dates back to the earliest Swedish settlement in this community, 1854. The modern facility was built in 1922, but the three church bells in the center of the lawn are relics of the original building, destroyed in the Chicago Fire. The Immanuel Church is located at the northwest corner of Elmdale and Greenview, a block east of Clark. Phone (312) 743-1820.

Annual Events/Community Celebrations

St. Patrick's Day Parade. Second or third Saturday in mid-March. Recognizing the international flavor of the community, the Andersonville Chamber of Commerce inaugurated the first annual St. Patrick's

Day Parade in 1988. Floats, marching bands, and well-known Chicago celebrities promise to take part in this new tradition. For dates and times, call the Chamber of Commerce at (312) 728-2995.

Midsommarfest (Midsummerfest). Last weekend in June, traditionally June 25–26. This is one of the great neighborhood festivals in Chicago. The business district of Clark Street between Foster and Berwyn in closed off to automobile traffic to raise the Maypole for the Swedish ethnic dancers and folk groups. For dates and times call (312) 728-2995. *Recommended.*

Leif Erickson Day. The Saturday closest to Columbus Day, October. Any Swede worth his salt herring will tell you that the famous Viking explorer crossed the Atlantic around the year 1,000 and stumbled across a country he named Vinland, four hundred years before Columbus. Well, at least the regulars at Simon's Tavern on Clark Street will tell you that. Call (312) 728-2995 for dates and information about the equally famous Viking performances in Andersonville.

St. Morten's Gos Day (St. Martin's Goose Day). Second   or third week of November. An ancient festival celebrating St. Martin of Tours has gained new meaning in Andersonville's Swedish community. For centuries this holiday was important to farmers, marking the end of the autumn harvest and the beginning of the Christmas season. Roast goose was the traditional meal, served with "svartsoppa" (black soup). For the past 150 years St. Morten's Gos Day has been observed in Skåne, Sweden—the southernmost provence.

Christmas Events

Andersonville has recreated the traditional Christmas holiday with banners hung from the street poles. Candles are placed in the storefronts, and roast goose dinners are the featured entrees in the restaurants. Goose liver pate is served in the shops along with the other Yuletide delight—Swedish glogg. Prizes and giveaways at selected retail establishments. Call (312) 728-2995 for a schedule of events.

Lucia Day. The Festival of Lights. Andersonville commemorates this most important of all Swedish holidays with a Lucia pageant sponsored by Ebenezer Lutheran Church. The Chicago Lucia queen and her court will, weather permitting, lead a procession down Clark Street from the

Philadelphia Church, 5437 Clark at Rascher. At the Swedish-American Museum the girls will lead the crowd in an hour of Christmas Carols and traditional holiday music. Santa Claus will drop by, with hot apple cider and ginger-flavored cookies known as pepperkakor. Call (312) 728-2995 for additional information.

Shopping in Andersonville

Andersonville is Chicago's very own Scandinavian community with a variety of charming little shops, delicatessens, restaurants, and bakeries easily accessible by car or public transportation. Many of the retailers are second and third generation children of immigrants who have maintained the family business down through the years. The business district of Andersonville stretches from Foster to Bryn Mawr, with the greatest concentration of stores south of Catalpa. (See map on p. 84.) The small shops remain open until 6:00 P.M., with extended holiday hours.

Interesting Shops
Swedish Items and Gifts

The Landmark of Andersonville. *5301 N. Clark St. at Berwyn, Chicago, (312) 728-5301.* Hours: 10:30 A.M. to 6:30 P.M. Tuesday–Saturday. 11 A.M.–4 P.M. Sunday. Closed Mondays. Opened in 1987, the Landmark is a gallery of 21 different boutiques under the roof of a renovated turn-of-the-century building. Antiques, collectibles, toys, books, health food, and a sweet shop make the Landmark a place to see in Andersonville. Be sure to see Jan Baxter's blue and yellow broom, tucked in a corner behind the cash register.

The Sweden Shop. *3304 Foster, Chicago, (312) 478-0327. Across the street from North Park College between Kedzie and Kimball.* Hours: 9:30 A.M.–8 P.M. Monday–Thursday. 9:30 A.M.–6 P.M. Tuesday–Wednesday. Closed Sunday. A department store of Swedish merchandise, and it's not even in Andersonville. For nearly forty years the Sweden Shop has imported the finest Scandinavian glassware from the glass-blowing regions of Småland. Each piece is carefully hand-crafted reflecting old-world detail and craftsmanship. Porcelain, hand-made wooden clogs, dolls, clothing, and pastries are available for sale. Gift items can be shipped directly to anywhere in the country. *Recommended.*

Books

The Fiery Clockface Bookshop, *5311 N. Clark Street, Chicago, (312) 728-4227.* Hours: 10 A.M. to 6 P.M. Monday through Saturday. Rare books, first editions, paperbacks, records. Book signings, poetry readings. "The store is an extension of myself," explains owner Sarah Lowrey. The name of her store is borrowed from an old English folksong, recently updated by a contemporary poet. "Songs and tales outlive time and set moments ablaze—read these things at the sign of the fiery clock face."

Books on Berwyn, *1476 W. Berwyn, Chicago, (312) 878-9800.* Hours: 10:30 A.M. to 6:30 P.M. Monday through Friday. 10:30 A.M.–6 P.M. Saturday. 11 A.M. to 4 P.M. Sunday. Part of the Landmark of Andersonville. Specializing in Dover books and cassettes.

Fine Jewelry

O.M. Nordling Jewelers, *5249 N. Clark, Chicago, (312) 561-9526* Hours: 9 A.M. to 5 P.M. Monday, Tuesday, Wednesday, Friday. 10 A.M. to 8 P.M. Thursday. 9 A.M. to 4 P.M. Saturday. Closed on Sunday. Ossian Nordling was a jeweler's apprentice when he decided to open his Andersonville store in 1935. The family business is conducted in the same location today by his son Tom, whose customers come from as far away as Iowa and Minnesota. And with good reasons. Nordling's is perhaps the only jeweler in Chicago who can order custom-made items directly from Swedish craftsmen. There is a distinct Swedish style, reflected in the elegant gold chains and the bridal crowns that have been sold to many a proud parent whose daughter was about to walk down the aisle. Hand-made crystal from Orrefors and Kosta-Boda, and other leading Swedish glass manufacturers are on display and available for sale. *Recommended.*

Erickson's, *5304 N. Clark, Chicago, (312) 275-2010.* Hours: 9:15 A.M. to 4:45 P.M. Monday through Saturday. 9:15 A.M. to 6:45 P.M. Saturday. Silver, Waterford crystal, Lalique. Discounts on retail sales.

Delicatessens

Wikstrom's Delicatessen (Formerly Schotts), *5247 N. Clark, (312) 271-6100.* Hours: 9:00 A.M.–6:00 P.M., Monday–Saturday. 11:00 A.M.–3:00 P.M., Sunday. Ingvar Wickstrom came to the United States in 1959 as an exchange student from Skåne. Thirty years later he's still here and serving up homemade "limpa" bread, imported smoked salmon, herring, Vasa bread and fine cheeses. Crawfish season is in August, and you can bet the old-timers who congregate in the front of his store will have their tables reserved. *Recommended.*

Erikson's Delicatessen, *4250 N. Clark, (312) 561-5634.* Hours: 9 A.M. to 6 P.M. Monday through Friday, 9 A.M. to 5 P.M. Saturday. Just an old-fashioned Swedish deli. No frills. Just lots of good food for sale. Fruk-soppa (fruit soup), potato sausage, herring, pea soup, crawfish (in season), and everything else needed for the perfect smörgåsbord.

Bakeries

The Swedish Bakery, *5348 N. Clark, (312) 561-8919.* Hours: 7 A.M. to 6 P.M. Tuesday through Friday. 7 A.M.–5:30 P.M. Saturday. Closed Sunday and Monday. Fancy marzipan cakes, "vort limpa" bread, pepperkakor, coffee cakes. Freshly baked on the premises. *Recommended.*

Nelson's Bakery, *5222 N. Clark, (312) 561-5494.* Hours: 9 A.M. to 6 P.M. Monday through Saturday. 9 A.M. to 4 P.M. Sunday. Specializing in seasonal bakery goods. Pepperkakor, strettkaka, cookies, pecan fudge pies. Wednesday is senior citizen's day, 10% off on all items.

Art Galleries

One Touch of Nature Gallery, *5208 N. Clark, (312) 561-3300.* Hours: 10:30 A.M.–6:30 P.M. Tuesday through Saturday. 11 A.M. to 5 P.M. Sunday. Chicago's only gallery devoted to art in nature, in all of its aspects. Limited edition prints, original art works, books, nature tools. Opened in 1989.

Swedish Restaurants

Ann Sather Restaurant (formerly Villa Sweden) *5207 N. Clark, (312) 271-6677.* Hours: 7 A.M. to 11 P.M. Completely remodeled and under new ownership, Ann Sather preserves all the warm memories of old-fashioned Swedish country kitchen. Enjoy a traditional Scandinavian meal of herring, meatballs, potatoes, and rice pudding topped by lingonberries in pleasant surroundings. Roast goose dinner served on St. Morten's Day. Two other locations: 929 W. Belmont, and 1329 E. 57th Street.

Svea Restaurant I, *5236 N. Clark, (312) 334-9619.* Hours: 7 A.M. to 8 P.M. Tuesday through Friday. 7 A.M. to 4 P.M. Saturday, Sunday, and Monday. "Simply the best Swedish pancakes in Andersonville," promises owner Kurt Mathiasson, cofounder of the Swedish American Museum directly across the street. Kurt is the resident Andersonville Viking. Costumed in traditional Viking clothing, he will, on occasion, lead the Saturday morning sweeping brigade.

Svea Restaurant II, *3258 W. Foster, (312) 539-8021.* Nothing fancy, just more of the same good cooking from the folks who brought you Svea I.

International Restaurants

Beirut Restaurant, *5204 N. Clark, (312) 769-1250.* Hours: daily, 10 A.M. to 12 A.M. Middle-Eastern cuisine, created with an artistic flair.

Calo Restaurant, *5343 N. Clark, (312) 271-7782.* Hours: 11:00 A.M.–1 A.M., Monday through Thursday; 11 A.M. to 3 A.M. Saturday. 2 P.M. to midnight Sunday. Italian cuisine. Entertainment Wednesday through Sunday.

Konak Restaurant, *5150 N. Clark, (312) 271-6688.* Hours: daily, 4 P.M. to midnight. Authentic, exotic Turkish cuisine.

Vahick's Chinese Cuisine, *5143 N. Clark, (312) 769-1300.* Hours: 11 A.M. to midnight, Monday through Saturday, 4 P.M. to midnight, Sunday. Chinese cuisine from all the provinces of China. Catering available.

A Neighborhood Bar

Simon's Tavern, *5210 N. Clark, (312) 878-0894.* Hours: 9 A.M. to 2 A.M., Monday through Friday. 9 A.M. to 3 A.M., Saturday. 12 noon to 11 P.M., Sunday. Simon's for glogg (pronounced "glewg"). Simon Lundberg, the founder, has gone to his reward, but his son Roy still brews up the homemade glogg for the regulars on Clark Street every November. Glogg is a potent mix of hot port wine blended with raisins, aquavit (Sedish vodka) and other spices. They come by the busload to purchase this traditional Yuletide drink. Simon's is a real Chicago bar, dimly lit in deep earthy tones. Old Simon opened his bar in 1934, serving the rough-hewn Swede carpenters who sat for hours talking business, always business, and in the lilting tongue of Skåne, Småland, Dalarna, Dalsland, and the other regions of Sweden whence they came. Those were the days when a man could eat a meatball sandwich and potatoes for the price of a beer. It's no longer possible to feed an army of hungry working men in a tavern, but Simon's retains the look and feel of a real prohibition bar. This is the way a tavern used to be—no ferns, glass, or peppy waitresses. Escape the cold of winter or the heat of summer to trade gossip with someone you know. Simon's on Clark.

Outside Andersonville

Swedish Days, *held at alternate sites in Geneva, located 36 miles west of Chicago (take I-29 west Ill. 88, to Kirk Road, exit north I-38, West).* The festivities begin with a street carnival near the courthouse at 4th and James Street the third weekend in June, closest to June 22. A two-day craft show, a "Kid's Day," with such activities as a parade, a Big Wheel derby, jump-rope and free-throw competitions in the afternoon kick off the extravaganza. Continuous entertainment on a central stage nearby. A 10-kilometer fun run begins on the morning of the third day. A "Swedish Days" parade closes out the festival on Sunday, beginning at 7th and State Streets. For additional information call (312) 232-6060.

Scandinavian Day, *Vasa Park, Route 31, in Elgin.*   The wooded glade has hosted many Swedish cultural activities and picnics over the years. Swedish heritage is celebrated with food, crafts, and entertainment the second week of September. Call (708) 774-SCAN for details.

Scandinavian Children's Day (Vasa Barnens Dag), *Vasa Park, Route 31, Elgin, Ill.*   One-day ethnic festival held the second week in June. Music, folk dancing, games, booths, and entertainment provided by the children's auxiliary of the Swedish fraternal societies. Admission: $2.50 for adults, $1.00 for children. Call (708) 679-4774 for additional information.

Annual Svithiod Day Outing at Vasa Park, *Route 31, Elgin, Ill., third or fourth Sunday in June.*   Varied entertainment and traditional refreshments served all day beginning at 10:00 A.M. In the old days, this was the one event on the Swedish social calendar that everyone circled. Salt herring. Cold beer. Mosquitos. The combination was irresistable. Free admission. $1.00 parking. Call: (708) 774-SCAN.

Swedish American Recreation Club Annual Picnic at LaBagh Forest Preserve, *Grove no. 1, off Cicero Avenue near Foster and the Edens Expressway.*   Herring breakfast, hamburgers, chips and things. Games for all with lots of prizes. The Swedish Male Chorus performs. Third or fourth Sunday in August. Contact the Swedish American Recreation Club at 3541 N. Clark, Chicago, (312) 281-0233.

The Andersonville Recipe for Swedish Glogg

1-1/4 cups of water
1 teaspoon cardamon seed or 8
  whole cardamoms
5 whole cloves
2 cinnamon sticks
1 piece of bitter orange peel
1/4 cup of raisins
10 almonds
1/2 to 3/4 cups of sugar
2 bottles of red wine
1-1/4 cups of cognac *or* unflavored aquavit (vodka)
1/4 cup of port wine

Directions: Bring the water, spices, raisins and almonds to a boil and let simmer for five minutes. Cover and let draw for at least half an hour. Strain and then add sugar stirring until dissolved. Add red wine, cognac, or aquavit and port wine. Heat gently. Serve the glogg in small mugs with a few raisins sprinkled in for added flavor. For a smoother consistency, substitute grain alcohol.

North Park College

When the Swedish Evangelical Mission Covenant College and Seminary opened in Chicago on September 18, 1894, a published announcement cautioned students residing near the Loop not to attempt to make the long trip at night. The best way to reach the distant North Side, they said, was to take the Chicago and Northwestern railroad to the Summerdale Station on Foster Avenue. Standing forlornly out in the middle of what was then empty farmland, the tiny college and theological seminary founded by Swedish immigrant members of the Evangelical Covenant Church was a lonely sight.

Their one building, affectionately known as the Old Main became the center of campus life for the modern North Park College and Theological Seminary, occupying twenty acres of land four miles west of Andersonville on Foster Avenue. David Nyvall founded the first Covenant school in Minneapolis in 1891. Classes were held in the cramped basement of the Swedish Tabernacle. The critical need for spacious new headquarters led Nyvall and his students to Chicago's North Side.

Today North Park is a four-year liberal arts college. Cultural ties to Sweden, Denmark, and Norway are fostered through the *Center for Scandinavian Studies* (CSS), which began a student exchange program in 1977. The school schedules a wide variety of events open to the public.

What to See

The Old Main, *3225 W. Foster Avenue, Chicago, 60625, (312) 583-2700.* The focal point of the campus is the Old Main, constructed in 1892 and opened two years later. Designated as a National Historic Landmark, the Old Main Preservation Society raised nearly $1.2 million to finance an extensive renovation project. In November 1986, the building was reopened to the public. The Old Main houses the campus hospitality lounge, the reception lobby, public relations, admissions, and alumni affairs.

The Center for Scandinavian Studies.   Located on the campus, the center serves the undergraduate student population and members of the community at large. Classes, lectures, special exhibits, and choral and dramatic performances are open to the public. Artisans, musicians, writers, and political figures from each of the five Nordic countries will appear from time to time. For more information and a calendar of events, call (312) 583-2700.

Getting to Andersonville

By car from the Loop: Drive north on Lake Shore Drive, exit Foster Avenue and proceed west past Sheridan and Broadway. When you reach Foster Avenue you have arrived. Look for a parking spot, not always the easiest thing to do, but the side streets of Balmoral, Berwyn, Farragut, and Summerdale are your best bet.

By Public Transportation from the Loop: Take the Howard (North-South) line. Exit Berwyn (a B stop) and walk west on Foster about four blocks. In January it is best to skip the walk and take the #92 Foster bus at the station. It is a short ride of about four blocks.

The Bishop Hill Settlement

Erik Jansson was a self-styled prophet. He believed that faith cleanses all sin and forgiveness follows. He ran into trouble with the leaders of the Swedish Lutheran Church who considered the Janssonites a love cult run by a religious heretic. It was 1846, and Jansson told his followers that peace could be found in the American west, whereas a "stern punishment shall descend on those inhabitants of Sweden." He envisioned a village based on communal ownership of land with absolute devotion to the leader and the ideal. Jansson and his flock sailed from Sweden in 1846 arriving in Chicago by way of the Great Lakes.

They walked the rest of the way, a distance of 160 miles to a land west of Chicago that they had only heard of. The farmlands of western Illinois offered rich opportunities long denied them in Hälsingland, Sweden. Jansson named his commune twenty miles northeast of Galesburg Bishop

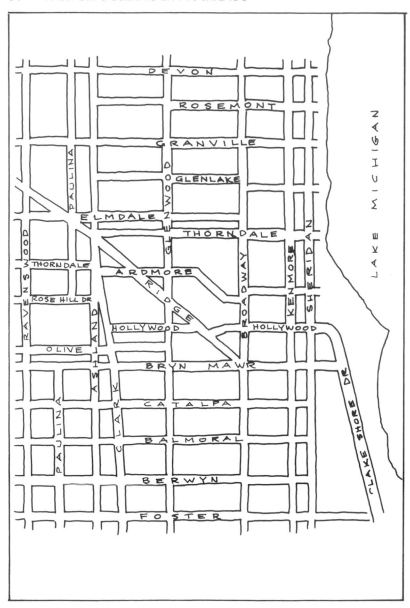

Andersonville

Hill after Biskopskulla, his ancestral home. The colony flourished for nearly fifteen years, but dissolved in a sea of controversy, financial mismanagement, and a breakdown in the religious unity that characterized the early years. A stranger named John Root came to town in 1848 to claim Jansson's cousin Charlotte for a wife. The marriage was sanctioned by Jansson with the proviso that if he left the colony his wife and children would remain behind. Root ran off with Charlotte two years later. Jansson followed him to St. Louis, where he sought help from the courts. Frustrated in his dealings with the American legal system, he returned to Bishop Hill and prophesied his own death. The very next day Root shot Jansson on the courthouse steps of a nearby town. Without the dynamic leader, members of the community carried on as best they could, but the board of trustees ran the community into the ground.

Bishop Hill survives as a uniquely preserved museum without the commercial glitz of Williamsburg or Greenfield Village, Michigan. The site has been listed as a National Historic Landmark in the Register of Historic Places. It is located 160 miles west of Chicago in Henry County, about a three-and-a-half-hour drive from the western suburbs. Swedish heritage is preserved year round, but Christmas at Bishop Hill is a special time for both the residents and tourists. Lucia nights are celebrated the second week of December. The Lucia queens serve pastries and coffee in the museums and shops—decorated for the holiday with brightly lit candles in the storefronts. The Nova singers and carolers serenade the Christmas revelers with traditional songs.

What to See in the Historic District

Steeple Building, a three-story Greek Revival building housing the Bishop Hill Heritage Museum. Pick up a copy of a Bishop Hill map and use it as a historical guide to the preserved district. A slide show explaining the history of the settlement and founding of Bishop Hill is shown several times each day. The clock on the Steeple Building has only one hand. No matter, the pace of life is slow and nobody really *cares* bout the time. The Steeple Building is open 9 A.M.–5 P.M., Monday through Sunday.

The Colony Church, built 1848. The paintings on the wall were painted by long-time resident Olaf Krans from memory. Krans lived in Bishop Hill until the Civil War, when he enlisted in the Union Army. He returned to neighboring Galva and recorded his impressions of the flourishing colony some 30 years later. His work is the only surviving depiction of life in Bishop Hill as it was lived by the Janssonites.

Colony Woodshed. Woodcraft demonstrations, antiques, and brooms for sale. 309/927-3571.

Abraham Florine House. Built 1867. Lace crochet, Swedish folk art. Four little shops inside including the Country Trunk, Calico Creations, the Little Brick Shed, and the Green Gables Shop. Hours: 10 A.M. to 5 P.M. (309) 927-3818.

Village Green. The Swedish settlers spent their first winter here, in dugouts built into mudbanks with only a timber front and a sod roof to protect them from the harsh midwestern snows. Nearly 100 died from the elements and deprivation. The village green is a stark reminder of a time in the distant past that was neither simple nor kind.

Vasa Order of America. Here are the national archives preserving Swedish culture in America. Hours by appointment. Call (309) 927-3523.

Guided tours of Bishop Hill are conducted by the Heritage Association by appointment. Call (309) 927-3899.

Annual Events

Old Settler's Day, second week of September, usually the 9th or 10th. Residents and visitors celebrate the founding of the colony with entertainment, dinner and demonstrations.

Jordbruksdagarna, or harvest celebration. The smell of cooking sorghum is in the air. The agricultural days of late September are celebrated with hayrides, harvest demonstrations, old-time crafts, children's games and good food. For a calendar of events call (309) 927-3345, or write to the Bishop Hill Arts Council, P.O. Box 47, Bishop Hill, IL 61419.

Julmarknad. The annual Christmas Market days, kicking off the Yuletide season. November 25–December 5. The shops of Bishop Hill are decorated for the season, special foods are prepared by the Swedish cooks residing in the village. Wandering carolers serenade the visitors to evoke a nineteenth century feeling.

Lucia Nights. The Festival of the Lights celebration. Second week of December. Young girls dressed in the traditional Nordic costumes of white, crowned with a wreath of candles, walk among the stores to serve pastries and coffee to visitors and residents.

Julotta. The six A.M. candlelight service at the Colony Church. The observance is nondenominational and in English. Coffee and rusks follow the service. Christmas Day.

Season Opening. Late March or early April. Music program, refreshments.

Midsummer Festival, known as the *sommarnoje* (summer pleasure) in Sweden. Warm days, the midnight sun, and the warm comradery of friends is what the mid-summer celebration on June 25 is all about. It is celebrated with a traditional dance around the maypole, and the preparation of Swedish ethnic food.

Other events to be announced. Call (309) 927-3899.

Shopping Bishop Hill

Swedish handicrafts, little red Dalarna horses, books, cookware, and gift items are available in the village from a variety of merchants.

The Colony Woodshed. Woodcrafts, gifts, antiques. Daily 10 A.M. to 5 P.M. Phone (309) 927-3571.

Abraham Florine House. Daily 10 A.M. to 5 P.M.
  Green Gables Shop. Antiques, florals, country wood.
  Country Trunk. Unique handmade gifts.
  Calico Creations. Sweatwear, wallhangings, country art.
  The Little Brick Shed. Crafts, antiques, handcrafted wood products.
  Phone (309) 927-3818.

Olson's Family Tree. Soda fountain, sundry items, gifts. Daily 10 A.M. to 5 P.M. Serving 11 A.M. to 3 P.M.

PJ's Needlecraft. Needle, fine Swedish embroidery.
Phone (309) 927-3304

The Prairie Workshop. Quilts, handmade items, antiques. Daily
10 A.M. to 5 P.M.
The Village Woodwright. Furniture, lathework, and treenware.
Langston's Milk House Antiques. Stoneware, kitchen collectibles.
(309) 927-3367. Daily 10 A.M. to 5 P.M.

The Red Oak. Swedish imported items. Daily 10 A.M. to 5 P.M.
Luncheonbord. Swedish-American cuisine. Serving 11 A.M. to 3 P.M.
(309) 927-3539.

Jultomten. Christmas collectibles from Sweden. Daily 10 A.M. to
5 P.M. Phone (309) 927-3539.

Bishop Hill Colony Store. Imported Swedish foods. Gifts, and
crafts. Daily 10 to 5:00. (309) 927-3596.

Holden's Administration Building. Gifts, souvenirs, and miscel-
lany Daily 10 A.M. to 5 P.M. (309) 927-3500.

Svenskt Hjarta Gift Shop. Linens, gifts, antiques. Daily 10 A.M. to
5 P.M. (309) 927-3302.

Antik Affar. Handcrafted gifts, collectibles. Daily 10 A.M. to 4 P.M.
(309) 927-3860.
Colony Cross Stitch. Supplies for the cross stitcher. Daily 10 A.M. to
4 P.M.
PL Johnson Dining Room. Serving 11 A.M. to 3 P.M. Phone (309)
927-3885.
Handwovens of Bishop Hill. Designing, weaving. Daily 10 A.M. to
4 P.M.

Market Day Baskets. Locally produced handwovens. Friday, Saturday, Sunday, 10 A.M. to 4 P.M. (309) 854-0531.

Colony Inn. Packaged liquors. Daily 1 P.M. to 5 P.M. (309) 927-3335.

The Singletree. Country crafts, ceramics. Daily 10 A.M. to 4 P.M. (309) 927-3514.

Village Smithy Gift Shop. Rug weaving, antiques, stitchery. Daily 10 A.M. to 4 P.M. (309) 927-3851.

Where to Stay in Henry Country

Bishop Hill is a three-and-a-half-hour drive from Chicago. It is a trip that can be completed in one day, via I-55. (See Directions.) For those desiring overnight accommodations there is a *guest house,* and a *bed and breakfast* establishment near the historic district. Because space is limited, it is recommended that reservations be made well in advance of your desired stay.

Historic Galesburg, site of a Lincoln-Douglas debate, was the boyhood home of Swedish American poet and historian Carl Sandburg. The Sandburg state historical site is a restored three-room cottage located at 331 E. 3rd Street. Admission is free, and the Sandburg home is open every day except New Year's, Thanksgiving, and Christmas Day. Galesburg is conveniently located 20 miles northeast of Bishop Hill on U.S. 34. There are several fine motels offering easy access to all the Galesburg and Bishop Hill attractions.

— In Galesburg —

The Winfield Inn (formerly the Holiday Inn). *Located three miles north of U.S. 34 bypass on U.S. 150.* The basic room rate for two persons is $43 per night. 143 Rooms, two stories. No weekend rates. Located north of downtown Galesburg. Bar. Restaurant. Entertainment. Coin laundry. All major credit cards. (309) 344-1111.

Days Inn (formerly Howard Johnson's). *Located adjacent to the Public Square in downtown Galesburg on U.S. 150.* Single bed, $37 per night. Double, $42. No weekend rates. 96 Rooms, seven stories. Indoor pool, 24 hour cafe. All major credit cards. (309) 343-9161.

Jumer's Continental Inn. *E. Main Street at I-74.* Single bed, $51. Double, $60. The weekend rate is $110. Cable TV, Indoor Pool.

Whirlpool, Sauna. Restaurant: Tavern on the Pheasant (continental menu). 149 Rooms, two stories. American Express, Diner's Club, Mastercard, Visa. (309) 343-7151 or (800) 635-8637 (Il).

— In Bishop Hill —

Holden's Guest House, *P.O. Box 95, Bishop Hill, Ill., 61419. (309) 927-3500.* A restored 1869 farm house located at the east end of the village that offers a magnificent view of the rolling hills of western Illinois. No TV, but you won't miss it. The Holdens will keep their guests entertained with old-time radio, Trivial Pursuit, and a sumptuous meal available through the hospitality pack. There is one suite and three antique appointed guest rooms. Available by the room, the floor, or the whole house. Rates: $180.00 full house; $125.00 second floor; $50 Emma's Room (double bed); $65 Margaret's Room (double beds, double occupancy). Per person: $20 extra. Complimentary breakfast. Hospitality packs including meal are available for cost. Your hosts: Linda & Steve Holden. *Recommended.*

Country Hills Bed & Breakfast, *P.O. Box 35, Bishop Hill, Ill., 61419. (309) 932-2886.* A modern two-story home located $1^1/2$ miles south of Bishop Hill. Two guest rooms furnished with quilt-covered antique beds. A comfortable family room with a fireplace and the engaging company of your hosts, Lawanda & Don England. Call for current rates and availability.

Getting to Bishop Hill From Chicago Take I-55 (the Stevenson) south to Joliet. Connect with I-80, and drive west to U.S. 82. Take this road south to the signs marked Bishop Hill. If you reach Nakoma you have gone too far and must turn back.

═══════════ Norwegian Chicago ═══════════

Did Leif Ericson *Really* Discover America?

Mayor William Hale Thompson had no use for King George of England. During the 1927 mayoral campaign, the blustering demagogue of city politics made an issue of School Superintendent William McAndrew's alleged pro-English biases which, according to the unabashed Thompson, posed a threat to impressionable young minds. "This fellow McAndrew

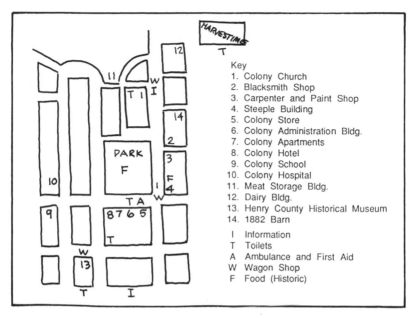

Bishop Hill

in the schools!" Big Bill thundered, "Teaching un-Americanism! If we don't look out our history books are going to have all kinds of things belittling George Washington, the great founder of our country!" The school text book issue struck a responsive chord with Chicago's 56,000-strong Norwegian community, who had felt the sting of history concerning the treatment of the legendary Viking explorer Leif Ericson.

The sons and daughters of Thor and Odin seized upon Thompson's fiery campaign rhetoric to petition the city for an official correction of the record. The "call to arms" was first sounded at the Norwegian Centennial Celebration of 1925. "It has been established as historical fact that Leif Eriksson (or Ericson) set foot on the eastern shore of the American continent 500 years before the voyage of Columbus," declared Mrs. Berthe C. Peterson, vice-president and spokesperson for the Norwegian National League.

According to Professor R.B. Anderson, a foremost authority on the life and times of the Norseman, Eriksson lost his way and landed on the New England coast between Massachusetts and Rhode Island sometime around the year 1000. The exact location was never established. The Norwegians based their claim on purely circumstantial evidence. Eriksson called the land "Vinland," because of the abundance of wild grapes he found growing on the shore. These same grapes are indigenous to New England. President Calvin Coolidge, speaking at the 1925 Norwegian League convention in Minneapolis, accepted the findings without reservation. Mrs. Peterson went ahead and drafted a resolution calling on Thompson to support the Leif Eriksson movement. Her motives appear to have been something less than altruistic. "Our request is particularly timely because of the present controversy about un-American school books and because a $10,000 prize has just been offered for the best new American history written for the Chicago Public Schools!"

The outcome of this controversy was never resolved to Mrs. Peterson's satisfaction, nor to that of the combined Norwegian fraternal societies that abounded in Chicago at that time. Weep not for Leif Eriksson. The memory of the intrepid Viking who established the first permanent European settlement in Greenland, was memorialized in Lincoln Park in the form of a curious nautical monument that arrived in the city in time for the 1893 World's Columbian Exposition. In honor of Leif Eriksson, Norway sent a replica viking ship under the command of Captain Magnus Anderson to Chicago. The tiny vessel set sail from the port city of Bergen on April 30, 1893. Anderson and his men crossed the Atlantic, passed through the canals, the Great Lakes, and toward Chicago. Off the coast of Evanston, the latter-day Vikings were greeted by a small flotilla of Chicago boats, which escorted the craft to the foot of Van Buren Street, where the captain and crew were greeted by Mayor Carter Harrison I. The viking long boat was placed on temporary display at the World's Fair, and was later donated to the Field Museum of Natural History.

Captain Anderson's boat was ignored, and nearly forgotten when a group of ladies from the Norwegian Women's Federation started a campaign to relocate the boat to a more visible location in Lincoln Park. Money was raised to reinforce the rotting timbers, and when work was completed, the long boat was presented to the state as a historic monument. There it would remain for another generation; a Chicago oddity most people took for granted, or simply didn't understand.

The Viking long boat is maintained by the Cook County Commissioners, but currently occupies a space behind the children's zoo in Lincoln Park. Over the years more than a few passers-by have wondered if this is the same vessel commanded by Leif Eriksson. Mrs. Berthe Peterson would have it no other way.

Czech Chicago

History and Settlement

Modern day Czechoslovakia was carved out of the remnants of the old Austro-Hungarian empire in October 1918. It is a Slavic nation composed of the former imperial provinces of Moravia, Bohemia, Slovakia, and Sub-Carpathian Ruthenia. No, not *all* Czechs are Bohemians, but that is what these immigrants have been called since they first set foot on these shores in the eighteenth century. The name "Bohemian," is derived from the Boli, an ancient Celtic people who inhabited western Czechoslovakia in the fifth century B.C. Bohemia is a lush region, with vast mountain ranges, fertile valleys, and rich deposits of coal, graphite, silver, iron ore, and uranium.

The history of Czechoslovakia is pockmarked by the violent struggles of a rebellious proletariat comprising the various ethnic groups who lived in the region. The Czechs, who accounted for 51 percent of the population were unable to pacify the Slovak, Hungarian, and Ukrainian minorities, who sought political, cultural, and social parity with the host government. In 1848 a nationalistic uprising against the Hapsburg monarchy to combat a rising tide of "Germanization" within the provinces, spurred the first wave of immigration into the U.S. The "48'ers" and all those who were to follow in the next 140 years were among the most literate and highly skilled Europeans to be processed through Castle Garden and (later) Ellis Island.

Their love of freedom echoed through the provinces in the long suppressed work of Jan Hus, the immortal fifteenth century author who championed the Czech language in his theological study, *De Orthographia Bohemia* (Czech Orthography, 1412). A new generation of thinkers awakened the national conscience and fueled the growing movement toward independence during the Victorian era. Journalist Jan Neruda (1834-91) encouraged the Czech people to improve their economic lot through public education. He penned colorful poetry and chronicled the lives of the Prague middle class in his work.

Tomas Garrique Masaryk, Czechoslovakia's greatest political figure who became the first president of the new republic in 1918, laid the foundation for a "new realism" that bridged the widening gulf between two schools of thought: the Parnassians, who weaved foreign themes into Czech literature, and the Nationalists whose most eloquent spokesman was the poet Suatopluk Cech (1846-1908).

A Czech, William Paca, was one of the signers of the Declaration of Independence. But the greater number of freedom-loving Czechs began arriving in the U.S. before the Civil War. They fanned out across the Midwest and the Plains states of Nebraska, Kansas, Wisconsin, and Texas; the terrain was reminiscent of the land they had recently left behind. Those who settled in Chicago in the 1870s established the first Czech community along De Koven Street—*Mala Jinzni Strana,* or "Little Prague."

After the Chicago Fire, the Czechs began to build on the open prairies near Eighteenth Street and Racine Avenue. One of the first buildings to be erected in the neighborhood was a Czech restaurant and saloon, owned by an immigrant from the West Czechoslovakian city of Plzen, which stands at the confluence of the Mze and Radbusa Rivers. The owner named his establishment the Pilsen Cafe, and gradually the name was adopted by the immigrants who inhabited Blue Island Avenue from Sixteenth to Twenty Second Streets.

The Pilsen neighborhood of Chicago was for many years an important manufacturing center. The McCormick Reaper Works at Blue Island Avenue and Western, and the Chicago, Burlington, and Quincy Railroads provided jobs and meager wages for the workers who crowded into modest two-story cottages with high basements, tiny grass plots in front of the dwelling, and a garden in the back yard. Describing the assimilation of his people into the Chicago culture, a W.P.A. writer penned these thoughts during the height of the Depression:

> The economic adjustment of the Czech community to American conditions seems almost to be perfect, due to a strong tendency for

economic cooperation. Here and there only minor conflicts arise with other nationalities, as for example with the Irish, whom the Czech hate on account of their Catholic religion, favoritism and rough dealing with their subordinates. They (the Czechs) are very anxious to get prestige in the group, knowing that there is much community spirit, patriotism, and solidarity among the people, which will be to their advantage. It is among the working men and among the intellectuals, where the Czech culture finds its place.

Pilsen was a highly secular, insulated neighborhood, hemmed in by railroad tracks, heavy industry, and a flourishing retail trade centered along 18th Street. For nearly eighty years English was the second language spoken here. The old timers organized mutual aid benefit societies to promote the culture, and the financial welfare of the immigrants who worked a variety of jobs at the Peter Schoenhofen Brewery at the east end of 18th Street, or the Chicago Stove Works Foundry. According to W.P.A. writer Theodore Przydryga, "the great mass of Czech people are skilled workmen and craftsmen. The second generation tends to prefer office employment, business and professional careers such as the law, dentistry, medicine, teaching and banking."

The immigrants received the latest news of the day through four daily newspapers representing the political extremes of the day. The main stream *Svornost Daily* (Harmony) was the first Bohemian newspaper published in the U.S. The "Free Thinkers," who were violently opposed to Roman Catholic clericalism published the *Spravedlnost* which advocated a liberal school system and socialism—unpopular views that contributed to the hard feelings existing between the Irish-run city administration and the fledgling trade unionist movement of the 1870s and 1880s.

The Czechs organized their "Sokols," or free thought schools that filled an educational gap in the immigrant community. The Sokol movement began in Czechoslovakia in 1862 in order to promote the physical, spiritual, and mental well-being of the people. Dissident poet and journalist Karl Havlicek (1821-56) was the prime mover of the Sokol ideal. Havlicek, whose statue was placed in Douglas Park on the West Side, was the editor of a Prague newspaper until he was imprisoned by the Hapsburg government for his views. In his memory the Chicago Czechs dedicated the Sokol Havlicek-Tyrs at 2619 S. Lawndale. The largest Sokol unit in the U.S. met here, in the heart of "Ceska California," the second most influential Czech neighborhood in Chicago. Bounded by California Avenue on the east, the city limits on the west, and from 14th St. on the north and 33rd on the south, Ceska California was inhabited by Czechs from the 1880s until the Mexican immigrants changed the ethnic composition of the neighborhood. Today, throngs of Mexican bakeries, restaurants, thrift stores, and community centers line the main business thoroughfares of Pilsen. For many newly arrived Mexicans, Pilsen is their first real encounter with American culture. The Czech residents abandoned these West Side neighborhoods by the 1950s, leaving behind only a few solitary reminders of their heritage, like the St. Procopius Catholic church at 18th and Allport, built in 1883, and the "mother parish" of Pilsen.

Ceska California (or Lawndale) was the political powerbase of Anton Cermak, Chicago's only Czech mayor, who was tragically shot down while in the company of President-elect Franklin D. Roosevelt at Miami's Bayside Park on Feb. 13, 1933. Cermak was the architect of the Democratic "machine" of legend. Born in Prague, Cermak came up the hard way—working for a few cents a day at the Braidwood mines. But he was resourceful and ambitious. This favorite son of Lawndale attracted the attention of George "Boss" Brennan, future Democratic kingmaker who came up through the coal mines, taught school for a time, and then drifted into state politics. In 1931, Cermak, whose personal wealth was estimated to be $7,000,000, was elected mayor by a majority of Chicagoans fed up with the antics of William Hale Thompson and his gangster coalition.

Cermak came down hard on the gangsters who turned the city streets into a shooting gallery. He was loved and respected by his Czech-Slavik constituency, the majority of whom supported his anti-Prohibition platform. Through his brief mayoral term, Cermak continued to reside in Lawndale at a modest residence located at 2338 Millard Avenue. The real estate office of Cermak and Serhant was located on the main thoroughfare of Ceska California at 3346 W. 26th Street. Further down the street stands the fortress-like Criminal Court Building and lock-up, constructed for the sum of $7.5 million and opened on April 1, 1929. Thanks to the log-rolling tactics of Cermak, the city bridewell was permanently located in the future mayor's home ward.

Appropriately, Twenty Second Street was renamed Cermak Road in honor of the martyred mayor who in his earlier years took an active role in community affairs as the Director of the Czechoslovak-American Chamber of Commerce. For it was here, in neighboring Cicero and Berwyn where the greatest number of Czechs settled after World War I. The steady westward drift into Cicero, Berwyn, Riverside, Brookfield, and other suburbs along the path of the old Burlington Railroad line continued into the 1950s and 1960s. But is was during the time of Cermak's political ascendancy that 22nd Street between Cicero and Harlem Avenues became known as the "Bohemian Wall Street."

"The neighborhood," according to author Norbert Blei, who grew up in Cicero during its halcyon days, "was a current, a circular field of motion. Much coming and going. Everything stood still, yet everything revolved (by the hour, the day, the season, the year) and came back to you. You departed and returned. And you were the same but different." For Miles Pancner, who arrived from Lisov, Czechoslovakia, in the 1920s to open an import business on 22nd Street, Cicero and Berwyn was the "Tailor City," for the many skilled garment workers who plied their trade on Bohemian Wall Street.

Evidence of the legendary Czech penchant for thriftiness abound. Up and down the street can be found the savings and loan institutions that do not bother to place withdrawal slips on the counter. For it was customary for the Czech families who lived in the red and brown brick bungalows off 22nd Street to visit the savings and loan every Saturday morning to deposit their paychecks—in cash. The dream of home ownership is alive and well in Berwyn, where the local real estate offices feature black-and-white photographs of two-flats and bungalows available for purchase in their windows. In good times and bad, the Czechs of 22nd Street are wary of the permutations of the stock market, putting their faith in the old adage that a penny saved is a penny earned. Or to quote Miles Pancner, described as "the last pioneer merchant" of 22nd Street, "You can lose your money, but you can't lose your education."

Cermak Road has been an extension of Czech folk life for nearly 80 years. The Western Electric Hawthorne Works in Cicero provided steady employment for many of the 40,000 Czechs living here, from 1903 until the doors of the old factory closed for the last time in the 1980s. Norbert Blei described the significance of Western Electric in his nostalgic memoir, appropriately titled *Neighborhood:* "though the boundaries of the town were fixed streets, addresses [and] directions were of less significance to a kid than the fact that Western Electric (the tower, the huge green and red sign that glowed from the roof at night) marked the spot where Chicago began; the Sanitary District (which you could smell when the wind blew from that direction) and the race tracks (Sportsman's Park and Hawthorne) and the Burlington Railway (home of the Silver Zephyr) and the Red Arrow (famous jazz joint) were south; the factories, the Dutch settlement, the Town and Ritz shows, [and] Columbus Park were north and also Chicago; and Cicero turned into Berwyn just after the Olympic show and Sokol around Lombard Avenue across the street from the Hole in the Wall Tavern . . ."

The neighborhood. It wasn't prettified or sissy. Al Capone sweated out four years of Mayor Dever's reform administration at the Hawthorne

Smoke Shop during the 1920s. And the all-night saloons of Cicero have raised the hackles of many a church-going reformer. But there have been greater threats in recent years. With the departure of Western Electric, Cicero and Berwyn face the usual economic drag that accompanies the defection of heavy industry from an area. How well the Czechs maintain their identity in Cicero and Berwyn remains to be seen, though the loosening of border restrictions and the retreat of communism in Eastern Europe fostered a new wave of immigration into the U.S. During the "Prague Spring" uprising of 1968, it was not uncommon to see twenty to thirty refugees a week step off the bus in Chicago with little more than the clothes on their back and a few dollars in their pockets. These new arrivals could count on the warm assistance of their American relatives, or the Czechoslovakian National Council of America (CNCA) to help them find affordable housing, a job at Western Electric, and neighbors of Bohemian descent to converse with in their native tongue. But this is a changing time, and the old rules no longer apply.

The Czechs will endure. They are a proud people who have embraced the American way of life in all aspects. George Halas of the Bears, sportscaster Chet Coppock, former Chicago Blackhawk center man Stan Mikita, actress Kim Novak, Assistant Public Defender Mary Jane Placek (a.k.a. "Empress of the Bohemians"), crime writer Gera-Lind Kolarik, and Cicero's former poet-in-residence, Nobert Blei, are Czech-Americans who have left their imprint on the community. There will certainly be more.

Annual Events and Celebrations

International Houby Festival. A "houby" (or *hribky*) is a mushroom. To the Czech people, this wild fungus, which we take for granted, is sacred. The houby is akin to the Irish shamrock, and every year around Columbus Day, the Cermak Road Business Association sponsors a week-long celebration of the houby. A Houby Queen is crowned; the ball and dinner-dance follow; the merchants sponsor a sidewalk sale during the week, which is followed by the centerpiece of the festivities: the Sunday parade, featuring food booths, floats, arts and crafts, horseshoe-throwing contests, and races. The Houby Festival has been going strong since 1969 from Central Avenue to Oak Park Avenue. According to local legend, and the wit and wisdom of Norbert Blei, the seasoned houby hunters will leave their homes in Cicero, Berwyn, or Riverside one morning in the early Fall, armed with a bushel basket, knife, and the fabled "houby stick." Then, with the quarry in hand, the hunter returns home to have his wife prepare mushroom soup, pickled mushrooms, sacred mushrooms . . . For more information, contact the Cermak Road Business Association, 2134 S. 61st Court, Cicero, 60650, or call (708) 863-8979.

Moravian Day (Moravsky Den). The ethnic traditions of Moravia, the central province of Czechoslovakia, are celebrated in song, dance, and colorful costumes during the annual Moravian Day at the Operating Engineers Hall, 6200 Joliet Road, in Countryside, Ill., the last weekend in September. The festival is one of the longest running ethnic events in Chicago, dating back to 1939 when the newly formed United Moravian Societies sponsored their festive outing at Pilsen Park, 26th and Albany, and then later at the Sokol-Havlicek Tyrs at 26th and Lawndale. In the early years a stately procession of horsemen decked out in Moravian folk costumes paraded to the fairgrounds. The pageantry and dash of those earlier times has been transplanted to the western suburbs under the auspices of the United Moravian Societies and the Moravian Folklore Circle. The finest Czech dance troops from Indiana, Wisconsin, and Canada assemble each year to perform a singing and dancing program depicting a different theme each year. A Welcome Dance at the Sokol Berwyn Hall, 6445 W. 27th Place in Berwyn precedes Moravian Day, to welcome the out-of-town performers. The following morning a Holy Mass conducted in the Moravian dialect at the Engineers Hall begins the day-long events. General dancing, and a rich harvest of Moravian food including tripe soup, dumplings and sauerkraut, dill pickles, and pastries, await the public, according to Alice Palach, Public Relations Co-ordinator for the Czechoslovak Fraternal Life (CSA). Admission prices are $10 on Sunday, and $6 per person on Saturday. For more information please call (312) 749-1346 or Rudy Liska, President of the United Moravian Societies, at (708) 442-7290.

Czechoslovak Day Festival, *at the National Grove No. 4, 27th and Des Plaines, North Riverside, Il., the last Sunday in July.* The day-long festival rekindles happy memories of Pilsen Park at 26th and Albany, where for years the Czech community of the West Side gathered every weekend to eat, drink, and dance. Pilsen Park had an outside stage and a dance pavillion with a wooden floor. On warm summer nights when the crocuses were in bloom, and the music soft and gentle, young people gathered under the stars to dream . . . and to romance. Pilsen Park was razed in the mid-1970s to make way for the Little Village Mall, which serves the Mexican community. The Czech Festival began in 1985 as a kind of Pilsen Park "revival." The event was an immediate success, attracting people from all over Chicago, Indiana, and one person from Australia. The picnic is held the last Sunday in July from 11:00 A.M. until dusk. There is music, dancing, entertainment and plenty of Czech food including potato pancakes, sausages, kolacky, and more. Phone: (312) 242-2224 or (312) 795-5800. Sponsored by the Czechoslovak American Congress.

American Sokol Organization Anniversary Celebration. The word Sokol means "falcon" in English—a symbol of strength and independence to the Czech people. In the U.S., roughly 10,000 adults and 50,000 children participate in American Sokol Organization activities. The movement was founded by Dr. Miroslav Tyrs, who was inspired by the customs of ancient Greece. The Sokol ideal—"Physical Fitness Through Gymnastics"—has been kept alive in the U.S. since the post-Civil War period. The anniversary celebration is held each year, featuring dinner, cocktails, and a cultural program. For location, ticket prices, and dates, call the American Sokol Organization, 6426 Cermak Road, Berwyn, (708) 795-6671.

Czechoslovak National Council of America Debutante Ball *(downtown)*. The Czechoslovak National Council of America was founded during World War I. It grew out of an urgent need for a united national war effort of Americans of Czech and Slovak descent. In recent years the CNCA has sponsored many worthwhile activities including Council-sponsored classes in English for newly arrived immigrants, the creation of a permanent chair of Czech and Slovak Studies at the University of Chicago, and numerous publications, including a 1976 bibliography, *Czechs and Slovaks In America,* and a monthly newsletter, *Vestnik.*

The CNCA is divided into six main districts: Washington, D.C., Cleveland; Chicago; Michigan; New York City; and the Pacific (San Francisco, Los Angeles, San Diego). Greater Chicago is the largest district, with six local chapters. Each year, since 1951, the CNCA sponsors a black-tie debutante ball, honoring local girls of Czech descent. The 1991 event was held in the Grand Ballroom of the Ritz Carlton Hotel in Chicago on February 2. In attendance were the Honorable Shirley Temple Black, U.S. Ambassador to Czechoslovakia, Illinois Governor Jim Edgar, and Mayor Richard Daley of Chicago. Tickets for this event are $50 per person. For further information, or to join the CNCA, please contact Olga Kovar, at 2137 S. Lombard Avenue, Cicero, (708) 656-1117. Annual membership is $7 per person.

Czechoslovak Allied Organizations in Chicago (Suburban Ball). The Czechoslovak Allied Organizations began holding formal dinner dances a few years after the CNC, but this group was the first to have debutantes. The tradition began in 1965, but unlike the CNC, which limits participation to girls of Czech extraction, the Allied Organizations will accept young women between 16-21 of any ethnic background. The main purpose of the ball is to formally introduce the debs to society, but is also aimed at bringing together recent arrivals from Czechoslovakia with the older and younger generations of Chicagoans whose links to the old country may not be quite so strong. Tickets for this gala event which include prime rib dinner, musical entertainment and debutante presentation is $40.00 per person, and is held at the Drury Lane Oakbrook, 100 Drury Lane, Oakbrook Terrace, Il., the first or second weekend of February. Please contact Jerry Rabas at Weber Travel, 6805 Cermak Road, Berwyn at (708) 749-1333.

Czechoslovak Independence Day. Observed on or about October 28 in Chicago and Cicero. The Chicago celebration occurs at the Daley Civic Center Plaza in a noon-time ceremony sponsored by the Czechoslovak American Congress and the Department of Cultural Affairs for the City of Chicago. The national anthems of both countries are sung, and various folk dance troops perform native dances. A second ceremony is held on the grounds of the Cicero Town Hall in conjunction with the Czech Congress. Colors are presented by the Cicero Police Auxiliary, and the national anthems are sung by the CSA Fraternal Life Singers. Please call (312) 656-1117 for details, or the village of Cicero, at (708) 656-3600.

Czech Language Radio Programming

"Sunday's Czechoslovak Radio Hour" 9 A.M. to 10 A.M. Sundays. Louis Kolarik has hosted this show for over 25 years. He doubles as the executive secretary of the CSA Fraternal Life, and is treasurer of the Czechoslovak American Congress.

"Czechoslovak-American Radio Show" 8:05 to 8:30 P.M. Wednesday and Thursdays. Host: Jerry Jirak, who is the director of the Bohemian American Concertina Association.

Both programs are aired on the voice of ethnic Chicago, WCEV Radio, AM-1450, located at 5356 W. Belmont Ave., Chicago, 60641. (312) 282-6700. The program director is Lucyna Migala.

Ethnic Museum

Czechoslovakian Society of American Heritage Museum and Library, *2701 S. Harlem Avenue, Berwyn, (708) 795-5800.* The CSA Fraternal Life (formerly the Czechoslovak Society of America) is a fraternal benefit organization founded in 1854 in St. Louis to provide its members with a full line of insurance products and annuities, and for the broader purpose of preserving the history and customs of the native land. The museum was started in 1974, when the CSA moved into its spacious new offices in Berwyn. The museum houses a colorful collection of authentic folk costumes from the many different towns and regions of Czechoslovakia. A fine collection of blown glass, and lead crystal in many colors and styles, are proudly displayed by the CSA side by side with decorative Easter eggs, embroidery, frame implements, musical instruments, and paintings and sculptures. The library houses a collection of papers and archives pertaining to rural village life in Czechoslovakia, and the Euro-American immigration which commenced in the late 19th century. The museum is located only a few minutes from the Harlem Avenue exits of I-55 and I-290, but the hours of operation are restricted to weekdays, 10 A.M. to 4 P.M. Call (708) 795-5800 for additional information.

Art Galleries

Jacques Baruch Gallery, *40 E. Delaware, Chicago, (312) 944-3377.* Jacques and Anne Baruch opened their Chicago gallery in 1968 after the unfortunate events surrounding the Soviet crackdown, which became known as the "Prague Spring." Anne Baruch continues her husband's work by featuring the work of previously "forbidden" Czech artists. Hours: Tuesday through Saturday, 10 A.M. to 5 P.M. No credit cards.

Shopping on 22nd Street

The dispersal of many second- and third-generation Bohemians into the distant suburbs of Cook and Du Page County has been a growing concern to many longtime residents who recall the original breakup of their cohesive ethnic enclave in Lawndale and Pilsen. Cicero and Berwyn still maintain a strong Czech identity, but the presence of other ethnic groups, notably the Hispanics and Asians, have changed the face of 22nd Street. In 1982, community leaders benefited from a $2.4 million-dollar renovation of the streets and sidewalks. The Czech bakeries, restaurants, and gift stores continue to dwindle, but as Norbert Blei suggests, the day may come when young "urbanites" discover 22nd Street, and gentrify this cozy, down-home neighborhood. "At times I entertain the notion that in years to come Cicero might become a kind of Old Town. Young professionals working in Chicago will discover the potential of this neighborhood as an "in" place to live—less than ten miles from downtown on the Eisenhower Expressway; minutes from the Loop on the Douglas Park El; minutes away, too, via the Burlington [Railroad]; excellent shopping, restaurants, services, an Old World atmosphere . . . an authentic ethnic culture which might be preserved and encouraged for its full European flavor, for truly there is no place, so self-contained, quite like it in all Chicago."

Pancner's, *6131 Cermak Road, Cicero. (708) 652-3512.* Miles Pancner opened his greeting card and stationary store at this location in October 1929—the same month the stock market crashed and plunged the nation into the worst depression in its history. Miles Pancner hung on gamely, and within a few years his small import business began to thrive. When he passed away on February 5, 1989, Pancner was hailed as the "last great pioneer merchant of 22nd Street," by the *Berwyn Life.* Pancner's is a gift shop specializing in fine imported glassware, crystal, Czech greeting cards, and an impressive collection of ornate dolls, and marionettes. The costumed dolls, imported from Czechoslovakia, are a delight to behold for children of *all* ages. Books by Czechoslovakia's President Vaclav Havel, and by Cicero's native son, Norbert Blei, are available for sale. The store is owned by Jean Pancner-Lundberg, the daughter to the founder, who maintains the family business with loving care. The creaking wooden floors and ancient display cases harken back to a time in American history when private entrepreneurship was the attainable dream for the poorest immigrant—when people did their shopping in the neighborhood and not at a distant suburban mall. *Recommended.*

F. Pancner, Inc., *6514 W. Cermak Road, Berwyn. (708) 484-3459.* The family opened a second store in 1948, four blocks west of the original location. Today, the two Pancner stores are under separate ownership, and the sense of rivalry here is unmistakable. But if healthy competition is the soul of American commerce, then the patrons of the two Pancner stores are well served. In many ways, the second Pancner facility retains more of an Old World flavor than its Cicero counterpart, which reminds one of an old-fashioned American five-and-dime store. Shoppers will find a wider assortment of foreign-language books and greeting cards in Czech, Italian, Polish, Slovak, and German. This store was originally located at 26th and St. Louis, until the changing demographics of Pilsen and Lawndale convinced him to follow his customers to Berwyn. Pancner's of Berwyn features a diverse selection of cookbooks published by the Sokol groups from across the U.S.; kitchenware; collector's figurines; and the classic Bohemian garnet—the sparkling red teardrop known to gem experts as the "pyrope." The mineral is unique to Bohemia. Unique to Chicago and to Pancner's of Berwyn, is the store manager, Olga Mitas. She is fluent in Czech, and was called on by the embassy in Washington to send several of her flags to decorate the table of President Havel during his state visit. Pancner's is *Recommended*.

Dining (Deluxe)

Old Prague, *5928 W. Cermak Road, Cicero, (708) 863-1106.* Since 1941, this Cicero landmark has served up delicious pajsl (veal hearts), svickova (beef strogonoff), and koprova (beef in dill gravy) to local residents and tourists . . . though the neighborhood people will tell you that Old Prague is strictly a tourist trap. Despite these complaints, we found the food to be very good and the prices reasonable. Old Prague has the look and feel of a European chalet, and its ties to the community are very strong. During the tumultuous days of 1968 when the Soviet tanks rumbled through Prague, owner Laddie Vala opened his doors and allowed the refugees to sleep in his banquet rooms. The atmosphere of the restaurant is very pleasing and the food even better. The mural depicting Hradcany Castle, the residence of the kings of Bohemia, adorns the walls. *Recommended*.

Klas Restaurant, *5734 W. Cermak Road, Cicero, (708) 652-0795.* In 1922 Adolph Klas opened his castle-like restaurant on 22nd Street, and it was an immediate hit . . . with Al Capone, who swapped stories, drank beer, and played gin rummy with the proprietor in the back room during the wild and woolly Prohibition days. The playing cards are on display in a glass cabinet near the front door, reminding patrons that Cicero was a lusty town in its heyday. The current owners of Klas advertise themselves as the "pork specialists" of Chicago, which is hard to refute. Hand painted murals in an Eastern European motif decorate the walls. Wood carvings and stained glass windows are featured in the "Dr. Zhivago" banquet room—upstairs. Is this where Al Capone hid from the police? Come and find out. Catering. Special luncheon prices. *Recommended.*

Moderately Priced Restaurants

Pelikan Restaurant, *5639 Cermak Road, Cicero, (708) 652-4105.* Open seven days a week. Bohemian smorgasbord. All you can eat from 11 A.M. to 3 P.M. daily. Dinner served from 3–8.

Chateau Rose, *5830 Cermak Road, Cicero, (708) 656-5690.* Open 11 A.M. to 8 P.M., Monday through Sunday. Credit cards accepted.

Pilsner, *6725 Cermak Road, Cicero, (708) 795-6555.* Open 11 A.M. to 8 P.M. Sundays, Closed Monday. Tuesday through Saturday, 11 A.M. to 9 P.M. Visa/Mastercard accepted.

Czech Plaza, *7016 Cermak Road, Berwyn, (708) 795-6555.* Open 11 A.M. to 8 P.M., Monday through Sunday. No credit cards accepted.

Home Restaurant, *6831 Ogden Ave., Berwyn, (708) 788-4104.* Closed Mondays. Open Tuesday through Sunday, 7:30 A.M. to 8 P.M. No credit cards accepted.

Czech Restaurants Outside of Berwyn-Cicero

Westchester Inn Restaurant, *3069 S. Wolf Road (near 31st St), Westchester, Ill., (708) 409-1313 or (708) 409-1391.* Bohemian-American cooking brought to you by Mary and John Bosela. Tuesday, Wednesday, Thursday, 11 A.M. to 8 P.M.; Friday, Saturday, 11 A.M. to 7 P.M. Luncheon served 11 A.M. to 4 P.M. daily. No credit cards accepted.

The Dumpling House, *4109 S. Harlem Ave., Stickney, Ill., (708) 484-6733.* Pleasant chalet exterior. Home cooking. Monday through Thursday and Sunday, 11 A.M. to 9 P.M. Friday and Saturday, 11 A.M. to 10 P.M.. Mastercard and Visa accepted.

Bohemian Garden Restaurant, *980 W. 75th St., Downers Grove, Ill., (708) 960-0078.* Luncheon menu from 11 A.M.–3 P.M. daily. Closed Mondays. Friday and Saturday, 11 A.M. to 10 P.M. and Sunday 11 A.M. to 9 P.M.

Moldau Restaurant, *9310 W. Ogden Ave., Brookfield, Ill., (708) 485-8717.* Bohemian-American cooking. Open daily 11 A.M. to 8 P.M. Closed Wednesdays. No credit cards accepted.

Little Bohemia Restaurant, *25 E. Burlington, Riverside, Ill., (708) 442-1251.* Tuesday–Saturday, 11 A.M. to 8 P.M. Sunday, 11 A.M. to 7 P.M. Closed Mondays. No credit cards accepted. Same menu the entire day with specials.

Czech Kitchens, *6731 Pershing Road, Stickney, (708) 749-7868.* Daily specials and fresh carry-outs. Open 11 A.M. to 6 P.M., Tuesday–Friday, 9–4 P.M. Saturday, Closed Sundays. No credit cards accepted.

Little Europe, *9208 Ogden Ave., Brookfield, (708) 485-1112.* Open Tuesday–Thursday, 11 A.M. to 9:00 P.M,. Fridays, 11 A.M. to 10 P.M., Sunday, 11 A.M. to 8 P.M. Closed Monday. American Express accepted.

European Village Restaurant, *11141 W. Roosevelt Road, Westchester, (708) 531-1115.* Closed Mondays. Open Tuesday, Thursday, Sunday, 11:30 A.M. to 8:00 P.M., Friday–Saturday, 11:30 A.M. to 9 P.M. Visa/Mastercard accepted.

Corner Restaurant, *9201 Broadway Ave., Brookfield, (708) 485-5660.* Open every day except Tuesday, from 11 A.M. to 8 P.M. Visa/Mastercard accepted.

Riverside Family Restaurant, *3422 Harlem Ave., Riverside, (708) 442-0434.* Large bustling restaurant owned by a Czech immigrant, Peter Stanga. Moderately priced. Hours: 11 A.M. to 8 P.M., Tuesday–Saturday. Closed Monday. Open until 7 P.M. on Sunday.

Zenona Restaurant, *3218 Harlem Ave., Riverside, (708) 442-1002.* A tiny little storefront restaurant. Very charming. Hours: Tuesday–Friday, 11 A.M. to 8 P.M.; Saturday, noon to 8 P.M.; Sunday, noon to 7 P.M. Closed Monday.

Bohemian Crown Restaurant, *7249 Lake Street, River Forest, (708) 366-8140.* Located west of the Oak Park mall, with convenient parking in the rear. Unpretentious decor, with good food at reasonable prices. Open Tuesday–Saturday, 11 A.M. to 8 P.M. Sundays till 7.

Bohemian Crystal, *639 N. Blackhawk, Westmont, Ill., (708) 789-1981.* Hearty portions of traditional Czech foods: duckling, pork with lots of dill gravy for the asking. Open Tuesday–Saturday, 11 A.M. to 8 P.M. Sundays till 7 P.M. American Express, Mastercard and Visa accepted.

Bakeries

Minarik's, *5832 W. Cermak Road, Cicero, Ill., (708) 652-2854.* "Chleb nas vezdejsi." The sign over the cash register reads "bread from us is best," and there are few people in Cicero and Berwyn who will argue the point with Stanley and Maria Zolnierczyk, who specialize in Czech pastries, cookies, and imported foods from Europe. Open 6 A.M. to 6 P.M. Monday through Saturday.

Vesecky's Bakery, *6634 W. Cermak Road, Berwyn, Ill., (708) 788-4144.* A fixture on 22nd Street since 1929. To understand the Czech culture, visit Vesecky's on a busy Saturday morning when the neighborhood people show up for their specially made "Bohemian Rye." Kolacky made from three kinds of dough, each filled with cheese, jam, or poppy seed is recommended for those with a sweet tooth.

Delicatessen and Sausage-Maker

Prague Delicatessen, *6312 Cermak Road, Berwyn, (708) 863-1106.* As you step into this old world deli, notice the copies of *Denni Hlasatel* (the Daily Herald) and other Czech language publications lying on the counter. The Prague Delicatessen caters to the needs of the Bohemians who live in the neighborhood. This is no tourist trap to be sure, just the finest sledzie, pierogi, kana, jaternice, and sery available in the neighborhood. Open Monday 10 A.M. to 6 P.M.; Tuesday through Thursday 9 A.M. to 6 P.M.; and Saturday 8 A.M. to 5 P.M.

Crawford Sausage Company, *2310 S. Pulaski Road, Chicago, (312) 277-3095.* It goes without saying that the wonderful Bohemian "prazsky," (favored by the Czechs of Berwyn, Cicero, and Riverside), must come from the old neighborhood in Chicago. Since 1925 Crawford has distributed their Daisy Brand sausage to many Chicago area stores, notably the grocers in the Czech neighborhoods. Prazsky is a derivative of "Prague." It is a stick-to-the-ribs kind of meat that goes best with rye bread and beer, and is not recommended for calorie counters or vegetarians.

Joseph A. Starosta Meat Market, *2617 S. Ridgeland Ave., Berwyn, (708) 788-2934.* Joe Starosta is one of the few butchers in the area who still makes his own sausages and meats.

Jim's Meat Market, *1538 S. 61st St., Cicero, (708) 863-6308.* Jim Ruda is another who does it the old fashioned way—he grinds the sausages himself.

Getting There: By car from the Loop: Connect with the Eisenhower Expressway (I-90), either by driving west on Congress Street which **becomes** the freeway just west of the Loop, or by exiting the Kennedy Expressway (from the North), or the Dan Ryan (from the South) at the clearly marked ramps. Head west on the Eisenhower until you reach Austin Avenue. Exit at Austin, turn left (going south) until you hit 22nd Street. Turn left and you are entering Cicero; right, and you are in Berwyn.

By CTA: From the Loop: Board a Congress-Douglas "B" train at a designated stop. Take this train to 54th and Cermak where you should board a No. 304 or No. 25 bus, which will take you to Austin and Cermak.

For additional information call the CTA at (312) 836-7000.

Romanian-Hungarian-Serbo-Croatian Attractions

These communities are too small, and much too scattered to list separately, but the following restaurants and cultural attractions are worth looking into.

Serbo-Croatian

Miromar's Serbian Club, *2255 W. Lawrence Ave., Chicago, (312) 784-2111.* Czech and Yugoslavian fare served daily from 5 P.M. to 2 A.M., except Saturdays when it is open 5 P.M. until 3 A.M. Entertainment and floor show, Fridays and Saturdays from 7 P.M. until 8:45 P.M. Visa and Mastercard accepted.

The Cafe Continental, *5517 N. Lincoln Ave., Chicago, (312) 878-7077.* Croatian specialties served, including sausages (*kobasice*), apple strudel and crepes (*palacinke*), and standard American fare. Entertainment nightly. Open Wednesday, Thursday, Sunday, 5 P.M. to 11 P.M. Friday–Saturday, 5 P.M. until 4 A.M.

Skadarlija Restaurant, *4024 N. Kedzie Ave., Chicago, (312) 463-5600.* Full Serbian menu, with entertainment nightly, beginning at 8 P.M. Closed Mondays and Tuesdays. Open 6 P.M. until 2 A.M. Wednesday through Friday. Saturday–Sunday, 6 P.M. to 3 A.M. All credit cards accepted.

Yugo Inn, *2824 N. Ashland Ave., Chicago, (312) 348-6444.* Serbian cuisine. Open 5 P.M. until 10 P.M., Monday–Thursday, Friday–Saturday, 5 P.M. to 11 P.M., Sundays, 3:30 P.M. to 9:30 P.M. Personal check accepted, but no credit cards.

Holy Trinity Croatian Church, *1850 S. Throop, between 18th and 19th Streets, Chicago, (312) 226-2736.* Built in 1914, this small-sized church and school in Pilsen served Chicago's Croatian community for many years. Mass is still conducted in Croatian, and it still serves as a cultural center for many Chicago residents of Croatian descent.

Hungarian

Hungarian Books and Records, *561 W. Diversey, Chicago, (312) 477-1484. Open 9 A.M. to 5 P.M., Monday–Friday, Saturdays, 9 A.M. to 2 P.M. Closed Sunday* Located on the second floor of a Hungarian travel agency, the shop sells Hungarian language books, videos, and English texts pertaining to the history of Hungary.

Kenessey's Wine Cellar Restaurant, *403 W. Belmont Ave., Chicago, (312) 929-7500. Entertainment Wednesday through Sunday beginning at 6 P.M. Open Monday, Wednesday, Thursday, 11 A.M. to 11 P.M., Friday–Saturday, 11 A.M. to 12 P.M., Sunday, noon to 9 P.M. All bank cards except Discovery accepted.* A coffee house on the first floor serves up Hungarian pastries and espresso. In the basement you'll find an ethnic Hungarian restaurant with Gypsy violinists playing in the background.

Kenessey's Cypress, *500 E. Ogden Ave., Hinsdale, Ill., (708) 323-2727. Open Monday–Saturday, 11 A.M. until 11 P.M., Sunday, 11 A.M. to 3 P.M. and 4 P.M. to 9 P.M. Accepts all credit cards.* American restaurant that serves certain Hungarian delicacies including beef *guylas* (stew).

Romanian

Romanian Folk Art Museum, *2526 Ridgeway, Evanston, (708) 328-9099.* With a small membership and a handful of dedicated volunteers, the Folk Arts Museum in Evanston has evolved into one of the most active Romanian cultural organizations in the U.S. Under the direction of Rodica Perciali, a teacher and collector of ethnographic and folkloric items from her native Romania, the museum houses an impressive collection of handwoven and embroidered textiles, pottery, wooden and metallic household items, new and old icons on glass, and assorted arts and crafts. The museum is also an important resource center about Romania, with a collection of 500 books dealing with aspects of history, the visual and performing arts, 500 slides, photos and video tapes of classical music, drama and poetry. A special archive deals with the Romanian immigration to the U.S. Hours: Open Saturdays, 2 P.M. to 6 P.M., or by appointment. Admission: $4.00. Students and senior citizens, $2.00.

Museum Special Events

"Romanian Evenings," a cultural program about Romania and a Round Table of discussion, with Romanian cuisine served prior to the meeting. During the year the museum also sponsors special exhibits, audio/visual presentations about Romania, performances of music, dance, and poetry readings. For a schedule of events, or information on how you can participate, please call Rodica Perciali at (708) 328-9099.

Folk Art and Tapestry Display at the Daley Civic Center, *Washington and Clark Streets, during the first week of May.* The display conveys a synthetic visual history of Romanian tapestry as it evolved from folkloric weavings, with geometric, floral, and anthropomorphic motifs to contemporary, stylized and abstract artworks. Hours: Monday–Friday, 9 A.M. to 5 P.M. Call (708) 328-9099.

Lithuanian and Latvian Chicago

History and Settlement

Not much is known about Antanas Kaztauskis, a resident of Chicago's Back-of-the-Yards community. He worked in "packingtown," side by side with hundreds of other disillusioned Lithuanian émigrés who abandoned the fertile valleys and lush woods of their Baltic state in search of political freedom and economic opportunity. Kaztauskis recorded the despair felt by his countrymen in an article appearing in the 1904 issue of the *Outlook,* titled: "From Lithuania to the Chicago Stockyards—an Autobiography." How different the city of smokestacks appeared. The sense of acute frustration was reflected in Antanas's impressions of Chicago; the real estate agents who attempted to cheat first-time home buyers looking to negotiate an installment plan.

Because of Kaztauskis's shocking accounts of grimy, disease-ridden packingtown, a 26-year-old journalist named Upton Sinclair decided to investigate the situation first hand. The hitherto unknown writer donned a set of shabby working clothes, and joined the immigrant work force to observe first-hand the true conditions inside the empire of Cudahy, Swift, Armour, and Libby, McNeill. The result of his year long investigation was the publication of the *Jungle,* the muckraking novel released by Doubleday in February 1906. The real-life inspiration for the fictional Jurgis Rudkis in the *Jungle* may in fact have been Antanas Kaztauskis. At the very least, elements of the 1904 exposé in *Outlook* formed the premise of the landmark novel which tugged at the heartstrings of America. The passage of the Pure Food and Drug Act followed.

Lithuania was a province of Imperial Russia before World War I, a free nation in the 1920s and 1930s, and an incorporated state of the Soviet Union after 1940. It regained independence in 1991, but Soviet troops were not slated to leave the country until 1994. With 100,000 immigrants living in Chicago and its adjacent suburbs, the city became the center of Lithuanian culture in the U.S.

It has remained that way since the 1920s when the population topped the 100,000 mark. Most of the early arrivals came to Chicago around the time of the 1893 World's Fair. The immigrants were, by and large, born on farms in Lithuania, where livestock breeding and dairy farming were the dominant agricultural activities. They came to Chicago equipped with healthy, strong bodies, keen minds, and a will to work hard—ideal qualifications for employment in the Union Stock Yard and Transit Company. The Lithuanians poured into the neighborhoods south and west of the Union Stockyards in the 1890s, following succeeding waves of Irish, German, and Polish workers into the South Side. Packingtown was a vigorous, thriving community, seemingly created overnight. The stockyards opened on Christmas Day 1865, on what was once a parcel of swampland formerly owned by Mayor John Wentworth. Within a few short decades, Chicago became the center of the meatpacking industry in the U.S. But the honor was not without a price, because poverty, high crime, polluted air and vermin-infested streets characterized Back of the Yards.

Like other European ethnic groups, the Lithuanians did not settle in just one neighborhood. There were scattered pockets of settlement in Bridgeport and Brighton Park—an Irish-German enclave west of the Yards along 43rd and 47th Streets. In 1892 they built their first church in Chicago—St. George's on Lithuanica Street. This roadway, which cuts through the heart of old Bridgeport was named in honor of a monoplane. In 1933 two Chicago aviators of Lithuanian descent took off from New York City in a celebrated race across the ocean with Wiley Post. The two flyers, Stephen Darius and Stanley Girenas took off in the *Lithuanica* without benefit of a parachute or radio, bound for Kaunas, one of the principal cities of Lithuania. The only concession to safety these two aeronauts made was to install an ice indicator to the wing. The *Lithuanica* was purchased by subscription from the *Chicago Daily News*. The two flyers never completed their mission. They crashed in a forest deep in the heart of Germany on July 13, 1933. A monument honoring the pilots was erected in 1934 at California Avenue and Marquette Road. It was designed by French artist Raoul Josset.

The building boom witnessed in Brighton Park in the 1920s lured many of the Back-of-the-Yards Lithuanians into this solid, working class neighborhood. In 1906 work began on the Immaculate Conception Church at 44th and California. Ten years later a parochial school was opened. Describing the notable achievements of his people, Joseph Elias, President of the Lithuanian-American Chamber of Commerce, wrote in 1927:

> They began their careers here very humbly. Yet it was a relatively short time before they were recognized as a valuable part of Chicago's melting pot of varied racial groups. Today the Lithuanian people have their own churches and parochial schools, newspapers, societies, and clubs, all of which foster the spirit of American ideals.

By the 1920s there were more than 200 Lithuanian societies and clubs with an aggregate membership of between 2,500 and 2,800. The oldest and most successful choral and dramatic society in the city was the Birute. Founded in 1907 and headquartered at the Lithuanian Association at 31st and Halsted Streets, the Birute has sponsored a number of concerts and stage plays. Indeed, the world of music and art embraced a number of Lithuanians who gained considerable prominence. Joseph Bobrovich, the noted opera tenor, for example, was born in Lithuania, where he grew up as a peasant fisherman. Bobrovich went on to become a member of the Russian Imperial Opera. After the 1917 Revolution he escaped to America, where his resonant voice echoed through the concert halls of Chicago and other cities. A highlight of one of his many tours was his celebrated appearance with Chaliapin at the Chicago Civic Opera Company. The Lithuanians are great lovers of the opera. Since 1956 the Lithuanian Company at Maria High School, 6727 S. California, has produced lyric opera on a grand scale. Such rarities as Amilcare Ponchielli's *I Lituani* premiered in Chicago.

Through hard work and thrift came the realization of the American dream: home ownership. By being able to earn more than the bare essentials for food, clothing, and shelter, the thrifty Lithuanians were able to pool their savings and climb the socio-economic ladder. By the 1920s there sprang up two Lithuanian state banks with deposits of more than $5,000,000. Building and loan associations were organized in the neighborhoods—grassroots banking for the community. Through these institutions, the immigrants were able to purchase homes in the expanding "bungalow belt" of Marquette Park on the city's Southwest Side.

Bungalow construction—inexpensive but durable housing—reached its peak in Chicago during the boom years of 1926–27. Prospective buyers who had accumulated money during the war years and early 1920s took advantage of easy credit terms and the availability of land. Improvements in public transportation, especially the electrified trolleys linked together the once isolated townships on the far Northwest Side and Southwest Side to the Loop.

Much of the land that formed the nucleus of the Chicago Lawn Community (Marquette Park) was owned by a real estate millionaire, Hetty Green, who kept the area undeveloped and decidedly rural until 1911, when she finally disposed of the property. Then almost overnight, new subdivisions were carved out of abandoned cabbage patches. The Lithuanians who settled west of Western Avenue beginning in the mid-1920s typically paid $5,500 for the distinctive "Chicago school" contribution to the architectural landscape—the much maligned but durable bungalow. For it featured deep overhangs, an unfinished basement, dormer attics, central heating, and a tiny one-car garage in the back yard.

By 1930 the combined population of Marquette Park and the adjacent community of Gage Park stood at 78,997. The numbers started to decline in Gage Park during the 1930s, but Marquette showed continuous growth right up to 1960. By virtue of their numbers the Lithuanians became the dominant ethnic group in the community by 1927. That year the Nativity of the Blessed Virgin Mary Parish opened at 69th and Washtenaw. Today it is the largest Lithuanian parish outside Europe, with 2,500 families.

Marquette Park reflects the outward shift of Chicago's white ethnics from older industrial neighborhoods like the Back-of-the-Yards which underwent profound racial and demographic changes after World War I. Today the heart of Chicago's Lithuanian community is centered near Western Avenue and Marquette Road. Lithuanian Plaza Court, a small commercial strip between Washtenaw and Western avenues features many charming ethnic restaurants and stores. Every Summer the Homeowners Association of Marquette Park sponsors a folk fare along West 69th Street, featuring the work of native craftsmen and merchants displaying their wares.

The Lithuanian community is one of the better organized, most cohesive immigrant cultures in Chicago today. The past is kept alive at the Balzekas Museum of Lithuanian Culture at 6500 S. Pulaski

Road. Founded by Stanley Balzekas, owner of a car dealership on Archer Avenue, this is one of Chicago's lesser known but more interesting folk museums, highlighting the history, customs, artwork, handicrafts, and armaments of Lithuania. It is definitely worth a visit.

Today Lithuania is fighting for the right of self-determination. The tiny Baltic state has experienced only two decades of precious freedom. During World War I, the German army occupied the country. The Treaty of Versailles established Lithuania's independence. This was affirmed by a vote of the constituent assembly in August 1922, which passed into law a constitution that proclaimed the existence of the republic. The U.S.S.R. annexed Lithuania on July 14, 1940, through a pro-Soviet government that took power the previous October. The Germans occupied the country from 1941 until the Russians reclaimed the land three years later. Freedom of religion was effectively snuffed out by 1949, when the Communist regime closed most of the churches and deported the priests. A numbing, uneasy calm descended like a curtain over Lithuania until the tense days of 1989–1990 when *glasnost* opened a crack in the door.

In Chicago the worshipers at St. George's gathered to celebrate Mass and pray for a free Lithuania. Some wore native costumes, while others carried the yellow, green, and red flag of the homeland. At the back of Tolius Slutas's bookstore in Marquette Park, an impressive array of audio equipment stood primed to receive telefaxed messages from Vilnius. Since 1988 Slutas and his wife Helen have broadcast the Lithuanian-American Hour, a news and information service for the Southwest Side community. Tolius fled Lithuania as a boy during the Nazi terror. Since that time he has kept his dreams alive, as he communicates with the *Sajudis,* the underground movement that has championed independence. Freedom is an eternal vigil for these Lithuanians. A dissident writer summed it up best when he titled a recent essay: "On the road to independence it's raining."

Ethnic Museum

Balzekas Museum of Lithuanian Culture, *6500 S. Pulaski Avenue, Chicago, (312) 582-6500.* It's really three museums in one. Upstairs, across the hall from the 13th Ward Democratic Organization, the Lithuanian Folk Art Institute offers valuable instruction in weaving sashes and national costumes from the seven ethnographic regions of Lithuania. The Folk Art Institute was founded in 1980 as a not-for-profit educational and cultural organization whose main goal is to preserve,

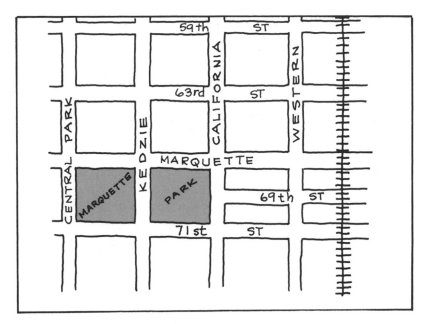

Chicago Lawn

research, and create Lithuanian folk art. Seventy to 100 members attend classes where they learn the skill of using the inkle loom under the direction of Vida Rimas and her artisans. For information about the lively decorative Lithuanian arts, call (312) 422-7147.

Downstairs, the main exhibit "Lithuania Through the Ages" transports the visitor through the history of the Baltic state, with special emphasis on folk costumes, amber jewelry (the stone is worn by Lithuanians for health), military items, Numismatics, and philately. The Balzekas Museum was formally opened on June 22, 1966, next to Stanley Balzekas's Chrysler showroom on Archer Avenue. The family moved into larger quarters at 6500 Pulaski in 1986. A Children's Museum of Immigrant History teaches school-age youngsters about the importance of their heritage through a tour of the Medieval World in the castle "Armory," and a journey back to the 19th century in the "Passport to Lithuania" exhibit. Children are permitted to dress up in authentic folk costumes and play the traditional musical instruments like the "kankles."

For serious researchers, the museum is the largest Lithuanian resource depository outside of Europe, housing 20,000 books, periodicals, monographs, and photo archives. The museum and gift shop are open daily, including weekends from 10 A.M. until 4 P.M. Free parking. Adults, $2.00, students and senior citizens, $2. Members free. Children under twelve, $1. *Recommended.*

═ Shopping and Touring Marquette Park ═

Marquette Park was the last of the pre-World War II neighborhoods to evolve out of the Union Stockyards, when the meat packing industry was still a vital concern to Chicago's economic well being. This Southwest Side community is home to 150,000 ethnic Lithuanians—more than any place outside Europe. Yet many of the younger generation have abandoned the "bungalow belt" for suburban Downers Grove, Clarendon Hills, and Lemont—where one can visit the Lithuanian World Center— which has been the nerve center for Lithuanian-Americans monitoring the political turmoil and fight for independence in the homeland.

The commercial district and unofficial center of Lithuanian culture in Chicago is 71st Street and Lithuanian Plaza Court (formerly 69th St.) between California (2600 West) and Western Avenue (2400 West). The small commercial/residential strip that comprises Lithuanian Plaza Court still features several ethnic-European restaurants and businesses, but increasingly these merchants are abandoning the neighborhood in light of a changing racial composition. The racial dynamics have adversely impacted the traditional Marquette Park Lithuanian Plaza Festival, which was held every summer until 1991, when it was postponed.

The little stores and the restaurants continue to serve the neighborhood people and Lithuanian visitors who return each day to sample the culture, irrespective of racial and ethnic differences that have cast Marquette and Gage Park into an unfavorable light over the last 25 years.

Lithuanian Youth Center (adjacent to the chapel of the Lithuanian Jesuit Fathers), *5620 S. Claremont Ave., Chicago (312) 778-7500.* The Youth Center serves Chicago's Lithuanian community as a cultural, educational, and social center, housing the Lithuanian World Archives, and the Ciurlionis Art Gallery (named for M.K. Ciurlionis, whose emblem of the Knight, Vytis, stands on the lawn outside the building.) Vytis is the Lithuanian national emblem. Special events, concerts, and dance troops scheduled periodically. Call for information.

Nativity of the Blessed Virgin Mary, *Lithuanian Plaza Court and Washtenaw Avenue, Chicago (312) 776-4600.* The late Mayor Richard J. Daley proclaimed 69th Street "Lithuanian Plaza Court" in 1966, to honor the ethnic Europeans who settled in this community. Many of them worshipped at Nativity B.V.M., founded in 1927. Begin your tour of the neighborhood here, and pay close attention to the colorful exterior mosaic murals, painted by Lithuanian artist Adomas Varnas. The modern church was dedicated in 1957, and designed by John Mulokas, who drew elements of the Baroque, Lithuanian folk themes, and Christian designs. Inside, the church maintains an impressive collection of artifacts and curios pertaining the Lithuanian history.

Parama Food and Liquors, *2534 Lithuanian Plaza Court, Chicago (312) 737-3332.* Fine imported chocolates are the specialty here, but this ethnic delicatessen and grocery also features fresh cut meats, a liquor section, imported foods, and foreign-language newspapers. Open Monday-Saturday 8 A.M. to 7 P.M., Sundays, 9 A.M. to 2 P.M.

Baltic Bakery, *2616 Lithuanian Plaza Court, and 4627 S. Hermitage Ave., Chicago (312) 737-6784 (on 69th St.) (312) 523-1510 (on Hermitage).* Nothing fancy about either store, but the Lithuanian and Polish residents of the South Side have patronized the Baltic Bakeries for years. A variety of fresh breads, imported cheeses, kolacky, stollen cakes, beer sausage, and a few German imports thrown in for good measure make this one of Chicago's best bakeries. Where else can you buy a freshly baked cheesecake for $2.00? Open Monday–Friday, 8:30 A.M.–6:00 P.M., Saturdays, till 6:00 P.M., and Sundays till 2:00 P.M.

71st Street,
══ Between California and Western ══

Two blocks south of Lithuanian Plaza Court, the 71st Street commercial district features a number of Lithuanian restaurants and cultural attractions. In some ways, Lithuanian Plaza Court has been eclipsed by the 71st Street merchants who have become recommitted to the neighborhood and continue to serve many of the Lithuanian senior citizens who refuse to abandon the neighborhood. According to Birute Jasaitis, Vice

President of the Lithuanian Community Organization in Chicago, few of these old-timers have ventured outside of the neighborhood even though they have raised their children to adulthood. Many of them can only speak a few words of broken English, but they count on the Lithuanian-American Community Organization to provide important social services, job referrals, and a conduit to the independence movement in Europe.

Lithuanian American Community and Human Services Council, *2715 W. 71st Street, Chicago (312) 476-2655.* Adjacent to the Seklycia Restaurant, the L.A.C. provides English language instruction to Lithuanian immigrants, a senior citizen aerobics class, medical lectures, and folk dancing for some of the 100,000 members who belong to this fraternal society dedicated to helping newly arrived immigrants to achieve self-determination. For the friends and relatives in need, the L.A.C. sends books and food supplies back to Lithuania. During the non-binding referendum conducted by Lithuanian voters over the question of separation with the Soviet Union (held over the weekend of Feb. 8–9, 1991) a telex number was set up to connect Chicagoans directly with the Parliament in Vilnius. Because all mail was routed through Moscow, local officials were concerned that printed telegrams would be confiscated by the officials.

Gifts International, *2501 W. 71st Street, Chicago (312) 471-1424. John Vaznelis, proprietor.* A neighborhood institution for 35 years, Gifts International specializes in Lithuanian books and publications, religious shrines, wood-marquetry plaques, greeting cards, and amber jewelry—the "Baltic Gold," cherished by Lithuanian-Americans for its clarity, beauty, and resonance. A bumper sticker for sale in the front of the store reads: "Lithuanians Aren't Coming— They're Here!" Open Monday–Saturday, 10 A.M.–5 P.M. Closed Sundays. *Recommended.*

Patria (Gift Shop), *2638 W. 71st Street, Chicago (312) 778-2100.* Store owner Fran Slutas discounts electronic appliances, sells religious statues, crystal, books, and Lithuanian recordings in addition to assisting community residents communicate with loved ones left behind in Lithuania, via her telex in the back of the store. Open Monday through Friday, 10:00 A.M.–5:15 P.M., Saturdays, to 4:30 P.M.

Sisters of St. Casimir Lithuanian Library, *2601 W. Marquette Road, Chicago (312) 776-1324.* Built in 1911, the Sisters of St. Casimir maintain a museum and archive of Lithuanian history that is open to the public by appointment only. The sisters also staff Holy Cross Hospital, opened at Lithuanian Plaza Court and Western Avenue in 1925.

Outside 71st St.

Lithuanian World Center, *511 E. 127th St., Lemont, Ill., 60439 (708) 257-6777.* Formerly St. Andreas Church. Lithuanian Mass is still conducted in this church and cultural center in south suburban Lemont, but in recent years it has served the dual purpose of museum and folk art institute. The basement houses a collection of folk art costumes, and works of art. Saturday school classes are conducted between nine and one for school children, and private parties are scheduled through the year.

St. George's Parish, *33rd St., and Lithuanica Ave., Bridgeport.* Here stands the mother church of Lithuanian immigration to the U.S., though the facility is closed now, and imperiled by the wrecker's ball. The handsome Gothic structure was built piecemeal between 1892 and 1908, or when money became available. The Rev. George Kolesinskas was appointed by Archbishop Patrick Feehan on Mar. 2, 1892, when it was determined by the Archdiocese that there were enough Lithuanians in Chicago to support their own parish. Nearly a hundred years later, the final Eucharist was celebrated by a handful of remaining parishioners. Irony of ironies: the archdiocese decided that there were no longer enough people in the community to keep the historic church open.

Restaurants

Tulpe, *2447 Lithuanian Plaza Court, Chicago (312) 925-1123.* Forget having a clandestine rendezvous here. The small, one room restaurant is not conducive for private conversation—especially during the lunch hour—but if Lithuanian food without the frill is your preference, it's definitely worth a look. The chalkboard over the counter lists the daily specials. Potatoes, in all shape and forms are staples of the Baltic diet. Kugelis is the timeless spud with meat tucked inside. The meat blintzes are wrapped in delicately cooked potato. Dumplings, pancakes, and smoked butt are other entrées.

Nida Delicatessen and Restaurant, *2617 71st St., Chicago (312) 476-7675.* The small restaurant is off the main bakery and deli, which sells bacon buns, kugilis, hazelnut cakes, Lithuanian "Andriulis" cheese, and some Polish delicacies. The restaurant, open from 10:00 A.M. to 5:30 P.M., Tuesday–Saturday seats only five to six people at a time. No credit cards accepted.

Neringa Restaurant, *2632 W. 71st St., Chicago (312) 476-9026.* Joseph and Janina Galica are your hosts, and if you want alcohol, they suggest you bring your own. No matter. The food and the soup—their specialty—are top drawer. The house specialties are kugilis, dumplings, and duck are highly recommended, in this, one of the largest Lithuanian cuisine restaurants in Chicago. Open 8 A.M. to 8 P.M., Monday–Sunday. Breakfast served 8–11:00 A.M. daily. No credit cards.

Daina, *2656 W. 71st St., Chicago (312) 434-9666.* Lithuanian and Polish food served by your hosts Elizabeth and Marion Czubiak. This family-owned eatery has been at this location since 1982. Banquet hall for any occasion (up to 140 people). Open Tuesday through Sunday, 8 A.M. to 8 P.M. Closed Monday. No credit cards accepted.

Seklycia Lithuanian Manor Inn, *2715 W. 71st St., Chicago (312) 476-1680, or 476-2655.* A favored gathering spot for Americans of Lithuanian descent—particularly for older people who have remained unassimilated into the community—the restaurant and its adjacent banquet hall have been serving the local residents for eight years as a dining establishment and meeting place. Specialties every day. No liquor served, or credit cards accepted. Open daily from 8 A.M. to 8 P.M.

Healthy Food, *3236 S. Halsted, Chicago (312) 326-2724.* Far removed from the Lithuanian community, but no less involved in the struggle to free the homeland from Soviet control, Healthy Food is located in Irish-Hispanic Bridgeport. The latest news of the community can be fbnd at the front counter in the form of handbills and notices. The standard Lithuanian dishes, Koldunai, Kugelis, and Blynai (pancakes with sour cream) are served with American entrées. Open seven days a week, 6:30 A.M. to 8:00 P.M.

Annual Events and Celebrations

Marquette Park Lithuanian Festival. The annual summer event until recently was held between Western Avenue and California on Lithuanian Plaza Court (69th Street) the last week of June. However, the 1990 event was suspended by the Homeowner's Association because of security problems. It was one of the largest and best organized summer festivals of its kind in the Midwest featuring crafts demonstrations, food booths, and folk dancing exhibitions by the renowned Lithuanian Folk Dance Group (7355 S. Whipple Street, Chicago (312) 496-4286), and merchandise exhibitors who sold amber jewelry in the streets. For further information about the festival, please call the Marquette Park Homeowner's Association at (312) 778-2233.

St. Casimir's Day *(Kaziuko Muge)*. In Lithuania, the coming of spring and the warm weather is marked by the annual St. Casimir celebration, honoring the memory of a canonized saint, born in 1458 in Krakow, Poland. St. Casimir was the grand prince of Lithuania, whose progressive social programs greatly benefited both Poles and Lithuanians. The annual event is something akin to the New Orleans Mardi Gras, according to Birute Jasaitis, community leader. The weekend festival is held the first weekend in March and is sponsored by a Lithuanian "scouting" movement similar, yet different from, the American Boy Scouts in that the members are in for life and are dedicated to the liberation of the eastern territories from Soviet control. Three floors of the Lithuania Youth Center at 5620 S. Claremont, Chicago, (312) 778-7500, are magically transformed into a market center from old Vilnius, featuring handicrafts, woodwork, decorated eggs, amber jewelry, and entertainment. The weekend celebration continues at the Balzekas Museum with a Sunday afternoon Lithuanian film festival, and a folk art show with depiction of key events from St. Casimir's life. *Recommended.*

Draugas **Community Festival,** *4545 W. 63rd Street, Chicago (312) 585-9500.* Run by the Marion Fathers, the *Draugas* Lithuanian-language newspaper is the only daily sheet to be published outside of Europe. The community fest is held the first Sunday in August at the Marion Fathers seminary at 63rd and Pulaski, and is a special fund-raising event to sustain the publishing venture. Food booths, book sale, raffle, and special exhibits.

Easter Brunch at the Balzekas Museum of Lithuanian Culture, *6500 S. Pulaski, Chicago (312) 582-6500.* Throughout the year, the Balzekas Museum sponsors many fine programs that promote Lithuanian culture. At Christmas time there are special workshops for designing and building candy houses. The Easter Brunch and egg decorating classes are community favorites. Call for details.

Brighton Park Lithuanian Homeowner's Festival, Mid-July, or the Friday and Saturday immediately following the Taste of Chicago Festival in Grant Park. A city-sponsored ethnic folk fair with a variety of musical styles to suit all tastes. Country, rock, Polish and Lithuanian folk music. In the past, the Brighton Park residents have brought in Lithuanian entertainers—eleven in 1991—to authenticate the real European flavor of this event. The Homeowner's Festival takes place on S. Western Boulevard between the 4300 and 4700 blocks. Call Bob Zebrauskas at (312) 778-5237 for information. Free admission.

Balzekas Museum Anniversary Dinner, *Amber Ballroom, 6500 S. Pulaski Road, Chicago (312) 582-6500.* Buffet dinner of Lithuanian cuisine. Dancing. Cash bar. Mid-June. Tickets are $25 per couple, or $15 per person.

Art Galleries

Gallery Astra, *308 W. Erie, Chicago (312) 664-6880.* Contemporary paintings, sculpture, ceramics, and tapestry from the Baltic regions of Latvia, Lithuania, and Estonia. Hours: Tuesday–Saturday, 10:00 A.M.–5 P.M. Credit cards accepted.

Lithuanian Language Radio Programming

"Rytmecid Ekspresas," with R. Zdanaviciute. Aired on WPNA-1490 AM, Monday through Friday, 11 to 11:30 A.M.

"Voice of Lithuania," hosted by Balys Brazdzionis. Aired on WCEV-1450 AM, Monday through Friday, 8:30 to 9:00 P.M.

"Margutis," hosted by Petra Petrutis. Aired on WCEV-1450 AM, Monday through Friday, 9:05 to 10:00 P.M. Long running program, first heard in the Chicago area in 1966.

"Lithuanian American Radio," Host: Anatolijus Slutas. Aired on WCEV-1450 AM, 7 to 8 A.M. on Sundays.

"Zeme L," hosted by Raimundas Lapas. Aired on OPNA-1490 AM, 8:30 to 10 P.M., Saturdays. Lapas receives his news directly from Radio Vilnius and the Lithuanian nationalist movement's newspaper *Atigiminas*.

An Immigrant's Odyssey

Stanley Balzekas, Jr., a dynamic leader of Chicago's Lithuanian community served as a director of the Chicago Public Library for twelve years, in addition to serving as president of the Ethnic Cultural Preservation Council. Balzekas is a first generation Lithuanian-American who is president of the Motor Sales agency bearing his name and of the Archer Advertising Agency. The following interview was originally printed in *Genealogija,* the newsletter of the Lithuanian-American Genealogical Society, in its spring, 1990, edition. In it Balzekas recounts the circumstances of his father's arrival in the U.S. His experiences are fairly typical of the hardships the Ellis Island generation encountered in the new land.

Q. Your father, Stanley Balzekas, Sr., is one of our most outstanding Lithuanian pioneers. Please tell us the story of how he came to the U.S.

A. He was a very unusual individual in the fact that in the little village of Ukmergé, where his family lived, he was the only one who could read and write. He used to answer all the letters for the people of Ukmergé. His father had died when he was a young boy, and when he got older, his sister gave him the choice of apprenticing as a tailor or a blacksmith. Since he was mechanically inclined, he decided to go into the blacksmithing business. He was a blacksmith for a number of years on one of the estates of the Lithuanian-Polish nobility. When he had an opportunity to go to the U.S. in 1912, he left Lithuania. He came here to make some money and learn more technology in order to open up a machine shop. When he was working in Lithuania, he was the one who put together the reapers and all the harvesting machinery because he was the only who could read the manuals and understand how these machines worked. He first got a job in New York City. He lived in Hackensack and he used to walk to work every day, five miles each way, to "save a nickel," as they would say. He was a concrete mixer for a company where everyone was Italian, and when they found out he was Lithuanian they fired him. He then came to Chicago to join his brother. This was 1913, maybe 1914. He worked as a blacksmith in a German place and of course when they found out he wasn't German, they let him go. Then he went to a Swedish blacksmith shop, and it was the same thing all over again. The reason I bring this up is because we forget how segregated everything was years ago by religion and ethnic origin, and how hard it was for a lot of the early immigrants to get established. From that point on he was a butcher. When the war started in 1914, he was working in three butcher shops and selling groceries as well. He soon realized that if he wanted to get ahead, he needed an education. So, he went to Valparaiso University in Indiana, which in those days was the "poor man's university." To support himself while he was in school, he sold automobiles, ran four movie theaters, and taught other Lithuanians to speak English. When he finished university, he returned to Chicago and made automobile batteries from wrecked cars—which in those days was a big business. This would have been around 1923 or '24. Between wrecking cars and selling cars, he soon was selling cars more. In 1926 he started ihs own automobile sales business on Archer Avenue, where we still are. His heart was still very much with Lithuania, although he was now completely Americanized. Throughout his life he helped many Lithuanian people and Lithuanian organizations. He was very involved in many business and civic associations beyond the Lithuanian community as well.

The Latvian Folk Art Museum

Chicago's Latvian population numbers less than 8,000, but this small but determined immigrant group shares common cause with the Lithuanians in liberating the Baltic states from Soviet rule. On August 5, 1940, the Soviet Union annexed the Latvian territories, effectively ending the republic's brief encounter with democracy. Thousands of Latvian citizens became refugees. Many of them settled on Chicago's Northwest Side between 1945 and 1950.

Today their needs are served by the Latvian Community Center, located at 4146 Elston Ave., near Hamlin St. The meeting hall is upstairs from the Latvian Folk Art Museum (see entry below), and it is where members of the Latvian Welfare Association, their senior citizen's group, and various community organizations meet in a congenial atmosphere. At various times during the year, the center sponsors concerts, art shows, and plays that are produced locally, and performed by visiting troops from Canada, Chicago and the Midwest.

Latvian Folk Art Museum, *4146 N. Elston Ave., Chicago (312) 588-2085.* The museum as it is constituted today is the outgrowth of an earlier effort by the Chicago Latvian Association and several artisan groups in Illinois and Wisconsin to establish a permanent home for a collection of archival artifacts *(Senmantu Kratuve).* Beginning in the mid-1960s, and continuing for the next decade, Osvalds Grins and his daughter Astra Revelins scoured the country in search of historic items brought back from Latvia. Osvalds Grins painstakingly assembled an impressive collection of folk art from all over the U.S., which made its way into the permanent exhibit, established at this location in 1978. As the years passed, Chicagoans of Latvian descent donated family heirlooms and artifacts. Today the museum features a collection that is particularly rich in textiles, but not to be overlooked are the less familiar items, such as the musical instruments: *kokle* (a string piece) and the *giga* (a monochord). An unusual collection of Latvian folk music, preserved through the decades on audio tapes, is available for the listening pleasure of museum visitors.

Admission is free, but donations are accepted with gratitude. Hours: Monday through Friday, 9:30 A.M. to 2 P.M. Other hours by appointment. Supported in part by the Illinois Arts Council.

Latvian Radio Programming

"Latvian Music," broadcast on WNIB-FM (97.1 on the dial) and WNIZ-FM (96.9, aired in Zion, Ill.) every Sunday evening at 10:00 P.M. Since 1985 the Folk Art Museum has produced this program.

Ukrainian Chicago

History and Settlement

Ukraine, a republic of the Commonwealth of Independent States, has ethnic traditions and a culture that dates back to the ninth century, when the lands southwest of Russia proper were known as the Kievan-Rus. The name Rus came to signify the lands around Kiev, an important trade center in Eastern Europe. Various other states existed in the region, and it wasn't until the late nineteenth century that the inhabitants began to think of themselves as a Ukrainian people with a similar culture and shared values. Those who lived under Austrian rule in Galicia fostered the nationalist movement—one that began as a literary revival and ended in a great awakening in 1917. The Russian Ukrainians established an independent republic in the aftermath of the Bolshevik Revolution. On November 1, 1918, Austrian Ukrainia proclaimed itself a republic and was federated into the U.S.S.R., as the ZUNR. In January 1919 warfare erupted in the Russian Ukrainian Republic. Under the leadership of Symon Petlyura, ZUNR was united with the Ukrainian National Republic. Between 1917 and 1921, several governments struggled for control of the Ukraine. The situation remained chaotic until 1924 when the Ukrainian Soviet Socialist Republic became one of the constituent republics of the Soviet Union.

There was widespread famine in the 1930s, which the Ukrainians blamed on Josef Stalin and his collectivization of agriculture. Some

5,000,000 persons perished. Many of them were victims of Stalin's dreaded secret police, which enforced a policy of "Russification"—the suppression of non-Marxist cultural and scholarly activities. The common thread of ethno-Ukrainian history through World War II was the growing awareness among these people that there was more to preserve than just a religious tradition being threatened by Bolshevism. The immigrants who escaped the Stalinist terror—and who have found a better life in America—continued the struggle to win freedom for their families back home. As they will tell you, the former Soviet Union was not Russia (though essentially dominated by Russians), nor are Ukrainians Russians.

The immigration to these shores began in the early 1870s with the arrival of the sub-Carpathian Rus (or Rusins—the ancient name of the Ukraine). Many of them were fleeing from the horrors of the Czarist regime; others were in search of a fortune in the mythical cities of gold. The political exiles settled in the cities for the most part. The others, who were seeking work in the industrial sector founded colonies in the iron manufacturing regions of Pennsylvania. In 1884 they organized the first Ukrainian church in the U.S.—St. Michael the Archangel in Shenandoah, Pennsylvania.

The first large settlement of Ukrainians arrived in Chicago around 1873. Dr. Volodymer Simenovych, a law student in his native land, was the Ukraine's foremost poet and a scholar in his own right. After emigrating to the U.S. in 1887, Simenovych edited *Ameryka,* one of the first Ukrainian newspapers to be published in this country. In Shenandoah, the early cultural center for these people, he organized a Ukrainian cooperative store, a children's theatre troop, and a reading circle. He left his mark on the community before moving on to Chicago where he was a vibrant force in ethnic-Ukrainian life until his death in 1932.

A small pocket of immigrants colonized Packingtown on the South Side. They erected a church that stood in the shadows of the large slaughterhouses in 1903. The First Greek Catholic Church of St. Mary's of Chicago featured a three-barred cross in the steeple. Beneath the cross was a crescent, symbolic of the "victory" of Christianity over Islam. St. Mary's soon became an integral part of Rusin-Ruthenian culture; predominant in Chicago's Ukrainian community. An important part of the service in those days was the plain chant of the congregation. No instrumental music was permitted. The Ukrainian church followed the forms of the Catholic Church of the Greek Rite.

By the 1930s there were five Ukrainian parishes dotting Chicago's neighborhoods, including the lovely Byzantine-Slavonic style of St. Nicholas's Roman Catholic Cathedral at Rice and Oakley streets on the Northwest Side. The Cathedral of St. Nicholas stood in the heart of an

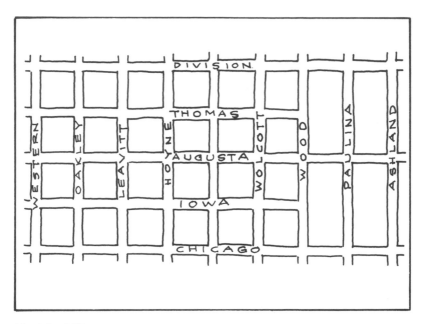

Ukrainian Village

emerging Ukrainian neighborhood south of Wicker Park and along Chicago Avenue. Built between November 1913 and January 1915, this fine old church emulated the style of the Basilica of St. Sophia in Kiev.

St. Nick's anchors Chicago's famous "Ukrainian Village," whose boundaries extend from Chicago Avenue to Division and from Damen to Western. This neighborhood north and west of the Loop was first settled by Polish and Slovak immigrants, but with the rise of Ukrainian nationalism, and the influx of political refugees during World War I, it assumed a Ukrainian cultural identity which lingers to this day. Among the folk traditions imported into the U.S. by the Ukrainian immigrants were the melodic native songs that date back to prehistoric pagan times. There are the *koliadky* (Christmas songs), mid-summer night songs *(kupalo)* and the harvest songs, most notably the *Kolo-miika,* which is accompanied by native dancing. The Kolo-miika portrays the sound of the waving wheat fields so familiar to the immigrant farmers. The dance steps of the Kolo-miika are intended to create a visual image of crossing swamp lands or stretches of arid deserts. In some of the more thrilling moments of the dance, the movements portray the life of the Tartar as he was chased through the woods by wolves and bears. It is said that when five or more

Ukrainians get together it is inevitable they should form a choral or dance group. The famous Ukrainian National Chorus under the direction of Alexander Koshetz introduced the translated version of the classic "Carol of the Bells," a Christmas melody.

No less important to Ukrainians is the plight of their countrymen, who have suffered under the yoke of oppression since the time of the czars. On Jan. 4, 1917, Dr. Simenovych led a delegation to the White House, where he prevailed upon President Woodrow Wilson to proclaim a national Ukrainian Day. Wilson, who was supported by both branches of the Congress, designated April 21, 1917 as Ukrainian Relief Day. A month later, on May 19, 1917, Simenovych and his colleague Dr. Stephen Hrynevetsky founded the first Ukrainian newspaper in Chicago— *Ukrayina*—which attempted to unify the various ethnic coalitions that were often at odds over religious and social matters into a common cause. Indeed, Dr. Simenovych was a driving force in Ukrainian Village during the early years. On May 30, 1918 he sponsored a massive rally at Pulaski Park (Noble and Blackhawk streets) that drew a crowd of 10,000 supporters of the democratic movement. At the time there were fewer than 40,000 Ukrainians residing in the city.

The Ukrainians settled in Chicago in three successive waves, the first occurring prior to World War I, the second in the 1920s, and the third between 1945 and 1950, when thousands of political refugees from war-torn Eastern Europe found their way to America. Included in this group were many people from the professional classes—physicians, lawyers, writers, and intellectuals who stood in opposition to the Stalinist regime. The population surge energized Ukrainian Village and spurred construction of new church parishes.

The new arrivals were a thrifty, self-reliant people who disdained the public dole in order to create a new life for their children in the U.S., while at the same time retaining much of their European heritage. The story of the First Security Federal Savings and Loan Association is a living reminder of Chicago's "I Will" spirit, and the faith of the Ukrainian immigrants in their public institutions. During the 1950s and early 1960s, the Savings and Loan pumped millions of dollars back into the Ukrainian Village, providing mortgages on easy terms to immigrants who otherwise had no chance of establishing credit in their new homeland. But in 1964 state regulators informed First Security that they were nearly insolvent when $360,000 in assets were reported missing. Julian Kulas, the embattled president of First Security appealed to the community for help. The residents answered the appeal. Borrowing a page from Jimmy Stewart's *It's a Wonderful Life,* they streamed into his office with cash gifts, some as high as $1,000. Kulas recalled that he had to "physically restrain" some of them so that he could write out receipts. Flushed with $300,000 in new investments, the Savings and Loan reopened its doors days later. In 1966 board members and depositors granted First Security three-year interest-free loans totalling $70,000 to replace the decrepit frame building which had served as office headquarters for years. First Security became a bank in 1985, and today controls assets of $136 million. On the occasion of the firm's twenty-fifth anniversary in March, 1989, board members conducted their meeting entirely in Ukrainian at a neighborhood youth hall.

The resurrection of First Security stabilized the Ukrainian Village at a time when many second- and third-generation residents were moving out to the suburbs. The neighborhood was "red-lined" by realtors. The Chicago business community was refusing to invest much needed dollars into the community, and many old-timers—the bedrock of the village—began to wonder whether the time had come to move their cherished cultural institutions.

In 1969 St. Nick's switched from the traditional Julian calendar to the Gregorian, which sparked an angry outcry of protest among the traditionalists in the congregation. A dissenting group of parishioners broke away and started their own church—Saints Volodymyr and Olha at Oakley and Superior streets. The church was dedicated in 1974 by the head of the Ukrainian Catholic Church—Patriarch Joseph Slidyi. The parishioners take credit for the resurgence of Ukrainian Village. With urban gentrification, many of the suburban Ukrainians began to return to the old neighborhood in the late 1970s to purchase homes and raise their children.

Ethnic pride is reflected in the various Ukrainian cultural centers that have opened in recent years. The Ukrainian Museum of Modern Art at 2453 W. Chicago celebrates the work of the Ukraine's contemporary artists. Many of these creative geniuses were outlawed by the Soviet government. In 1988, after nearly ten years of hot debate with some of the other European groups that permeate the Northwest Side community west of the Kennedy Expressway, the $2.5 million Ukrainian Culture Center opened at Chicago and Oakley.

Each year on January 22, Ukrainian Independence Day is celebrated in Chicago. It is a symbolic event that commemorates that all too brief period following the Bolshevik Revolution, when the republic was established.

The Ukrainians take pride in their Americanism. At the same time they were mindful of the diminution of their national identity under the Soviets. In the 1930s, a Ukrainian writer who was asked to prepare a brief history of his people for the Works Project Administration (WPA) summed up the hopes and dreams of ihs people by saying: "This new generation, with its modernistic tendencies for progress, will no doubt in time be the making of Ukrainia as one of the world nations." That goal began to be realized in 1991 as the Ukraine decided to declare its independence from the Soviet Union.

Getting There: By car or taxi from the Loop, drive north on Michigan Avenue to Chicago Avenue, where you make a left turn. Continue west to Ashland or Damen, which places you in the middle of Ukrainian Village. The CTA elevated line stops at Chicago and Division where you can transfer to the #66 bus. By bus: From Michigan Avenue, take the Chicago Avenue bus (#66, which originates on Fairbanks) to either Damen or Ashland. Connecting buses run on Milwaukee Avenue (#56 beginning at Michigan and Madison), Damen (#50 begins on the West Side at 18th Street) or Division Street (#50, starting on State Street).

Ethnic Museum

Ukrainian National Museum, *2453 W. Chicago Avenue (312) 276-6565.* Housed in a modest, three story townhouse constructed in the late 19th century, the museum is located in the heart of the Ukrainian settlement between Western and Hoyne. Olha Kalymom (who will remind you that O*l*ha is Ukrainian, Olga is Russian) is your host and guide during the half-hour long tour into the customs, history, and folk art of the Ukraine. Olha will show you a wonderful collection of wood carvings, costume dolls, sculptures, and bas-reliefs of modern Ukrainian artists. Pay particular attention to the intricate and highly detailed Easter eggs *(pysanky)*—a staple of Ukrainian folk art. The oldest designs are called ideograms, but the painted eggs share a common theme; the sun represented by a tripod, a rose, and stars in various patterns. Ukrainian embroidery, a highly developed folk art, is included in this collection. Many of the articles were made by village women to satisfy their innate sense of decorative beauty. The art can be found in such common household items as tablecloths, scarves, and smocks. Upstairs in one of the back rooms can be found 17,000 Ukrainian language books received in donation from immigrants and visitors coming from Europe. A military room and a room dealing with the history of Chicago's Ukrainian community are included. Plans are afoot to relocate to larger headquarters, but so far the budget has not supported such a move. Therefore, donations are requested. Hours: Tuesday—Saturday, 11 A.M. to 4 P.M. Sunday, 11 A.M. to 4 P.M. Closed Mondays. *Recommended.*

Ukrainian Institute of Modern Art, *2320 W. Chicago Avenue (312) 227-5522.* UIMA, as it is called, was opened in 1971 in a rehabbed storefront. Since that time, the museum has presented an average of five major art exhibitions each year, and has featured the work of independent artists whose avant-garde style has come to the attention of the Arts Committee, which consists of a curator and a panel of professional artists. UIMA is the only Chicago art museum located outside of the downtown business district. Hours: Tuesday through Sunday, 12 A.M. to 4 P.M. Donations accepted. Annual memberships available for $10 and up.

Annual Events and Celebrations

Ukrainian Heritage Festival, *Smith Park, 2526 W. Grand Avenue, Chicago.* Food booths, dance troops outfitted in colorful Ukrainian costumes (the women all wear knee-high boots), folk art, wood carvings, and *pysanka* eggs are featured in this celebration held the second weekend of September at Smith Park in Ukrainian Village. Sponsored by the Ukrainian Congress of Chicago, the highlight of the festival is the main stage event held on Saturday night, where a variety of performers ranging from traditional to popular entertain. The Ukrainian Festival has been profiled in *National Geographic,* and is the centerpiece of the calendar year in the village. For additional information and a listing of times and scheduled events, please call the Ukrainian Congress at (312) 252-1228, or stop by their office at 742 Oakley Avenue, Chicago. Or call the Chicago Park District (Smith Park) at (312) 227-0020.

Acres of Fun Festival *at St. Joseph's Ukrainian Catholic Church , 5000 N. Cumberland, Chicago (312) 625-4805.* Six days of entertainment featuring country and western bands and 1950s rock revivalists is capped off by a special presentation of the St. Joseph's Ukrainian dance troop on Sunday. The festival takes place at this far Northwest Side parish for six days in mid-August. The Sunday festivities mark Ukrainian Day and the anniversary of the parish. St. Joseph's was founded in 1956. Admission and parking are free. Plenty of food booths, games and rides for the kids.

Ukrainian Independence Day Celebration, *the Ukrainian Cultural Center, 2247 Chicago Avenue.* On January 22, the Ukrainian community celebrates its independence. A banquet is held each year at the Cultural Center in conjunction with other ethnic groups. A short-lived independence was achieved on Jan. 22, 1918, and to mark this day, the Chicago Ukrainians participate in a symbolic flag-raising ceremony at St. Volodymyr and Olha Ukrainian Church at Oakley and Superior streets. The dinner and ceremony are sponsored by the Ukrainian Congress. Call (312) 252-1228 for details.

Taras Shevchenko Festival, *various locations in March, including the Ukrainian National Museum, the American-Ukrainian Youth Association, Inc., 2455–59 W. Chicago Avenue, (312) 486-4204; St. Andrew's Church, 22 W. 349 Army Trail Road, Bloomingdale, (708) 980-5769; and St. Joseph's, 500 N. Cumberland Ave., Chicago, (312) 625-4805.* Taras Shevchenko was the Ukraine's greatest poet, who championed the independence movement at the expense of his own personal freedom. Shevchenko was exiled to Siberia for his beliefs, but his memory is preserved in the Ukrainian schools across the U.S. Shevchenko was born on March 9, 1814, and died on March 10, 1861. The museum features month-long exhibitions of Shevchenko's art work, his writings, and depictions of his life. The churches feature tributes during March. Please call for details.

Christmas celebration, January. The 20-member children's choir from St. Nicholas Ukrainian Cathedral School, dressed in traditional costumes, sing Christmas Carols in English and Ukrainian on the Christmas Holiday, which falls on the first week of January. The choir performs at local business establishments on Chicago Avenue, including the National Security Bank at 1030 W. Chicago Avenue. Call St. Nicholas School at (312) 276-4537.

East European Arts and Crafts Exposition, *mid-December at the Ukrainian Village Cultural Center, 247 W. Chicago Avenue.* Icons, paintings, hand-carved wooden boxes, ceramics, glass, and some great foods are offered for sale. Admission prices vary with the hours of operation. Weekend: $15 per person, weekday, $4. Call (312) 276-3990.

Interesting Places to Visit in the Village

Ukrainian American Publishing Co., *2315 W. Chicago Avenue, (312) 276-6373.* What began as a printing house disseminating newspapers and political pamphlets to newly arrived Ukrainian immigrants is now a gift shop, selling Easter Egg coloring kits, greeting cards, embroidery, and school books for children attending St. Nicholas. The spirit of those former times is not lost, however, because the store also sells copies of the *Independent Ukraine*, a political journal published quarterly out of Toronto, Canada, where there is a sizable Ukrainian population. The U.A.P. has been at this location for 30 years, and is open Monday through Friday from 9:30 to 5:30 P.M., Saturday, 9 A.M. to 5 P.M., and Sunday, 10 A.M. to 2 P.M.

Stauropegion Bookstore, *2226 W. Chicago Avenue, (312) 276-0774.*   Icons are used in the Divine Liturgy of the Eastern Christian Church, presented to children at baptism, to couples when they exchange wedding vows, to soldiers about to engage in mortal combat, and to the individual who seeks communion with those beings depicted in the image. The Stauropegion Bookstore sells these beautiful handcrafted images to its customers and the parishioners of St. Nicholas and St. Volodymyr. This is a bookstore, to be sure, but in some ways also a museum, cared for by Irene Gajecky, who explains the significance of the icons, many of which are sent to the Ukraine directly from Chicago. The Soviets denied many Ukrainians the right to worship as they please. Irene understands the community history, and is saddened by the religious divisions that still exist among the Ukrainians. The store itself was once a printing company, until it was converted to a retail emporium in 1987. Until 1987, Stauropegion's distributed parish literature and invitations for St. Nicholas. Hours: Monday, 10 A.M. to 2 P.M.; Tuesday through Friday, 10 A.M. to 6 P.M.; Saturdays, 9 A.M. to 4 P.M. *Recommended.*

Delta Import Company, *2242 W. Chicago Avenue, (312) 235-7788.*   Since 1963, the Delta Importing Company has sold folk jewelry, figurines, fabrics, crystal, greeting cards, decorative eggs, and sundry other items from the Ukraine. The trident is the national symbol of the Ukraine, and the nautical image abounds at Deltas, in rings, posters, T-shirts, and pennants. Irene Bodnar, the third of three owners, will ship parcels to the old country. Hours: Tuesday–Friday, 10 A.M. to 6 P.M.; Saturday, 9 A.M. to 5:00 P.M.; Sunday, 10:00 A.M. to 1:30 P.M. *Recommended.*

American Ukrainian Youth Association, Inc., *2455–59 W. Chicago Avenue, (312) 486-4204.*   Busloads of school age children attend Ukrainian language classes here every week and practice their folk dancing—the Hutzuk and Hopak are the traditional steps. The building is home to the famed dance ensemble "Ukrainia," which has performed at Epcot in Orlando, Florida, the Trump Castle, and Las Vegas. The

45-member troop performs in July. For times and dates, call the UAYA. Hours: 2 to 4 P.M. weekdays, 6 to 9 P.M., evenings. Yearly enrollment for children and adults is $12.

St. Nicholas Ukrainian Catholic Cathedral, *Oakley Boulevard and Rice Street, (312) 276-4537.*   This beautiful Byzantine-style cathedral was modeled after the Basilica of St. Sophia in Kiev, but only thirteen of the original 32 copper-clad domes were built into the Chicago version. When a serious rift over the proposed adaptation of the Gregorian calendar split the followers of the Eastern Rite (called Uniate Catholics) from the immigrants of the Western Ukraine, the decision was made to construct a second parish. Those who observe the Gregorian calendar chose to remain at St. Nicholas, when the decision was made in 1968.

SS. Volodymyr and Olha Church and Cultural Center, *Superior Street and Oakley Boulevard, (312) 276-3990.*   Built between 1973 and 1975, St. Volodymyr features gilded Byzantine domes set off by a two-story high mural on the façade. The mosaic commemorates the conversion to Christianity in 988 A.D. by St. Volodymyr. The saints of the church were painted on a lovely mural in back of the nave by an 82-year-old neighborhood resident named Dickey. Church and community planners envisioned a time when the Ukrainian community could take advantage of the spacious Cultural Center and auditorium constructed adjacent to the church on Chicago Avenue. But according to several of the St. Nicholas parishioners, this is more illusion than reality. Theological differences still stand in the way of reconciliation.

Restaurants

Sak's Ukrainian Village Restaurant, *2301 W. Chicago Avenue, (312) 278-4445.*   Nothing fancy, no pretension, just lots of good food. Sak's is for people on a budget, or, as one person told me, where the real Ukrainians eat. Try the borsch soup and the holubtsy (cabbage rolls). You won't leave hungry. Hours: Tuesday through Sunday, 11:30 A.M. to 7:30 P.M. Closed Mondays.

Galan's Restaurant and Lounge, *2212 W. Chicago Avenue, (312) 292-1000.*   For a slightly more upscale atmosphere, try Galan's, and be sure to order the Kozak Feast, which is a random sampling of borsch, holubtsi, varenyky (filled dough dumplings), kovbassa and kapustka (Ukrainian sausage and mild sauerkraut), kozak spys (tenderloin of beef and pork on a skewer), and kartpolyanyk (potato pancakes). In the "Land of the Trident," Galan's lovingly adheres to the old world customs and features Ukrainian music on Fridays and Saturdays from 7:30 P.M. until 10:30. Cool jazz is featured afterward. *Recommended.*

(A popular anecdote tells of a Zaporozhian Cossack who died several centuries ago and found himself in hell. Though not perturbed by his new surroundings, he considered his plight a sorry one only because there was no borsch in hell!)

Bakery and Grocery

Ann's Bakery, *2158 Chicago Avenue, (312) 384-5562. Second location at 2923 Milwaukee Avenue, (312) 489-6562.* A neighborhood institution specializing in wedding cakes, fine pastries and Ukrainian twist bread. Monday through Friday 6 A.M. to 10 P.M., Saturday, 6 A.M. to 9 P.M., Sunday, 7 A.M. to 9 P.M.

Self Reliance Co-op Grocers, *2204 Chicago Avenue, (312) 252-9092.* The co-op is a European concept that is practiced here in Ukrainian Village. This independent grocer offers a wide array of items from beets to borsch, dried mushrooms from Yugoslavia, kutiya for the Christmas celebration, Ukrainian-language publications, and the usual staples of American food. Monday through Friday, 9 A.M. to 7 P.M., and Saturday from 8 A.M. to 6 P.M.

Ukrainian Language Radio Programming

"Ukrainian Variety Hour," hosted by Maria Chychula. Aired on WCEV-1450 AM, Mondays, Wednesdays, and Thursdays, 7:05 to 8:00 P.M.

"Voice of Hope," religious programming. Aired on WCEV-1450 AM, Mondays, 8:00–8:30 P.M.

Religious programming from St. Volodymyr and Olha Ukrainian parish. Aired on WPNA-1490 AM, Tuesdays, 8:00–9:00 P.M.

Ukrainian Evening Tribune. Aired on WPNA-1490 AM, Fridays, 8:00–9:00 P.M.

Religious programming from St. Nicholas and St. Volodymyr. Aired on WPNA-1490 AM, 3:00–5:00 P.M., Saturdays.

"Ukrainian Voice of the Gospel," religious programming. Aired on WSBC, 1240 AM, Tuesday evenings at 9:00 P.M.

Ukrainian Easter Egg Design Symbols

Each section of Ukraine has its own basic Pysanka designs, although the symbols and their meanings often vary from one village to the next. In the Carpathian Mountains the Hutsuls have patterns that are intricately geometric, while across the great steppes, in Eastern Ukraine, design patterns are more baroque, with floral designs predominating.

No two Pysanky are identical. Although the same symbols are repeated, each Pysanka is different in its pattern arrangement and color. The symbols most often used include:

 Triangle *(trikutnik)*: any trio; air, fire, and water

 8-pointed star *(zvizda)*: star, ancient sun god

Sun *(sontse)*: good fortune

Rooster *(piven)*:⟩ fruition (of egg) denotes fulfillment of wishes
Chicken *(kurka)*:

 Deer *(olen)*: wealth, prosperity

Fir tree *(sosna)*: eternal youth

Flower *(tsvitka)*: love, charity

 Endless line *(bezkonetchnik)*: eternity

Checkerboard:⟩ used to fill in border designs

Dots, sieve:

Polish Chicago

═══════ History and Settlement ═══════

If Chicago was once the center of Irish-Gaelic culture in the Midwest, it is today the most important port of entry for thousands of Polish immigrants who share the same hopes and aspirations as the earlier arrivals from the English-speaking lands. Indeed, more than one million Poles and the descendants of the people of Polish heritage call Chicago home. They are the largest of the non-Hispanic white ethnic groups, followed by the Irish and Germans. They come from all backgrounds and socio-economic classes. A cousin of Lech Walesa—the Democratic conscience of Eastern Europe during the days of political and economic discord following the declaration of martial law in December 1981—lives in suburban Park Ridge, just across the city boundary line.

Since 1980, the year that Walesa and his band of patriots launched the Solidarity Movement, courageous Poles possessing the wherewithall to buck the system have come to Chicago to live under less-than-ideal circumstances, if only to breathe the fresh air of freedom for the first time. Back home, many of these immigrants were pillars of the local community—lawyers, teachers, and skilled craftspeople. But they suffered under a stagnant economy and high unemployment. During the height of the Solidarity crackdowns in 1982–1983, thousands of Poles arrived at O'Hare Airport as political refugees. Members of the professional classes, including lawyers and accountants, were forced to accept menial employment, cleaning other people's houses or scrubbing the floors of towering Loop office buildings. They do it happily—for now. Freedom and economic opportunity exact a heavy price, but one that must be paid, even at the risk of deportation. Between 50,000 and 100,000 Poles are thought to be living in the Chicago area illegally. Most arrive in the U.S. as tourists, but they actually come here to work, and when their visas expire, it is not reported to the immigration authorities. Others sometimes enter into a marriage with a U.S. citizen, which permits them to remain in the country legally.

The crossroads of Chicago's "old Polonia" was once located at Milwaukee and Division streets, directly northwest of the Loop. Today Milwaukee Avenue is still very much the "Polish Main Street," but the new arrivals now settle farther north in Avondale, or "Jackowo," (which borrows its name from St. Hyacinth's Roman Catholic Church at 3636 W. Wolfram Street) stretching from Central Park to Pulaski. The Milwaukee Avenue corridor is a rich tapestry of sights and sounds that meanders through some of Chicago's most colorful, ethnically diverse neighborhoods—from West Town at the foot of the Loop, up through Wicker Park, Logan Square, Avondale, Portage Park, and Jefferson Park—where many second- and third-generation Poles live—all the way to the Illinois-Wisconsin state lines.

The residents of Jackowo speak Polish and attend St. Hyacinth's. The average weekly attendance at mass numbers 8,000—which is double the turnout at any other parish in the Chicago Archdiocese. These immigrant Poles have little in common with their American-born countrymen whose parents arrived before World War II. But they are united in thought and spirit, as they funnel roughly $1 billion in cash and material goods back to Poland. Very often these private "foreign aid" packages sent through the U.S. postal system make up the only hedge against starvation in a land that too often has known only deprivation and want.

Chicago's Polonia—the name is derived from an ancient Slavic tribe known as the "Polanie" (field or plain we live in)—first took shape in 1851, when Anton Smarzewski escaped the Prussion regime that had enslaved his homeland. He became the first settler from that region to establish residence in Chicago. A carpenter by trade, Smarzewski decided to add the German-sounding "Schermann" to his last name. He opened up a small grocery store near Division and Noble streets. Thus, the first Polish colony was born on the near Northwest Side.

In 1864, Peter Kiolbassa, a Pole from Texas who fought in the Civil War, came to Chicago where he hoped to make his mark in public life. He was to become one of the notable men of the Midwest, whose personal integrity and charisma are well known.

When "Honest Pete" was elected city treasurer in 1891, he established the precedent that was later incorporated into law, making it obligatory for state, county, and city officials to pay into the public treasury all interest on public money. Kiolbassa believed in his heart that he was ethically bound to teach the lessons of citizenship not only in word, but in deed. His political advisors reminded him that he was not legally required to do so, but Kiolbassa made good on his promises at a time when politicians were not always circumspect in their dealings.

Kiolbassa and Smarzewski-Schermann organized the St. Stanislaus Kostka Society in 1864, which, five years later evolved into Chicago's first Roman Catholic parish. The St. Stanislaus Kostka church, standing at the corner of Noble and Evergreen streets on the Northwest Side is the oldest and grandest Polish Catholic parish in the archdiocese. It was designed by Charles Keely, who is best remembered as the principal architect of Holy Name Cathedral. Forty of the first fifty-six houses of worship erected for Chicago's Poles were replicas of the great churches of Europe, with paintings, statuary, stained glass and wood carvings handcrafted by artisans. St. Stanislaus in Chicago houses a masterpiece painting by the famous Polish artist Stanislaus Zukctynski during one of his visits to the city. To a generation of Poles who attended services at this Parish, the church will always be equated with the memory of Father Vincent Barzynski, who helped found the Polish Roman Catholic Union in 1874.

The arriving immigrants fanned across the greater Northwest side in record numbers, especially after 1871, when Otto von Bismarck enforced a policy of "Germanization" in the Polish provinces. During that time of brutal repression, many ecumenical figures were exiled or jailed, and the German language was required learning for all Polish school children. The tide of immigration between 1871 and 1918 was fostered by the desire to escape political subjugation and the quest for greater economic opportunity.

They found jobs in the industrial basin along the North Branch of the Chicago River—Goose Island, the Lower West Side near the Burlington Railroad, and the Bridgeport and Back-of-the-Yards neighborhoods on the South Side. The Polish ghettos that sprang up in the waning years of the nineteenth century circled the factories and slaughterhouses. The unskilled poles were happy to accept jobs in heavy industry, which paid an average of $8 per week. With these meager earnings they clothed and fed their families while paying for the upkeep of the neighborhood parish, even though it involved tremendous self-sacrifice. St. Hedwig's, founded in 1888 at Webster and Hoyne, was built and paid for by the immigrant parishioners who absorbed 90% of the construction costs. In 1904, Poles were again called upon to finance the construction of a monument to the Revolutionary War hero Thaddeus Kosciuszko. In that year, the statue, sculpted by Casimir Chodainski, was unveiled amid much fanfare in Humboldt Park. (It has since been moved to Achsah Bond and Lake Shore Drive, west of Adler Planetarium.) To participate in such a worthy cause was seen as a great honor, and was encouraged by the political and religious societies, which fostered closer ties to the mainstream American establishment.

There were two major Polish settlements in Chicago at the turn of the century, with smaller pockets on the South Side at 47th and Ashland; 32nd and Morgan; and 88th and Commercial in South Chicago. The "Polonia Triangle" at the intersection of Division, Milwaukee, and Ashland formed the nucleus of the original "Polish Downtown." It was a cohesive neighborhood about three-quarters of a mile long and a half-mile wide. Eighty-six percent of the population was composed of foreign-born Polish immigrants, according to 1898 census figures. At 1520 W. Division Street stands a modest gray building that once housed the Polish National Alliance (PNA), an ethnic-political fraternity organized in 1880 by a group of exiles committed to the liberation of the homeland from the various occupying powers. By 1927, the PNA membership in the U.S. stood at 250,000, with assets totaling $17,000,000, and a publishing house at 106 W. Division. The PNA first published *Zgoda* (Harmony) in 1880, and was less concerned about religious and moral issues than a rival organization that sprang up six years earlier—the Polish Roman Catholic Union (PRUC), which sought to promote religious ties between the immigrant community and the church. For years these two powerful fraternal organizations were at cross-purposes with each other. The PNA was assailed as a Godless collection of anarchists, unbelievers, and troublemakers. Following the collapse of the Central Powers in 1918, the Poles moved rapidly toward statehood. In November of that year, the short-lived republic was established on democratic principles, and a government was installed the following January. With the goal of unity achieved, the religious PRCU and the nationalistic PNA closed ranks. The cultural gap that previously separated them dissipated.

By 1920, Chicago's Polish community had moved ahead of every foreign-born immigrant group in the strength of their numbers. Catherine Sardo Weidner of Butler University estimates that 31% of all European Poles over the age of 21 became American citizens in the 1920s. The attainable dream of home ownership in the expanding "Bungalow Belt" on the Southwest and Northwest Sides during this period was a powerful lure, and it convinced many of the new arrivals to invest in property, instead of saving their money for the inevitable trip back home.

To preserve the links in the face of "Chicagoization," community leaders officially dedicated the Polish Museum at 984 Milwaukee Avenue on January 12, 1937. Under the direction of its first curator, Mieczyshaw Haiman, the museum has become an important repository for items of historical significance pertaining to the Polish settlement of Chicago. The museum has expanded from two to three floors in the PRCU building, and it features a wide assortment of ethnic folk costumes, religious art, and murals depicting the scientific accomplishments of its people.

One of the most popular exhibits over the years has been the Paderewski collection, honoring the famed classical pianist who made three celebrated visits to Chicago during his illustrious career. Paderewski performed for the first time on New Year's Eve, 1891 at Sullivan and Adler's Auditorium Theater. He collect $300 for the performance, but left the city with some vivid impressions. He would recall the metropolis on the lake as a city of colossal dimensions—rivaled in the U.S. only by the majestic Niagara Falls. Paderewski returned for the second time in 1893 to play at the World's Colombian Exposition. This time he struck up a lifelong friendship with Theodore Thomas, Chicago's famed symphony director. Then in 1916, Paderewski played Chicago for the last time before embarking on a political career. The Polish pianist performed before 4,000 people. The proceeds went to the Polish relief fund.

To honor Paderewski's 100th birthday in 1960, the Chicago Polish Museum completely restored the New York hotel room where he had passed away. The significance of Chicago as a Polish-American cultural center is illustrated by the recent visits of Pope John Paul in October 1979, and Lech Walesa, the Solidarity leader who scheduled a visit to the city in 1989 to appeal for financial aid for Polonia. But even as the last vestiges of communism were swept away, the exodus out of Poland continued unabated. In 1989, 150,000 people traveled to Chicago where 25 U.S. dollars converted into Polish currency would be worth about two months' pay in Warsaw.

Today there are two Polonias in Chicago. Jackowo is representative of the earlier 19th century immigrant settlement. Polish is spoken here, and the parents of school age children see to it that their youngsters receive instruction in the Polish language and customs. Small grocery stores, travel agencies, and other shops carry Polish newspapers and conduct business in the Polish language. There is a sense of togetherness in Avondale—pride amid despair. Triumph over adversity. But there is still a long way to go.

This is inner-city living; a noisy congested urban kalaedescope of sights, sounds, and smells. A few miles to the north, the landscape changes ever so slightly. Here in Jefferson Park, Norwood, and Edison, the more affluent Poles who arrived before and after World War II manicure their lawns, keep a watchful eye on the property values, and drive to the suburban malls to do their shopping. Few, if any, go back to Milwaukee Avenue and Central Park unless it is by necessity. There is a friendly rivalry between the newcomers and the old timers.

Younger Poles profited from an improved postwar educational system, but have chosen to emigrate to the suburbs in recent years for purely economic reasons. They do not dance the polka (some have never *heard* of the polka), and look upon the quaint folk traditions of the far Northwest Siders as relics of a vanished era of Polish history. The older residents, for their part, may view the new immigrants as communists or free-thinkers. For years they were represented in the City Council by long-time 41st Ward Alderman Roman Pucinski, whose office on North Milwaukee Avenue was a favored gathering spot for Polish Americans eager to share in the latest news of the old country. Pucinski, a former news reporter and wheel horse in the two Daley mayoral administrations, is a personal friend of Lech Walesa and has visited him in Poland.

The far Northwest Side still retains its Polish identity. Przyblo's White Eagle banquet hall skirts the city boundary line on Milwaukee Avenue in Niles. Przyblo's is built on the site of an old ethnic picnic ground. It stands across the street from St. Adalbert's Cemetery, arguably the largest Polish burial ground in the city. It can be said of restaurateur Ted Pryzblo that he gets them coming and going. Hundreds of young couples have celebrated their nuptials in the banquet hall by donning aprons featuring baby toys. It is an old Polish custom that foretells of many children and a long, prosperous life. The White Eagle also hosts the numerous funeral processions that file in and out of St. Adalbert's every day. Ted Pryzblo, a second generation Pole, is quick to point out, however, that two presidents and Pope John Paul have been feted in his eating establishment. The White Eagle is a great ethnic restaurant that celebrates Poland's national symbol in its name.

According to popular legend, Lech, Czech, and Rus, three brothers who were said to have lived in Central Europe 1,500 years ago, were at one time betrayed to their common enemy by their sister. They fled the ancestral home in order to escape their persecutor and to find a fortune wherever it may lie. After crossing the Danube River they parted, each continuing in a separate direction. Lech and his followers came upon the Wartha River where one of the Slavic tribes dwelt. Lech, who was an ancestor of Poland's first ruler, Miecrzslaw I, came upon a nesting white eagle. Startled by the presence of Lech, the eagle fluttered its wings and flew off toward the sun. Observing the graceful beauty of the soaring eagle in flight at sunrise, Lech settled near the spot and founded a city which he called Gniezo (the Nest). A popular and benevolent ruler, Lech's people honored him by identifying themselves as "Polaki" (derived from "po Lochu" or followers of Lech). For a national symbol they selected the white eagle on a red background, which down through the centuries has become Poland's national symbol.

Getting There: By public transportation, take the CTA O'Hare Rapid Transit Line to Belmont Station, where you can connect with the #77 bus, or Addison street (#152), which conveniently serves this Northwest Side neighborhood. Take either bus to Milwaukee Avenue, which places you in the heart of Avondale. For a real slice of ethnic culture, you may wish to consider a leisurely bus ride on the CTA Milwaukee Avenue line (#56), which begins at Michigan Avenue and Madison, and ends at the Jefferson Park station on the far Northwest Side. The hour-and-a-half ride will take you through some of the oldest immigrant settlements in the city, including West Town, Logan Square, Avondale, Portage Park, and Jefferson Park. You can trace the outward expansion of the Polish community from "Dinner Pail Row" (lower Milwaukee Avenue near the Polish Museum) right through Avondale and Jefferson, a solid middle-class neighborhood anchored by the Lawrence Avenue business district and the Copernicus Center, located on Lawrence Ave. The Milwaukee Avenue bus makes plenty of stops along the way and at times it might be slow going, especially if there is heavy traffic. But this self-guided tour will provide you with a fresh perspective on city life. In West Town and Humboldt Park you will be passing through Chicago's largest Puerto Rican community. Then as you cross Central Park, the ethnic transformation is quite profound, as it reverts entirely to Polish. This dividing line is characteristic of the historic immigrant settlements of Chicago.

Ethnic Museum

The Polish Museum of America, *984 N. Milwaukee Avenue, Chicago, 60622 (312) 384-3352.* With 60,000 volumes housed in the lending library, a collection of rare and unusual historical artifacts, and a gallery of paintings and sculptures, the Polish Museum is one of the oldest and largest ethnic museums of its kind in the U.S. Located in West Town, the hub of the original "Polish Downtown," the museum is a tribute to the many struggles of this immigrant group in adjusting to the hardships of American life. It has on display the sword presented to Poland's King Bolesaw the Brave by Holy Roman Emperor Otto III in the year 1000 A.D., books that were printed in the 1500s an 1600s, and some personal effects of Ignacey Paderewski, pianist, statesman, and composer.

The Main Hall features a Casimir Pulaski exhibit; a Maritime Room contains scale ship models. There are ethnic and military costumes, and a gift shop selling souvenirs and Polish folk art. The Art Gallery on the fourth floor features the works of some noted Polish painters including Jozef Czapski, Leon Polzycki, Wojciech Kossak, Konstanty Mackiewicz, and Eugeniusz Geppert.

The museum is sponsored by the Polish Roman Catholic Union of America (PRUCA) which shares offices in the building. The lending library is open Monday and Friday from 1:00 P.M. to 7:30 P.M., Tuesday, Wednesday, Thursday, from 10 A.M. to 6 P.M., and Saturdays from noon until 5 P.M. Museum hours are Monday through Sunday, noon to 5 P.M. Admission is free, but donations are encouraged. Special exhibits throughout the year. *Recommended.*

Ethnic Centers and Cultural Societies

The Copernicus Foundation Cultural and Civic Center, *5216 W. Lawrence Ave., Chicago, (312) 777-8898.* Founded in July 1972 by the Illinois Division of the Polish American Congress, the Copernicus Foundation is a nonprofit corporation that sponsors a wide variety of programs and activities aimed at preserving and celebrating a rich ethnic heritage. In 1973, the Foundation presented the City of Chicago with the Nicolaus Copernicus Monument, honoring the 15th century Polish astronomer who advanced the theory that the earth and the other planets revolved around the sun. The monument commemorates the 500th anniversary of the astronomer's birth, and is situated on the grounds of the Adler Planetarium.

The most ambitious project to date has been the conversion of the old Gateway Theatre at 5216 W. Lawrence Avenue into a community arts and cultural center. The Foundation completed its purchase of the former movie palace on June 17, 1979. Six months later the first major renovation took place when the original theater lobby was converted into a three-story area that now houses offices, conference rooms, and a small ballroom. Funding for the project was obtained from private individuals, organizations, and corporations who wanted to invest in the future of the Northwest Side Jefferson Park community, while at the same time preserving Polish culture for future generations.

The center sponsors an annual Taste of Polonia, the Spring Copernican Award Ceremony, a Christmas Holiday Festival, art exhibits, Mother's Day Concert given by Majki Jezowski's dance troop, lectures, musical events, senior citizen seminars, and classes in the Polish language. Members receive the *Copernican Observer,* a quarterly newsletter, special reduced rates at the yearly events, and voting privileges (with a donation of $500 or more). The cost: activities member, $25 yearly; supporting member, $100 yearly; regular member, $500 yearly; life member, $2,500 and up.

Polish Highlander Alliance, *4808 S. Archer Ave., Chicago, (312) 523-7632.* Founded in October 1929 by Zigmund Lokanski, the Highlander Alliance is a South Side not-for-profit cultural society representing 5,000 members (4,500 reside in Chicago alone) who were born in the extreme southern regions of Poland, or who descend from families who resided in the Carpathian Mountains and its foothills. The Highlander Home on Archer Avenue is an educational and cultural center that offers English language classes three times a week to immigrant Poles, sponsors a Sunday afternoon radio program on WPNA, provides studio space for the dozen or so folk dance troops that regularly practice here, a reference library of Polish literature and nonfiction books, several banquet halls, and a restaurant. During the year, the alliance sponsors a number of cultural activities including a Fall Festival, a February Christmas Pageant, a "Queen of the Highlanders" contest in August, and regularly scheduled performances given by the "Hyrni" and "Szkolka" dance troops, plus other worthwhile events to help pay for a scholarship fund established by the alliance in 1984.

Annual Events and Celebrations

Polish Constitution Day Parade. On or about May 3, commemorating the signing of the short-lived constitution in 1791, which established a democratic monarchical government with a senate, a house of deputies, and a judiciary. The document included the concepts of people's sovereignty, majority rule, religious freedom, and most importantly, universal liberty. The Poles modeled their democratic constitution after that of the United States, which ratified into law two years earlier. However, Poland was invaded by Catherine II of Russia in 1792, and by 1795, the fledgling democracy was partitioned into three spheres of influence controlled by the Russians, Austrians, and Prussians. Poland did not become an independent state until after the first World War, and then came the long period of Nazi occupation followed by forty-four years of Soviet repression. The first glimmer of hope came in 1980, when the Solidarity movement was founded. In 1989 the archaic, repressive Communist government fell, and now the Polish people are working to restore the 1791 constitution.

In 1891, the Polish National Alliance (PNA) decided to mark the anniversary of the signing of the constitution with a gala parade and celebration. The PNA's observance has continued more than twenty-five times as long as the constitution was in effect. The big downtown parade, featuring 12,000 marchers in traditional Polish costumes, drum and bugle corps, and 100 floats, proceeds along Dearborn Street from Wacker to Van Buren. The day begins with a 9:30 A.M. wreath-laying ceremony at the Thaddeus Kosciuszko monument at Lake Shore Drive and Solidarity Drive, near the Adler Planetarium. The parade kicks off at 11:30 A.M.

Constitution Day Banquet, *at the Chicago Hilton and Towers, 720 S. Michigan Avenue, Chicago.* Sponsored by the Polish National Alliance. The annual dinner held on May 3 (or 4) includes testimonial speeches given by notable Illinois politicians of Polish descent after dinner dancing and refreshments. Tickets are $45 per person, and may be purchased from the PNA, located at 6100 N. Cicero Ave., Chicago, (312) 286-0500, ext. 312.

Taste of Polonia, *annual event held during the Labor Day weekend outside of the Copernicus Foundation, 5216 W. Lawrence Avenue, Chicago.* Continuous entertainment on two stages (a variety stage and a polka stage), featuring such musical acts as the "Average Polka Band," Grazyna Auguscik (Polish jazz), and an array of 1950s-60s nostalgia groups. Special performances by the Lechici Folk Dancers of the Polish Youth Association are held at various times during the festival. The food vendors are representative of the restaurants and delicatessens that proliferate on the Northwest Side, and have participated in this event since its inception in 1979. They sell such traditional menu items as potato and meat *pierogi, nalesniki* (blintzes), cabbage rolls, mushroom soup, *bigos, zurek,* and *flaczki.* Local merchants will allow patrons to use their parking lots at specified times. Call (312) 777-8898 for scheduled times.

Annual Copernican Award Ceremony, *held at the Copernicus Center, 5216 W. Lawrence Avenue, Chicago,* the first or second Friday in May. The foundation has paid tribute to an outstanding member of the Polish-American community each year since 1979. The 1991 recipient was Robert F. Martwick, former assistant state's attorney and noted trial lawyer in Chicago. The award is presented during a concert given by the Lake Shore Symphony Orchestra. A lavish buffet supper is served in honor of the recipient beginning at 6 P.M. Tickets for the buffet supper and the concert are $45 per person. The concert begins at 8 P.M., and the cost for that event alone is $20. All tickets may be purchased at the center during normal office hours, or concert tickets (only) will be available at the door one hour prior to the concert. For additional information please call (312) 777-8898.

Copernicus Center Holiday Festival, *the first Saturday in December at the Copernicus Foundation, 5216 W. Lawrence Avenue, Chicago.*   Arts and crafts booths, featuring the works of Polish artisans from the Chicago area. The handmade items (which do not always pertain to Christmas themes) are offered for sale to the public. Admission to the one-day event is free. Hours: 10 A.M. to 2 P.M.

Pulaski Day Reception. *every March 4 at the Polish Museum of America, 984 N. Milwaukee Avenue, Chicago, (312) 384-3352.* Pulaski day is a city and county holiday. On the 150th anniversary of the Polish martyr's death in 1929, President Herbert Hoover proclaimed March 4 Pulaski Day. But few people who are given the day off work have the slightest idea what they are supposed to celebrate. The answer may be found at the Polish Museum, where a special exhibit chronicles the life and times of this freedom fighter who helped save George Washington's army from disastrous defeat at Brandywine and West Tavern in 1777. Casimir Pulaski was living in exile in Paris when he was recruited by Benjamin Franklin to join the war for independence in America. Pulaski, known as the "father of the U.S. Cavalry," met a hero's death while leading French and American troops in the attack against Savannah, Georgia.

An overflow crowd usually attends the reception, concert, and museum tour on the afternoon of March 4. In the past, public notables, including Governor James Edgar, have scored points with Polish-American voters on the Northwest Side by appearing at the museum to spread the good word about this forgotten hero. Admission is free.

Polish Art Fest, *at the Polish Museum of America, 984 N. Milwaukee Avenue, Chicago, (312) 384-3352.*   An annual art fair held in conjunction with the Chicago International Art Expo, beginning the second week of May. The fair spotlights the work of contemporary painters, graphic artists, sculptors, and weavers. This major ethnic event is viewed as the presentation of various trends and generations in modern Polish art. Lectures in the Polish language will be give on two consecutive Sundays by renowned experts from Europe, and an art auction conducted by a sponsoring gallery takes place one Saturday in the month. Most of the work exhibited at the fair is for sale, as are posters, graphics, and books on Polish art. The festival is open daily from noon until 5:30 P.M. and admission is free, but a $2 donation is suggested.

Festival Polonaise, *a three-day outdoor folk fair held in Grant Park (Arvey Field, across from the Field Museum of Natural History) the second weekend in July, sponsored by the Polish National Alliance.*   Continuous entertainment provided by Polish jazz musicians, polka bands, the Lechici ethnic dance troop, and some of the famous 1950s and '60s rock groups, such as the Surfaris, Coasters, Mark Lindsey, and Herman's Hermits. On Sunday, "Miss Polonaise" is crowned after the outdoor Mass. Tickets are $6 at the gate, or $5 in advance if purchased through local Dominick's Food Stores. For show times and additional information, call the PNA at (312) 631-3300. *Recommended.*

Polish-Spanish Ethnic Festival. Next to the last Sunday in August. This one-day street fair is sponsored in part by the Milwaukee/Diversey Chamber of Commerce. Beginning in 1992, the Polish Avondale community joins with their Hispanic neighbors in Logan Square and West Town to stage an extravaganza of food, dancing, ethnic bands, rock n'roll, and sales of merchandise around the statue of General John Logan and Milwaukee Avenue and Logan Boulevard. The fair will actually encompass the Milwaukee Avenue business district from Belmont to Logan Boulevard. For additional information call (312) 235-6403.

Holy Trinity Polish Church, *Christmas Bazaar, 1118 N. Noble, Chicago, (312) 489-4140.*   Arts and crafts booths, Polish foods for sale, and musical entertainment in the parish hall. The event is held for the first Sunday in December, and is free to the public. Food and merchandise are offered for sale.

"Rendezvous With Music," *a series of concerts given throughout the year by famed classical pianist Henry Wawrzyczek, at the*

Polish American Congress, Illinois Office, 5844 N. Milwaukee Avenue, Chicago, (312) 631-3300. Pianist Wawrzyczek has performed twenty-seven concerts through 1991, all of them well attended by the community. For times and dates, call the P.A.C.

"Christmas in Poland," *held the Sunday before Christmas at the Museum of Science and Industry, 5700 S. Lake Shore Drive, Chicago, (312) 684-1414.* The holiday traditions of Poland are celebrated in song and dance during the museum's annual "Christmas Around the World" festival held throughout the month of December. A special one-hour appearance by the Lechici Folk Dancers of the Polish Youth Association of Chicago is featured. This famous dance troop, founded by Czeslaw Orzel-Orlicz, marked its twenty-fifth anniversay in 1991. The troop consists of forty-five teenagers and young adults who perform the regional dances of ten Polish provinces under the direction of choreographer Ted Wiecek.

Polish National Alliance Debutante Ball. *Since 1967. Held the second Saturday in November, (most recently) at the Hyatt Regency O'Hare, 9300 Bryn Mawr Ave., Rosemont.* Formal presentation ball for young women between the ages of 16 and 22 who are members of the PNA. Dance music, presentation, and dinner. Tickets are $40 per person, subject to change. Call (312) 286-0500 for details.

"Bal Amarantowy" *(White and Red Ball). A formal debutante presentation ball, held at the Chicago Hilton Towers, 720 S. Michigan Avenue, Chicago, the last Saturday in February.* Sponsored by the Legion of Young Polish Women, the White and Red Ball (the color symbolizes the debutante before her formal introduction into society, the red represents the post-deb) is regarded by many as the "crown jewel" of the Polish-American social season in Chicago. The annual fund-raising event, which benefits various Polish charitable causes, dates back to 1941, when the Legion of Young Polish Women donated the proceeds of the Ball to the exiled Polish armies and resistance movement battling Nazi aggression. The league was founded in Chicago by Helen (Lenard) Pieklo on Sept. 2, 1939—the day after the Nazi armies invaded Poland. In 1945, the first debutante cotillion was held for young women of Polish extraction between the ages of 16 and 20. The tradition continues into the 1990s. Even though the league does not have an office or phone listing, interested parties are encouraged to contact the Copernicus Foundation at (312) 777-8898, where many of their meetings are held. The cost of a ticket to the White and Red Ball is $75 per person. Formal attire requested.

"Cinderella-Prince Charming Ball." *Annual cotillion sponsored by the Polish Roman Catholic Union of America, and held at the Drake Oakbrook Hotel, 22nd and York Road, Oakbrook, (708) 574-5700.*   The Presentation Ball is given for both the young men and women of high school age who belong to the PRCUA. The teenagers are taught the social graces and formal ballroom dancing prior to their "presentation" at the dinner dance, held the first Saturday in November. The cost is $45 per person. In addition to the Prince Charming-Cinderella Ball, the PRCUA offers other social activities during the year, including athletic tournaments, bus tours to Polish cultural events outside Chicago, the traditional Easter *Swiecone* and a Christmas *Oplatek*. Please call the PRCUA at (312) 278-3210 (1-800-772-8631 outside Illinois) for times.

"Traditional Easter Celebration," *sponsored by the Polish Women's Alliance of America, 205 S. Northwest Highway, Park Ridge, (312) 693-6215.*   Held at alternating restaurants on the North Side and South Side the Sunday afternoon closest to Easter. The Polish Women's Alliance (which is not affiliated with the PNA) has been in existence for ninety-four years, and has 63,000 members in a seventeen-state area. It is a fraternal benefit society offering life insurance to its members and a calendar of social events. The Easter celebration includes the traditional blessing of the food, singing of Polish Easter carols, folk dancing in colorful ethnic costumes, and children's events. Every other year the Easter party is held on the South Side at various banquet halls and restaurants including the Landmark, the Mayfield, and the Polonia. The sponsoring North Side halls include Przyblo's White Eagle, and Aqua Bella. To find out where the event will be held in a given year, please call Helen Wojcik at the Polish Women's Alliance of America, (312) 693-6215. The cost of the dinner ranges from $20 to $25 per person.

"Traditional Christmas Celebration," *sponsored by the Polish Women's Alliance of America, 205 S. Northwest Highway, Park Ridge, (312) 693-6215.*   Held the first Sunday afternoon in December, between noon and 4:30 P.M., at alternating restaurants on the South and North Sides. Includes dinner, a Santa Claus for the youngsters, ethnic dancers in folk costumes, and the blessing of the food. The cost is $20 to $25 per person. Call (312) 693-6215 for times and location.

"Swietojankie," *(St. John's Day Festival). Annual picnic held on or about June 24, at Allison Woods Forest Preserve, Des Plaines. (The grove is located on Milwaukee Avenue between Sanders Road and River Road.)*   The League of Young Polish Women hosts this charming ethnic event, which recreates the folklore and customs of St. John's Day. The eligible young women of the Polish community are given plastic wreaths to float down the Des Plaines River. According to ancient European customs, the young man who "rescues" the wreath from the churning river is sure to become the fair maiden's betrothed. The Des Plaines River is a tepid, polluted artery nowadays, but the quaint custom is interesting to observe anyway. A Polish kitchen serves food on the grounds. Prize drawing. Music. Admission is free. Hours: noon to dusk. Call the Legion of Young Polish Women, c/o the Copernicus Foundation, (312) 777-8898.

Fall Festival at the Polish Highlanders Home, *4808 S. Archer Avenue, Chicago, (312) 523-7632.*   A two-day ethnic festival held the second weekend of November in the Highlander Hall, featuring an assortment of ethnic foods from twelve different nationalities. Folk dancing contests and sales of Polish ethnic costumes are included in the festivities. Admission is $6 per person.

"Przeglad Zespolow Koledniczych," *(Polish Christmas Traditions), at the Polish Highlander Home, 4808 S. Archer Avenue, Chicago, (312) 523-7632.*   Christmas in February? Because the Highlander folk dance troops are so busy in December, the Alliance postpones the Christmas pageant until the first Sunday in February. Among the dozen or so dance troops based at the Highlander Home are the "Szolka," (children from 3 to 14 years old), and the "Hyrni," (young adults, 16–25). They perform for cash prizes of $100 and $200 at the Christmas festival, held from noon to 10 P.M. in the hall. Admission is $5 per person. For times and dates, call the Highlander Home at (312) 523-7632.

"Frontline Poland," *on-going series of film presentations held in January, March, May, July, and November, at the Film Center of* *the Art Institute, Columbus and Jackson, Chicago, (312) 443-3737.* Featuring Polish-language movies and documentaries. The Polish Film Festival takes place in late September or early October, with lectures given by visiting Polish filmmakers, showings of restored cinematic classics, and the latest contemporary movies direct from Eastern Europe. The cost of admission is $5 per person for each showing. Call the Film Center for a calendar of events.

Milwaukee Event

Polish Fest, *at the Henry W. Maier Festival Park, along the Milwaukee lakefront.* An annual celebration of Polish food, music, and ethnic customs held since 1981. Held in mid-June, and sponsored in part by local advertisers and Polish Festivals, Inc., the three-day extravaganza features some of the famous local dance troops, polka lessons, a Miss Polish Fest Pageant, fireworks, celebrity appearances, a market place, historical and cultural exhibits, a carnival midway, and plenty of fabulous *pierogi,* kielbasa, *czarnina, golbacki,* and pastries. Presale adult admission is $5 per person. Admission at the gate is $6. Advance admission includes a raffle ticket. For tickets and information, contact Polish Festivals, Inc., at 7128 W. Rawson Avenue, Franklin, WI, or call (414) 529-2140.

═══ Avondale: Chicago's Little Warsaw ═══

A twisting Indian trail that was once home to a handful of farming families who arrived in the 1840s is today the site of the largest, most concentrated Polish neighborhood in Chicago. The community of Avondale is bounded by Addison Street, Pulaski Road (formerly Crawford until several Northwest Side aldermen pushed through a bill in the City Council to rename the thoroughfare in honor of the Polish military hero after years of heated debate going back to 1933), Diversey, and the Kennedy Expressway. Until large numbers of Germans, Scandinavians and Poles began settling the area in the 1890s, Avondale was a distant farm community stretching along an old Indian trail. In the 1840s a plank road was built to expedite the transfer of produce, and dairy products to Chicago's Randolph Street market.

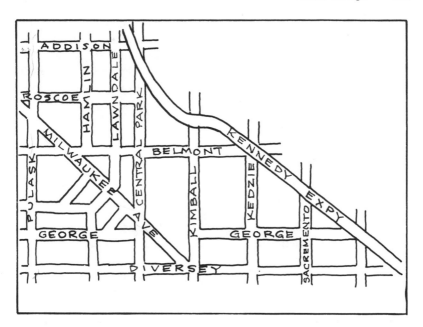

Avondale

The arrival of the Europeans in the late 1890s, signaled the beginning of a building boom which lasted into the 1930s. Thousands of sturdy, but unassuming brick two-flats and frame houses were built during this period, and have been carefully maintained ever since by the owners. On Saturday and Sunday afternoons, Milwaukee Avenue between Central Park and Pulaski is a hub of commercial activity, as the residents attend to their shopping needs in congested delicatessens, retail and grocery stores, dine at the small but intimate Polish restaurants, and meet and greet each other before the bells of St. Hyacinth signal the call to Mass.

It is a slice of Eastern Europe that peacefully coexists with the Puerto Rican and Mexican communities to the immediate south on Milwaukee Avenue. Yet, like so many other Chicago neighborhoods, natural or manmade barriers tend to separate and isolate the nationalities from one another, much like an invisible wall or dividing line. In this case the Kimball-Diversey-Milwaukee confluence offers a stark contrast between *el barrio* and the new Polonia. Travel south of this intersection and the overhanging signs are all in Spanish. To the North, it is Polish, though

Hispanics began moving into Avondale in sizable numbers during the 1970s. Real estate people will tell you that Avondale is one of the three "affordable" neighborhoods in Chicago (Humboldt Park and Rogers Park are the other two) for prospective home buyers. They will hasten to add that the distinctive European flavor gives Avondale a real sense of community.

Shopping and Dining Guide

Delicatessens

Joe and Frank's, *5620 S. Pulaski, Chicago, (312) 581-0639.* Located on the northern tip of Avondale. Old fashioned bakery and delicatessen that manufactures its own homemade sausages. Brought to you by Frank Ratulowski and Joe Ligas. Hours: Monday to Thursday, 9 A.M. to 6 P.M.; Friday, 8 A.M. to 7 P.M.; Saturday, 7 A.M. to 5 P.M. Closed Sunday.

Teresa Deli, *3184 N. Milwaukee, Chicago, (312) 282-5515.* Freshly cut meats, imported gourmet items, homemade sausages, and baked goods. Hours: Monday to Thursday, 8 A.M. to 9 P.M.; Friday and Saturday, 9 A.M. to 8 P.M.

Iry's Inc. Deli and Liquors, *2924 N. Milwaukee, Chicago, (312) 227-5424.* Iry's is the kind of place you remember from the old neighborhood. They always used to be on the corner. This place isn't, however. It's tiny, and cluttered, and the owners will probably give you the big eye if you happen to be 9 or 10 years old and just want to hang around. It is also helpful if you speak Polish. Gift baskets, liquors, baked goods, and meats. Hours: Monday to Saturday, 7 A.M. to 10 P.M.; Sunday, 9 A.M. to 9 P.M.

Wiosna Fruit Market, *3037 N. Milwaukee, Chicago, (312) 227-5417.* Owner Barbara T. Pieniazek sells bulk produce and imported foods from this sparsely decorated, yet surprisingly busy, grocery store. Hours: Monday through Sunday, 9 A.M. to 9 P.M.

Bristol Liquors, Deli, & Lounge, *3084-86 N. Milwaukee, Chicago, (312) 545-7072, and 5205 W. Belmont Avenue, Chicago, (312) 545-6097.* The delicatessen is in the front, the restaurant area in the back, just like the old-fashioned neighborhood places used to be. Polish foods and newspapers are sold at both locations. Hours: (Milwaukee Avenue) 8 A.M. to 2 A.M., seven days a week; (Belmont Avenue) 8 A.M. to 10 P.M., also seven days a week.

Piast Delicatessen, *3125 N. Milwaukee, Chicago, (312) 604-4315.* An old-world market place that does not pretend to be anything more than a place where neighborhood people shop. Baked goods, import items, and fresh meats. Hours: Monday to Friday, 8:30 A.M. to 9:00 P.M.; Saturday, 8 A.M. to 9 P.M.; Sunday, 9 A.M. to 9 P.M.

Czerwone Jabuszko Deli, *3127-29 N. Milwaukee, Chicago, (312) 583-3982 and 3427 W. Diversey Avenue, Chicago.* Deli, produce, and green goods sold inside. Outside on the sidewalk, vendors sell *jablka* (apples) and other eat-as-you-walk foods. The store is always busy on Saturdays and Sundays. Ferdinand Hebal, proprietor.

Mulica's Deli & Liquors, Inc., *3118 N. Milwaukee, Chicago, (312) 777-7945.* Wally Mulica's place is one of the busiest gathering spots on the street. The deli is located in the rear. Frozen foods, liquor, pastry, produce, and Polish magazines and newspapers are sold in the front. Hours: Monday to Friday, 9 A.M. to 9 P.M.; Saturday and Sunday, open until 8 P.M.

Bacik's Super Meat Market, *3038 N. Milwaukee, Chicago, (312) 489-0994 and 4249 S. Archer Avenue, Chicago, (312) 247-2253.* Pierogi, lunch meats, liquors, dairy products, Polish imports, newspapers and magazines. Hours: Monday to Sunday, 9 A.M. to 9 P.M.

Andy's Deli, *3055 N. Milwaukee, Chicago, (312) 486-8160, and 1737 W. Division, (312) 486-8870, and 5438 N. Milwaukee, (312) 631-7304.* The place is nearly always busy. The overextended clerks sell imported food items, greeting cards, and Polish newspapers. Hours: Monday through Saturday, 8 A.M. to 9:00 P.M.; Sunday, 10 A.M. to 8 P.M.

Bakeries

Pasieka Home Quality Bakery, *3056 N. Milwaukee, Chicago, (312) 278-5190.* A real old-fashioned Chicago bakery with wooden cupboards, and sales clerks who smile at you. Pastries. Cakes for all occasions. Bread. Hours: Monday through Saturday, 6 A.M. to 9 P.M.; Sunday, 7A.M. to 7 P.M.

Forest View Bakery, Inc., *3034 N. Milwaukee, Chicago, (312) 342-9456 and 6454 N. Milwaukee, Chicago, (312) 775-7740.* Two locations: one in Avondale, and the other further north near the Chicago-Niles boundary. Fancy tarts, cakes, and homemade baked breads. Hours: Monday to Sunday, 7 A.M. to 6 P.M.

Ann's Bakery, *2923 Milwaukee, Chicago, (312) 489-6562.* Sister store to the one in Ukrainian Village. Baked goods, delicatessen items, Polish newspapers and candy. Hours: Monday through Friday, 8 A.M. to 8 P.M.; Saturday, 8 A.M. to 5 P.M.

Retail and Gift Shops

Avondale Department Store, *3025 N. Milwaukee, Chicago, (312) 235-9446.* Wholesale and retail general merchandise, including men's and women's clothing and leather goods. Some Polish import items. Hours: Monday through Sunday, 10 A.M. to 8 P.M. No credit cards.

Toys and Gifts Store *(Paczki do Polski), 3114 N. Milwaukee, Chicago, (312) 685-1517, and 4406 N. Milwaukee, (312) 545-4300.* A fine little toy shop, with a large inventory of Lego kits, Polish greeting cards, and ethnic dolls. Hours: Monday to Friday, 9 A.M. to 9 P.M.; Saturday, 9 A.M. to 8 P.M.; Sunday, 10 A.M. to 6 P.M. No credit cards.

J.D. Jewelers, *3022 N. Milwaukee, Chicago, (312) 252-6140.* Jewelry items. Gold bought and sold, and Polish music on cassettes. Repairs while you wait. Hours: Monday through Saturday, noon to 8 P.M.

Calisia Imports, *3026 N. Milwaukee, Chicago, (312) 222-3268.* Dimly lit, cluttered gift store with the look and feel of an old-fashioned neighborhood rummage and resale shop. The gift items are imported from Poland, India, and China, among other places. Some of the merchandise is expensive, some of it is not. Cards, jewelry, and Czech and German crystal pieces, religious icons, woodcarvings, and dolls. Hours: Monday to Saturday, 10 A.M. to 7 P.M.; Sunday, 10 A.M. to 4 P.M.

Syrena Department Store, *3004 N. Milwaukee, Chicago, (312) 489-4435.* Before there were suburban shopping malls, interstate highways to whisk you there, and coldly impersonal retail chains that swallowed their competition like a Pac-Man character gone berserk, there were cozy, intimate neighborhood department stores with creaking wooden floors and merchandise displays that did not titillate the visceral senses. They were not supposed to. Your parents took you there on Thursday nights (never on Tuesday—that was when *I Love Lucy* was on, and the slowest night of the week for retailers) to buy school clothes, a Sunday-go-to-meeting outfit, and sensible Oxfords. The Avondale Department Store and Syrena's evoke powerful childhood memories. The customers and sales clerks are all Polish, so it might help if you speak the language. Hours: Monday through Saturday, 10 A.M. to 8 P.M.; Sunday, 10 A.M. to 6 P.M.

Nabill Gifts, *3069 N. Milwaukee, Chicago, (312) 267-6643.* No credit cards, please. Toys, electronics, women's handbags, clothing, watches, and CD's. Hours: Monday through Sunday, 10 A.M. to 8 P.M.

Anna's, *2992 N. Milwaukee, Chicago, (312) 227-5221.* Children's and adult's clothing in the same kind of neighborhood setting that makes Avondale Department Store and Syrena's so interesting. Hours: Monday through Saturday, 11 A.M. to 8 P.M.; Sunday, 10 A.M. to 6 P.M.

Books and Video

Polonia Bookstore and Publisher's Co., *2886 N. Milwaukee, Chicago, (312) 489-2554.* The largest Polish bookstore in America offers a wide selection of books in Polish; fiction, and poetry, historical and religious books, books for children and students, dictionaries, travel guidebooks, books in English on Polish subjects, both paperbacks and hardcover, records, albums, and music cassettes. Hours: Monday and Thursday, 10 A.M. to 7 P.M.; Tuesday, Wednesday, and Friday, 10 A.M. to 6 P.M.; Saturday 9:30 A.M. to 5:30 P.M. Accepts credit cards.

Polish Record and Video Center of America, *2942 N. Milwaukee, Chicago, (312) 486-6700.* Polish and Eastern European films available for rental or sale, including the historical epic, "Knights of the Black Cross," and the children's special "Bolek and Lolek on the Western Frontier." Music cassettes, albums, and CDs. Hours: Monday through Friday, 10 A.M. to 9 P.M.; Saturday, 10 A.M. to 9 P.M.; Sunday, 10 A.M. to 7 P.M. No credit cards.

Batman Video, *3932 W. School Street, Chicago, (312) 777-3129, and 4195 Archer Avenue, Chicago, (312) 927-6991.* Located one block east of Milwaukee near Pulaski. A Polish-American video center that stocks the classic black and white films made during Poland's "golden age" in the 1930s. In addition to the latest U.S. films available for rental, the owner also carries contemporary Polish films with English subtitles. Foreign films can be ordered into the store within seven days. Hours: Sunday through Thursday, 11 A.M. to 10 P.M.; Friday and Saturday, 11 A.M. to 11 P.M.

Polish-American Video, *5229 W. Belmont, Chicago, (312) 725-1025.* Over 600 Polish and American-made movies for sale or rental. Hours: Monday, Wednesday, Friday, 11 A.M. to 10 P.M.; Tuesday and Thursday, 11 A.M. to 9 P.M.; Saturday, 10 A.M. to 10 P.M.; Sunday, noon to 8 P.M.

Restaurants and Ethnic Nightclubs

Teresa I and II Polish Restaurant, *3938 W. School, Chicago, (312) 286-5166, and 4751 N. Milwaukee, Chicago, (312) 283-0184.* Very inexpensive little Polish kitchen, located next to Batman Video. You can order a full dinner for under $6.00. The *gollabki* (stuffed cabbage) and *naiesniki serery* (cheese blintzes) are house specialties. Hours: Monday through Sunday, 11 A.M. to 9 P.M.

Orbis Restaurant, *2860 N. Milwaukee, Chicago, (312) 342-7800.* Marai Jagla is your host, and the traditional Polish dishes are top drawer: pork tenderloin with pepper sauce, cabbage rolls, sausages, and potatoes. Very small, intimate dining room. Hours: Monday through Sunday, 7 A.M. to 10 P.M.

Wigry Restaurant, *3027 N. Milwaukee, Chicago, (312) 342-5636 or 278-1311.* The truly amazing thing about the restaurants in Avondale is the prices. A full meal can be ordered at the Wigry for $4 to $7.50. Breakfast, lunch and dinner are served. Cocktail lounge on premises, Hours: Monday through Sunday, 10 A.M. to 10 P.M. No credit cards.

Senkowski Home Bakery Delicatessen and Restaurant, *2931 N. Milwaukee, Chicago, (312) 252-3708.* Eat and shop at the same time. The delicatessen sells baked goods, sausage, candy, imported foods and newspapers. The restaurant, featuring herring blanketed by onion and cucumber sour cream, potato pancakes, bigos (hunter's stew), is open Monday through Saturday, 6 A.M. to 9 P.M.; and Sunday from 9 A.M. to 9 P.M.

Czerwone Jabluszko Restaurant, *3121-23 N. Milwaukee, Chicago, (312) 588-5781, and 6474 N. Milwaukee, Chicago, (312) 763-3407.* Two locations, one in Avondale, the other a stone's throw away from Roman Pucinski's old office in the 41st Ward. The Hebals promise that you will never leave hungry, simply by dipping into their big smorgasbord, with a variety of pierogis and crepes, pork chops, roast beef and pork, goulashes, sauerkraut, potato pancakes and fritters. "If you get tired of the smorgasbord, you can choose something else from our small menu," they say, and I believe them. The prices are a real bargain at $4.25 on weekdays, and $4.95 on weekends. Hours: 11 A.M. to 10 P.M., seven days a week.

Congress Restaurant and Nightclub, *3200 N. Milwaukee, Chicago, (312) 286-5105.* Located at Belmont and Milwaukee, the Congress is one of the hotspots of Avondale. The Polish music and dancing goes on from 8 P.M. to 4 A.M. every Friday, Saturday, and Sunday. The restaurant is open from 7:00 A.M. to 11:30 P.M., Monday through Friday, and on Sundays from noon until 4 A.M.

Made In Poland Entertainment Center, *3336-42 N. Milwaukee, Chicago, (312) 283-6606.* A bar, restaurant, and nightclub that features disco, rock music, and comedy acts from 8 P.M. until 2 A.M. On Wednesday, Krzysztof Zakreta invites the local musical acts to come in and perform. The center is the only teen club in the city open to young people of high school age on Friday nights. Restaurant hours: Monday through Sunday, 11 A.M. to midnight.

Eurodisco Cisza Lesna, *3356 N. Milwaukee, Chicago, (312) 794-0401.* Two disc jockeys spin the records—Maciej Lojewski and Robert Kobryn. Hours: 8 P.M. to 4 A.M., Monday through Friday; Saturday, 8 P.M. to 5 A.M.

Polanaise Nightclub and Restaurant, *3196 N. Milwaukee, Chicago, (312) 545-4152.* Restaurant and dance club. The weekend entertainment kicks in at 8 P.M. and goes until 4 A.M. on Friday and Saturday, and till 5 A.M. on Sunday. Restaurant hours are from 7 P.M. to 4 A.M.

Cardinal Club, *5155 W. Belmont, Chicago, (312) 736-4662.* Big-name guest stars from Poland and musical bands perform on the weekend at this show lounge and saloon with two bars. Hours: Monday through Friday, 8 P.M. to 4 A.M.; Saturday and Sunday, 8 P.M. to 5 A.M.

═ Dining and Shopping, Outlying Areas ═

Restaurants

Taste of Europe, *6247 N. Milwaukee Avenue, Chicago, (312) 792-1492.* A tiny, family owned restaurant where mom, dad, and the kids strive to make your visit a pleasant one. The food is served buffet style, and is always warm and fresh thanks to the extra attention shown by the owners. Not to be missed is the Polish-style cabbage casserole, the thin-sliced roast pork, or the sweet tasting blintzes. You'll also enjoy the prices. During the week, the buffet is $3.95 per person, and on weekends, $4.95. Buffet hours: Monday through Friday, 11 A.M. to 4 P.M.; Saturday and Sunday, 11 A.M. to 6 P.M. No credit cards.

Pierogi Inn, *5318 W. Lawrence Avenue, Chicago, (312) 725-2818.* Owner Richard Zawadzki has a Cable-TV cooking show, and he once served as Hugh Hefner's personal gourmet cook. The servers are not well versed in the English language, but a chalkboard listing the day's specialties (including, no doubt, pierogi) will help you make the right selection. The dinners are moderately priced, as is the case with most Polish dining rooms. You can eat well for under seven dollars. No live entertainment, but there is background music. Hours: 10 A.M. to 9 P.M., seven days a week. Cash only.

Sawa's Old Warsaw Restaurant and Banquet Facility, *9200 W. Cermak Road (at 17th Avenue), Broadview, (708) 343-9040.* A chain of four family-owned restaurants is now reduced to one. The 1978 recession hit the Sawa family very hard, according to the owner, who started his business at Clark and Ashland in 1963. Sawa's is still a good bargain for a meal, buffet, or private party. There are three private halls. Lunchtime hours: 11:00 A.M. to 2:30 P.M., Tuesday through Saturday; dinner from 4 P.M. to 9 P.M., Tuesday through Saturday; Fridays and Saturdays until 10 P.M.; and Sundays 11 A.M. to 8 P.M. Credit cards accepted.

Przyblo's White Eagle, *6839 N. Milwaukee Avenue, Niles, (708) 647-0660.* There must be something to this large airy banquet hall and restaurant if it attracted such luminaries as the President (Carter) of the United States, the Governor, and a host of lesser celebrities. Since 1948, the Przyblos have probably hosted more funeral luncheons than any restaurant in the metropolitan Chicago area. Don't interpret that as an omen; St Adalbert's Cemetery is across the street. Seven banquet halls. Dinners are served family style. Restaurant hours: lunch, Tuesday through Saturday, 11:30 A.M. to 3 P.M.; dinner, Tuesday through Saturday, 4 P.M. to 9 P.M., Sunday, 11:30 A.M. to 7:30 P.M. Credit cards accepted.

L.M. Sava, *3802 W. Diversey, Chicago, (312) 486-2881.* Hot buffet, all you can eat all day. Sava's is new to this area, but the prices are still reasonable. The buffet is $4.50 with soup, Monday through Friday, and a dollar more on the weekends. Hours: 12 P.M. to 9 P.M., Monday through Sunday.

Little Europe, *160 W. North Avenue, Villa Park, (708) 530-4979.* Serving Polish food since 1988. Accordion player entertains on weekends from 4:30 P.M. to 12:00 P.M. Other hours: Tuesday through Sunday, 11 A.M. to 10 P.M. Closed Monday. Credit cards and entertainment coupons accepted.

Staropolska Restaurant, *5249 W. Belmont, Chicago, (312) 736-5230.* Buffet smorgasbord, all you can eat. Prices range from $4.50 on weekdays to $5.50 on weekends. Affiliated with the Jolly Club (see following entry). Hours: Monday through Thursday, 11 A.M. to 9 P.M.; Friday and Saturday, 11 A.M. to 10 P.M.; Sunday, 11 A.M. to 9 P.M. Credit cards accepted.

Jolly Inn, *6501 W. Irving Park Road, Chicago, (312) 736-7606.* Adjacent to the Jolly Club, one of the most popular banquet halls on the Northwest Side. Low-priced buffet served all day. Hours: 10:30 A.M. to 9:00 P.M.; Monday through Thursday, Friday and Saturday until 10 P.M. Credit cards accepted.

Polo Restaurant and Bar, *8801 N. Milwaukee Ave, Niles, (708) 470-8822.* A dinner restaurant, so the prices here are somewhat more than you would pay at an all-you-can-eat establishment on the Northwest Side. Halibut in dill sauce, stuffed cabbage, and real potato pancakes are the recommended entrees. Hours: 4 P.M. to 10 P.M., Tuesday through Friday, and Saturday until 11 P.M. Sunday brunches served from 10 A.M. to 3 P.M. Credit cards accepted.

Warsaw Inn, *217 N. Route 31 (one mile south of Route 120), McHenry, (815) 344-0330.* Open for breakfast, lunch, and dinner. Low-priced Polish restaurant. Hours: breakfast, Monday through Friday, 7 A.M. to 11 A.M.; lunch 11 A.M. to 4 P.M., Monday through Friday; dinner 4 P.M. to 10 P.M. Saturdays, noon to 10 P.M.; Sunday, 10 A.M. to 9 P.M. Credit cards accepted.

Nightclub

Baby Doll Polka Club, *6102 S. Central Avenue, Chicago, (312) 582-9706.* Owner Irene Korosa bubbles over with enthusiasm when she describes her off-the-beaten path nightclub and cocktail lounge, with its panoramic view of Midway Airport's majestic runways. We don't know of any other club in the city that caters to the polka set, which makes this place so unusual. Irene has been at this location for over ten years, and seems to be doing well despite the fact that she does not charge an admission fee to the seventy-five or so patrons that can be squeezed onto the dance floor. Hours: 5 P.M. to 2 A.M. daily. The house polka band starts playing at around 9:30 P.M. *Recommended.*

Delicatessens

John & Ray's Market, *5760 N. Milwaukee, Chicago, (312) 774-1924.* Specializing in choice meats, and Harczak sausages. Located a few doors down from the busier Kalinowski market. Hours: Monday through Friday, 8:30 A.M. to 5:00 P.M., Saturday, 8:30 A.M. to 6 P.M.

Kalinowski European Style, *5746 N. Milwaukee, Chicago, (312) 631-4640* All foods made on the premises. Serving the Gladstone neighborhood of the 41st Ward, this deli is busiest on Saturday mornings. Fresh meats, party trays, and catering. Open Monday through Friday, 8 A.M. to 6 P.M.; Saturday, 7 A.M. to 6 P.M.; Sunday 7 A.M. to 1 P.M.

Sobczak's Avondale Sausage, *8705 N. Milwaukee Ave., Niles, (708) 470-8780.* A slice of the Avondale neighborhood transported to serene, tranquil Niles, a world removed. European-style homemade sausage, salads, and party trays. Extensive catering menu for house parties, graduations, banquets, showers, and anniversaries. A real favorite of the suburban Poles. Hours: Monday through Friday, 9 A.M. to 6 P.M.; Saturday, 8:30 A.M. to 5 P.M.; Sunday, 9 A.M. to 3 P.M.

Polish-Italian Deli, *5712 W. Fullerton, Chicago, (312) 622-4588.* They say a Pole will often marry an Italian, or an Irishman. Here's one deli at least where they recognize that simple Chicago truth. European style, homemade sausages, pierogi, flaczki, and Italian foods. Hours: Monday through Saturday, 8:30 A.M. to 7:30 P.M.; Sunday, 8 A.M. to 1 P.M.

Kasia's Polish Deli, *2101 W. Chicago Ave., Chicago, (312) 486-6163.* Kazimiera Buber sells imported foods from Poland and Greece, but takes cash only. Hours: Monday through Saturday, 9 A.M. to 6 P.M.; Sunday, noon to 3 P.M.

Cragin Sausage, *5145 W. Diversey, Chicago, (312) 637-1730.* Homemade sausages, pierogis, bigos, and golabki. Hours: Monday through Friday, 9 A.M. to 8 P.M.; Saturday, 8 A.M. to 8 P.M.; Sunday, 9 A.M. to 1 P.M.

Gilmart Quality Food and Liquors, *5050 S. Archer, Chicago, (312) 585-5514.* The South Side's choice for imported Polish, Yugoslav, Czech, and German delicatessen foods. Anna and Jozef Gilowie also serve smorgasbord style foods in a small dining area in the store, which is open from 11 A.M. to 6 P.M. Other hours: Monday through Saturday, 7 A.M. to 10 P.M.; Sunday, 9 A.M. to 8 P.M. No credit cards.

Gifts

Petrov Enterprises, *6203 W. Montrose Avenue, Chicago, (312) 545-2277.* Offering the finest Polish, Yugoslav, German, and Austrian crystal and imported Italian figurines to the public for wholesale prices. Hours: Monday through Saturday, 9:30 A.M. to 6 P.M.

Bakeries

Dunajec Bakery and Delicatessen, *3601 S. Paulina, Chicago, (312) 247-4175, and 5060 S. Archer, Chicago, (312) 585-9611.* Homemade bakery and Polish deli foods; sausages, pierogi, etc. Hours: Tuesday through Friday, 7 A.M. to 4 P.M.; Saturday, 7 A.M. to 3 P.M. Closed on Sunday and Monday.

Gorski Bakery and Deli, *5222 W. Diversey, Chicago, (312) 736-0805.* Roman Gorski, proprietor. The sausages are not homemade. Hours: Monday through Saturday, 6 A.M. to 9 P.M.; Sunday, 8 A.M. to 4 P.M. No credit cards.

Kolatek's Bakery, *5405 S. Kedzie, Chicago, (312) 737-2113.* Old fashioned South Side Polish bakery where the layer cakes, fruit slices, cookies and breads, are all homemade. Hours: Monday through Friday, 5 A.M. to 8 P.M.; Saturday, 5 A.M. to 6 P.M.; Sunday, 9 A.M. to 2:30 P.M. No credit cards.

Polish Language Broadcasting

WCEV-1450 AM, with offices in Chicago, is a foreign-language station owned by Migala Communications. WCEV ("Chicago's Ethnic

Voice") is a time-sharing station with WXOL, featuring black-oriented programming.

"Voice of Polonia," Host: George Migala, who doubles as the station manager and vice president. Migala invented the concept of ethnic radio by introducing this format to Chicago in 1979. Migala and his wife Slawa first aired the "Voice of Polonia," in 1950 as an independent producer at WLEY-FM, 107.01 in Chicago. It is the longest running daily Polish radio program in the city. Mondays through Thursday, 4:30 P.M. to 6:00 P.M.; Saturday 4:05 P.M. to 6:00 P.M.

"Young Polonia," Host: Diana Maria Migala. Monday through Friday, 4:30 P.M. to 6:00 P.M.; Saturday 4:05 P.M. to 6:00 P.M.

"World in Music," Host: Lucyna Migala. Tuesdays, 6:05 P.M. to 6:45 P.M. and Thursdays, 6:05 P.M. to 6:35 P.M.

"Poland In Music and Song," Host: Adam Grzegorzewski. Mondays and Wednesdays, 6:30 P.M. to 7:00 P.M.; Saturdays, 6:05 P.M. to 6:45 P.M.

"Moments in Polish History," Host: Dr. Joseph Migala. Tuesdays, 6:45 P.M. to 7:00 P.M.

"Words of Life," religious. Fridays, 6:30 P.M. to 7:00 P.M.

"American Czestochowa," religious. Saturdays, 6:45 P.M. to 7:00 P.M.

"Polish Catholic Pastoral Mission," religious. Saturdays, 7:00P.M. to 7:30 P.M.

"Polish Apostleship of Prayer," religious. Saturdays, 7:30 P.M. to 8:00 P.M.

"Polish Voice of the Gospel," religious. Saturdays, 8:05 P.M. to 8:30 P.M.

"Roman Catholic Mass and Polish Apostleship of Prayer," religious. Sundays, 8 A.M. to 9 A.M.

WCEV, Polish Programming

"Polonia Today," Hosts: Chet and Delores Schafer, Mondays, 3:30 P.M. to 4:30 P.M.

"Patrick Henry Polka Show," Host: Patrick Henry Cukierka, Tuesdays and Wednesdays, 3:30 P.M. to 4:30 P.M. and Sundays, 2:05 P.M. to 3:00 P.M.

"Johny Hyzny Show," Hosts: Johny and Lorrie Hyzny, Thursdays, 3:05 P.M. to 4:30 P.M.

"Eddie Blazonczyk Polka Show," Hosts: Eddie and Tish Blazonczyk, Fridays, 3:05 P.M. to 4:30 P.M.

"Bob Maczko's Polka Program," Host: Bob Maczko, Sundays, 10:05 A.M. to 10:30 A.M.

"Polka Hit Parade," Hosts: Stas Bulanda & Chet Schafer, Sundays, 10:30 A.M. to 11:30 A.M.

"Happy Hearts Polka Show," Host: Joe Walega, Sundays, 11:30 A.M. to 12:00 P.M.

"Noon Time Polkas," Host: Frank Samoraj, Sunday, 12:05 P.M. to 1:00 P.M.

"Chet Schafer Show," Host: Chet & Delores Schafer, Sundays, 1:05 P.M. to 2:00 P.M.

"International Polka Association Show," Host: Leon Kozicki, Sundays, 4:05 P.M. to 4:30 P.M.

"Li'l Wally Radio Show," Host: Walter 'Maly Wladziu' Jagiello, Sundays, 4:30 P.M. to 5:30 P.M.

WSBC and WEDC-WCRW

WSBC, 1240 AM and WEDC-WCRW are two of the last "time sharing" stations in Chicago. Founded in 1925 by Joel Silverstein, owner of the World Storage and Battery Company (hence the call letters, WSBC), the station features a variety of ethnic programming serving the Polish, Asian, and Hispanic communities.

"The Bob Lewandowski Program," Host: Bob Lewandowski, a pioneer to Chicago ethnic broadcasting, whose career dates back to 1963. Lewandowski, who emigrated to the U.S. in 1944, interviews guests, plays some music, and discusses the latest news from Poland. His radio program airs Monday through Friday, from 7:00 A.M.-8:30 A.M. Mr. Lewandowski can also be seen on WCIU-TV, Channel 26, on Sundays from 5:00 P.M. to 5:30 P.M.

"Zlobin-Rylski Program," Sundays, from 3:00 P.M. to 3:30 P.M.

"Li'l Richard Polka Show," Sundays at 7:30 A.M.

Father Justin Polish Rosary Catholic Program. Religious. Aired at 9 P.M. on Saturdays.

WEDC, 1240 AM

"Sunshine Hour," (*Godzina Sloneczna*), formerly hosted by the late Lidia Pucinski, mother of former 41st Ward Alderman Roman Pucinski. Aired daily from 8:30 A.M. to 9:30 A.M.

WPNA, 1490 AM

"Muzyka Noca," Host: Helena Wantuch, Tuesday through Saturday, midnight to 1 A.M.

"Nocne Muzykowanie," Host: S. Zukowski, Tuesday through Saturday, 1 A.M. to 2 A.M.

"Nocny Pan," Host: Jarek Obrecki, 2 A.M. to 6 A.M. weekdays.

"Muzyka Na Dzien Dobry," Host: Marek Kulsiewicz, Thursdays, 6:00 A.M. to 6:30 A.M.; 6 A.M. to 7 A.M., Monday, Tuesday, Wednesday, Friday.

"Poznaj Swiat," Host: S. Tomczynski, Thursdays, 6:30 A.M. to 7:00 A.M.

"Morning Drive Time Polka," Host: Chet Gulinski, 7 A.M. to 10 A.M. weekdays.

"Wokol Nas," Host: Barbara Oralowska, 2:00 P.M. to 3:00 P.M. weekdays.

"O Nas, Ola Nas," Host: Sylwester Skora, 3:00 P.M. to 4:00 P.M. weekdays.

"Slowo I Piesn," Host: Sophia Boris, 4:00 P.M. to 5:00 P.M., weekdays.

"Otwarty Mikrofon," Host: Lucia Sliwa, 5:00 P.M. to 7:00 P.M. weekdays.

"Program Pol Zartem, Pol Serio," Hosts: Andrzej Szopa and Barbara Choroszy. 7:00 P.M. to 7:30 P.M., weekdays.

"Program Rozmaitosci," Host: Marian Czeriecki, 7:30 P.M. to 8:00 P.M. daily.

"Poznaj Swiat," Host: Stefan Tomczynski, Mondays, 8 P.M. to 9 P.M.

"Turystycny Wademecum," Host: Helena Wantuch, Wednesdays, 8 P.M. to 9 P.M.

"Jackowo Story," Host: Zofia Mierzynska-Miszczak, Thursdays, 8 P.M. to 9 P.M.

"Program Na Serio," Hosts: Z. Banas, & B. Lanko, 9 P.M. to 11 P.M. weekdays.

"Studio M," Adriana Petri & Daniel Malinowski, weekdays, 11 P.M. to midnight.

"Johnie Baski Polka Show," Host: Johny Baski, Saturdays, 6:30 A.M. to 7 A.M.

"Eddie Blazonczyk Polka Show," Host: Eddie Blazonczyk, Saturdays, 1 P.M. to 2 P.M.; Sundays noon to 1 P.M.

"Emilie's Sunshine Polka Show," Saturdays, 2:00 P.M. to 2:30 P.M.

"Lucy's Sunshine Polka Show," Saturdays, 2:30 P.M. to 3:00 P.M.

"Your Polish Heritage," Host: Chris Gulinski, Sundays, 8:00 A.M. to 8:30 A.M.

"Chet Gulinski Polka Show," Host: Chet Gulinski, Sundays, 10 A.M. to noon.

"Zwiazek Podhalan," Hosts: Joe Bafia, & Andrew Gendlek, who report on the news from the Polish Highlands, and play music from that region of the country. Hours: Sundays: 1:30 P.M. to 2:30 P.M.

"Cultural Radio Magazine," Host: Dr. W. Wierzewski, Sundays, 2:30 P.M. to 3:00 P.M.

"Polish Panorama," Host: Stan Lobodzinski, Sundays, 3 P.M. to 4 P.M.

"Red Poppies," Host: Feliks Konarski, Sundays, 4:00 P.M. to 4:30 P.M.

chapter eight

Jewish Chicago

History and Settlement

Crowded, chaotic, noisy and dirty—such are the fading images of the Maxwell Street open air market that lingers in the shadow of the tall buildings on the West Side. You recall this peculiar slice of ethnic culture on Sunday mornings, when the shabby glory of those former times comes alive once more. It is the world's largest flea market, where Gold Coast Yuppie rubs elbows with the hustlers and con men eager to make a few bucks selling hub caps, bootlegged video movies, and the kitchen sink. The bark of the carnival huckster and flimflam man fill the early morning air as the short order cooks grill Polish sausage and the famous Maxwell Street pork chop for the Sabbath bargain hunters.

Maxwell Street: a symbol of Chicago's past vitality and Jewish immigrant culture is about to be swallowed by the encroaching University of Illinois, Chicago, campus which displaced that Italian and Greek quarter in the early 1960s. Maxwell Street has survived a hundred years, but now its character—its essential *shtetl* character—is imperiled by what urban planners glowingly refer to as progress.

The old Maxwell Street ghetto, bounded by Canal, Halsted, Polk and 15th streets, was densely populated by Eastern European Jews who lived in one- and two-story tenements in the back of Kosher meat markets and in second-hand furniture stores. Until 1923, when the city enacted stiff regulatory laws, real estate promoters would capitalize on the zoning loopholes by constructing two houses on one lot. Two, three, sometimes four families would be packed into these flimsy wooden lean-tos seemingly held together by bailing wire and tar paper.

For the grandparents of longtime Chicagoan Nathan Kaplan, their destiny was intertwined with that of thousands of other Eastern European Jews who settled Maxwell Street from the 1880s until the outbreak of World War I. The odyssey began in the tiny village of Bransk in Poland. "Myths of the new world stirred dreams," Kaplan writes in his family genealogy. "My grandparents, parents, aunts and uncles were part of the historic European migration that poured into the U.S. between 1881 and 1923. The Jewish immigration differed from that of other Europeans in one major respect: Jews turned their backs on the land of their origin. Other Europeans came, but not all intended to stay. One of every three returned. Ninety-five out of a hundred Jewish arrivals stayed. The Orthodox Jews perceived America as a heathen country where Judaism would be endangered. Apparently my grandparents, though firm believers, did not have such fears."

Grandmother Shifrasrah Brinsky and Grandfather Nathan Brinsky, instilled with a sense of awakening and guided by their faith in the God of Abraham, settled on Maxwell Street. The Eastern European Jews faced the usual poverty, economic despair and ethno-religious prejudices previously reserved for the Irish Catholics and Italians. The earliest arriving Jews came from the Germanic corridor—Prussia, Austria, Bohemia, and sections of modern-day Poland. The growth of the Jewish population in Chicago was spared by historic oppression aimed against Jews in their native lands. By 1900 the Yiddish-speaking Jews outnumbered the earlier arriving German Jews, whose presence in Chicago was noted as early as 1832—five years before Chicago's incorporation. In 1845, the first Yom Kippur services were conducted above a storefront at the southwest corner of Wells and Lake streets. A year later the "Jewish Burial Society" was organized to provide for the dead. They purchased an acre of ground on the present site of the baseball field in Lincoln Park. This was Chicago's first Jewish cemetery. Within two years a deadly outbreak of Asiatic cholera filled the available plots. This of course only served to discourage future newcomers from settling along the banks of Lake Michigan. As the crisis worsened, community leaders welded together the Kehilath Anshe Mayriu (Congregation of the People of the West) (K.A.M.). In June, 1851, the congregation built the first Jewish synagogue at Clark and Adams—a site now occupied by the Kluczynski Federal Building. By 1857 there were four congregations, but they were bitterly divided along ethnic lines. The Bavarian Jews, still the predominant group at this time, had little regard for their struggling counterparts from Eastern Europe.

Henry Greenebaum, an important figure in early Jewish Chicago objected to the divisiveness of his own people, and wondered what steps might be taken to attain religious and cultural unity. Greenebaum was one of four brothers who arrived here in the midst of the cholera epidemic.

Greenebaum belonged to the Bavarian K.A.M. group, but vocalized his opposition to its exclusionary policies by joining the B'Nai Sholom Congregation. He served as the group's first secretary until the K.A.M. threatened him with expulsion. Young Greenebaum was vociferous in his criticisms. "And another thing, why so much concern about cemeteries? Why not provide for the living?" So, in 1857, he founded the first B'nai B'rith lodge—Number 33—proclaimed a new era of cooperation between peoples as they united for common cause. "Here," Greenebaum exclaimed, "some of the best minds of German and Polish Jews joined hands to remove miserable provincial barriers existing in Chicago." In 1856 Greenebaum's organizational genius was rewarded with election to the Chicago City Council. He became the first Jewish alderman, representing the old Sixth Ward.

A close friend of Stephen A. Douglas, Greenebaum was an ardent Unionist during the Civil War. He was one of the notable men in Illinois, not only in the political realm, but in the world of finance as well. When his bank smoldered in ruins during the Chicago Fire, he informed his depositors that they could come and receive their money once the vaults cooled down. It was an uncommon expression of charity and good will at a time of widespread looting and rapacity, when the civil authorities were hard put to safeguard the city.

The expansion of the Jewish community after the great fire of 1871 was steady if not spectacular. The flames swept away many German-Jewish residences near the downtown business district, forcing many of these people to move farther south along Michigan Avenue, Wabash, and Indiana Avenues. By the 1920s, Washington Park, Kenwood, Hyde Park, and South Shore were heavily populated by prosperous German Jews. The University of Chicago, located in staid, austere Hyde Park, benefited from the warm financial support of such philanthropists from the retail business community as Julius Rosenwald and Leon Mandel. In science and the humanities Albert Michaelson (physics), Saul Bellow (literature), and Milton Friedman (economics) won Nobel prizes during their tenure at the University of Chicago. Professor Michaelson won the coveted Nobel Prize in 1907 for his studies of light, which contributed to Albert Einstein's theory of relativity. Bellow, who was actually born in Lachine, Quebec, a suburb of Montreal, captured the humorous and touching sides of Jewish life in Chicago in the *Adventures of Augie March* (1953). By the time he was eight years old young Bellow was fluent in French,

English, Yiddish, and Hebrew. His Nobel Prize came in 1976, for *Humboldt's Gift.* Economist Friedman joined the University of Chicago faculty in 1946. He was awarded a Nobel Prize in 1976 for "achievements in the fields of consumption analysis, monetary history, and theory, and for his demonstration of the complexity of stabilization policy."

Reflecting the outward movement from the central city, the K.A.M. Congregation relocated from downtown to Indiana and 26th Streets, the first of seven moves in its long and storied history. The South Side German Jews were prosperous, upscale and innovative. Despite claims to the contrary, they identified more closely with German culture than with the strict Orthodoxy practiced by the Eastern Europeans who lived in the Maxwell Street ghetto.

The assimilated German Jews published several newspapers, notably the *Jewish Advocate,* a weekly journal devoted to social issues and progressive Judaism. In 1880 the cornerstone for what was to become the future home of Michael Reese Hospital was laid at 29th and Ellis streets on the South Side.

The first Jewish hospital was erected at Schiller and Goethe streets on the North Side in 1868, through the efforts of the Hebrew Relief Association. When the facility was reduced to a pile of smoldering rubble in the 1871 fire, the relatives of Michael Reese set out to obtain a desirable site location on the South Side. Michael Reese, oddly enough, never set foot in Chicago. He made his fortune in the California Gold Rush, and willed his estate to his civic-minded kin back in Chicago for worthy causes. The opening of the Michael Reese Hospital in 1882 on the site of the old Sherman Stockyards marked the beginning of an era of unbridled scientific accomplishment and service to the community. By the 1940s, the prestigious facility, with its 718 beds, had become the largest voluntary hospital in the Chicago area. However, much of the surrounding neighborhood became engulfed in urban blight in the 1960s. Hospital administrators were forced to make a hard decision about their future role in the community. The choice boiled down to denying the low-income residents essential medical services, or re-committing the available resources in their familiar urban setting. The planning board hired a professional staff to oversee a neighborhood expansion project, and today Michael Reese remains one of Chicago's major medical centers, even though the German Jewish "Golden Ghetto" is no more.

Before 1880 the Eastern European Jews represented only a very small fraction of the city's Jewish population. The handful of Russian Jews who lived in Chicago before 1871 resided in an area near Federal and Harrison streets. The uprooting caused by the Chicago Fire and the period of civic rebuilding that followed pushed these people to the west of the central business district, and the Germans to the South Side. Events taking shape on the continent spurred a tide of immigration that was to last a full fifty years (1880–1930).

Following the assassination of Czar Alexander II in 1881, the Russian government instituted a brutal crackdown against the Jews, who were falsely accused of subversive activity. The Jews were charged with the systematic murder of Christian children during the festival of Pesach or Passover. The "pogrom"—A Russian word meaning devastation—was an invention of the czarist government to divert political and social discontent from existing conditions toward a convenient scapegoat—the Jew. The suppression of Jewish culture and the murder of thousands of peasants occurred at a time of rising Jewish nationalism.

The movement to create a Jewish homeland of Zion was outlined by Leo Pinsker (1821–91) in Russia and by Theodor Herzl in Austria. The Zionist movement ultimately led to the creation of the modern state of Israel in 1948, but not before decades of persecution at the hands of the host governments of Europe and Russia. Driven from their homelands with only the shirts on their backs and whatever could be carried in a torn and tattered valise, thousands of Russian and Polish Jews flooded into the near West Side of Chicago, displacing many Germans and Irish who once lived there. The Jewish ghetto encompassed much of the area between Canal and Halsted streets—the Maxwell Street market—which was an embodiment of Russian Poland. Yiddish was spoken here, and the members of the community who subscribed to the Orthodox and Conservative movements of Judaism were free to worship as they pleased. Hebrew schools and Yiddish theaters were organized. Forty Orthodox synagogues were all within walking distance of the heart of the ghetto—the intersection of Halsted and Maxwell Street. By the early 1910s, it was estimated that 50,000 Eastern European Jews lived in close proximity to their houses of worship on the West Side.

Year	Chicago Population	Jewish Population	Percentage
1880	503,185	10,000	2.0
1900	1,698,575	75,000	4.5
1910	2,185,283	135,000	6.0
1920	2,701,705	225,000	8.0

The "ghetto" featured kosher food stores, matzo bakeries, and hundreds of peddler wagons and pushcarts, where down-and-out entrepreneurs tried to hustle a few cents selling fruit and vegetables in the muddy streets. Above the storefronts of the dilapidated wooden tenements hundreds of

Jews worked in the most squalid conditions, manufacturing garments for all Chicagoans. The city's clothing industry quickly grew into a $50,000,000 business by 1900. Jews accounted for 68.6 percent of all Chicago tailors in 1910, but they earned less than $8 a week and were often required to put in 12 to 18 hours a day. The famous clothing strike against Hart, Schaffner, and Marx and other large clothiers in September, 1910, capped off an era of growing disenchantment among these laboring classes. The strike was spearheaded by Sidney Hillman, Jacob Potofsky, and Bessie Abramovitz, who organized Jewish workers against a powerful Jewish manufacturing concern—a phenomenon in those days when labor and capital represented different races, nationalities and religions. Under the leadership of Hillman and Abramovitz—who were later wed—the newly organized Amalgamated Clothing Workers Union of America won important concessions from management, concessions which led to a better standard of living for the men and women who toiled into the night at the Maxwell Street sweatshops.

Maxwell Street will soon exist only in the collective memories of the people who earned their livelihood there. In its heyday, the street represented the trappings of free enterprise. The liveliest debate in town was not in "Bug House" Square, where orange crate orators espoused socialism, but between buyer and seller haggling over the price of a pair of knickers on Sunday morning at Maxwell and Halsted. It was a congested, overcrowded, reeking tenement. Many of the residential dwellings lacked proper ventilation, plumbing, and in some cases, a bathtub or commode. By 1900 the Jewish population strained at the seams. In his 1952 survey of economic conditions in Chicago, Erich Rosenthal of Queens College in New York estimated that 50 percent of the Russian Jewish immigrants lived in ghetto conditions by 1915. The community was replete with gambling dens, houses of ill repute, and low cesspools of vice—which coexisted alongside synagogues and the *beth hamedrash,* or house of learning. Along Morgan and Green streets on the near West Side, Mike "de Pike" Heitler procured women of easy virtue, dice, liquor, and even cocaine, while paying a fealty to the Irish police captains who commanded the Des Plaines Street District. The rise of the Jewish gangster after the turn of the century—Ike Bloom (née Gitelson), Jack Guzik, Davey Miller and Samuel "Nails" Morton—was an alarming, but not so surprising, development. The ghetto was tough and mean, and fostered lawlessness in varying degrees when the teachings of the rabbi fell on deaf ears. Some, like Morton and Miller, were roguish Robin Hoods, interested to a certain extent in the welfare of their own people. Miller operated a restaurant and gym, and could always be counted on to come to the aid of elderly Jews who were attacked and beaten in Douglas Park by gangs of young hooligans. Nails Morton was another product of Maxwell Street. During World War I he was awarded the Croix de Guerre after leading a raiding party "over-the-top" against a trench of German soldiers who had pinned down an entire company of American soldiers. Morton flushed them out, but met an untimely death several years later on the Lincoln Park bridle path, when his horse kicked him to death. Gangsters like Heitler, Bloom, and Guzik were vicious white slave traffickers who lacked the élan of Davey Miller. The Jewish *Courier,* founded in 1887 as a weekly (but later converted to a daily sheet), cautioned its readers to remain vigilant against this class of men and the "moral filth" of the ghetto.

After 1905 overcrowding and a changing economic picture resulted in an exodus from Maxwell Street for the safer, more pleasant residential neighborhoods of the South Side, and the Douglas Park-Lawndale communities farther west. Douglas Boulevard, fronting a fully landscaped park designed and laid out by architect William LeBaron Jenney in 1880, became the Jewish "Main Street" by the 1920s. At first the German and Irish landlords refused to rent apartment flats to the Jews, but through their sheer numbers and the availability of low-cost mortgages, Lawndale became a predominantly Jewish neighborhood by 1920. The Congregation Ansae Kneseth Israel was opened on Douglas Boulevard in 1913. It soon became known as the "Russian Shul" for the many Eastern European Jewish families that worshipped there. The rabbi of this temple was Ephraim Epstein, who rescued many Jewish exiles from Europe shortly before the outbreak of World War II. Epstein served his temple from 1876–1960.

By 1927, there were more than 125 Jewish congregations scattered across the city. About 100 were Orthodox; the rest were Conservative or Reform. Yiddish newspapers were founded to emphasize the principles of Orthodox life in the U.S., but increasingly the language underwent a subtle transformation, until a distinct Americanized Yiddish emerged. No doubt the change was a consequence of the desire among older Jewish residents of Chicago that the newer arrivals become more quickly assimilated. In a remarkably short time, the immigrants and their children absorbed American customs and participated directly in American institutions.

No longer excluded from the political process, the Jews of Lawndale exerted considerable influence at City Hall through their benefactors Mike and Moe Rosenberg, the 1920s patron saints of the 24th Ward Democratic machine. The brothers owned a junkyard and an iron metal company, but their rightful bailiwick was Chicago politics. The Rosenbergs pushed the selection of Governor Henry Horner in 1933, no small achievement

during those highly partisan times. A decade earlier, the brothers succeeded in placing 28-year-old Jacob Arvey in the alderman's chair.

Henry Horner, a distinguished probate judge who sat on the bench from
1914 to 1932, earned a reputation as Cook County's last "professional
honest man." His compassion for widows, orphans, and the city's down-
and-out was well known in legal circles. Horner was the grandson of one
of Chicago's original Jewish settlers. In 1841, a young man, guided by
ambition and instilled with the kind of forward-thinking outlook on life
that turned dreams into reality, arrived in frontier Chicago. Harry Horner
laid the foundation for what was to become one of the city's largest
wholesale grocery firms. He was also one of the founding members of the
Chicago Board of Trade, and was well known among the old-timers until
his illustrious grandson dwarfed his accomplishments a generation later
in the political arena.

The generation of 1848 produced a number of business leaders less
inclined to sully their reputations in the back alleys of Chicago politics.
In the years that followed, German-Jewish parents encouraged their sons
to pursue careers in law, finance, and the retail trade. Emanuel, Leon,
and Simon Mandel founded a State Street department store that anchored
the downtown shopping district for many years. Morris Selz and Sigmund
Florsheim began their respective footwear businesses in Chicago.

Chicago's Jews were never a nationalistic people in the sense that the
Germans were. The Russian, Polish, and Hungarian Jews who came later
shared a common religious bond, and also a keen motivation to prosper
within their chosen fields. Such was the case with the Rosenbergs, who
succeeded in placing 28-year-old Jacob Arvey in the alderman's chair in
the 1920s. Through the sheer force of his personality, Arvey, a Rosenberg
protégé, became the floor leader of the city council and chairman of the
finance committee. Arvey was a fixture in Chicago politics for many
years, and might have become governor himself if not for the fact that the
political sachems in the hall considered it politically expedient to avoid
having one Jew in the mayor's office and another in the state house. To
this day, there has not been a Jewish mayor of Chicago, though LaSalle
Street businessman Bernard Epton waged an unsuccessful campaign
against the late Mayor Harold Washington in 1987.

Mike Rosenberg served as 24th Ward committeeman and trustee of the
Sanitary District until his death in 1928. Brother Moe succeeded him, and
went on to reshape the Democratic Party into the modern "machine" that
endured in one form or another until the 1980s. Moe spent money like a
drunken sailor in order to promote the election of friendly judges. He
supported an ally from the Czech-Bohemian neighborhood, Anton J.
Cermak, as the next mayor in 1931. Later, Moe Rosenberg outlined his

strategy to a Congressional subcommittee that was investigating a powerful crony of his, utility magnate Samuel Insull: "We were not only looking to those judicial elections, to have Cermak become leader, but then we were looking to put Cermak in the mayor's chair, which we did."

Greater Lawndale remained a bustling Jewish community well into the 1940s, when it began to undergo profound racial changes. Erich Rosenthal estimated that 102,470 Jews resided here in 1940, but the numbers dropped by nearly half just six years later. The expansion of the black community and the desire of many second- and third-generation Jews to leap-frog to the far North Side communities of Albany Park and Rogers Park, stripped the Lawndale community of its Jewish identity. The opening of the Ravenswood elevated line in 1907, and the Kedzie trolley seven years later, spurred the growth of Albany Park, annexed to the city when much of the property was farmland. Near the principal business district at Lawrence and Kedzie, thousands of transplanted Polish and Russian Jews from Lawndale and the greater West Side purchased two- and three-story flats and worshipped at the Orthodox, Reform, and Conservative synagogues that served the community's needs. Jewish business from Lawndale were clustered along Lawrence Avenue between Pulaski and Kedzie for many years. By 1945, the Jewish population of Albany Park topped out at 35,000, but the area went into a slow decline, hastening the exodus to neighborhoods farther north. In the late 1960s and early 1970s, Asian Indians, Greeks, and Arabs began buying up commercial property. By 1979, there were only 13,000 Jews counted in Albany Park, most of them retired pensioners and senior citizens. Today Chicago's Jewish community numbers some 240,000, but is widely scattered across the metropolitan area and into the suburbs and collar counties. The largest concentration can be found in West Rogers Park between Kedzie, Western, Peterson and Howard streets, where a number of synagogues, bakeries, book stores, restaurants, and fraternal associations keep alive the sense of community that seems to diminish each year. West Rogers Park, like so many other diverse Chicago neighborhoods, is not restricted to just one group. Increasingly, the Jewish population is experiencing slow decline, while the Indian, Assyrian, and Asian presence is slowly transforming the composition of the area. Devon Avenue, from Ridge to California, resembles a miniature United Nations. Indicative of the rapidly changing patterns of settlement was the decision on the part of the Jewish community to sell Temple Mizpah (built at 1615 Morse in 1924) to the Koreans, who converted the facility into the Korean Presbyterian Church. Where did they all go? To Skokie, Lincolnwood, and the North Shore suburbs for the most part. By 1975, 40,000 of Skokie's 70,000 inhabitants were Jewish. The suburbanization of Chicago Jewry continues into the 1990s.

Many of Chicago's newer Jewish residents emigrated from Russia to escape Soviet discrimination and religious repression. The Soviet government listed their nationality as Jewish rather than Russian on their passports. With the doors of opportunity slamming shut in their face, the Soviet Jews who were fortunate enough to secure exist visas very often arrived in Chicago via the Joint Jewish Distribution Committee in Vienna. From there to Rome, and finally Chicago, where Rogers Park, adjacent Skokie, and parts of Des Plaines, Palatine, Wheeling, and Buffalo Grove have become "ports of entry." Some 15,000 Soviet Jews have poured into Chicago in recent years. Many have found well-paying jobs in the industrial sector, and have saved up for the day when they can make their first down payment on a home in the quiet residential suburbs. Many older Jewish residents bemoan a corresponding loss of culture and tradition, perhaps forgetting that the younger generations often reassert their ancestral identities within the boundaries of the American value system.

Getting There: The Howard Street elevated line links downtown with the Rogers Park community. The el makes eight scheduled stops between Foster and Howard Street (at the city limit). The Devon (#155) bus begins at the Morse Avenue elevated stop. Or you can transfer to the Touhy Avenue (#290) bus at Howard Avenue in Evanston. Both lines connect with West Rogers Park.

Ethnic Museum, Historical Society, Theatre and Film

The Spertus Museum of Judaica, *618 S. Michigan Avenue, Chicago, (312) 922-9012.* Chicago's Spertus Museum teaches us the history of the Jewish people through traveling exhibition, workshops, paintings, sculpture, costumes, and religious artifacts on permanent display. Founded in 1925 for the purpose of providing recent high school graduates with a basic program on Judaic studies, the museum was renamed in honor of Maurice and Herman Spertus in 1970. These gentlemen were the world's largest manufacturers of retail and wood frame pictures. Now in its seventh decade, the Spertus College of Judaica is an accredited graduate institution and a major learning resource center in the Midwest, offering classes in religious philosophy, Hebrew and Yiddish art, music, and culture. The Norman and Helen Asher Library on the fifth floor houses one of the great collection of Judaica in the nation, with over 70,000 volumes, back periodicals, musical collections, video, and the Chicagoland Jewish Archives, which are available to serious researchers.

The Bernard and Rochelle Zell Holocaust Memorial on the first floor of the museum relates the history of the Nazi persecution (1933–1945) through surviving artifacts, photographic documentation, and interesting sidelights into this darkest period of the human experience. The six pillars at the entrance record the names of Holocaust victims whose families reside in the Chicago area. The Paul and Gabriella Rosenbaum Artifact Center is considered to be a "hands-on" innovator in children's museum education, offering many classes and workshops for youngsters stressing the spiritual values of Jewish holidays. During the Hanukkah season, for example, children over the age of seven are taught how to construct menorahs. Through this kind of direct participation, they learn the significance of the holiday, which dates back to 165 B.C. (Before Common Era), when a small army of Jews led by Maccabees reclaimed the second temple after it had been pillaged by the Syrian Greeks. With only a small jar of pure oil left behind, the Jews lit their menorah. According to legend, the lamps remained lit for a period of eight days. The miracle is celebrated by the Jewish people during the last week of December. Admission: adults, $3.50; children, $2.00. Spertus memberships are available in increments of $30, $40, $50, $100, $500, and $1,000. Museum hours Sunday–Thursday, 10 A.M. to 5 P.M.; Friday, 10 A.M. to 3 P.M.; closed Saturday. Artifact Center hours: Sunday–Thursday, 10 A.M. to 5 P.M.; Friday, 10 A.M. to 3 P.M.; closed Saturday. Library hours: Monday through Thursday, 9:00 A.M. to 6:15 P.M.; Friday, 9 A.M. to 3 P.M. (2:30 P.M. in winter); and Sunday, 11 A.M. to 5 P.M. *Recommended.*

Chicago Jewish Historical Society, *618 S. Michigan Avenue, Chicago, (312) 663-5634.* Located on the second floor of the Spertus Museum, the Chicago Jewish Historical Society is interested in neighborhood settlement, the preservation of local archives and issues of historical importance to the Jewish community. The Society sponsors a series of bus tours during the summer (see Annual Events), conducts monthly meetings, publishes a bimonthly periodical, and bestows a $1,000 cash prize each year for the outstanding published monograph dealing with an aspect of Chicago Jewish history. Recently, the Jewish Historical Society reissued Hyman L. Meites 1924 book a *History of the Jews in Chicago,* in a joint venture with Wellington Publishing. The cost of membership is $15 (and up) for individuals, and $25 for families.

National Jewish Theater (Mayer Kaplan Jewish Community Center), *5050 W. Church Street, Skokie.* A performing arts center featuring the works of Jewish playwrights, with themes of Jewish community. Four plays are given each year between October 2 and late June in a subscription series that has previously included such critically acclaimed presentations as *The Golem, Minnie's Boys* (a reverent look at the life of the Marx brothers), and *The Dybbuk*. Performances are given Wednesday, Thursday, Saturday, and Sunday afternoons at the 256-seat auditorium in the Mayer Kaplan JCC. It is important to know that the plays are performed in English, not Yiddish. Ticket prices range from $17 to $24. To purchase season tickets, call (708) 675-5070. Credit cards accepted.

Jewish Film Foundation, *6025 Christiana, Chicago, (312) 588-2763.* The JFF arranges special screenings of independent documentaries and dramatic films of special Jewish interest, at various commercial theaters throughout Chicago. These films would probably not reach a wider suburban audience if they were limited exclusively to the city's "art houses," like the Music Box at 3733 Southport Avenue, or the Fine Arts Theatre, 410 S. Michigan Avenue, in Chicago. JFF sponsors two exhibitions a year. While there is no membership or enrollment procedure, persons interested in being included on the mailing list are encouraged to contact Beverly Siegal at (312) 588-2763.

Jewish Community Centers of Chicago

The seven neighborhood Jewish Community Centers of Chicago promote Jewish values in American life through a broad spectrum of educational, cultural, social and athletic programs available to individuals, families, and groups. Each center is an independent Group Services Agency, with its own calendar of special events that may include dramatic presentations, lectures, classes, physical fitness, self-help sessions, counseling, child care, and various recreational programs. For more information, contact the appropriate center or the central offices of the Jewish Federation of Chicago, at 1 S. Franklin Street, Chicago, Ill., 60606, or call (312) 346-6700.

Bernard Horwich JCC, *3003 W. Touhy Avenue, Chicago, IL, 60645, (312) 761-9100.*

Mayer Kaplan JCC, *5050 Church Street, Skokie, IL, 60077, (708) 675-2200.*

Florence G. Heller JCC, *524 W. Melrose Street, Chicago, IL, 60657. (312) 871-6780.*

North Suburban JCC, *633 Skokie Boulevard, Northbrook, IL, 60062. (708) 205-9480.*

Northwest Suburban JCC, *Jacob Duman Jewish Community Building, 1250 Radcliffe Road, Buffalo Grove, IL, 60089. (708) 392-7411.*

Anita M. Stone JCC, *18600 Governor's Highway, Flossmoor, IL, 60422. (708) 799-7650.*

B'Nai Zion Senior Adult CJE-JCC Center (Rogers Park), *6759 N. Greenview Avenue, Chicago, (312) 764-6191.*

Historic Places

Adler Planetarium, *1300 S. Lake Shore Drive, Chicago.*   In the 1920s noted Chicago businessman and philanthropist Max Adler traveled to Munich, Germany, with an architect to examine an astronomical exhibit at the Deutsches Museum. When he returned, Adler (a brother-in-law of Julius Rosenwald) went ahead with his plans to construct a museum of astronomy for the benefit of all Chicagoans. The Adler Planetarium was dedicated in his honor in 1930.

The First Synagogue in Illinois *is memorialized on a plaque that is affixed to the new Federal Building on Dearborn Street, between Adams and Jackson and extending to Clark.*   On this site stood the first Jewish house of worship in the state. The plaque was originally dedicated on October 9, 1918, but when the old federal courthouse was razed, it was moved to its present location.

Henry Horner Memorial Monument, *Horner Park: Montrose Avenue and California.*   Dedicated on Oct. 27, 1948 to the memory of the first Jewish governor of Illinois, who died in office in 1940 after serving for eight years. Governor Horner was born in Chicago. He served as a judge on the Cook County Probate Court from 1914–1932, and was elected to the governorship on the strength of President Franklin Roosevelt's coattails. He was in many respects a visionary politician who attempted to shelve partisan causes in order to serve all of the people of Illinois fairly and without bias. For this, he was castigated by members of the Chicago Democratic "machine," who demanded equal control of the patronage and spoils in return for their continued support.

The monument to Horner was authorized by an act of the legislature in 1942, and at the formal dedication ceremony, famed Illinois poet Carl Sandburg delivered the keynote address.

Sidney Hillman Center of the Amalgamated Clothing Workers of America, *333 S. Ashland Boulevard, Chicago.* A Russian-born Jew, Sidney Hillman was one of the founders of the CIO. He served as the president of the union from 1914 until his death in 1946, and was actively involved when the CIO split with the AF of L. During World War II, Hillman was the number-two man in the War Production Board. The bust of this famous Chicagoan stands in the reception room of the Ashland Boulevard center. It was sculpted by Jo Davidson.

Lessing Monument, *located in the Rose Garden of Washington Park, 57th Street and Cottage Grove Avenue, Chicago.* Gotthold Ephraim Lessing was not Jewish, but this German writer who lived during the great Enlightenment did much to help the plight of 18th century Jews through such published works as *Nathan the Wise.* His contributions were a factor in the emancipation of Jews in Western Europe. The Lessing monument was presented to the city in 1930 by Henry C. Frank.

Museum of Contemporary Art, *237 E. Ontario, Chicago.* One of the more recent additions to the Chicago museum world, the MCA was founded in 1967 by Joseph Shapiro, a Russian Jew who decided to share his vast collection of modern art with the public in a convenient, central location.

Museum of Science and Industry, *57th Street and Lake Shore Drive, Chicago.* The fascinating history of Chicago's most famous public institution dates back to 1893, when it opened as the Fine Arts Building for the World's Columbian Exposition. When the World's Fair closed, the Fine Arts Building became known as the Field Museum, until the collection of natural history artifacts moved to its present location farther north, at Roosevelt Road and Lake Shore Drive. Philanthropist and business tycoon Julius Rosenwald became greatly concerned that this architecturally significant building be preserved for future generations. Rosenwald, who purchased controlling interest in Sears, Roebuck & Company from its founders several decades before, donated $3 million to pay for the renovation of the Fine Arts Building. It was reopened as the Rosenwald Museum of Science and Industry, but the founder was an exceptionally modest man who did not wish to see his name attached to the worthy philanthropic causes he sponsored. The Rosenwald name was quietly dropped. In his lifetime, Chicagoan Julius Rosenwald was person-ally responsible for the construction of 5,357 schools, shops, libraries, and residential homes in 993 counties of the rural South. These projects benefited impoverished southern blacks.

Haym Solomon Monument, *Heald Square.*   Officially known as the George Washington, Robert Morris, Haym Solomon Memorial. Ded-icated on December 15, 1941 to commemorate this 150th anniversary of the ratification of the Bill of Rights, this memorial to our freedom depicts Haym, a Polish Jew who helped finance the revolution, with George Washington and Robert Morris. It is the only statue of Washing-ton in the country where the first president is not standing alone. The base of the statue contains the following inscription, taken from Washington's letter to the rabbis at the Newport, R.I. synagogue. "The government of the U.S., which gives to bigotry no sanction, to perse-cution no assistance, requires only that they who live under its protec-tion should [conduct] themselves as good citizens in giving it on all occasions their effectual support." Solomon died broke at age 45 after contracting a lung disease while he was incarcerated by the British for spying.

Jewish Waldheim Cemetery, *located in southwest suburban Forest Park, between the Des Plaines River on the west, Harlem Avenue on the east, Roosevelt Road on the north, and 16th Street on the south.*   Waldheim is one of the largest burial grounds in the world for people of the Jewish faith. There are roughly 175,000 graves located here, including those of the anarchist lecturer Emma Goldman (buried near the five condemned Haymarket men in the German section), her lover, and the self-styled "King of the Hobos," Dr. Benjamin Reit-man, former Illinois governor Sam Shapiro, theatrical mogul Michael Todd, and Clara Peller, who is well known for her comedy routine in the Wendy's TV commercials of the mid-1980s. The Waldheim cemeteries have always served as a burial ground in one form or another, going back to the time when the Illini and Pottowatomi Indians buried their dead here. The first Jewish interment took place in 1875, according to official re-cords. Located due west of the old Maxwell Street ghetto, a trip to the cemetery was an arduous all-day journey before the Metropolitan Ele-vated constructed a "funeral car" route out of the city in 1914. For twenty years, these customized train cars conveyed coffins and mourners to Waldheim, until they were put out of public service. These railroad cars were later used as examination rooms for motormen.

Selected Annual Events and Celebrations

"Yom Ha'Atzmaut," annual celebration of the founding of Israel in 1948. The community-wide observance at Orchestra Hall, 220 S. Michigan Avenue, Chicago, is sponsored by the Jewish Community Relations Council of the United Fund, and the Chicago Zionist Foundation, and is held in mid-April. Special performances are given by the Combined Day Schools Choir, Israeli folk dancing troops, and pop singers such as Aric Lavie. More than fifty organizations and synagogues participate in the traditional parade of organizations. The event is free, but admission is by ticket only. Tickets are available through the city's major Jewish organizations. For additional information, please call the JCRC at (312) 346-6700, ext. 7620.

"Yeshiva/Taste of Kosher Chicago," *Labor Day, from noon to 6 P.M., on the grounds of the Yeshiva Women of Hebrew Theological Seminary, 7135 N. Carpenter Road, Skokie, (708) 267-9800.* Meals and "noshes" by Chicagoland kosher restaurants, including La Misada, Selig's, Yonatan's Delectibles, and Chaim's Kosher Catering. Activities for children and adults including pony rides, carnival games, a "moonwalk," and a shopping bazaar featuring Jewish folk art, household items, women's wear, and jewelry. Music and entertainment are free, and so is the admission. Tickets to the food booths and rides may be purchased separately.

"Annual Walk With Israel," fund-raising walkathon held at seven locations in the Chicagoland area to provide financial support for essential humanitarian services in Israel, and for the care and feeding of Jewish refugees emigrating from the Soviet Union and Ethiopia. This event has been held annually the first Sunday in May since 1971, and is a project of the Chicago Jewish Youth Council in cooperation with the Chicago Jewish Community Centers and the Leadership of the Jewish United Fund. For additional information about the walkathon, please call the JUF at (312) 444-2860.

Annual Interfaith Dinner, commemorating the anniversary of the State of Israel, and benefiting the Israeli Red Cross. Sponsored each year since 1966, by the Chicago Chapter, Magen David Adom, and in recent years has been held in the Westin O'Hare Hotel, 6100 River Road, Rosemont. The event is scheduled the second Sunday in June or the first Sunday in July. Banquet, oratory, and musical concert marking the founding of the Jewish state. Ticket prices: $100 per person. For advance reservations and the date, call (312) 465-0664.

Jewish Community Center Hall of Fame Induction Banquet, *held the first Monday afternoon in June at the Grand Ballroom of the Chicago Hilton and Towers, 720 S. Michigan Avenue, Chicago.* Banquet and ceremony honoring Jewish leaders who have demonstrated a commitment to worthy local causes and community service. Special guest speakers and presentations. Luncheon tickets can be purchased for $35. Patron: $35. Benefactor: $175. For tickets and information, contact Arlene Shafton at (312) 761-9100.

Chicago Jewish Historical Society Bus Tours. Throughout the summer months, the Chicago Jewish Historical Society sponsors a series of day-long bus tours on Sundays to significant locations in the city that pertain to the early Jewish settlement of the community. The "Chicago Jewish Roots" guided tour explores the history of Maxwell Street, Lawndale, Humboldt Park, Logan Square, Albany Park, and the Rogers Park neighborhoods. A "Summer Safari" to Northwest Indiana winds its way through Hammond, Michigan City, and Gary, and makes periodic stops at some of the local synagogues. An excursion through the "Southern Suburbs," takes you through Homewood, Olympia Fields, and Flossmoor. The history of the Jewish movement in Chicago and its surrounding suburbs is discussed by local experts, including retired University of Illinois professor, Dr. Irving Cutler. The cost of these tours ranges from $14 to $34 for adult members, and $7 to $29 for children. Advance reservations are always necessary. Please call (312) 663-5634 for information. *Recommended.*

Raoul Wallenberg Humanitarian Awards Ceremony, *at the Spertus Museum, the first Sunday in April.* Swedish diplomat Raoul Wallenberg saved an estimated 100,000 Hungarian Jews from extermination at the hands of the Nazis in the closing months of World War II. This "righteous Gentile," as historians have tagged him, vanished without a trace in 1945, fueling speculation that the occupying Soviet armies arrested him and placed him a gulag deep in the heart of Russia. Wallenberg's achievements are commemorated each year, with the presentation of a series of awards to community figures who best exemplify the spirit of the courageous Swede. A buffet reception follows the awards ceremony and speeches. The awards are sponsored by the Raoul Wallenberg Committee of Chicago. Tickets are $6 per person, and reservations can be made by calling (312) 726-3555.

"A Buffet of Jewish Thought," *a monthly lecture series on contemporary Jewish issues and concerns at the North Conservatory (Lobby Level) of the Hyatt Regency Hotel West Tower, 151 E. Wacker Drive, Chicago.* Sponsored by the Chicago Community Kollel, the thought-provoking lectures are delivered by leading members of the religious and academic community of Chicago and abroad on the last Tuesday of the month from noon to 1:15 P.M. A brunch and buffet follow. Reservations are recommended, and a monetary donation is optional. Audio and video cassettes of the talks are available for purchase ($5.00 for audio cassette, and $12.50 per video plus $1.00 to $2.50 shipping and handling) through the Chicago Community Kollel, 6506 N. California Avenue, Chicago, IL, 60645. For information about upcoming lectures, please call (312) 262-9400.

Jewish Community Center Literary Series, *at the Mayer Kaplan JCC, 5050 W. Church Street, Skokie, (708) 675-2200.* Outstanding lecture series featuring contemporary Jewish-American authors discussing their careers and current projects. The annual literary series is presented on Sunday evenings at 7:30 P.M., in April and May, and is supported in part by the Robert S. Fiffer Memorial Fund, established by his family and friends. In 1991, the featured speakers included Joyce Carol Oates, author of twenty novels and the winner of a National Book Award; Chaim Potok, whose most famous works include *The Chosen, The Book of Lights, My Name Is Asher Lev,* and *In the Beginning.* Mordecai Richler, author of *The Apprenticeship of Duddy Kravitz,* rounded out the 1991 program. Tickets may be purchased at the door or by phone using Visa or Mastercard. Prices range from $12 to $15 per person. For additional information, call (708) 675-2200, or (708) 675-5070 to purchase tickets directly.

"Yom Hashoah" Commemoration (Holocaust Memorial Day), *Anshe Emet Synagogue, 3760 N. Pine Grove, Chicago, (312) 281-1423.* Dramatic readings, memorial service, candle lighting ceremony, and community singing of Yiddish and Hebrew songs marking the events of the Holocaust. Each synagogue in the city pays homage to those who perished in Nazi death camps, but the services at the Anshe Emet Congregation are among the most notable in Chicago. This annual event is open to the public (regardless of religious affiliation) and is held on or about April 10 each year beginning at 7:30 P.M. Admission is always free, and parking is available.

"Dr. K. Jeffrey Kranzler Memorial Concert," *at the Anshe Shalom B'nai Israel Congregation, 540 W. Melrose Street, Chicago, (312) 258-9200.* A different cantor each year presents a program of cantorial renditions, and traditional Yiddish and Israeli folk songs. The concert is held the first Sunday in June at 7:30 P.M. Individual tickets are available for $10 each, or $36 for a group.

Prism Gallery and Performance Center, *June exhibition, 620 Davis Street, Evanston, (708) 475-7500.* A performing arts center and gallery that spotlights ethnic art, music, and culture at different times of the year. In June, Prism features an exhibition of fine arts and craft holography, jewelry, and a mixed theme of artwork by Russian and Jewish artists. Live entertainment by the Chicago Klezmer Ensemble and the singing comedian Allan Lieberman, whose act is a blend of Jewish humor and parody, is featured on the weekend. Lieberman is best known for his satire of the John Denver song, "Thank God I'm a Country Boy." Lieberman croons: "Thank God I'm a Jewish Boy." Admission to the Prism Gallery is free, but a $4–$5 cover charge is applicable for the live entertainment. Paintings, sculpture, holography, textiles, pottery, jewelry and furniture offered for sale. Hours: Tuesday–Wednesday, noon to 7 P.M.; Monday, Thursday, noon to 9 P.M.; Friday–Saturday, noon to midnight. Usually closed on Sundays.

West Rogers Park:
═══════ A Community In Transition ═══════

The West Rogers Park neighborhood on the city's Far North Side has been home to thousands of Jewish families since the end of World War II, when Lawndale underwent significant social and racial changes. Settled in the mid-nineteenth century by the Swedish and Irish, West Rogers Park was a part of the village of Rogers Park until it was annexed to Chicago in 1893. The growth of the community was accentuated by the addition of a Northwestern L line that was constructed in the 1900s, linking downtown Chicago to Wilson Avenue. Bounded by Howard Street and Western Avenue on the north and south, and Kedzie and Peterson on the east and west, it is a quiet residential community revolving around devotion to the family and religious traditions. Orthodox Jewish families began settling West Rogers Park as early as the 1920s, but the numbers increased significantly during the 1950s. By 1963 there were more than 48,000 Jewish residents living in the 50th Ward, represented in the city council by two of the most flamboyant aldermen of the day: Jack Sperling (1955–1973), and Bernard Stone (1973–   ). Both men championed the neighborhood's best interests with only a passing regard for partisan issues.

The growing Jewish community that moved into West Ridge purchased Georgian, ranch, and bungalow style homes and two-flats closest to the nearly two dozen synagogues serving the area; many of them originally located along Maxwell Street and in North Lawndale. On Sabbath days, Orthodox Jews are prohibited from driving, and therefore must walk to the congregation nearest their homes. The Jewish businesses centered near Devon and California avenues are closed on Saturdays, which is the traditional day of prayer and meditation.

West Rogers Park has undergone significant changes in recent years. This highly insulated Jewish community is no longer immune to changing residential patterns and neighborhood displacement which have upset the kind of traditional ethnic boundaries once associated with Chicago. In recent years, dozens of Indian and Pakistani grocery stores, video rental shops, restaurants, and sari stores have opened on the congested Devon Avenue commercial strip between Leavitt Street and California Avenue, which seems to serve as an unofficial "dividing line" between the Middle East and southern Asia. More recently, the Assyrian-American Association, representing Chicago's small but growing Iraqi-Christian community, established headquarters at 1618 W. Devon. They are the city's newest addition to the great melting pot.

The remaining kosher delis, Hebraic bookstores, and small retail shops are concentrated in a narrow strip between California and McCormick Boulevard, but in time even that may change. The Croatian Cultural Center of Chicago occupies a large building at 2845 Devon Avenue, suggesting that the "most cosmopolitan" of Chicago's North Side streets may undergo yet another ethnic transformation.

Shopping and Dining, Chicago and North Suburban

Book Stores

Rosenblum's World of Judaica, Inc., *2906 W. Devon Avenue, Chicago, (312) 262-1700.* Books on Israel and the Holocaust. Judaic video cassettes priced at $29.98 and up. Cantorial and Yiddish music. Games for youngsters. This is the Midwest's largest and oldest distributor of Judaica. Hours: Monday through Thursday, 9 A.M. to 6 P.M.; Friday, 9 A.M. to 4 P.M.; Sunday, 10 A.M. to 4 P.M. Credit cards accepted.

Chicago Hebrew Bookstore, *2942 W. Devon Avenue, Chicago, (312) 973-6636.* Paperback and hardcover books. Tapes, gift items, religious goods. Hours: Monday through Wednesday, 9 A.M. to 6 P.M.; Friday, 9 A.M. to 4 P.M.; Sunday, 10 A.M. to 4 P.M.

Gift Shops and Art Galleries

Hamakor Gallery, *4150 W. Dempster Street, Skokie, (708) 677-4150.* Full-service gift store and art gallery that sells ritual and ceremonial objects, limited edition prints and sculpture by American, Israeli, and other European artists, Jewish books and audio and video cassettes are also available. Periodic art exhibitions scheduled throughout the year. Hours: Monday and Thursday, 10 A.M. to 9 P.M.; Tuesday and Wednesday, 10:00 A.M. to 5:30 P.M.; Friday, 10 A.M. to 4 P.M.; Sunday, 10 A.M. to 5 P.M.

Laverne & Shirley, *281 Waukegan Road, Northfield, (708) 446-4888.* Gift items imported from Israel. Personalized gifts, monogramming, custom artwork and hot stamping. Hours: Tuesday and Wednesday, 10 A.M. to 4 P.M.; Thursday, 10 A.M. to 7 P.M.; Saturday, 9 A.M. to 4 P.M.

Arthur M. Feldman Gallery, *1815 St. Johns Avenue, Highland Park, (708) 432-8858.* Antique and contemporary Judaica; furniture, fine art, bridal registry, and appraisal service available. Hours: Monday through Saturday, 10 A.M. to 5 P.M.; closed Sunday.

Art Gallery Inn, *7514-7520 N. Skokie Boulevard, Skokie, (708) 676-0111.* Artwork, lithographs, and paintings from all over the world. Selected Hebraic items. Auctions scheduled at different times of the year. Hours: Tuesday and Wednesday, 10 A.M. to 5 P.M.; Thursday and Friday, noon to 9 P.M.; Saturday, 10:00 A.M. to 5:30 P.M. Credit cards accepted.

Maya Polsky Gallery, *311 W. Superior, Chicago, (312) 440-0055.* Features the work of contemporary Soviet and Jewish artists, with a heavy emphasis on oil paintings and drawing. Maya Polsky, a Russian émigré, opened her gallery in February, 1990, in River North. Since that time she has featured the first solo exhibition of Alexander Gazhur and Ukrainian painter Vladimir Bovkun. Hours: Tuesday through Friday, 10 A.M. to 5 P.M.

Bakeries

Gitel's Kosher Bakery, *2745 W. Devon Avenue, Chicago, (312) 262-3701.* Breads, wedding cakes, pies and pastry baked under the supervision of the Chicago Rabbinical Council (CRC). Hours: Monday through Friday, 5 A.M. to 5 P.M.; Sundays, 5 A.M. to 5 P.M. Checks, but no credit cards.

Kaufman Bagel Bakery, *4411 N. Kedzie, Chicago, (312) 267-1680.* Cakes, pastries, bagels, and breads. Affiliated with the Kaufman Dempster St. deli. Hours: Monday through Saturday, 6 A.M. to 6 P.M.; Sunday, 6 A.M. to 3 P.M.

Tel Aviv Kosher Bakery, *2944 W. Devon, Chicago, (312) 764-8877.* Kosher, cakes, pastries, and breads. Hours: Monday through Wednesday, 6 A.M. to 6 P.M.; Thursday, 6 A.M. to 8 P.M.; Friday, 6:00 A.M. to 5:30 P.M.; Sunday, 6 A.M. to 6 P.M. No credit cards.

Levinson's Bakery, *2856 W. Devon, Chicago, (312) 761-3174.* Without doubt, the earliest opening bakery in Chicago. Pastries and breads. Hours: Tuesday through Saturday, 4 A.M. to 6 P.M.; Monday, 9:00 A.M. to 2:30 P.M.; Sunday, 4 A.M. to 5 P.M. No credit cards.

Delicatessens & Grocery

Selig's Kosher Delicatessen, Inc., *209 Skokie Valley Road, Highland Park, (708) 831-5560.* Located in the Crossroads Shopping Center, west of the Edens Expressway. Full line of kosher foods, including bakery products and import items. The restaurant area serves up to forty people for a home cooked lunch, dinner, or a quick snack. CRC approved. Hours: Monday through Thursday, 9:00 A.M. to 7:30 P.M.; Friday, 8 A.M. to 5 P.M.; Sunday, 8 A.M. to 7 P.M. Checks, but no credit cards.

The Original North Shore Bakery & Deli Restaurant, *2919–21 W. Touhy Avenue, Chicago, (312) 262-0600. Tehiya Benezra, proprietor.* A delicatessen in the front sells a full line of kosher foods, and a restaurant in the rear of the building serves hungry patrons. CRC endorsed. Hours: Monday through Friday, 6 A.M. to 6 P.M.; Sundays, 6 A.M. to 4 P.M. No credit cards.

Ada's Famous Deli & Restaurant, *405 Lake Cook Road, Deerfield, (708) 654-4446.* Delicatessen in the front, a restaurant serving lunch and dinner located in the rear. (Not kosher.) Hours: Sunday, 7:00 A.M. to 8:30 P.M.; Monday through Thursday, 6 A.M. to 9 P.M.; Friday, 6 A.M. to 10 P.M.; Sunday, 7:00 A.M. to 10:30 P.M. Accepts credit cards.

Door County Fish & Deli, *N.E. corner of Lake Cook Road at Waukegan, Deerfield, (708) 940-0140, and Grove Point Plaza, Route 83 and Lake Cook Road, Buffalo Grove, (708) 459-7040.* Famous for their smoked fish, which is prepared on the premises. A small lunch counter serves the lunchtime crowd. This Jewish delicatessen is better known for catering bar/bat Mitzvahs, Bris, Shiva, graduations and Mother's Day celebrations. Hours: Monday through Friday, 7 A.M. to 8 P.M.; open until 7 P.M. on Sunday at the Deerfield location and until 6 P.M. in Buffalo Grove. Credit cards accepted.

Fine's Market, *3935 W. Touhy Avenue, Lincolnwood, Ill., (708) 676-4590.* Full line butcher shop specializing in homemade soups, prepared foods, matzo ball, kishke, kreplach. Fresh fish delivered daily from the Chicago Fish House. Hours: Monday, Tuesday, Thursday and

Friday, 9 A.M. to 6 P.M.; Wednesday and Saturday, 8 A.M. to 2 P.M.; closed Sunday. No credit cards.

Hungarian Kosher Foods, Inc., *4020 W. Oakton Street, Skokie, (708) 674-8008.* Full-line delicatessen and grocery, selling kosher foods. Hours: Monday through Thursday, 8 A.M. to 9 P.M.; Friday, 8 A.M. to 4 P.M.; Sunday, 8 A.M. to 7 P.M. No credit cards.

Kosher Karry, *2828 W. Devon, Chicago, (312) 973-4355.* A carry-out deli serving home cooked gourmet kosher food including meat blintzes, gefilte fish, and sandwiches. CRC supervised. Hours: Monday, 8:30 A.M. to 6:00 P.M.; Tuesday through Wednesday, 8:30 A.M. to 7:00 P.M.; Thursdays until 8 P.M. Friday and Saturday hours vary. No credit cards.

Kaufman's Bagel & Delicatessen, *4905 Dempster St., Skokie, (708) 677-6190.* Imported foods from Israel. Kosher foods available for carryout. Hours: Monday through Friday, 7 A.M. to 9 P.M.; Saturday, 7 A.M. to 11 P.M.; Sundays until 7 P.M.

New York Kosher, *2900 W. Devon, Chicago, (312) 338-3354.* Smoked fish, salmon, groceries, and kosher foods direct from the warehouse. Hours: Monday through Wednesday, 8 A.M. to 7 P.M.; Thursday, 8 A.M. to 9 P.M.; Friday, 8 A.M. to 6 P.M.; Sunday, 8 A.M. to 6 P.M. No credit cards.

Restaurant Dining (North Shore and Outlying)

Kosher City Deli & Grill, *3353 W. Dempster, Skokie, (708) 679-2850.* Owner Ken Hechtman promotes his deli as a kind of "Kosher Ed Debovic's"—patterned after the kitschy 1950s motif that made the River North diner famous. People come from all over the Midwest to partake of the food (certified by the Chicago Rabbinical Council, CRC) and festivities. Music. Pinball games, and "Comedy Night" every Tuesday. This is the home of the "Burger Buddy," if you didn't already know. Hours: Monday through Thursday, 8 A.M. to 8 P.M.; Friday, 8 A.M. to 3 P.M.; Sundays, 8 A.M. to 8 P.M. Free parking. No credit cards.

What's Cooking? *6107 N. Lincoln Avenue, Chicago, (312) 583-3050.* Jewish-American cuisine located in the Lincoln Village Shopping plaza. Breakfast, lunch, and dinner. Hours: Monday through Friday, 6 A.M. to midnight; Saturday, 6 A.M. to 1 P.M.; Sunday until midnight. Credit cards accepted.

The Bagel Restaurant and Deli, *3000 W. Devon, Chicago, (312) 764-3377, and 50 Old Orchard Shopping Center, Skokie, (708) 677-0100.* Non-kosher Jewish-oriented restaurant formerly located in Albany Park. Specializes in blintzes and stuffed whitefish. Hours: Monday through Friday, 6:30 A.M. to 11:00 P.M.; Sunday 6:30 A.M. to 10:00 P.M. No credit cards.

Falafel King Israeli Restaurant, *4507 W. Oakton Street, Skokie, (708) 677-6020.* Kosher meat and vegetarian dishes. Hours: Sunday, Wednesday and Thursday, 11 A.M. to 9 P.M.; Tuesday till 8:30 P.M.; Friday, 11 A.M. to 2:30 P.M. No credit cards.

Lox Around the Clock, *2625 N. Halsted, Chicago, (312) 929-9909.* The "ultimate lox experience" if you happen to fancy choice, textured angle cut Norwegian Nova. Serving kosher corned beef and pastrami and a variety of dinner entrees, including meat, fish, poultry, pasta and vegetarian. Hours: Monday through Thursday, 6 A.M. to 11 P.M.; around the clock on Fridays and Saturdays.

Belden Restaurant and Deli, *four locations: North, 7572 N. Western Avenue, Chicago, (312) 743-4800; West, 8630 W. Golf Road, Des Plaines, (708) 699-1930; Arlington Heights, 902 W. Dundee Road, (708) 398-7750; Deerfield, 708 1/2 Waukegan Road, (708) 940-0200.* A Jewish deli reminiscent of the old days, even though they have been in existence only twelve years. Noisy and very crowded during the noon hour, Belden sells sandwiches to go, fancy bakery items, and kosher foods in the front of the restaurants. Catering available. Hours: Monday through Thursday, 7 A.M. to 1 A.M.; Friday and Saturday, till 2 A.M.; and Sundays, 7 A.M. to 1 A.M. Credit cards accepted.

Tel Aviv Kosher Pizza, *6349 N. California, Chicago, (312) 764-3776.* Pizza and dairy restaurant that is CRC supervised. Hours: Monday–Thursday, 11:30 A.M. to 9:00 P.M.; Saturday, 10 P.M. to 1 A.M. Closed Fridays. No credit cards.

Pita House, *6242 W. California, Chicago, (312) 465-4635*
Serving Middle Eastern and Arabic cuisine from the entire region.
Hours: noon to midnight, seven days a week. No credit cards.

Manny's Coffee Shop, *1141 S. Jefferson, Chicago, (312) 939-2855.* Years ago when there used to be a "real" Maxwell Street, and it spilled over onto Roosevelt Road where there stood hundreds of tenement buildings, discount clothiers, and butcher shops, afternoon shoppers would satisfy their appetite at either Lyon's Deli (now known as Nate's, 807 W. Maxwell Street) or Manny Raskin's, where you could feast on lamb shanks, matzo soup, baked chicken and fish, and other kosher-style foods that made the strip famous. Manny went on to his reward, but his son Ken continues to run the business at 1141 S. Jefferson. He moved to this location in 1965, a few years after the Dan Ryan Expressway tore through the neighborhood and sapped Maxwell Street and Roosevelt Road of much of its local color. No matter; the food is still good, and the new-old Manny's remains one of the favorite lunchtime spots west of the Loop. Hours: open Monday through Saturday from 6 A.M. Credit cards accepted for catered orders only. *Recommended.*

— Ethnic Recipe —

Traditional Rosh Hashanah Meals: **Brisket and Gefilte Fish**

Brisket
Ingredients

1 (12-ounce) jar of chili sauce
1/2 cup of brown sugar
2 tablespoons lemon juice
2 tablespoons of yellow mustard
Several garlic cloves
1 (10 ounce) package of frozen baby lima beans, thawed
Beef brisket (six pounds) trimmed of all fat

Directions

Combine chili sauce, brown sugar, lemon juice and mustard. Add 2-1/2 jars of water from chili jar. Chop garlic coarsely in roasting pan. Add lima beans and brisket. Pour chili sauce mixture over brisket, cover tightly with foil and roast in preheated 350-degree oven about four hours. After two hours remove foil and continue roasting. Baste brisket occasionally with pan juices. Makes about 12 to 18 servings.

Gefilte Fish
Ingredients

Fish
4 carrots, scraped and pared
4 celery stalks, cut into two or three pieces
1 onion, halved or quartered
Several white peppercorns
2 to 3 eggs
1/4 cup of water, optional
2 medium onions, finely minced with all liquid pressed out
Salt and freshly ground pepper to taste

Directions

Purchase enough whole fish to yield three pounds of skinned and boned edible fish (suggestion: a proportion of half white fish, one-fourth trout, and one-fourth pike). Reserve the head, bones, and skin. Begin with a fish stock: place head, bones, and fish skin in a large pot. Add carrots, celery, and quartered onion. Season with peppercorns and add enough water to cover vegetables. Bring mixture to a boil. Reduce heat to low, and simmer while making gefilte fish. Place fish pieces in a wooden bowl. Make a well in the fish. Add one egg, a little of the water, a little salt and pepper. Using a hand-held chopper, chop fish finely, gradually adding remaining 2 eggs if necessary and minced onions. If mixture seems dry, add water as necessary. Season with salt and pepper. Mixture will begin to stick to the blade of the chopper. When finely minced and mixed, wet hands and mold fish into a dozen large oval dumplings.

Ease dumplings into fish stock. Make one layer and cook for five minutes. Then add a second layer to prevent gefilte fish from sticking together. Simmer for one hour, running spatula through fish cakes occasionally to separate them. Cool, then refrigerate. Serve cold with a little of the pan liquids (which may solidify into a jelly). The carrots may be sliced and served with the fish. The scraps, celery, and onion should be discarded. Makes 12 servings. Note: The amount of eggs used will depend upon the natural moisture in the fish. The mixture should be pasty. Also, use only enough water to make a pasty mixture. Some cooks use a food processor to grind the fish. Do this in small batches and don't over-process, or the fish will become mush.

Italian Chicago

═══════ History and Settlement ═══════

The family matters. Ask Chicago Italians and they will tell you so. This sense of family and community spanning the generations is what the Italian-American experience is about, dating back to the 1880s when they began arriving in Chicago in great numbers. Regional identification in Italy was so strong that the newcomers did not consider themselves Italians until the Americans began calling them that. Before 1890, the Italians entering the U.S. came from the prosperous, economically advanced regions of the north: Venetia, Piedmont, Genoa, and Tuscany. After 1899, the new arrivals were for the most part southerners attempting to escape the feudal structure and class stratification of the Old World. Economic opportunity—that great equalizer among peoples—fostered the first wave of emigration. Ironically though, the first significant population shift from the Kingdom of Italy during the early years of the nineteenth century was toward Latin America, not the U.S. Brazil and Argentina were economic magnets until the industrial revolution reached the shores of America and the need for unskilled laborers willing to work for a few pennies a day encouraged a northerly exodus.

The Italians were latecomers. In 1850 U.S. census figures showed that only forty-three of them lived in Illinois compared to 27,000 Irish, 38,000 Germans, 18,000 English and 4,000 Scandinavians. By the 1860s there were only 100 Italians in Chicago. But this would change drastically by the turn of the century, with the arrival of the *contadini,* or peasant farmers. Very often the Italian immigrants processed through Castle Garden in New York were following the footsteps of their relatives who had settled in Chicago to work as shoemakers, tailors, grocers, meat packers, and in construction. Many were "sojourners," who stayed only long enough to earn money to purchase farm land in Italy. Others waited months, even years, but then found that peasant life, which seemed so idyllic from their tenement building in the core of the city, had changed. These nomadic "Americani," who were torn between two divergent cultures, very often returned to the U.S. It was a phenomenon of the Italian immigration.

The early arriving northerners who were counted in the 1850 census followed the Germans, Irish, and Swedes into the central city. Frank and August Lagorio were two important figures in the development of the first Italian community in Chicago. The brothers left their native Genoa in 1852. Following a perilous seventy-day ocean voyage, they passed through Castle Garden in New York, and made their way to Chicago. The Lagorios purchased a home at Kinzie and Kingsbury streets and opened a small neighborhood import business that sustained them for many years. In 1857, Frank Lagorio's wife gave birth to a son, named Antonio. Years later, this son of the Genoese immigrants completed his studies at the Rush Medical College. He later served as president of the Chicago Library Board. The other brother, August Lagorio, was a member of the city's volunteer fire department, which was composed entirely of businessmen and civic leaders. Chicago in the early 1850s was still an overgrown village, struggling to become a modern metropolis. The unification of the two police constabularies and the formation of the paid fire department were still several years away.

The trail-blazing Lagorios encouraged their friends and relatives to emigrate, and within a few years a thriving Genoese colony was founded near Kinzie Street.

In 1870, there were Italians in all twenty wards except the Irish Seventh. Ominous political events taking shape in the Kingdom of Italy that year contributed directly to the second wave of immigration. As a result of Giuseppe Garibaldi's defeat by a French force at Mentana, many refugees from Naples, Tuscany, Piedmont, Venice, and Sicily poured into the city. Less than a year later, on July 2, 1871, Italian unification was completed when the Roman people overwhelmingly approved a union with the kingdom. The price of peace was economic deprivation, and widespread unemployment. On the brink of starvation, thousands of Italians made their way to the U.S. and its large urban centers.

An 1884 Board of Education survey determined that the largest concen -
tration of Italian immigrants resided south of the Chicago River near
Harrison and 12th Street. Later, just as thousands of immigrants poured
into the city from Southern Italy, the poorest of them settled between Van
Buren and 12th Street. This was the longtime political domain of Republican Alderman Johnny "de Pow" Powers, saloon keeper, gambler, and
sachem of the Nineteenth Ward, who ruled the neighborhood from 1888
until the 1920s.

Known as the "Prince of Boodlers" for his rapacious tactics in the city
council, Powers greeted the new arrivals with characteristic swagger. "I
can buy the Italian vote with a glass of beer and a compliment," he
snorted. The nineteenth ward was a classic Chicago melting pot, populated by twenty-six different nationalities. In 1898 there were 48,190
residents living in squalid tenements along Ewing, Forquer, Taylor, and
DeKoven (between Halsted and Canal). The 5,784 Italians were viewed
with a mixture of suspicion and mistrust by the firmly entrenched Irish
and native Anglos. "Here the urbane expression gave way to a censorious
one," commented a *Tribune* reporter who tramped down the wooden
cinder blocks of the ward on May 13, 1898. "And the change was
reflected in the countenance of a sympathetic friend. ' 'Tis a shame,' said
the friend, 'I thought the laws had been passed to keep them out.' 'They
are a noisy, quarreling set,' continued the first speaker, 'They are not
even friendly with one another.' "

It was a polyglot community. Few of the southern Italians owned
property. They crowded together in poorly lit hovels, sometimes housing
three families per floor. Economic deprivation and unfamiliarity with
the language and the customs created despair and a feeling of powerless-
ness. Beginning in the 1890s, several key figures within the community
joined forces with Jane Addams, the founder of Hull House, to elect
candidates more inclined to represent their interests. In 1898, for example, the community rallied behind aldermanic candidate Simeon S. Armstrong, an Irishman who was endorsed by Addams. Responding to the
insults heaped upon them by Powers, *L'Italia* and *La Tribuna Italiana*
launched an ambitious registration drive. The initial results were dis-
couraging. Powers rolled on to victory by a 2-1 margin and continued
to rule into the Prohibition era. "I am what my people like, and neither
Hull House nor all the reformers in town can turn them against me,"
Powers gloated.

The inevitable revolt against the Irish boss began after 1910 and it was
led by a man of dubious character—the unfrocked priest Anthony
D'Andrea, whose ties to the Black Hand and criminal elements within the

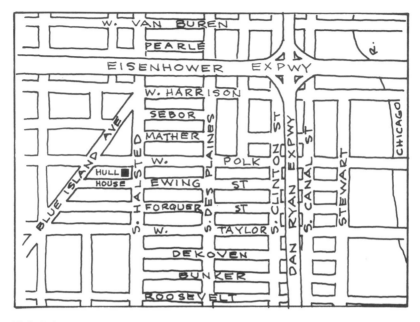

Little Italy

neighborhood were well known. D'Andrea was a force in labor union politics and president of the Unione Siciliana, the largest, most influential Italian fraternal society in Chicago, founded at the turn of the century. On April 13, 1920, D'Andrea ran unopposed for the office of ward committeeman and was elected. the Italians had made important strides working within the system only to have the results invalidated by the state supreme court under the 1919 primary law. Powers, of course, regained his former position of committeeman, leaving D'Andrea out in the cold.

By 1921 the Italians were the single largest ethnic group in the ward, yet had no real say-so in policy-making. Powers employed a handful of Italians in his own organization, but they were viewed with suspicion and mistrust by the *paesani* (fellow countrymen).

D'Andrea challenged Powers in the aldermanic election that year in a violent, bloody political campaign characterized by the free use of the bomb and shotgun. The Municipal Voter's League refused to endorse either candidate, though D'Andrea commanded immense popularity among the members of the Chicago Building Trades Council. The vendetta raged through the spring and summer months. In March, Paul Labriola, one of the Powers men who served as bailiff of the Municipal

Court, was ambushed and killed. "Labriola was my best friend," Powers sobbed. "I don't know of any enemies he had."

Symbolic of the murderous intent of these two groups was a poplar tree which stood on Loomis Street in the heart of the "alky cooking" district. Here the rivals would post the names of their next victims. Nearly thirty men who lost their lives in the Powers-D'Andrea feud saw their names carved on the "Dead Man's Tree" at one time or another. One of the last was D'Andrea himself, who was cut down at the height of his career on May 10, 1921, in front of his doorstep on Ashland Avenue. The Italian-language newspapers decried the violence, but reserved its judgments. On election day, several months before his untimely death, D'Andrea went down to defeat by a scant thirty-eight votes. The Nineteenth Ward vendetta presaged the rise of the modern crime syndicate, and illustrated the sense of despair many earnest, hardworking Italians felt as they attempted to rise above the nightmare of poverty, discrimination, and exclusionary laws they encountered in the U.S.

In the minds of many native Chicagoans, the new arrivals were either mainland Communists or Sicilian Black Handers, who had imported an ancient feudal system to America. The North Side Italian community, bounded by the industrial districts of Goose Island, North Avenue, Wells Street and Chicago Avenue, became known as "Little Hell." According to Chicago census statistics published in 1920, Little Hell was taken over by the Italians who comprised 28 percent of the area's population. In the shadow of the opulent Gold Coast, less than a mile to the east, lived thousands of Sicilians who worked on Goose Island, formerly the home of Irish laborers who cluttered the north branch of the Chicago River with their shanties and wild geese (hence the famous nickname). They arrived in the neighborhood in the 1880s, displacing many Swedes who moved farther north along Belmont Avenue. The majority of these Italians from the Kingdom of Italy came for the island of Sicily. They established autonomy along Gault Court and Milton Avenue between Chicago Avenue and Division Street. Then later they pushed across Division to North Avenue.

The intersection of Oak and Milton (now Cleveland) gained a fearful notoriety in the first decade of the twentieth century. Here the Black Hand gangsters practiced their extortions, impervious to the police. In this tightly woven ethnic Italian enclave, thirty-eight victims of the Black Hand met death in a fifteen-month killing spree between January, 1910, and March, 1911. There was little a shopkeeper or private citizen could do if he received the dreaded letter with the hand imprint on it. Pay up or die. From the pages of *La Tribuna Italiana Transatlantica,* editor Allessandro Mastro-Valerio decried the violence. "Yesterday this one, today that one; tomorrow it may strike even you!" The Chicago Police were often blamed by community leaders for their complacency and inertia. The implication, of course, was that the police were "on the take." The Black Hand flourished in Chicago until the early 1920s, when the modern crime syndicate organized to reap the bountiful harvest of Prohibition. Compared to the fabulous profits from bootlegging, the activities of the old-fashioned "Mustache Petes" was strictly small-time. With the assassination on May 11, 1920, of James Colosimo, a rotund gangster fond of Enrico Caruso and the Chicago Opera Theater, an era of terror ended— only to be replaced by something altogether different. The rise of Johnny Torrio, Al Capone, and their minions deeply embarrassed the community at large. During the height of the "booze wars" in the 1920s, the Italian periodicals went out of their way to minimize and downplay the significance of the crime problem. The 1929 St. Valentine's Day Massacre, in which eight Irish gangsters were lined up against the wall and shot by the Capone mob, received no attention from the community press. Instead, *L'Italia* championed Judge Bernard Barasa of the Municipal Court as a role model for the community. In 1923 Barasa became the first Italian American to announce his intention to run for mayor of Chicago. He entered the Republican primary after Mayor William Hale Thompson dropped out, due to the taint of scandal that surrounded his eight-year reign. Unfortunately, Barasa's name was linked to "Thompsonism," and despite carrying the Nineteenth Ward, the judge was swamped in the primary. The non-Italians proved unresponsive to the Barasa campaign. Since 1923, no Italian has seriously challenged the office of mayor in a city that was until recently dominated by Irish politicians.

Political progress was slow. In the 1920s, four Italians sat on the bench of the Municipal Court: Judge John J. Lupe, Judge Francis Allegretti, Judge Francis Borrelli, and Judge John Sbarbaro (who also owned the city's most famous undertaking parlor). By the 1980s, Chicago's Italian community was well represented in the City Council by Aldermen Vito Marzullo, William Banks, and Michael Nardulli. In Congress, Frank Annunzio of the Eleventh Congressional District was recognized as a leader and as an eloquent spokesperson for the National Italian-American Foundation, a lobbying group.

In the scientific realm, one name stands alone, that of Enrico Fermi (1901–1954), the architect of the nuclear age. Fermi was born in Rome, and educated at the Reale Seuola Normale Superiore at a time when Benito Mussolini's Blackshirts were coming to power in Italy. Fermi was a brilliant physicist who conceived the idea of inducing artificial radioactivity through a new and ingenious method of reducing the speed of neutrons by passing them through paraffin. In 1938, Fermi was named a Nobel laureate in physics for his work with radioactive elements. The Fascist government granted him permission to attend the award ceremonies in Stockholm, Sweden, but Fermi and his Jewish wife, Laura Capon, fled Italy for a safe haven in the U.S. As the war clouds gathered over Europe, Enrico Fermi and two of his colleagues alerted President Franklin Roosevelt to the grave dangers posed to the U.S. if the Nazis should succeed in developing an atomic bomb. The letter to the president, dated October 11, 1939 convinced Roosevelt of the necessity of developing the bomb before the Nazis did so. The top secret Manhattan Project was launched in 1942, with Fermi heading a team of scientists who worked around the clock in a makeshift laboratory constructed on the squash court under the stands of Stagg Field on the University of Chicago campus. On December 2, 1942, Fermi and his associates produced the first self-sustaining chain reaction. The testing of the bomb occurred at the Alamogordo Air Force Base in New Mexico on July 16, 1945.

At the Argonne National Laboratory in Chicago's western suburbs, a one-foot section of common graph paper recording the first atomic reaction is on permanent display—a tribute to the genius of an Italian immigrant who only desired to raise his children in a country free of tyrants, a country that would permit all its citizens, regardless of nationality, religion, or color, to live together in peace.

North Side Italians attended Mass at the Assumption of the Blessed Virgin Mary Church. Construction of this magnificent edifice began in 1880, but the city's first Italian parish was not officially dedicated until August 15, 1886. The second Italian congregation was formed six years later, when St. Mary's of Mount Carmel opened its doors at 67th and Page streets on the South Side. For years church parishes have filled a vital social and religious role in the lives of their Italian constituents. The *festa* was an expression of devotion to a particular saint and also an important social occasion in the "ghetto," much like an old-fashioned country fair. Dating back to the 1890s, the Chicago street fest is patterned after the traditional religious celebrations in Italian villages. Those celebrations included the procession through the streets and prominent display of the saint in whose honor the feast was conceived. As the statue was carried through the town on the shoulders of those leading the parade, happy villagers would pin money to the image as a token of respect and appreciation for past favors granted.

The religious festival in Chicago embodied the old world flavor in a modern urban setting. The "Flight of the Angels," in honor of the Blessed Virgin Mary, was an annual summer ritual on the near North Side beginning at the church of St. Philip Benizi. The men of the parish would pull a float in the shape of a sailing vessel with the statue of the patron saint sitting on top. To be selected one of the two "angels" was the highest honor accorded an Italian family, for the two girls chosen not only had to read and write, but they also had to be fluent in the native tongue. The honor carried with it a $20 prize, put up by the sponsoring fraternal society. Dressed in ornamental white gowns, the two "angels" were affixed to a mechanical pulley strung across the rooftops of the convent school and an adjacent building. The girls slowly advanced toward each other suspended as they were, in mid-air. Below them, the bugler would sound three notes to alert the people and remind them to be quiet while the girls recited a prayer in Italian to the patron saint. The tableau of the angels was the high-point of the summer season, and was traditionally held in late August. When the ceremony was over, the immigrants would sample the gourmet delicacies of the outdoor booths—tasty Italian dishes, such as *graticola*—fished soaked in vinegar or lemon and then grilled above an open fire. It was the traditional Friday meal in Little Italy. The Flight of the Angels is a memory today, but similar festivals, such as the Our Lady of Mount Carmel celebration in Melrose Park in July, and the Santa Maria Lauretana fest in the Harlem-Cermak neighborhood in September, are but a few reminders of this rich heritage imported from across the ocean.

The number of Italians living in Chicago has dwindled in recent years. Construction of the University of Illinois campus in the early 1960s displaced thousands of second- and third-generation immigrants residing in the Taylor-Halsted neighborhood on the near West Side. Little Hell is also gone. The Francis Cabrini-Dwight Green housing project, completed in 1962, occupies much of what was once the living, breathing heart of Little Italy. But the culture—the fests—are preserved on the lower West Side near 24th Street and Blue Island Avenue. At the turn of the century this neighborhood was settled by Italians from the Tuscany region who were lured by the promise of good-paying jobs at the McCormick Reaper Works (now International Harvester). In 1903 historic St. Michael's was built on the foundation of what was formerly a Swedish Methodist-Episcopal church. On the South Side, "La Colonia del Sessantanove Strada" (the Colony of 69th St.) near Hermitage was developed in 1890 by the *contadini* from Oliveto Citra, a village in the province of Salerno. St. Mary's of Mount Carmel, built in 1892 at 67th and Page became the city's second Italian parish.

Like other immigrant groups before them, the third-generation Italians began to leave the city neighborhoods for improved housing and economic opportunity in the suburbs. It began in the era of rising expectations in the 1920s and continued through the 1960s, when River

Forest, Melrose Park, Riverside, and Oak Park took on a decidedly Italian character.

The Italians have been characterized as an ethnic group that remains behind in the "old neighborhood" forever, seemingly unresponsive to the realities of change. *Campanilismo,* or the sense of place, tied the Italians to their communities, be it through the fraternal societies, the ethnic press, or the magnet-like influence of the church parish. Attitudes and perceptions change, however, and as the sociologist Robert Park observed, "In America the peasant discards his habits and acquires ideas."

Suburbanization accelerated after World War II, but it had its roots in the 1890s, when a small group of Italians moved into Chicago Heights, thirty miles south of the city. The 300 Italians listed in the 1900 census worked at the brickyards or for Gaetano D'Amico, a former railroad section hand, who was the founder of "Mama Mia" spaghetti products.

Italians moved into Melrose Park as early as 1890. Ten years later they accounted for nearly 70 percent of the village population. Smaller, but still viable Italian neighborhoods can be found in North Suburban Highwood, Riverside, and in the Chicago neighborhoods of Belmont-Cragin on the Northwest Side, Bridgeport on the South Side, and the storied Tri-Taylor District, which endures in the shadow of the sprawling University of Illinois campus. The new Little Italy, though, is concentrated on the far western outskirts of the city, along Harlem Avenue between Irving Park Road and North Avenue. The residents call it *Corsa Italia,* (the Italian Boulevard), and it bares little resemblance to the congested inner city ghetto that existed on the near West Side at the turn of the century. The Harlem Avenue commercial strip, with its Italian banquet halls, beef stands, and small, independently owned businesses front blocks of single-family bungalows and ranch-style houses that are neatly maintained in a neighborhood that is relatively crime free.

There is no scarcity of Italian culture in Chicago despite the frequently heard lament of community residents, who harken back to a time when the Sicilians, Neapolitans, and Calabrians celebrated the festivals of the saints, the birth of their children, and the passing of the elders in the "city of immigrants." "Neighborhoods were missed by folks who had moved to the suburbs," complained Dominic Candeloro, a research associate at Governor's State University. "They looked back and saw a time when everybody knew everybody else and helped everybody else." It has been said that in the heart of every man there is one small corner that is Italian. Some of the neighborhoods may be gone now, but the belief in spirituality, love of family, and the inner dignity Chicago's Italians hold will never be destroyed.

Ethnic Museums

The National Italian American Sports Hall of Fame, *2625 Clearbrook Drive, Arlington Heights, (708) 437-3007.* George Randazzo is an Italian-American who satisfied his passion for professional boxing, and the pride he felt in the achievements of his people in the athletic arena by founding a Boxing Hall of Fame in 1977. From these modest beginnings, various sports-minded Chicagoans of Italian descent urged Randazzo to expand the Hall of Fame to honor Italians whose noteworthy contributions to all fields of sport captured the imagination of the American public. In 1978 the immortal "Yankee Clipper," Joe De-Maggio, became the first inductee in Randazzo's revamped Hall of Fame, which was originally headquartered at 7906 W. Grand Avenue, in Elmwood Park, Illinois. Present at the ribbon-cutting ceremony were such luminaries as Dodger manager Tom Lasorda, former Yankee catcher Yogi Berra, Mary Ann Marciano, daughter of prize fighter Rocky Marciano, and Willie Mosconi.

In 1980, the highly successful *Red, White, and Green* was launched, a monthly sports tabloid dedicated to promoting Italians in sports. The publication has a national circulation. On April 4, 1987, thanks to the generous support of Edward J. DeBartolo of Youngstown, Ohio, the NIASHF moved into spacious new quarters located on seven acres of land in Arlington Heights, where the latest in state-of-the-art technology permits visitors to experience a "hands-on" approach to sports history. Thousands of pieces of memorabilia are on display, including the race cars driven by Mario Andretti and his son Michael; Rocky Marciano's heavyweight championship belt, and Olympic gold metal momentos won by Matt Biondi, Mary Lou Retton, and Mike Eruzione.

Throughout the year, the museum hosts a number of special events, including the March Annual Awards Ceremony honoring the athlete of the year (or decade) from the prep, college, and professional ranks. The induction ceremony and sports memorabilia auction is held in July or August, with refreshments served on the grounds. Contact Public Relations director David Alonzo for details. The museum is open from 8:30 A.M. to 4:30 P.M., Monday through Friday. Free admission. Closed on weekends. *Recommended.*

Italian Cultural Center (Under the Aegis of the Scalabrini Fathers and Brothers) *1621 N. 39th Ave., Stone Park, (708) 345-3842.* Two blocks east of bustling Mannheim Road (Route 45) and two blocks south of North Avenue (Route 64), the Italian Cultural Center has enhanced the appreciation of the literary, religious, and artistic endeavors of Chicago's large Italian community. The three-story museum was opened in May 1970 when the original seminary of the Scalabrini Fathers and Brothers moved into a newly constructed wing on Division Street, in Stone Park. Tucked away on 22-acres of ground in a quiet residential neighborhood, the Cultural Center features a first-floor library, an important research archive that contains 113 oral history transcripts, 2,500 volumes of Italian history, biography, philosophy, religion, and arts. Second floor exhibits chronicle the Italian settlement in Chicago, with particular emphasis on neighborhoods, the working experience, and the "festa." The John Cadel Art Gallery is down the hall, featuring the works of this celebrated painter, who died in 1977. Various oil paintings, bronzes, ceramics, original prints, and Italian crafts are included in the collection. The Savoia Exhibit, a 1:100 scale model of St. Peter's Basilica in Rome and St. Mark's Square in Venice, Italy, occupies much of the available floor space on the third level. Italian language classes for children and adults are held during the week and on Saturdays. The center is open Monday through Saturday, 10 A.M. to 4 P.M. Free admission, but memberships are available: family, $20.00; lifetime, $300.00; guarantor: $1,000. *Recommended.*

Taylor Street: A Touch of Italy
═════ on the Near West Side ═════

The old neighborhood dwells in the hearts and minds of Chicago's Italian community. Much of this West Side enclave was swallowed up by the University of Illinois campus in the early 1960s, and the Cabrini Housing Project on Taylor Street occupies land where Italian homes and businesses once stood. Though diminished in stature, Taylor Street retains its essential Italian character despite an increasingly wider ethnic diversity. A collage of elegant southern Italian (Calabrian) restaurants can be found between Halsted on the east and Racine on the west. While most of the 500,000 Italian-Americans live in the outlying neighborhoods and suburbs, many of them come back each year to relive the customs, and celebrate Mass at Our Lady of Pompeii Church, especially on Columbus Day. According to Anthony Sorrentino, former Executive Director of the Joint Civic Committee of Italian Americans, "They begin to recall their rich memories, not only of the hard times, but of their varied social life in the family, church, club, neighborhood and world of work. These and other thoughts came to mind when hundreds attended the Mass for the Columbus Day Parade at Our Lady of Pompeii Church. One Italian-

American who attends this event every year said: 'I bring my children here every year so that they will have some link with my roots and my heritage.' It is true that you can't turn the clock back, but I believe that this proves that you can go home again—if only to discover who you are and where you should be going."

Al's Italian Beef, *1079 W. Taylor, and Mario's Lemonade Stand. (Taylor, between Aberdeen and Carpenter).*   Al's, a four-star chain, started here. During the summer buy your sandwich and stroll the street to sample a frosty Italian snowball and lupini at Mario's— where the Gray Line tour buses make an obligatory stop as they make their rounds in Chicago. Mario's opens for the season on May 1.

Trattoria Roma Terza, *1119 W. Taylor Street, Chicago, (312) 226-6600*   Small, unpretentious dining room amid the artful Roman-ruins faux finishes. Appetizer table. Daily specials. Open Monday through Friday, 11:30 A.M. to 3:00 P.M. for lunch, 5 P.M. to 11 P.M. for dinner. Saturdays, 5 P.M. to 11 P.M., Sunday 4 P.M. to 10 P.M. All major credit cards accepted.

Mategrano's, *1321 W. Taylor Street, Chicago, (312) 243-8441.* A twenty-year institution on Taylor Street renowned for its "all you can eat" buffets on Thursday and Saturday. Mildred Miccucio and Annette Mategrano cook their Neapolitan dishes, and serve it proudly to the famous and not so famous. Mayor Richard M. Daley and Senator Paul Simon have sampled Mategrano's delights. So has Al Capone's former bodyguard. We wonder what Mayor Daley would say about that, given his opposition to a proposal to establish a Chicago gangster museum celebrating "Al Capone's Chicago." Mategrano's is open Monday through Thursday, 11 A.M. to 9 P.M., Friday, 11 A.M. to 10 P.M., Saturday, 4 P.M. to 10 P.M., and Sundays, 1 P.M. to 8 P.M. All credit cards accepted.

Scafuri Bakery, *1337 W. Taylor Street, Chicago, (312) 733-8881.*   Luigi Scafuri immigrated from Naples and opened this bakery in the 1890s. Today it is owned and operated by Mildred and Annette who were born on nearby Loomis Street and lived above the bakery. The sisters still use Luigi's traditional recipe for bread. The fresh, unusual flavor comes from the way the bread is prepared: in old fashioned boxes. According to Mildred, Italians come from all over the Midwest to buy the bread, which can be frozen and stored. Open 7 A.M. to 5 P.M., Tuesday through Saturday. *Recommended.*

New Rosebud Cafe, *1500 W. Taylor Street, Chicago, (312) 942-1117.* This is without doubt one of the most popular Italian eateries in the city, catering to the patrons of the Chicago Stadium, who fill the place to overflowing after the Bulls and Blackhawk games. The homemade pastas are served in huge ceramic bowls. Reservations strongly suggested. Open for lunch Monday through Friday, 11 A.M. to 3 P.M., dinner, Monday through Thursday, 5 P.M. to 10:30 P.M., Saturday 5 P.M. to 11:30 P.M.

Falbo's, *1335 W. Taylor Street, Chicago, (312) 421-8915.* Delicatessen and submarine sandwich shop that sells imported Italian sausage, olive oil, and cheeses. Established 1912. Open Tuesday through Friday, 9 A.M. to 5 P.M. Saturdays, 9 A.M. to 2 P.M., Sunday, 9 A.M. to 2 P.M.

Chiarugi's, *1447-1449 W. Taylor Street, Chicago, (312) 666-2235.* Where else but in the near West Side can you find a retail emporium that displays toilet seats in the front window? Keep an open mind. Chiarugi's is a charming, old-fashioned hardware store with creaking wooden floors and display cases containing a variety of goods including wine-making tools, bottles and corks. Closed on Sunday. *Recommended.*

Conte Di Savola, *1438 W. Taylor Street, Chicago, (312) 666-3471.* Italian grocery store with a small self-service cafe in the front that caters to the weekday lunch crowd. Vito Cambio started the business at Taylor and Halsted in the 1930s, until the university bulldozed acres of private and commercial buildings in 1960. Mike DiCosola, the current owner, is one of the third-generation Italians who fled to the suburbs, but was lured back to the old neighborhood when the Tri-Taylor district underwent gentrification. Imported sausages, pastries, tortellini, cavatelli, fine wines, and standard American groceries are sold here. Open Monday through Saturday, 9 A.M. to 6 P.M., Sundays 9 A.M. to 4 P.M.

Gennaro's Restaurant, *1352 W. Taylor Street, Chicago, (312) 243-1035.* One of the old-line Taylor Street eateries since 1959. Pasta and pizza are the standard fare. Open: Thursday 5 P.M. to 9 P.M., Friday and Saturday, 5 P.M. to 10 P.M., Sunday, 4 P.M. to 9 P.M. Closed Monday through Wednesday.

D'Amato's Bakery, *1124 W. Grand Avenue, Chicago, (312) 733-5456.* One of the city's legendary Italian bakeries, located about two miles north of Taylor Street. D'Amato's bakes the best sour dough bread,

according to *Chicago Tribune* columnist Bill Granger, and will sell you
uncooked pizza dough if you ask for it.

Architecture

The Near West Side, despite its changed character, offers a pretty good
glimpse of what Chicago used to be like in the heyday of the great Eastern
European immigration before the post-World War II land boom, which
brought with it the implementation of the Chicago Plan Commission's
Master Plan of Residential Land. That plan called for the demolition of
miles of low-income slum housing on the near South and West Sides—
one of the most densely populated regions *in the world.* In 1894 it was
estimated that the Polish neighborhood on the West Side was more
crowded than the worst sections of Tokyo or Calcutta. The average slum
district on the West Side housed 270 persons per acre, crowded together
in dimly lit, unsanitary brick slum buildings known as "double deckers."
These buildings were three or four stories high, and typically extended
over the entire lot. A 1901 survey found 127 people huddled together in
a set of three small rooms.

The West Side neighborhoods remained stagnant and squalid until the
process of renovation took hold, beginning in 1943 with the construction
of the Robert Brooks Homes at 14th and Loomis. In 1955, the year that
Mayor Richard J. Daley won his first mayoral election, the Grace Abbott
Homes opened on a ten-block site near Roosevelt Road and 12th Street,
not far from the Maxwell Street Market. This was only the tip of the
iceberg, as Daley and his team of energetic civic planners looked to a
brighter day, when poverty might be abolished entirely. The solution to
the problem was deceptively simple: build low-cost, yet sturdy public
housing amid the rubble of the old immigrant tenement houses. Certainly Daley could not foresee that "urban renewal," as he envisioned it,
would create more problems than it was intended to solve, for within a
few short years, the bland public housing projects became seedbeds
of crime, drugs, and gang mayhem. And then, on February 24, 1961,
came the announcement that the new Chicago campus of the University
of Illinois would be built under the auspices of Skidmore, Owings
and Merrill adjacent to the Congress (Eisenhower) Expressway. This
occurred at a time when community and business leaders were attempting to reclaim and gentrify sections of the old Italian neighborhood. The
fight against the university was waged in part by Florence Giovangelo
Scala and the Near West Side Planning Board, who fought to preserve

their neighborhood as they knew it. The legal wrangles continued into the mid-1960s, but were unsuccessful because the $27 million campus opened to the public on February 22, 1965. That same year, the West Side Medical Complex, encompassing Cook County Hospital, the University of Illinois Medical Group, Presbyterian-St. Luke's Hospital, and Convalescent Park opened its doors. Though a significant portion of Chicago's ethnic history had been obliterated in the span of five short years, the university and medical center proved to be a boon to the Taylor Street merchants, and stabilized single-dwelling housing. In fact, by 1980, housing prices soared in the Tri-Taylor Historic District, which was buoyed by young homeowners eager to rehab their buildings in order to live in a historic, yet modern urban setting.

Tri-Taylor District

Located between Oakley Avenue (2300 W.) and Taylor Street (1000 S.), and the Penn Central Railroad tracks, the Tri-Taylor Historic District features a charming, wonderfully preserved collection of row houses and two- and three-story flats, typical of the kinds of buildings that existed in this neighborhood in the 1880s and 1890s. Tri-Taylor was added to the National Register of Historic Places in 1983, and it continues to be rehabbed under historic guidelines established by the government. The homeowners are for the most part young Italians, Mexicans, Germans and Irish who have banded together to preserve the architectural aesthetics of one of the oldest residential communities in Chicago.

Our Lady of Pompeii, *Lexington and Lytle Streets, Chicago, (312) 421-3757.*   A storied Italian church constructed in 1910, and rebuilt in a Romanasque style thirteen years later.

Jackson Boulevard Historic District

Jackson Boulevard east of Ashland, in the 1500 block (near Halsted). At a time when the West Side was little more than an inner-city slum with little chance of revival, a group of visionary Chicagoans rescued this block of Victorian mansions from the wrecker's ball, and in the process set the tone for urban renovation in the years to come. Thirty-one Victorian row houses were saved, which stand as a reminder of a simpler, more elegant era. It is doubtful that the poor southern Italians who crowded

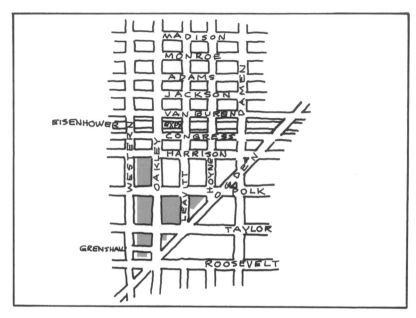

Tri-Taylor Historic District

along Taylor Street could have afforded homes like these, but it is important that we understand the class differences of the era through its architecture. The Chicago Architecture Foundation conducts a two-hour walking tour of the district on three Sunday afternoons in June, July, and September. Call (312) 326-1393.

Oakley Avenue and 24th Place in Pilsen: ===Northern Italian Restaurant Row===

Thousands of northern Italian immigrants, primarily from the Tuscany region, poured into this industrial neighborhood in the 1890s. They were lured by the promise of jobs at the McCormick Reaper Works (later International Harvester) on nearby Blue Island Avenue, and affordable housing once occupied by the Germans, Swedes, and Irish. After World War II, a second wave of Italian immigrants poured into this corner of Pilsen which comprises the 25th Ward, from the Piedmont region.

Through the 1950s, 1960s, and 1970s, the first and second generation immigrants were represented in the Chicago City Council by Alderman Vito Marzullo, a Sicilian politician who sat at the throne of Mayor Richard J. Daley. Marzullo was chairman of the powerful transportation committee and an important cog in the Daley machine through six terms. It was fitting therefore, that the council should reward Marzullo's loyalty by renaming Oakley Avenue, from Blue Island to Cermak Road, Vito Marzullo Avenue. After all, Charles Oakley (1792-1849) for whom this street in Chicago was originally named, set an early standard for Chicago's ward characters by turning the Illinois-Michigan Canal project into a massive patronage trough, in his capacity as a state-appointed trustee.

Today, the Twenty-Fifth Ward has lost much of its Italian character. Thousands of Hispanics now reside in Pilsen, but for several blocks along Oakley (Marzullo) Avenue it is still possible to experience Northern Italian culture, at least in the fine cuisine served by these restaurateurs.

La Fontanella, *2414 S. Oakley Avenue, Chicago, (312) 927-5249.* Family owned and operated. A small, out of the way Italian eatery. Open for lunch 10:30 A.M. to 3:00 P.M. for lunch Monday through Friday. Dinner served from 3:00 P.M. to 9:30 P.M., Monday through Thursday, Friday, 3:00 P.M. to 11:30 P.M.; Saturday, 4:30 P.M. to 11:30 P.M. Checks accepted, but no credit cards.

Bacchanalia Ristorante, *2413 S. Oakley, Chicago, (312) 254-6555.* The tortellini and chicken Vesuvio are the house specialties. Open Monday through Friday, 11 A.M. to 10 P.M., closed Tuesdays. Open on Saturday 4 P.M. to 11 P.M., Sunday, 3:30 P.M. to 9:00 P.M. No credit cards, but personal check accepted.

Alfo's, *2512 S. Oakley, Chicago, (312) 523-6994.* Family style, informal surroundings. Specialties include *vitello* (veal), *Fritto Misto* (fried veal) and chicken á la Alfo. Open: Tuesday–Thurs., 11 A.M. to 11 P.M.; Friday, 11 A.M. to 2 A.M.; Saturday, 4:30 P.M. to 2:00 A.M.; Sunday, 2 P.M. to 9 P.M. Closed Mondays.

Toscano, *2439 S. Oakley, Chicago, (312) 376-4841.* Seafood specialties. Tuesday, Wednesday, Thursday, 11 A.M. to 10 P.M., Friday, 11 A.M. to 11 P.M., Saturday 4 P.M. to 11 P.M., Sunday, 3 P.M. to 10:00 P.M. Closed Monday.

Bruna's Ristorante, *2424 S. Oakley, Chicago.* Bruna Cane and her husband opened this small neighborhood restaurant in 1934. It's a neighborhood kind of place specializing in veal and fettuccini. Open: Monday, Wednesday, and Thursday from 11 A.M. to 10 P.M.; Sunday, 2 P.M. to 10 P.M.; Friday and Saturday, 11 A.M. to 11:00 P.M.

Villa Marconi, *2358-2354 S. Oakley, Chicago.* Traditional northern Italian cuisine. All major credit cards accepted. Closed Sundays.

Bakery

Fontana Brothers Bakery, *2404 Oakley, Chicago, (312) 847-6697.* John Toschi, an Italian baker, opened his business more than seventy years ago. Like other ethnic Italian bakers, this family-owned business specializes in bread; be it twists, ryes, or sticks. Cookies, but no fine pastries. Open Monday through Friday, 6 A.M. to 6 P.M.; Saturday, 6 A.M. to 5 P.M.; Sunday, 6 A.M. to 1 P.M.

Gifts and Import Shops

Milieu, *2422 S. Oakley, Chicago, (312) 847-7766.* Porcelains, dinnerware, potpourri.

Italian Records and Video, *7172 W. Grand Avenue, Chicago, (312) 637-5300.* Charming family-owned store now at its third location near Elmwood Park. The business began more than sixty-seven years ago on the West Side, but is now owned by Pompeo Stillo, author of three books about Italian life. Flags, jackets, greeting cards, Italian cassettes and records are available for purchase. Ermida Cassano, one of the employees, is a wealth of information about Chicago's Italian community. Hours: Monday, Thursday, Friday, 10 A.M. to 8 P.M.; Tuesday, 10 A.M. to 6:00 P.M.; Sunday, 10 A.M. to 6 P.M. Credit cards accepted. *Recommended.*

Capodimonte Imports, *5958 W. Addison, Chicago, (312) 283-2412.* Flowers and assorted gift items attractively presented in this small, independently owned store. Hours: Monday through Saturday, 10 A.M. to 6 P.M.; Sundays, 10 A.M. to 2 P.M.; Closed Thursday.

Gino's Italian Imports, Ltd., *3420-22 N. Harlem, Chicago, (312) 745-8310.* Gino Bartucci built his Mediterranian-style shopping plaza in 1981 to house the specialty imports he offers for sale, including cheeses, sausages and pasta, kitchen tools and handmade china. Hours: Monday through Friday, 9 A.M. to 7 P.M.; Saturdays, 8 A.M. to 6 P.M.; Sundays, 8 A.M. to 4 P.M. Credit cards accepted.

Minelli Brothers Italian Specialties and Liquors, *7780 N. Milwaukee Avenue, Niles, (708) 965-1315.* Homemade roast beef, pizza, and Italian sausages. Hours: Monday through Saturday, 8:30 A.M. to 6:00 P.M.; Sundays, 8:30 A.M. to 2:00 P.M. No credit cards.

Lappetito Imported Italian Foods, *30 E. Huron Street, Chicago, (312) 787-9881.* Complete line of Italian imported groceries. Deli service, party trays. No liquor products. Hours: Monday through Saturday, 10:00 A.M. to 6:30 P.M.; closed Sundays.

La Bomboniera, *3429 N. Harlem, Chicago, (312) 725-9000.* Imported gifts, party favors for all occasions. Hours: Monday through Friday, 10 A.M. to 8 P.M.; Saturdays, 10 A.M. to 7 P.M. Credit cards accepted.

Via Moto Ltd., *835 N. Michigan Avenue, Chicago, (312) 943-1700.* Plan on registering for the Marchetti family's "Concours d'Elegance." You can stock up on all your automotive needs (if you happen to drive an Alfa Romeo or a Ferrari), at this interesting boutique catering to the race-car set. The gifts and supplies are nearly all imported from Italy. Monday through Friday, 10 A.M. to 7 P.M.; Saturday and Sunday, 10 A.M. to 6 P.M. Credit cards accepted.

Pasta Fresh Co., *3418 N. Harlem, Chicago (312) 745-5888.* Located next to Gino's in the "Piazza Italia" plaza on Harlem Avenue. Pasta and delicatessen products imported from Italy. Hours: Monday through Saturday, 8 A.M. to 6 P.M.; Sundays, 8 A.M. to 3 P.M.

Neighborhood Festivals and City Celebrations

Columbus Day Parade, annual event scheduled on the Monday closest to October 12. Each year Chicago's Italians pay tribute to the great navigator whose voyage of discovery led to the permanent settlement of the New World. Whether the Vikings preceded Christopher Columbus or not remains a hotly debated issue. It is a moot point on Columbus Day, of course, as thousands of people line the parade route, which stretches along Dearborn Street between Wacker Drive on the north to Van Buren on the south. Lavishly decorated floats, some 175 marching bands, and a score of politicians and celebrities have turned out each year since 1952 to laud the accomplishments of Columbus. "It's a great day to be Italian!" exclaimed former Lieutenant Governor Neil Hartigan—an Irishman—who was in attendance at the 1990 parade. For more information about the parade, call (312) 828-0010.

The night before the gala downtown parade, the Sons of Italy sponsor a Columbus Day Banquet, traditionally held at a suburban hotel. Call the Order Sons of Italy in America, 7222 Cermak Road, Riverside, (708) 447-6304.

Festa Italiana, *a three-day folk fair held at Arvey Field, the south end of Grant Park at 12th Street and Columbus Drive during the third weekend of August.*   Since 1976, this popular family event has become a perennial favorite of Chicagoans. That year, the event was a side attraction to the Columbus Day weekend festivities, and was held in relative obscurity at the O'Hare Hyatt Regency in suburban Rosemont. In 1979, under the direction of attorney Anthony J. Fornelli, Festa Italiana moved to Navy Pier to become the city's first important ethnic folk fair. Fornelli envisioned more than just an arts and crafts, eat-all-you-want festival. He did not want to lose sight of the cultural and religious aspects of Italian-American life. Sculptors, painters, and artisans from the Chicago area display their work during the weekend in order to educate and inform the public about the achievements of Chicago's Italians. Festa Italiana features more than the usual food booths and balloons. There are two main stages showcasing such local and national talents as Frankie Avalon, the singing restauranteur Tony Spavone, and Rick "Elvis" Saucedo. An impressive fireworks display presented by the Bartolotta Company of Milwaukee caps off the festivities on Friday and Saturday. Tickets are available at local Dominicks and Butera Finer Food stores for $5 or at the gate for $6 the day of the event. For further information and times, call (312) 829-8888. *Recommended.*

Annual Italian Heritage Ball and Cotillion, *Grand Ballroom of the Conrad Hilton Hotel, 720 S. Michigan Avenue, Chicago.* The Joint Civic Committee of Italian Americans (JCCIA) is an umbrella organization of leaders representing more than forty fraternal societies who joined forces in 1952 to combat bigotry and prejudice against Americans of Italian descent. The Women's Division, organized in 1966, sponsors an annual Heritage Ball and Cotillion held the second Friday of December. The black-tie event began in 1966, and it marks the debut of the prettiest and most talented Italian-American debutantes between the ages of 15 and 21. The young ladies and their escorts perform a sequence of choreographed dance routines before the assembled guests which may include the Bishop or Cardinal. Ticket prices (subject to change) can be purchased for $65 per person. Call the JCCIA at (312) 828-0010.

A Touch of Italy, *food fest and entertainment on the Near West Side along Taylor Street between Halsted and Morgan Streets.* Two stages of continuous entertainment featuring such Italian-American entertainers as Al Martino. An annual event in the old neighborhood since 1989. Donations requested. Call (312) 243-3773.

Memorial Day Weekend and pancake breakfast *at Smith Park, 2526 W. Grand, Chicago.* Sponsored by the Italian Cultural Society in conjunction with the Northwest Civic Committee. Held every year since 1989 on the Sunday of Memorial Day weekend, from 10 A.M. to 1 P.M. Entertainment, games art exhibit, merchandise sales, memorial service in the afternoon. Bocci ball tournament, seven special contests. Tickets: $5 for adults, $3 for seniors and children under twelve. For more information call (312) 421-7505.

Outside Chicago

Festa Italiana, *Henry W. Maier Festival Park, Milwaukee, Wisconsin, located off of I-794, east of Harbor Drive.* Billed as "America's Greatest Italian Event," the Milwaukee fest is indeed a show-stopper, held for four days in mid-July along the scenic lakefront. Eight stages appropriately named "Roma," "Folonari," "Tenda," and the obligatory Milwaukee breweries, feature some of the biggest names in show business. Anna Maria Alberghetti, Buddy Greco, Al Martino, Julius LaRosa, and Dick Contino are among the performers who have entertained and delighted audiences since Festa Italiana was conceived in 1977. Mass and procession on Sunday. Bocci tournament. Drum and bugle and flag-throwing drill team. Continuous entertainment. Tickets are $6 in advance or at the gate. To receive a free brochure and additional information, contact Festa Italiana, 631 E. Chicago Street, Milwaukee, WI 53202, or call (414) 223-2180.

Italian Community Center *at 631 Chicago Avenue, Milwaukee, Wisconsin.* Opened in the fall of 1990, the center fosters an awareness of Italian culture, and dedicates itself to making available charitable, educational, social, and recreational activities for the greater Milwaukee community.

Rockford Days Festa Italiana, *Rockford, Illinois.* A three-day festival of Italian top name entertainment, folk dancing, cultural displays and Italian food. Held at Boylan Catholic High School, Campus Hills Boulevard, Rockford, (815) 877-2573, or contact Eugene Fedeli at (815) 966-2531. Admission: $1. Traditionally held the first weekend in August.

Religious Fests

The Annual Feast of Our Lady of Mt. Carmel Outdoor Mass and procession *through the streets of Melrose Park.* Since 1893, members of Chicago's Neapolitan communities have observed this important religious festival in various surroundings. It began in the inner city neighborhoods north of the river, but with the suburban population shift, the traditions have been imported. The Saint's Day Procession is held on the Sunday closest to July 16. After the Sunday noon Mass, the statue of Our Lady of Mount Carmel is carried through the streets of Melrose Park from the grounds of the Civic Center, at 25th and Lake Street. The sacred image, which stands six feet tall, was brought to the U.S. in 1894, and is held aloft by six strong men. The procession sometimes stretches eight blocks or more. Call (708) 865-9746 for details.

St. Francesco di Paola Society, *Italian Cultural Center, 1621 N. 39th Avenue, Stone Park.* An outdoor feast accompanies the Sunday outdoor Mass, held in mid-August on the grounds of the Cultural Center. Entertainment. Italian food may be purchased on the grounds. Call (708) 345-3842 for details.

Feast of Santa Maria Lauretana Society, *22nd and Harlem, Berwyn.* A three-day festival held on the last weekend of August, featuring food, entertainment, fireworks, and the time honored "Flight of the Angels" procession on Saturday and Sunday at 5 P.M. Call (312) 736-3766 for details.

Feast of St. Anthony of Padua. *Solemn High Mass conducted at Our Lady of Mount Carmel Church, 1101 N. 23rd Avenue, Melrose Park, the second Sunday of June.* Religious procession following the Mass. Refreshments served in Carmel Hall following the procession. St. Anthony's bread is also blessed. Call (708) 345-0630 for details.

St. Joseph's Day Celebrations

According to religious scholars, the custom of offering a "St. Joseph's Table" of food and beverage to the hungry and the homeless began in Sicily, when the people, appalled by the treatment shown the Holy Family, restaged the biblical event in their towns and villages. Others claim that it recalls St. Luke's account of the Nativity, in which Mary and Joseph found only the barest of essentials when they arrived in Bethlehem to give birth to the Christ child. The Sicilians adopted March 19 as the traditional St. Joseph's Day; a time when they opened their doors and their hearts to the street people, offering unlimited food in a symbolic anticipation of the Holy Family's arrival. The custom is recreated at several Chicago-area parishes in March as both a feast and fundraising event.

Scalabrini Village, *480 N. Wolf Road, Northlake.* Mass at Villa Scalabrini Chapel (procession to Casa San Carlo dining room afterward). Noon to 7 P.M. Donations requested. Call (708) 562-0040.

Immaculate Conception, *Monsignor Plunkett Hall Parish Center, York and Archer, in Elmhurst.* Table open from 1 P.M. to 4 P.M. Donations accepted. Call (708) 833-1759.

St. Symphorosa Church, *5940 W. 62nd Street, Chicago.* Table open from noon to 3 P.M. Donations are sent to the St. Rose School for Special Children. Donations: Adults $6; children $3. Call (312) 667-1523.

Our Lady of Pompeii Church, *1224 Lexington Avenue, Chicago.* Mass celebrated at 11 A.M. Table open from noon till 3 P.M. Call (312) 421-3757.

St. Anthony's Holy Rosary Society, *11533 S. Prairie Avenue, Chicago.*   Table open 10 A.M. to 3 P.M. Donations accepted. Call (312) 928-6460.

St. Callistus Parish, *2167 Bowler Street, Chicago.*   A tradition since 1957. St. Joseph's Table is open from 1 P.M. to 5 P.M., Sundays in the school gym. Festivities begin with a procession to the statue followed by noon Mass. Donations accepted. Call (708) 823-2550.

Our Lady of Ransom Parish, *Paluch Hall, 8300 N. Greenwood, Niles.*   Table is open from 1:30 P.M. to 5:00 P.M. Donations accepted.

Selected Italian Restaurants in Outlying Areas of Chicago and the Suburbs

There are hundreds (probably thousands, if the truth be known) of Italian restaurants in Cook and the collar counties, ranging from beef stands to elegant formal dining. Our purpose here is to list the establishments which have earned the critics praise, either because of the quality of the food served, or the ambient decor which suggests a touch of Italy within Illinois.

Tony Spavone's Ristorante, *266 W. Lake Street, Bloomingdale, (708) 529-3154.*   It's where the owner sings to his customers—but you can only catch Tony Spavone's act on weekends, so it's best to call ahead for reservations. Tony, a fixture at Festa Italiana, has been featured on WBBM-TV's "Two On Two" segment. His restaurant is consistently rated among the best in metro-Cook County. Open Monday through Friday, from noon to 11 P.M. Saturday, 4 P.M. to 2 A.M.; Sunday, 2 P.M. to 10 P.M. Credit cards accepted.

Italian Village, *71 W. Monroe, Chicago, (312) 332-7005.*   A downtown institution housing three restaurants in one. On the main level you'll find the "Viviere," which is gourmet cooking at its best. Viviere is actually the old Florentine Room. The "Village"—most popular with opera aficionados—is less expensive and is on the second floor. The basement "La Cantina" is a wine cellar grotto and ideal for a quick lunch.

Open: Monday through Thursday, 11 A.M. to 1 A.M.; Friday and Saturday, 11 A.M. to 2 A.M.; Sunday, 11 A.M. to 1 A.M. Major credit cards accepted.

Carlucci's, *2215 N. Halsted, Chicago, (312) 281-1220.* Elegant decor, and sophisticated Italian cooking. Open Monday through Thursday, 5:30 P.M. to 10:30 P.M.; Friday and Saturday, 5:30 to 11:30 P.M.; Sundays 5 P.M. to 10 P.M. Credit cards accepted.

Da Nicola, *3114 N. Lincoln Avenue, Chicago, (312) 935-8000.* Pricey family-style portions served in a pleasing, homey atmosphere. The appetizers are considered exceptional. Open: Sunday, Monday, Wednesday, and Thursday, 4:00 P.M. to 11:30 P.M., Friday and Saturday, till 12:30 P.M. Major credit cards accepted.

Pizzeria Uno and Due, *29 E. Ohio and 619 N. Wabash, Chicago, (312) 321-1000, and (312) 943-2400.* Two of the best deep-dish pizza parlors in the city are only a block apart. Both restaurants are usually crowded, so it's best to phone your order ahead. Off-times tend to be the best. Uno is open Monday through Thursday, 11:30 A.M. to 11:00 P.M.; Friday and Sunday till midnight. Due is open Monday through Thursday 11:30 A.M. to 1:00 A.M.; Fridays till 2:30 A.M.; Saturday, noon till 2:30 A.M.; Sunday till 11:30 P.M.

Ristorante Italia, *2631 N. Harlem, Chicago, (312) 889-5008.* This is the place to go for pasta—twenty-four varieties in all. They are cooked al dente and most are homemade. The restaurant is busy and crowded during peak times, so it is best to call ahead. Open Sunday, Tuesday, and Thursday, 4 P.M. to 9 P.M.; Friday and Saturday till 11 P.M. Closed Monday.

Scoozi! *410 W. Huron, Chicago, (312) 943-5900.* Large Italian eatery that seats 320 people is usually crowded during the dinner hour, but roasted meats and smoked pheasant dishes are worth the wait. Luncheon served from 11:30 A.M. to 2:00 P.M. Monday through Friday. Dinner: Monday through Thursday, 5:00 P.M. to 10:30 P.M.; Friday and Saturday, 5:00 P.M. to 11:30 P.M., Sunday, 5 P.M. to 9 P.M. *Recommended.*

Spiaggia, *980 N. Michigan, Chicago, (312) 280-2750.* The decor is impressive, the servers are well versed and attentive, but the prices of the pasta are high—as pastas go. Spiaggia on Boul Mich is certainly worth a look, though it is a far cry from the homey little places along Oakley (Marzullo) Avenue. Luncheon served Monday through Saturday, 11:30 A.M. to 2:00 P.M.; dinner, Monday through Thursday, 5:30 P.M. to 9:30 P.M.; Friday and Saturday, 5:30 P.M. to 10:30 P.M.; Sunday till 9 P.M. Credit cards accepted. *Recommended.*

Va Pensiero-Margarita Inn, *1566 Oak Avenue, Evanston, (708) 475-7779.* At center stage is the cooking of executive chef Peggy Ryan, whose superb pastas and veal shank are highly recommended. Wonderful desserts and an exceptional wine list. A Northshore delight. Lunch, Monday through Friday, 11:30 A.M. to 2:00 P.M.; dinner, Monday through Thursday, 5:30 P.M. to 9:00 A.M.; Friday and Saturday, 5:30 P.M. to 10:30 P.M. Credit cards accepted.

Lou Malnati's, *(four locations) 441 N. Wells, Chicago, (312) 828-9800; 6649 Lincoln Avenue, Lincolnwood, (708) 673-0800; 1050 E. Higgins Road, Elk Grove Village, (708) 439-2000; 88 S. Buffalo Grove Road, Buffalo Grove, (708) 980-1525.* Lou Malnati is a top-drawer, down-home, deep-dish pizzeria that is a favorite of Chicago sports fans. Autographed posters and photographs of Chicago sports greats line the walls of the restaurants. In Buffalo Grove there is a miniature museum on display. But the décor is not the reason to drop by; the pizza's the thing. Open seven days a week. Hours vary with location.

The Como Inn, *546 N. Milwaukee Avenue, Chicago, (312) 421-5222.* The story begins in 1920, when "Papa" Giuseppe Marchetti left his home in the Tuscan village of San Ginese near Lucca. He arrive in Chicago at the age of 17, ragged, hungry, and filled with ambition. Joe Marchetti became a partner in a small restaurant at Grand and Halsted. In 1924 a nearby grocery store suddenly became available, and young Marchetti, realizing the golden opportunity that comes to each man but once, bought out the business and founded the Como Inn Restaurant. In the early days it was your typical white tablecloth Italian restaurant, but after World War II, the Como Inn evolved into its present neoclassical design. Today the Como Inn is a restaurant *complex*, with thirteen dining rooms. The Marchettis serve Northern Italian cuisine, and can accommodate large private parties. The Como Inn, tucked away in the sleepy West Town neighborhood bounded by Grand Avenue, the Kennedy Expressway, Division, and Ashland, is open Monday through Thursday,

11:30 A.M. to 11:30 P.M., Friday and Saturday, 11:30 A.M. to 12:30 A.M., Sundays, noon till 11:30 P.M. The restaurant is only *part* of the story, so please read on. *Recommended.*

La Gondola, *2425 N. Ashland, Chicago, (312) 248-4433.* Southern Italian cooking served in a pleasing old-fashioned family atmosphere. The paintings of familiar Venetian scenes grace the walls and provide an interesting European backdrop as you dine on steamed mussels, fresh ravioli, and fried calamari. Nothing fancy here, just a down-home style in West Lincoln Park. Hours: Monday through Friday, 11 A.M. to 11 P.M.; Saturday and Sunday, 4 P.M. to 11 P.M. Credit cards accepted. Parking in rear.

Galleria Marchetti, 825 W. Erie Street, (312) 829-7065

A few years after launching the Como Inn, Giuseppi Marchetti decided to invest a portion of his earnings in a cherished prize: a 1929 Cord automobile. Marchetti and his four sons had a lifelong love affair with the automobile, especially sleek, high-performance racing cars.

Ferraris. Joe Jr. began collecting them in 1963. His fixation with the vintage Italian racing machines began that year when he housed his collection in a garage across the street from the Como Inn. The garage at Erie and Halsted was first a showroom and dealership, and then a showcase for art exhibitions and a banquet hall for private parties of up to 250.

The Galleria Marchetti is a unique and picturesque spot within the old industrial corridor of West Town. In October, 1989, the Marchettis hosted an extravaganza of Italian design—called the Oggi exhibit, featuring a display of contemporary furniture, home accessories, painting, film, and fashion from Milan. Oggi '89 (the literal translation means "today") was magnificently received, with the proceeds going to the Rinascimento Foundation, which promotes cultural exchanges between Italy and the U.S. The Oggi exhibit promises to become another Como tradition. The ticket prices are $65 per person, and interested parties should call the Galleria Marchetti at (312) 829-7065.

In 1980, Joe Marchetti founded the Chicago Historic Races at Road America at Elkhart Lake, Wisconsin. Fifty drivers and 500 visitors turned out the first year to preview a fine collection of sports and racing cars built prior to 1973. Since that time the International Challenge for the Chicago Historic Races has attracted 330 cars and drivers, and

10,000–15,000 spectators a year. The annual event, held the second weekend in July, features a stunning "Race Car Concours D'Elegance" exhibition at Elkhart Lake, a dinner at Siebken's Resort, qualifying sessions, and an awards ceremony capped off by the Sunday feature races. Each of the events are separately priced, and inquiries should be directed to the Galleria Marchetti, at (312) 829-7065. They will be happy to send a registration form and information about entry requirements. The Marchettis abide by a simple philosophy when it comes to vintage racing: "Winning is not the sole purpose, and thoughtless driving will not be allowed."

Montefiori: Re-defining An Exotic, Lost Age

The air is still, the setting reminiscent of West Egg, and the Long Island estate of F. Scott Fitzgerald's fictional playboy Jay Gatsby, who welcomed the jazz babies and high living millionaires from the big city to share in the revelry of the times. Montefiori, a sprawling 55-acre retreat located 25 miles southwest of Chicago near the Cal-Sag Channel in Lemont, harkens back to that opulent era of champagne and roses, especially when Joe Marchetti sponsors the International Concours D'Elegance, featuring vintage car collectors showing off their road machines in Gatsby-era costumes. In 1989, Baron Hans Freiherr von Richthofen, grandson of the Red Baron, was in attendance at Montefiori to lend his name to the festivities.

Montefiori was added to the growing Marchetti empire in 1924, when Giuseppe decided he had to construct a Palladian-style replica of his birthplace in San Ginese. The summer home now belongs to Paul Marchetti, who maintains the estate in style. A camel, twelve llamas, six species of swans, and forty exotic birds ensure that the Montefiori estate lives up to its name—"mountain of flowers." The Marchetti family opened Montefiori to the public ten years ago, and during the summer months the family hosts a series of festivals evolving around collector automobiles, jazz dance, the Lyric Opera, and the beauty of flowers. A schedule of events, beginning in May and continuing through September, include "Festa Campagnola," an Italian-style picnic, the Great Gatsby Weekend, and International Concours D'Elegance, performances of Shakespeare, and classic Italian opera. In mid-September the Marchettis celebrate "Immagini di Toscana" in the beauty of the countryside. Montefiori is located along Routes 83 and 171. For additional information about seasonal events at the estate, please call Karen Baker at (312) 829-7065.

— An Italian Delight —
Stuffed Squid

4 tablespoons oil
1 clove garlic, minced
1 (no. 2) can plum tomatoes
8 medium-sized squid
2 cloves garlic, minced
1 cup bread crumbs
1 tablespoon minced parsley
2 tablespoons grated Romano cheese
salt and pepper to taste
1 egg, beaten

Sauce: Brown the garlic in oil; mash the tomatoes with a fork or put through a blender. Add to the garlic and simmer for one-half hour.

Squid: Clean the squid thoroughly. Combine the remaining ingredients; fill the cavity of each squid with the stuffing. Sew the squid closed or fasten with toothpicks. Place in baking pan; cover with sauce. Bake at 400 degrees for 35 minutes or until tender. Serves eight.—"Italian American Ways," by the Elenian Club of New Orleans.

Italian Language Radio Programming

"L'Ora della Famiglia," 2:30–3 P.M., Monday through Friday. Religious programming aired on WEEF-1430 AM. Hosted by Father Dino Cecconi, associate director of the Italian Cultural Center.

Greek Chicago

History and Settlement

"When Greek meets Greek they start a restaurant!" or so wrote Peter Lambros, founder and editor of the *Star*, Chicago's oldest established Greek newspaper. Lambros was recalling a time in the 1890s when his countrymen were first making their mark in the city.

The great exodus from the Pelopponese began in the late nineteenth century when the price of currants—a staple crop of the peasant farmer— fell to record lows. These Greeks had heard all of the familiar stories about the favorable prospects for Europeans seeking their way in America. Years earlier, during the Greek War of Independence (1821–28), hundreds of orphaned boys whose parents had been slaughtered by the rampaging Turks were sent to the U.S., where they were given good homes with American families. Many of these youths prospered in their new surroundings as they grew to adulthood.

Prior to 1871, there were only a few Greek immigrants in Chicago. One of the earliest arrivals was Captain Nicholas Pappas who settled on Kinzie Street in 1857. He lived in Chicago until his death in 1927. The first Greek marriage in Chicago took place shortly after the Civil War, when Nicholas Brown, owner of a Kinzie Street barber shop, married an American-born girl.

The cataclysmic fire of 1871 was the milestone event in the history of the Greek settlement of Chicago. The terrible disaster that scorched miles of prime city real estate encouraged large numbers of strong-bodied Greek men to come to Chicago to take part in the great rebuilding. Word of mouth—that great intangible of the European immigration—was important in luring the Greeks. Christ Chacona, known as the "Columbus of Sparta," was a pied-piper in his own right. Realizing that there was money to make here, Chacona returned to his home in Tzintzina, Sparta, to convince his relatives to sell the farm and come back with him to Chicago. Because of Chacona and others like him, the Greek colony near Clark and Kinzie Streets on the near North Side became the largest of its kind in the U.S., numbering 1,000. The immigrants for the most part, came from Laconia and Arcadia.

The Greek experience in Chicago in many ways paralleled that of the Chinese. Until 1885, there was not one woman counted by the census takers. This began to change with the arrival of Mr. and Mrs. Peter Pooley (Panagiotis Poulis) from Corfu, Greece, in 1885. Peter Pooley was a sea captain who was familiar with the city from his earlier excursions up the Mississippi River from New Orleans. Impressed with Chicago and all it had to offer, Pooley returned to Corfu where he was joined in marriage to Georgia Bitzis. Together they crossed the ocean and headed straight to Chicago, where in 1885, this spirited, dynamic woman organized the Greco-Slavonian Society, the first benevolent association of its kind. In 1887, the Therapnon Society was formed to promote the religious ideals of the homeland. Its members were instrumental in bringing to the U.S. the Reverend Peter Phiambolis, the first Greek Orthodox priest to emigrate to America. The church was located in modest surroundings—a rented loft space in a building at Randolph and Union Street. The church was consecrated by Greek Orthodox church leaders on March 25, 1893 during a visit to the World's Columbian Exposition by Bishop Dionysius Lattas of Zante. The oldest Greek Orthodox congregation in the U.S. worshipped in a converted Episcopal Church at 1101 S. Peoria from 1897 until 1963. Here in the West Side "Delta," (bounded by Halsted, Harrison, Blue Island, Polk Street and named for the triangular Greek letter), Chicago's largest, most important Greek settlement, generations of devout worshipers attended services and paid their dues to support the *koinotis* (community).

The role of the Greek Orthodox Church in the koinotis was paramount. Every Greek immigrant who resided in the Delta was automatically a member of the *paroikia* (colony). But only those persons who contributed a share of their earnings to support the church and its sponsoring institutions could be said to belong to the koinotis. This rigid social structure bounds its members to the neighborhood and it provided an important identity through the benevolent, fraternal, and social organizations. Despite their inherent factionalism, Chicago's Greeks were united in their support for Jane Addams, founder and director of Hull House from 1885 until her death in 1935. Addams was a friend to the community. She encouraged the Greeks to preserve their rich cultural heritage—so crucial for the survival of the folk traditions. The first Greek play in Chicago was presented at the Hull House Theater in December, 1899. It was a classical tragedy titled *The Return of Odysseus,* sponsored in part by the Greek fraternal societies. The play attracted favorable attention from the newspaper critics, which no doubt encouraged a number of the society women, including Bertha Honore Palmer, to purchase tickets. In May 1900, the play was transferred to the spacious Studebaker Theater for the benefit of all Chicagoans.

At Hull House, the Hellenic League For the Molding of Young Men was organized in 1908 to provide paramilitary and athletic training for young Greek men. Instruction was provided by former Greek army officers, who had the unit whipped into shape for the visit of former President Theodore Roosevelt in 1911. Commenting on the president's visit, the Chicago *Tribune* noted that he had come to Hull House "not to teach, but to learn." When Jane Addams died, she was mourned by the Greek community, which eulogized her as the "Saint of Halsted Street."

The Delta attained significance beginning in the 1890s, when thousands of immigrants poured into the city. Many of them became fruit and vegetable peddlers, or pushcart vendors, dispensing smoking sausages on a bun to lunchtime patrons in the Loop. Competition was often fierce between the Greeks and the Italians. Sometimes it evolved into fistfights between these two immigrant groups familiar with each other's culture and language. In 1904 the Grocer's Association complained to the City Council that the Greek peddlers were undercutting their business. The pushcart entrepreneurs defended themselves against their upscale competitors by telling the aldermen that they provided an indispensable service to the community, selling produce at reduced prices. In 1909 the city restaurant lobby attempted to ramrod through the council a bill that would raise the license fee from $25 to $200 a year. The street peddlers only postponed the inevitable, for Mayor Carter Harrison II put his stamp of approval on a City Council measure to ban the sale of food on the streets of Chicago.

The Greek merchants engaged in the fruit, vegetable, confectionary, and ice cream trade re-evaluated the options open to them. All those who could scrape together a few dollars did so—very often mortgaging their lands back in the old country to pay the first month's rent. Chicago's Greeks were to become in a few years some of the city's most skilled restaurateurs. They began selling food in the streets, then realized the business potential of storefronts. Some were pioneers in their respective industries. The first soda fountain was opened in a Greek-owned ice cream parlor in the Security Building. By 1927, according to Peter Lambros, the Greeks operated 10,000 stores—500 of them in the Chicago Loop—paying an aggregate monthly rental that exceeded $2,500,000. Typical of the many success stories in the food service industry was that of John Raklos, whose chain of restaurants numbered forty-five by 1930. During the war years and through the 1950s, Chicago's best-loved Greek restaurateur was "Billy Goat" Sianis, whose lower Michigan Avenue cafe was the favored watering hole of the city's left bank. Sianis, as the story goes, tried to purchase a seat in the grandstand for his pet goat, who very much wanted to see the Cubs play the Tigers in the 1945 World Series. When owner Phil Wrigley denied the ornery goat his place in the sun, Sianis placed a curse on the ballclub that has endured to this very day. Sam Sianis took over after his father passed away, but could do little to assist the hapless Cubbies, who have yet to win another pennant.

The Greeks were also prominent in banking, real estate, and Chicago's burgeoning commercial business, then located at South Water Street and Randolph. An estimated $250,000,000 was annually transacted with Greek merchants. Prominent in the entertainment field was the man who was to become synonymous with the big band sound. Andrew Karzas, who arrived in Chicago in 1904, erected a monument to the immigrant spirit in 1922—the magnificent Trianon Ballroom—on the same location where he began his career hustling newspapers and candies. The Trianon at 63rd and Cottage Grove Avenue on the South Side is gone but certainly not forgotten by those old enough to remember it. Later, Karzas gave to the North Side the Aragon Ballroom, where Paul Whiteman, Guy Lombardo, Wayne King, Glen Gray and his Casa Loma Band played to starry-eyed romantics for so many Saturday nights.

The Delta was synonymous with Greek culture in Chicago until the late 1950s, when the Eisenhower Expressway and the new University of Illinois campus displaced thousands of residents and forced the closing of Holy Trinity in 1963. The congregation had dwindled to only a handful of parishioners, but the faithful few re-established the church on the far Northwest Side, where it is now located. The Socrates School followed the congregation, moving from 42 S. Ada Street, where it was replaced by a statue of Christopher Columbus. The children who attended classes at the Socrates School were the offspring of first-generation immigrants.

Today all that remains of the dismantled Delta is a string of ethnic Greek restaurants in a two-block stretch along Halsted Street. At the Parthenon Restaurant at 314 S. Halsted, a passerby is often reminded of those former times by the sight of a whole pig or lamb roasting on a spit in the window.

After 1904 a second Greek settlement sprang up along 63rd Street between Wentworth and Cottage Grove avenues. It was founded by a group of malcontents from the Delta, who were instrumental in the formation of SS Constantine and Helen at 61st and Michigan in 1904. The church stood until 1926, when a fire gutted the interior. It was rebuilt with the help of Washington Park's most famous Greek citizen, Andrew Karzas. The church continued to serve the neighborhood until 1948, when the building was sold to the Episcopal congregation of St. Edmunds. The changing racial makeup of Washington Park hastened by the influx of southern blacks into the city before and after World War I influenced the decision to abandon the neighborhood for a new location farther south at 74th and Stony Island Avenue. In 1972, the congregation again moved for much the same reason—this time to south suburban Palos Hills.

The Washington Park Greeks are but a memory today. The spirit of those former times are being kept alive by the priest's son, novelist Mark Petrakis, who has written a string of award-winning books, including *Pericles on 31st Street, Hour of the Bell,* and *Nick the Greek.* Petrakis lives in Indiana now, but like other Chicago expatriates, the city is never very far from his thoughts. Today's Greektown encompasses much of the Lincoln Square neighborhood along Lawrence Avenue on the far North Side. The Greeks account for 10 percent of the population according to 1980 census statistics. But there is a distinctive Mediterranean presence here, reflected in the mural-decorated restaurants specializing in traditional lamb dishes.

Since 1928 St. Demetrius Greek Orthodox Church at Winona and Washtenaw has kept Greek religious traditions alive in Lincoln Square, a neighborhood noted for its wide ethnic diversity. The Greeks share living space with the Germans, Asians, Irish, and Hispanics. It is a latter-day melting pot. The church complex contains a community center, a library, and the Solon Afternoon Greek School, fostering a dual pride in classic Greek culture.

Chicago's 250,000 Greeks are widely dispersed through the Chicagoland area. They are linked together culturally, socially, and politically by the United Hellenic American Congress, an umbrella group founded in 1974 to coordinate the diverse activities of the community. Every May since 1965 the societies have sponsored the annual Independence Day Parade, a festive event featuring ecumenical leaders, the Greek "evzones" attired in colorful folk costumes, floats, and, of course, the queen.

Hellenism has survived and indeed prospered in the urban ethnic frontier of Chicago . . . or Chicagonopolis, if you will. Hellenic traditions have been preserved and handed down to a younger generation, thus preserving the duality of two worlds.

Getting There: By cab or bus, the Little Italy section (Halsted and Taylor) and Greektown (Halsted and Van Buren) are only minutes from the Loop. If you elect to take the CTA, catch the Madison Street bus (#20), and take it several blocks west to Halsted Street. You are within walking distance of both neighborhoods.

Parades, Celebrations, and Neighborhood Festivals

Greek-American Parade, *second Saturday in May, Michigan Avenue, from Lake Street to Van Buren.*   Everyone loves a parade, especially Chicago's Greek community, which turns out in full force every year to celebrate their independence from Turkey, which actually took place on March 25, 1821. However, the yearly threat of inclement weather in Chicago, and the health risks posed to the 10,000 or so children who participate in this event prompted officials to wait until May and the customary end of the school year. The parade is sponsored by the United Hellenic American Congress (UHAC), which was organized in 1975 to promote ethnic ideals and tradition, and to foster support for tiny Cyprus, which was cruelly invaded by an ancient foe in the region—Turkey—on July 20, 1974. Beginning with the very first parade in 1965, UHAC has attached a yearly theme to the festivities. In 1981 the parade tied in with the "Search For Alexander" exhibition that was touring the U.S. Three years later promoters again paid homage to the ancient world with "A Salute to the Olympics." The 1991 event marked "25 Years of Hellenic Unity!" Thousands of celebrants lined the parade route to hear traditional ethnic music, view the visiting Evzones—the presidential guard of honor guards from Athens outfitted in their colorful costumes— and to greet the "Queen of Greek Heritage Week," chosen in a contest held every year during the first week of May. For more information, call Helen Alexander at UHAC (312) 822-9888, or write to the organization at 400 N. Franklin Street, Suite 215, Chicago, IL 60610.

Greek Heritage Night, held at alternating churches the night before the annual parade in May. Free admission. Greek Heritage Week begins with a historical pageant recalling the 1821 War of Independence. The parade queen and her court are introduced, followed by a presentation given by the Evzones, and the Greek dance troops, including the Opa

Dancers of the Hellenic Society, and the Greek Macedonian Society of Chicago. The yearly pageant rotates between the North, West, and South Side Greek Orthodox churches in Chicago, and is sponsored by the Greek Heritage Committee. Two days before the actual parade, the Evzones will perform a series of Greek dances at the Chicago Civic Center, 50 W. Washington Boulevard, beginning at noon. Call UHAC at (312) 822-9888 for the specific times and location of these events.

Annual UHAC Banquet, *held at the Chicago Hilton and Towers, 720 N. Michigan Avenue, Chicago.*   Since 1975, the United Hellenic American Congress has sponsored an annual fund-raising dinner the second week of November, honoring notable Greek personages from Chicago, the U.S., and abroad. The proceeds generated from this event are channeled into the UHAC coffers for cultural, religious, philanthropic, and charitable programs. Keynote speaker, music, and entertainment. Call UHAC for the time, date, and price (usually $125, but this may vary from year to year). Call (312) 822-9888.

St. John Chrysostom Oratorical and Arts Festival. A two-day festival of poetry, iconography, and oratorical expressions of faith, sponsored by the Greek Orthodox Diocese, and held at the end of April in different churches in Chicago and the surrounding suburbs. The categories of participants are the Junior Division (7th to 9th grades); Senior Division (10th–12th grades); and a Young Adult Division (ages 19 to 35). Includes breakfast, awards luncheon, and divine liturgy. The recitations and poetry readings' are open to the public. Please call the Greek Orthodox Diocese at (312) 337-4130 for times and locations.

Greektown Festival on Halsted Street, *between Monroe and Van Buren, the second weekend of August.*   In 1991, the Greektown Merchants Association launched their first open-air summer festival, with specialty foods prepared by the master chefs of the restaurants, music, merchandise, and plenty of Greek culture. For additional information call Pete Liakouras, president of the Greektown Association at (312) 726-2407. *Recommended.*

Annual Celestial Soirée and Debutante Cotillion, *sponsored by the St. Helen Women's Philoptochos (club) of Sts. Constantine and Helen Church, 11025-45 S. Roberts Road, Palos Hills, (708) 974-3400.*   Annual charity ball and debutante presentation held at the Grand Ballroom of the Chicago Hilton and Towers the last weekend in June. The year 1991 marked the twenty-eighth anniversary of this gala formal black-tie affair, which features many notable guests, including the bishop or archbishop, the Consul General of Greece, and celebrity emcees, including Bill Kurtis and Maryann Childers. The Philoptochos is a woman's organization founded in New York. However, every Greek Orthodox Church in Chicago sponsors its own chapter, which promotes many worthwhile causes. Dinner. Two dance bands. Price: $65 to $75 per ticket.

St. George Holy Day Dinner Dance, *sponsored by the St. George Church at 2701 N. Sheffield Avenue, Chicago, and held at the Golden Flame Restaurant at 6417 W. Higgins, Chicago, the last Sunday in April.* A social hour begins at 5:30 P.M. from an open bar, which will continue throughout the evening. A complete prime rib dinner is served at 6:30 P.M. The donation is $30 for adults and $15 for children under twelve. For reservations call (312) 525-1793.

Neighborhood Church Festivals

"Greek Fest," *at the Annunciation Greek Orthodox Cathedral, LaSalle and Oak, Chicago, (312) 664-5485.* The first Greek Orthodox Church was also called the Annunciation (or "Evangelismos," meaning happy message), and it was located in a small wooden building at Kinzie and Clark. Philosophical differences and festering internal rivalries between religious factions within the community led to the closing of the first Annunciation Church, but a second one was built in 1910. The lovely yellow-brick Orthodox Church which borrows the earlier name, symbolizes the parallel between the Annunciation of the Virgin and the establishment of freedom in the motherland. Many other Greek churches in the U.S. trade upon the same theme: "Evanelismos-Hellenismos" salvation and freedom. The last weekend in July is a time to celebrate the enduring ideas that the Greek Orthodox Church in the U.S. was founded upon. The festival takes place every year on church grounds, and it features entertainment, Greek bands, singers, food booths, but no carnival rides. A liturgy is celebrated on Sunday. Admission is free, but there is a charge for food and beverage.

St. Demetrios Greek Fest, *Winona and Washtenaw Ave., Chicago, (312) 561-5992.* The church sponsors the oldest annual Greek Fest in the city, one that dates back to 1949. Each year hundreds of parishioners, many of whom abandoned the area years ago, come back to rekindle a few good memories, sample traditional Greek food under the tent, and listen to the dance music of Harry Karoubas and his band. The festival takes place the weekend following the Assumption, usually the second week in August. Admission is $2 per person.

St. George Orthodox Church Greek Fest, *Sheffield and Schubert, Chicago, (312) 525-1793.*   The parish of St. George originally opened at this North Side location as a German Evangelical Lutheran church, but with changing patterns of immigration it became a Greek Orthodox Church. The church has sponsored an annual Greek Fest for the last ten years in the rear parking lot, the second weekend in June around Father's Day. No rides, but plenty of good food, music, and ice cream. Admission: $1 per person.

St. Basil Greek Orthodox Church Greek Fest, *733 S. Ashland Avenue (at Polk), Chicago, (312) 243-3738.*   Formerly the Anshe Sholom Jewish synagogue, until the Greek community converted it into an Orthodox Church in 1927. The church has played an important role in the Near West Side Greek community, and still manages to hold on to its congregation, even though neighborhood displacement has caused many Greeks to leave the area. The traditional Greek festival is the last one on the calendar, and is held the weekend after Labor Day in the church hall and adjoining back yard. Music and entertainment. Food booths, merchandise displays, and Greek pastries are sold on the grounds. Admission is $1 per person.

St. Andrews Greek Orthodox Church, Annual Greek Fest, *5649 N. Sheridan Road, Chicago, (312) 334-4515.*   One of the newer churches to be built in the Chicago area (1956), St. Andrews has hosted a Greek Festival since 1960 on the church grounds at Hollywood and Sheridan near Lake Shore Drive. The one-day event is held on the second Sunday of July from noon to 11 P.M. Food booths, carnival rides, games, Greek food and dancing. Admission: $1.50 per person.

St. John the Baptist Greek Fest, *St. John's Orthodox Church, 2350 Dempster Street, Des Plaines, (708) 827-5519.*   Churches in the Northwest and south suburbs also feature colorful weekend festivals promoting Greek heritage. One of the best is sponsored by St. John's, the weekend following Father's Day. Food booths, Greek music, dancing, and an import booth in the church Social Center, where gift items from around the world are sold during this three-day extravaganza. Admission is $2. Parking is available in the Maine East High School parking lot at Dempster and Potter Roads, with shuttle bus service available.

Saints Constantine and Helen Greek Orthodox Church Greek Fest, *11025 Roberts Road, Palos Hills, (708) 974-3400.* Two-day festival held the weekend on, or immediately after August 15. Carnival rides, Greek food, clowns, musical entertainment, and dance troupes. One of the South Side's oldest church festivals. Admission: $1 per person.

St. Nicholas Church, Father's Day Festival, *10301 S. Kolmar Avenue, Oak Lawn, (708) 636-5460.* An annual south suburban Greek festival held on the weekend of Father's Day in the parish parking lot. Food booths, games, music, and dancing. Prices and times will change from year to year, so it is best to call the church in late May.

St. Spyridon, *12307 S. Ridgeland Ave. Palos Heights, (708) 385-2311.* Since 1972, the annual Greek Fest has been held in mid-July, and it features games, food booths, and ethnic dancing. The cost of admission is $1 per person.

St. Nectarios, *133 S. Roselle Road, Palatine, (708) 358-5170.* The three-day St. Nectarios Greek Fest takes place in mid-July in the church parking lot. Pony rides, food booths, ethnic dancing, pastries, and an "agora" (market place) where imported items are sold. Admission is $1 to $2 per person.

St. Sophia Greek Festival, *St. Sophia Greek Orthodox Church, 525 Church Road, Elgin, (708) 888-2822.* Greek culture celebrated through food, music, games, and a shopping boutique. The St. Sophia dance troupe also performs traditional dances. Held the second weekend in July. Hours: Friday, 6 P.M. to 11 P.M.; Saturday, noon to 11 P.M.; Sunday, noon to 10 P.M. Free admission.

St. Haralambros Greek Orthodox Church Foodfest, *7373 Caldwell Avenue, Niles, (708) 647-8880.* Second or third weekend in July. A real taste of Greek Chicago, with healthy servings of Athenian chicken, roast lamb, shishkabob, and pastichio (Greek lasagna). This annual fundraising event is hosted by Father Dean Botsis. All proceeds benefit the church. Free admission.

Ethnic Society

The Hellenic Museum and Cultural Center, *offices at 400 Franklin Street, Suite 215, Chicago, (312) 822-9888.* Incorporated in 1989, the Hellenic Museum and Cultural Society regularly schedules art exhibitions, and cultural presentations of general interest to the Greek community in Chicago. In the Summer of 1991, a traveling exhibition from the Art Gallery of Thessaloniki was brought to Chicago's Athenaeum Gallery in the Hancock Building under the auspices of the Museum, the Pan-Macedonian Association, and the Hellenic Professional Society of Illinois. The board of directors has explored various sites in Greektown for a permanent home for the museum, but for now, special exhibitions and programs of this nature must be held at alternate locations around Chicago. If the proposed "Greektown U.S.A." development goes through as planned, the museum, a gift shop, and a chapel will be headquartered in one of the buildings. Talks with the city continue. Membership in the society is open to persons with an abiding interest in Greek history and culture. To receive the Museum's recent publication, *A Guide to the Icons of Chicago,* and to be added to the mailing list, please call (312) 822-9888 during business hours.

Shopping and Dining in the
═══ Halsted Street Greektown ═══

Spurred by the construction of the Presidential Towers, a 2,346 unit apartment complex located in the West Loop, Chicago's Greektown is making a strong comeback following a period of economic decline in the mid- to late 1960s, when some 30,000 immigrant residents living near Halsted and Harrison were forced to abandon the neighborhood in order to make way for the new University of Illinois campus. With the arrival of many single, upscale professionals who live in the neighboring high rises, business is better than ever for the Greek restaurateurs and small shopkeepers along Halsted Street between Monroe on the north and Van Buren on the south. Chicago's Greektown blends the best of the old and the new. The St. Basil Greek Orthodox Church at 733 Ashland Avenue has anchored the community since 1927 when it was purchased by the Greeks for the benefit of those who stood in opposition to the Royalists of the older Holy Trinity Church at 11th and Peoria. During World War I, a rift developed between the staunch conservative Royalist party, which supported King Constantine, and the followers of the liberal-thinking Prime Minister Eleutherios Venizelos, who circulated rumors that the monarch was "pro-German" during the time the Greek government professed its neutrality. King Constantine's wife, Queen Sophie, was a sister of the German Kaiser, which placed the ruler in an untenable position. The king was exiled by the allies during the war, was brought back by a vote of the Greek people, and exiled a second time before passing away in Italy in 1923. This ideological split had deep repercussions across the Atlantic. The anti-Royalist sentiments led to a permanent rift in Chicago's Greek ecumenical community, and it contributed to the founding of St. Basil's by the Venizelists, who were inspired by the diplomat's historic visit to the city in October, 1921. Venizelos, who was described by former President Woodrow Wilson as "one of the greatest men at the [Paris] peace conference," was escorted on a guided tour of the Greek churches by the Hellenic Post of the American Legion.

In the 1960s, the congregation of St. Basil's dwindled to less than sixty families. Today it has grown to more than 250. Many of the parishioners are lured from the distant suburbs by the energetic young priest, Father Chris Kerhules, who took over his duties in 1989. St. Basil's, originally

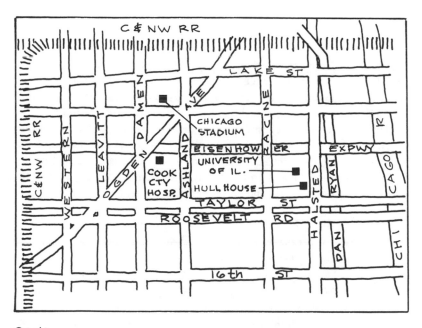

Greektown

built as a Jewish temple in 1911, has undergone extensive renovation in recent years. New icons prepared in the traditional Byzantine style have replaced the Renaissance images, favored by the founding members of the congregation back in the 1920s. The inside dome has been repainted, with a bright new molding and stenciling.

Several new dining establishments have opened in the last few years, and a real estate developer's ambitious plan to create "Greektown U.S.A.," a residential, commercial, and tourist complex centered along Halsted Street, points to the economic revitalization and seemingly limitless future of the community. The multipurpose center that will provide a permanent home for the Hellenic Museum and Cultural Center is still several years away. The impact of the 1990 recession temporarily put the plan on hold, but the lingering concerns that the last vestiges of the old Greek "Delta" would fade into memory have been put to rest.

Pegasus Restaurant and Taverna, *130 S. Halsted, Chicago, (312) 226-4666.* Pegasus is the latest addition to the Greektown restaurant row, opened in November, 1990. An attractive wall mural painted by Bora Guanovich depicts three of the Greek islands, Mykonos, Paros, and San Torini. The mural provides an appropriate backdrop for the elegant dining. House specialties include souvlaki, lamb, sinagrida (snapper), octopus, and some delectable appetizers. Valet parking. Hours: daily, 11 A.M. to 1 A.M. Bank cards accepted.

Santorini, *138 S. Halsted, Chicago, (312) 829-8820.* Named for one of the islands in the Aegean Sea. Seafood, especially broiled fish, is the order of the day at this charming but rustic eatery in Greektown that was opened in 1988 by Jim Kontos, owner of the Tempo Coffee Shop on Chestnut Street. The lunchtime menu is the best bargain, but it's advisable to call ahead for reservations since the restaurant critics around town have been falling all over themselves in praise of Kontos. Hours: Sunday through Thursday, 11 A.M. to midnight; Friday and Saturday, 11 A.M. to 1 A.M. Free valet parking, and credit cards are accepted.

Greek Islands, *200 S. Halsted, Chicago, (312) 782-9855, and 300 E. 22nd St., Lombard, (708) 932-4545. Formerly located at 766 W. Jackson.* The owners of this restaurant joined in a partnership to open Santorini, which is just down the street. The Greek Islands is one of the busiest locations on the street, and is not recommended for a quiet, late evening repast. During peak hours, the Greek waiters (no other nationalities will do) can serve up to 1,000 people. Hours: 11 A.M. to 11 P.M. daily.

Dianna's Opaa! *212 S. Halsted, Chicago, (312) 332-1225.* *Philo-xenia,* Greek meaning love for the stranger, is in abundance at Dianna's, one of Halsted Street's landmark restaurants. In 1961 Petros Kogiones opened the Diana Grocery and Restaurant in the 300 block of Halsted Street. It was nothing fancy as far as ethnic neighborhood restaurants go. But the personal magnetism of the owner ensured that this former school teacher from Nestani, Greece, would be around for a long time. Petros claims to have kissed more women than any man alive. He would dance with them, too, earning the well deserved sobriquet "King of the Opaa." The Kogiones brothers would douse their cheese appetizers with brandy and then set it on fire. "Opaa!"

Petros would personally greet each and every one of his female "cousins" to his Halsted Street restaurant, and would keep the festivities moving at a fever pitch. Sometimes the waiters got into the act, and a few dishes would occasionally be broken. But it was a small price to pay to experience Opaa! Hours: 11 A.M. to 1 A.M., every day. All credit cards accepted, valet parking. *Recommended.*

It's Greek To Me, *306 S. Halsted, Chicago, (312) 977-0022.* Opened in 1985. Owner Deni Salafatinos likes his patrons to feel as if they were among old friends by greeting them at the door. He used to be a meat salesman, but wanted to "be around his people more," so he decided to open a restaurant. It's the kind of hospitality that has made Greektown a favorite of both tourists and Chicagoans. Hours: Monday through Saturday, 11:30 A.M. to 1 A.M.; Sundays till midnight.

Parthenon, *314 S. Halsted, Chicago, (312) 726-2407.* The oldest restaurant on the strip, dating back to 1968 when Chris and Bill Liakouras bought out a small gyros restaurant that was about to go under. Complete with music, shouting waiters, dancing, and tasty flaming saganaki. (They even say Opaa!) Hours: Open 11 A.M. to 2 A.M. every day. All credit cards accepted.

Neon Greek Village, *310 S. Halsted, Chicago, (312) 648-9800.* Formerly George Mitchell's Greek Village, but now completely redecorated and under new ownership. The Village features the only continuous live entertainment in Greektown, (which means belly dancing, in case you didn't know) with music every night at 9 P.M. Panos Lambropoulos sings Greek ballads, George Sofos plays the bouzouki. Hours: Wednesday through Friday, 5 P.M. to 4 A.M.; Saturday and Sunday till 5 A.M. Closed Monday and Tuesday. All credit cards accepted.

Courtyards of Plaka, *340 S. Halsted, Chicago, (312) 263-0767.*
Laid back, understated elegance. Named for the old quarter of Athens,
near the slopes of the Acropolis. Owned by the Liakouras family, who
also run the Parthenon. The piano music of Dimitri Marinos is featured
nightly. Hours: Monday through Thursday, 11 A.M. to midnight; Friday
and Saturday, 11 A.M. to 1 A.M.; Sunday, 11 A.M. to midnight.

Rodity's, *222 S. Halsted, Chicago, (312) 454-0800.*   Rodity stands
for "red wine," which is served here. Greek rose wine is lighter, and
easier to take in large doses so be careful. If you're unfamiliar with Greek
food, try the Rodity's combination plate. Homemade bread. Wood pan-
eled bar. Hours: Open Sunday through Thursday, 11 A.M. to 1 A.M.;
Friday and Saturday, 11 A.M. to 2 A.M. Free parking.

Shops

Panellinion Meat Market, *804 W. Jackson, Chicago, (312) 726-
1081, or 454-9873.*   Bustling Greektown butcher shop. Baby back ribs,
spring lamb, and goat meat cut to specifications on an ancient wooden
chopping block. Open Monday through Saturday, 8 A.M. to 6:30 P.M.

Athenian Candle 6. , *801 W. Jackson, Chicago, (312) 332-
6988.*   Off-the-beaten-path religious gift store that sells icons, bibles,
exotic spices, mints, and uncut oil by the pound. Hours: Monday and
Tuesday, Thursday and Friday, 9:30 A.M. to 5 P.M.; Saturday, 9:30 A.M.
to 4 P.M. Closed Wednesday and Sunday.

Nikos Imports, *330 S. Halsted, Chicago, (312) 263-6342.*   One of
the new additions to the Greektown scene. One of the two brothers who
owns the business attends Harold Washington College. They specialize in
Greek video movies, CDs, albums, and cassettes. Silver gift items, pins,
religious icons, wedding gifts, jewelry, and figurines also stocked. Hours:
Monday through Saturday, 10 A.M. to 8 P.M.; Sunday, 11 A.M. to 6 P.M.
Checks, and credit cards accepted.

Athens Grocery, *324 S. Halsted, Chicago, (312) 332-6737.*   Owned by Jim and Bill Siannis, who opened the business a few doors down in
1962. The shelves are lined with imported Greek foods, olive oil, feta
cheese (made from goat's milk and sheep's milk), grapes, leaves, and
several foreign-language newspapers, including Chicago's own *Hellenic*

Life, published at 7902 Maple Street, Morton Grove, IL 60053. Hours: Monday through Saturday, 8 A.M. to 8 P.M.; Sunday 8 A.M. to 8 P.M.

Pan Hellenic Pastry Shop, *322 S. Halsted, Chicago, (312) 454-1886.* Owned by Louis Manolakos, an immigrant from Sparta who cooks his own special version of the sweet and gooey desert treat, baklava. *Galactoburiko* is a custard filled pastry, worth a try; ditto for the Kadaifi (shredded wheat with walnuts). You can order these delights and eat them in the shop. Hours: Monday through Saturday, 9 A.M. to 8 P.M.; Sunday, 1 P.M. to 6 P.M. No credit cards.

= The New Greektown at Lincoln Square =

An estimated 40,000 Greek Americans reside in a polyglot community directly west of the Lincoln Square shopping mall between Talman and Maplewood, along Lawrence Avenue. The Germans originally laid claim to this neighborhood, but with the breakup of the Delta in the years following World War II, many Greek families relocated to the North Side. A steady flow of immigrants from the old country found the numerous courtyard apartment buildings and two-stories very affordable and within walking distance of the church and the Lawrence Avenue commercial business. St. Demetrios Greek Orthodox Church at 2727 W. Winona Avenue, a basilica-style structure built in 1928, anchors the North Side Greektown. The 500-student Solon School is the largest afternoon school in the city, and it helps keep the traditions alive for second- and third-generation youngsters who attend classes until the age of sixteen. Their foreign language instruction is fully certified by the Greek government, and is transferable credit. The church library serves much the same cultural functions for the 1,500 families who worship here.

Less touristy than Halsted Street, the new Greektown is fighting to preserve its Hellenic identity amid a growing influx of Koreans, who have opened grocery emporiums, video rental agencies, and restaurants on West Lawrence Avenue, very often in vacated storefronts formerly occupied by Greeks and other Eastern European groups. The offspring of the Greek immigrants who settled Lincoln Square after World War II began leaving the community in the 1960s and 1970s in order to purchase single family dwellings north of Foster Avenue. According to George Stamos, who coordinates the St. Demetrios Festival, the new Greek immigrants are following close behind. Yet the church itself has maintained its congregation and still has a high percentage of "walk-up" traffic from the neighborhood for services.

Lincoln Square is indeed a "Touch of Europe," as it has been promoted by the local Chamber of Commerce in recent years, but increasingly this diverse community has also become a window to East Asia.

Shopping and Dining

Grecian Taverna, *4761 N. Lincoln Avenue, Chicago, (312) 271-4419.* A Greek restaurant the way they used to be. Two chefs cook the gyros over a hot spit in the front, while attending to the delicatessen. In the rear, Greek waiters provide for the luncheon and dinner patrons. Homemade gyros, carry out foods. Hours: 11 A.M. to 1 A.M., Sunday through Thursday. Closed Friday. Bank cards accepted.

Hellas Cafe and Restaurant, *2603 Lawrence Avenue, Chicago, (312) 561-9517.* Located at the intersection of Lawrence and Rockwell. The cafe is open for early morning breakfast from 6 A.M.. Open until midnight, Monday through Saturday. No credit cards taken.

Hellas Pastry Shop, *2627 Lawrence Avenue, Chicago, (312) 271-7500.* Weddings, birthday cakes, and assorted Greek pastries for all occasions. Hours: 8:30 A.M. to 9 P.M. Monday through Sunday.

New Hellas Imports, *2558 W. Lawrence, Chicago, (312) 271-1125.* Gift shop specializing in party favors for Greek religious observances. Candles, glassware, greeting cards, Greek language newspapers and magazines. Hours: Monday through Friday, 9:30 A.M. to 8 P.M.; Saturday, 9:30 A.M. to 5 P.M.; Sunday 11 A.M. to 2 P.M. No credit cards.

Parthenon #2, *4754 Rockwell Avenue, Chicago, (312) 989-0595.* Specializing in needlepoint and picture frames, with a limited selection of religious paintings and general merchandise. Located across the street from the Psarpoula Fish House, off Lawrence Avenue. Hours: Monday through Saturday, 10 A.M. to 7 P.M. Closed Sunday.

The Athenian, *4748 Western Avenue, Chicago, (312) 334-5698.* Imported shoes for men and women. Hours: Monday and Thursday, 10 A.M. to 7 P.M.; Tuesday–Wednesday, 10 A.M. to 6 P.M.; Fridays and Saturdays, 10 A.M. to 6 P.M. Bank cards accepted.

Psarpoula Fish House, *4755 N. Rockwell, Chicago, (312) 728-5415.* Where the neighborhood Greeks go to buy sea bass, squid, shrimp, and octopus for their cooking needs. Hours: Monday through Friday, 9 A.M. to 8 P.M.; Saturday, 9 A.M. to 5 P.M. No credit cards.

Delphi Food Market and Restaurant, *2655 W. Lawrence, Chicago, (312) 878-4917 for the restaurant, and (312) 271-0660 for the market.* Another throwback to the days when the Greeks were both grocers and restaurant owners. Hours: 9 A.M. to 9 P.M. Monday through Saturday; 9 A.M. to 5 P.M., Sunday.

Danny's Foodmart and Bakery, *2707 W. Lawrence, Chicago, (312) 561-9292.* Well-stocked grocery store and delicatessen that sells imported Greek foods, liquor, and newspapers, and rents the latest movies from Greece on video cassette. Hours: Monday through Saturday, 8 A.M. to 9 P.M.; Sunday, 8 A.M. to 5 P.M.

Outlying Restaurants and Stores

Billy Goat Tavern, *Hubbard and (Lower) Michigan Ave., Chicago, (312) 222-1525.* The "curse of the Billy Goat" has haunted the Chicago Cubs since 1945, the year that Phil Wrigley decreed his ballpark off-limits to Sonovia, a cantankerous horned mammal that was the pride and joy of William Sianis, popular West Side restaurateur and bon vivant. During the '45 World Series, Sianis, an ardent Cub fan, purchased a ticket for Sonovia so that the beast could bring good luck to the North Siders. Phil Wrigley, a rather straight-laced, priggish owner who inherited his daddy's chewing gum empire, decided that his ballpark was no place for shaggy, foul-smelling Sonovia. Ticket or no ticket, the goat wasn't going to get in. The Cubs went on to lose the series to the Detroit Tigers, which afforded Sianis the perfect chance to get in a few last digs. He sent a telegram to Wrigley, demanding to know: "Just who stinks now?" It certainly wasn't the mountain goat. Billy Sianis prophesied that the Cubs would never again win the pennant, and the rest, as they say, is history.

Sianis emigrated to Chicago from a rural village in the mountains of Greece in 1909, and within a few years, he opened his first tavern and restaurant at 1855 W. Madison Street, directly across from the Chicago Stadium. A stable of baby goats occupied the rear of the building, but by decree of the owner, no Republicans were allowed to enter the domain. Sports writers and Democrats were always welcome to come in and quaff his Pilsner at thirty-cents a glass (or three for a dollar . . . Billy never was very good at arithmetic), while the neighborhood urchins played with the pet goats. Eventually the old tavern was bulldozed in order to make way for a parking lot, but this did not deter Sianis from moving to the high rent district. Billy's East opened up on Lower Michigan, and it soon became the poor man's lunchtime alternative to the glitzy Ric Riccardo's, where the journalistic élite gathered to swap war stories.

The Billy Goat attracted its own literary clientele over the years. Columnists Jack Griffin, Arch Ward, Mike Royko, Studs Terkel, and Dave Condon spent a fair amount of time ingesting greasy "cheezeborgers," chips, and Coke (no Pepsi!) between deadlines. Actor John Belushi and the rest of the Second City cast ate here, too. Years later, Belushi mimicked the short-order cooks who worked for nephew Sam Sianis, in his own comedy sketches for "Saturday Night Live."

You won't find traditional Greek food here. To sample the finer dishes from the islands, you'll have to backtrack to Halsted Street—but the old fashioned atmosphere of Billy Goat's makes this Michigan Avenue landmark one of a kind. Hours: Monday through Thursday, 7 A.M. to 2 A.M.; Fridays till 3 A.M.; Saturday, 6 A.M. to 3 A.M.; Sunday, 11 A.M. to 2 A.M. Credit cards? Forget it! *Recommended.*

Nikos Restaurant & Lounge, *7600 N. Harlem Avenue, Bridgeview, (708) 496-0300.* Greek and continental cuisine. Sunday brunch from 10 A.M. to 3 P.M. Hours: Monday through Friday, 11 A.M. to 10 P.M.; Saturday, 5 P.M. to midnight. Sunday brunch, 10 A.M. to 3 P.M.

Green's West, *8624 W. 95th Street, Hickory Hills, (708) 598-6688.* Greek and American cuisine. Hours: Monday through Saturday, 7 A.M. to midnight. Credit cards taken.

Deni's Den, *2941 N. Clark Street, Chicago, (312) 348-8888.* Features live entertainment: Greek singers and music every Friday and Saturday night, 8:30 P.M. to 4:30 A.M. Other hours: Monday, Wednesday, and Sunday, 5 P.M. to 4 A.M.; Saturdays until 5 A.M.; and Sundays until 4 A.M. Credit cards accepted. Advance reservations recommended.

Central Gyros, *3127 N. Central, Chicago, (312) 622-5288.* There are hundreds of gyros stands in Chicago, but we recommend Central

Gyros on the Northwest Side, owned by the Apostolou brothers, as our personal favorite. Beer and Greek wine served. Open 11 A.M. to 1 A.M. daily. Friday and Saturday, 11 A.M. to 2 A.M.

Parragon Restaurant and Lounge, *Roselle and Algonquin Roads, Palatine, (708) 705-9300.* Greek and continental food. Your hosts: George, Paul, and Vasilios Sourounis. Hours: Monday to Thursday, 11 A.M. to 3 A.M.; Friday and Saturday, 11 A.M. to 4 A.M.; Sunday, 8 A.M. to 11 P.M.

Sparta Grocery, *6050 W. Diversey, Chicago, (312) 637-8073.* Greek foods, meat, produce, and newspapers. Hours: Monday through Thursday, 8 A.M. to 8 P.M.; Friday, 8 A.M. to 9 P.M.; Saturday and Sunday, 8 A.M. to 5 P.M.

Greek Bakery, *6113 W. Diversey, Chicago, (312) 889-6222.* Hours: Monday through Saturday, 9 A.M. to 7 P.M.; Sunday, 9 A.M. to 5 P.M.

S & H Food Mart, *5733 Cicero Avenue, Cicero, (708) 656-9757.* Goat meats, roast pork, lamb, and grocery items from Greece. Hours: Monday through Friday, 9 A.M. to 8 P.M.; Saturday, 9 A.M. to 6 P.M.

Crystal Palace Imports, *9292 Waukegan Road, Morton Grove, (708) 965-7844.* Imported gift items, including Greek ceremonial clothing, baptism candles, and crystal from all over the world. No credit cards. Hours: Monday through Friday, 10 A.M. to 8 P.M.; Saturday, 10 A.M. to 6 P.M.; Sunday, noon to 3:30 P.M.

Greek Language Radio Programming

"Hellenic Heartbeat," Sounds of Yesterday and today, produced and presented by Vicky Kournetas every Sunday from 2:00 P.M. to 4 P.M., on WONX-AM, 1590.

— A Recipe For Kakavia, a Traditional Fish Soup —
This hearty fish soup is a traditional favorite on the Greek islands. After the fishermen had returned from the sea with their daily catch, they would build a roaring fire and place all of the unsold fish into a large pot called

a "kakavia" and feast into the night. To recreate the Greek fisherman's meal, you'll need the following items:

4–6 pounds of whole fish suitable for boiling. Stripped bass, red snapper or striped bass are best.

1/2 cup of olive oil
4 large chopped onions
2 stalks of celery, cubed
2 leeks, sliced
3 cloves of garlic, sliced
3 large carrots, pared and cubed
2 tablespoons of salt
1 teaspoon of pepper
juice from 1 whole lemon
1 pound can of plum tomatoes with juice
6 cups of water
1 cup of white wine
3 bay leaves
1/2 teaspoon dried thyme
1 tablespoon minced parsley
1 (2 pound) lobster cut into serving size pieces (include shells)
12 clams scrubbed
12 shrimp, shelled and deveined
12 mussels, bearded, scrubbed, and cleaned

Clean and cut the fish into small pieces. Heat the oil in a large pot. Sauté the onions, garlic, celery, and leeks over medium heat for five minutes. Add the remaining ingredients except the seafood and bring to a boil. Reduce the heat and cover. Cook for fifteen minutes. Add the fish and cover for another fifteen minutes. Add shellfish and simmer for 10 minutes, or until clams and mussels open. Remove the fish from the pot and clean it, removing the skin and bones. Discard the shells from the shellfish. Return fish and shellfish to the pot and reheat briefly. Serve in deep bowls with crusty garlic bread. Serves up to twelve.

African-American Chicago

History and Settlement

A sea of windswept prairie grass, a sky of leaden gray, and an expanse of lake, left there by an ancient, retreating glacier that extended as far as the eye could see—this is how Chicago appeared in 1779 when Jean Baptiste Point du Sable established a trading post in what is now Pioneer Court.

Du Sable, a French-speaking mulatto, was the son of a prominent Quebec merchant and a former slave woman from Santo Domingo. His trading post on the banks of the lake was the hub of commercial activity in the Northern Illinois territory in the years before Fort Dearborn was established to guard the waterways from the French and the Indians in 1803. The settlement of Chicago, and the African-Americans who were to follow in the intervening decades rightfully begins with the itinerant fur trapper and "voyageur," Jean du Sable.

Seventy-three years later, the Illinois legislature passed a law forbidding blacks to enter the state. Slavery was expressly forbidden in the state constitution, but the racial issue had simmered in Illinois since the French period. In 1824 a proslavery faction in the legislature ordered a referendum on the calling of a constitutional convention to legalize slavery in the state. Led by Edward Coles, a Virginian who became the second Illinois governor, the antislavery forces triumphed by a margin of 6,640 to 4,972. Coles, who freed his own slaves before leaving for Illinois, spent $4,000 of his own money to see to it that the "peculiar system" would not infect Illinois politics in the years to come.

Despite the noble intentions of Coles and other sympathetic legislators, a black man had no real legal rights in Illinois, and very often freed slaves would be abducted by hired thugs and returned to their former owners in the cotton South. Blacks could not vote, serve on a jury, or join a militia. With the passage of the second Fugitive Slave Law in 1850, the city became an important stop on the "underground railroad" for fugitive slaves making their way north to freedom. Consequently, the black population tripled in the 1850s, and continued to grow steadily until 30,150 African-Americans were counted in the 1900 city census. Most of them worked as low-paid household domestics, and though they accounted for only 1.3 percent of the population in 1890, the black community supplied 37.7 percent of the male, and 43.4 percent of the female, servant class.

Blacks were denied the opportunity to join the skilled trade unions, and when better jobs in construction and manufacturing became available, it was usually the result of a bitter labor strike or management lock-out which forced frantic employers to meet their production demands by hiring blacks as strikebreakers. This, of course, contributed to the ill will that already existed between whites and blacks.

The fledgling black political movement began to take shape during this period, when the patterns of neighborhood segregation in Chicago first became evident. The South Side "Black Belt," an expanding self-contained community whose borders were defined by Michigan Avenue on the east to Cottage Grove Avenue on the west, and from 31st Street (north) to 51st Street (south), was given definition in the 1890s when half of the city's black population resided in three economically depressed wards.

In the immediate post-Civil War period the most eloquent spokesman for black causes was John Jones, a tailor, the son of a freed slave woman and a German immigrant who brought his family to Chicago in 1845. In 1871 Jones was elected county commissioner on Joseph Medill's "Fire Proof" ticket, which was swept into office as a result of the calamitous fire which leveled the city in October. Jones was defeated in his re-election bid four years later, but by virtue of his victory in 1871, he became the first black to hold public office in Chicago. In

1876, grocer John W. E. Thomas was elected to the Illinois legislature, but after the Reconstruction period ended, a political backlash against black candidates negated the advances made by Jones, Thomas, and other blacks nationwide.

The period of black activism began in 1893, the year that a college-educated New Yorker named Edward "the Iron Master" Wright was elected president of the Afro-American League, which was aimed at promoting blacks for public office. Wright served several terms on the county board, and finally succeeded in securing the committeeman's post from the Second Ward in 1920, following a protracted battle with the white political establishment that ran things in the Black Belt. Wright was a canny political organizer, and despite his numerous setbacks, he paved the way for other up-and-coming black leaders who profited from his tutelage. Through some rather astute backroom dealing, Ed Wright negotiated the appointment of Ferdinand L. Barnett, who became the first assistant Cook County State's Attorney. It was a payback for the vote Wright had delivered to candidate Charles Deneen, who was elected state's attorney in 1896.

The black population of Chicago increased from 30,140 in 1900 to 44,103 just ten years later. It was during this time that the nation's most influential black newspaper, the *Chicago Defender* was founded by a Georgian named Robert S. Abbott. An earlier sheet, the *Chicago Conservator*, was founded by Ferdinand Barnett in 1878 to crusade for the rights of former slaves. In 1895, the year before Barnett was appointed assistant state's attorney, he married Ida B. Wells. She had come to Chicago after a mob of whites had destroyed her Memphis *Free Press* newspaper, which protested the lynching of blacks. Wells was a gifted, but fiery muckraker who drew attention to the appalling mistreatment of Chicago blacks, who were denied entrance to the World's Fair grounds because of their color. By 1915, however, the *Conservator* had folded, leaving Abbott, the "Lonely Warrior," as the spokesman for black Chicago. He began his paper with twenty-five cents to his name, and a single card table as a desk. Within a decade the *Defender* was a successful, albeit sensational, newspaper that was read by blacks all over the country. Abbott painted an unrealistic picture of conditions in the industrial North, pleading, in some cases, for blacks to turn their backs on the "Jim Crow" South to come to Chicago, which he called a mecca of opportunity.

The *Defender* offered unsolicited advice on resettlement, the housing market in Chicago, and the job prospects for blacks once they stepped off the train. Abbott struck a responsive chord, as Chicago's black population swelled to 109,458 by 1920. The outbreak of World War I resulted in a temporary job shortage in the stockyards and steel mills, which Abbott was quick to exploit. On May 17, 1917, scarcely a month after the U.S. entered the war on the side of the Allies, the *Defender* announced its "Great Northern Drive." Abbott encouraged blacks to flee the poverty and oppression in the South, and he was joined in this crusade by Chicago's vocal and flamboyant mayor, William Hale Thompson, whose most powerful ally on the South Side was Second Ward Alderman Oscar DePriest. Thompson pandered to the black vote; and in return for black support he dropped hundreds of patronage jobs into DePriest's lap to dispense as he saw fit. Encouraged by a sympathetic white mayor, a strong NAACP branch opened in Chicago in 1911; and, lured by the soothing words of Abbott, Southern blacks "went North"—by the thousands.

With little in the way of financial reserves, but instilled with unbridled optimism, they boarded trains that took them only as far as their money permitted. African Americans from the southern coastal states of Virginia and Georgia very often ended up in New York or Philadelphia. The Illinois Central "Green Diamond," servicing Mississippi, Arkansas, and Louisiana, conveyed blacks from their rural backwater towns directly to the bustling Illinois Central Station at 12th Street, which commentator Clarence Page likened to a "Midwest Ellis Island." Here Abbott's Chicago was stretched out before them. The smokestacks of the factories belched out billowing soot. The stockyard stench was equally foul, especially in the disagreeable July heat. Acres of ramshackle wooden housing in the Black Belt barely kept out the cutting January winds, as two, three, sometimes four families huddled together in the darkness. Overcrowding was a chronic problem. But it was their new home, this Chicago, city of promise.

The reverse of ghetto life were the glitzy jazz honky tonks up and down State Street, and in the last vestiges of the old South Side levee. After the war, Chicago became the Midwest mecca of jazz music, an emerging art form popularized in New Orleans at the turn-of-the-century. Jazz was something new and daring; a hybrid of West African rhythms, southern banjo music, and the barrelhouse piano styles practiced by midwestern tavern musicians. The fusion of popular ragtime and blues with these earlier musical forms occurred around 1900, when Bunk Johnson, "Jelly-roll" Morton, Danny Parker, and Alphone Sicou experimented with the curious new music in the brothels of "Storeyville," a legal, thirty-eight-block controlled vice district in New Orleans. Because black musicians were denied the opportunity to perform in legitimate vaudeville houses, they were forced to find their audiences elsewhere. Often those audiences were made up of chemise-clad strumpets and their well-heeled white customers who patronized the sporting houses dotting Canal Street.

Louis Armstrong, Kid Ory, and Joseph "King" Oliver appeared nightly in the bistros, until the reformers had enough and abolished the district for good on November 12, 1917. Out of work, the young musicians headed north where they assembled their own bands. King Oliver organized his famed Creole Jazz Band, which was recognized as the first black group to record jazz music. In 1922, Louie Armstrong stepped off the train in Chicago. He, too, had read Abbott's *Defender,* and decided to come northward where he joined up with Oliver's Creole Jazz Band. Armstrong plied his trade in the Black Belt, where the Elite, the Schiller Cafe, the Dreamland, the Royal Gardens, and the Onion, which routinely booked such top-notch acts as Baby Dodds, Jimmy Noone, and Sidney Bechet. The Near South Side pulsated with the sounds of Dixieland and with Armstrong's *Gut Bucket Blues,* which he recorded with the Hot Five. A unique Chicago sound—fusing jazz and blues together—had been born. Moralists decried what they called "shameless iniquity" going on within the doors of the "Black and Tan" cabarets—so named because of the free association between white patrons and the African American performers and clientele. The indignation of the white establishment was best summed up by Captain Max Nootbaar of the Chicago Police Department, whose detail closed down several of the Second Ward cabarets in October, 1917:

"No place is respectable where young white girls are allowed to drink and dance with Negro men," Nootbaar told the police trial board when he was brought up on charges of racial discrimination by Alderman Louis Anderson and by the old political war-horse, Edward Wright, who was serving as a corporation counsel. "I would shoot my wife or daughter if I found them in such places!" Nootbaar roared. The commission found the police captain "justified" in closing down immoral places, but in a rare conciliatory gesture toward the black politicians, Nootbaar was transferred out of the district.

The white jazz impresarios like Bix Beiderbecke, Benny Goodman, Art Hodes, and the Austin High School Gang were unfazed by prevailing narrow-mindedness. They preferred to learn their craft in a dozen gin-soaked, smoke-filled cafes of the Second Ward. The Austin High School Gang, led by Jimmy McPartland, Bud Freeman, Muggsy Spanier, and Mezz Mezzrow took jazz in a new direction, and broadened its popularity with white audiences.

The South Side Black Belt was a thriving, self-contained neighborhood throughout the 1920s. Jesse Binga founded the first black-owned bank at 35th and State Streets, the hub of what was then known as the "Black

Downtown." In its heyday, the bank held $1.5 million in assets, representing one-third of all money deposited in savings institutions by Chicago blacks.

In 1928, Oscar DePriest became the first popularly elected black man to win a seat in Congress since the Reconstruction era. (In 1915, DePriest had become the first black to take his place in the Chicago City Council.) DePriest was a skillful political organizer and businessman. He owned the largest painting and decorating business of any African-American community in the industrial North. The success of DePriest, Wright, and Binga in the political and business arena belied the growing racial tension between anxious whites facing a shrinking job market and the economic consequences of neighborhood integration, and the city's 109,000 blacks, who demanded an equal share of the pie. Random acts of violence against the homes of blacks in the summer of 1918 foreshadowed the calamity that was to come a year later. On July 27, 1919, an outing at the 29th Street Beach on the South Side became a battleground when a 14-year-old boy named Eugene Williams was stoned to death as he crossed the invisible "race line" separating the white and black bathers. When a white policeman named Dan Callahan refused the arrest the perpetrators, angry blacks vented their outrage by hurling stones and bricks at their antagonists. Before it was all over with a week later, Chicago had become an armed camp. The Illinois National Guard was deployed along the Black Belt to keep white South Side street gangs like Ragen's Colts from setting fire to the wooden tenements east of Wentworth Avenue. Thirty-eight people died in the rioting, including twenty-three blacks and fifteen whites. A biracial commission empanelled by Governor Frank Lowden examined the cause and effect of the riots, recommended an end to job discrimination, improved educational opportunity for young blacks, and open housing. The noteworthy recommendations of the panel were ignored for the next forty years, until the same vexing issues confronting the races again threatened to overturn the peace.

In the 1920s, blacks continued to penetrate predominantly white neighborhoods. Washington Park on the South Side was a microcosm of social and ethnic displacement; a pattern of mobility that was duplicated in many Chicago neighborhoods for decades to come. In 1920 blacks comprised 15 percent of Washington Park's 38,076 residents. The "white flight" in the next ten years was dramatic. By 1930, scarcely 10 percent of the Washington Parkers were white. Much the same scenario was later repeated in East and West Garfield, North Lawndale, and Austin on the West Side.

Political power in the black wards was vested in William Levi Dawson, inheritor of the Wright-DePriest legacy. Dawson was one of two black aldermen to occupy a place in the City Council in the 1920s. Dawson was a Republican at the outset of his career, like so many of his constituents who equated the Democratic Party with the antebellum South and slavery. Dawson was a machine politician who pacified his supporters with jobs and patronage. He served the Thompson forces loyally when the Republicans were the only game in town. That game changed overnight when Anton Cermak, a Czech from Lawndale, was elected mayor in 1931. Cermak counted on the black vote, but to change their way of thinking and to convince them to vote Democratic was another matter. Cermak and his successor Edward Kelly used essentially a carrot and stick approach to bring the balky Dawson into the fold. Cermak threatened Dawson with grave political reprisals, and to illustrate this point, the mayor ordered his most capable police officers into the Second Ward strongholds to clean up illegal gambling—an important source of revenue to members of the South Side Dawson machine.

Finally, Kelly offered Dawson a deal. He offered him the Democratic committeeman post in return for black support on election day. Dawson's people worked the five predominantly black wards tirelessly; going door to door trying to convince voters to shift their allegiance to the Democratic Party. When the process was complete, Dawson found himself in the enviable position of commanding a vast patronage army. Dawson was the master of all he surveyed, a situation that would not change until the volatile 1960s. The Cook County Democracy reciprocated with jobs and relief benefits for thousands of blacks caught in the grind of the Depression. Under Kelly's stewardship, William Dawson was elected to Congress in 1942, and would serve fourteen continuous terms until his death in 1970 at the age of 84. Dawson, by his very nature, was an amenable politician that the white aldermen and mayor could "work with." Mayor Richard J. Daley counted on Dawson's South Side clout through his first four terms of office. It was only after Dawson had passed the staff of leadership to a younger, more outspoken generation of black leaders, who were less impressed with plantation-style politics, that this situation began to change.

During this era of passivity, there were powerful, but still muted voices in the black community who were expressing the collective frustrations of a generation raised in poverty, and suffering the stigma of oppression. Richard Nathaniel Wright was born in Mississippi, but came to Chicago in 1935, where he found work on the Federal Writer's Project. In 1938, Wright published his first book, *Uncle Tom's Children,* which was a collection of essays dramatizing racial prejudice. His most important work, *Native Son* (1940), explored the horror of ghetto life and its impact on a young Chicago black named Bigger Thomas, who was driven to commit murder. Wright was the spokesman for a generation, and his other notable books, *Black Boy* (1945), *The Outsider* (1953), and *White Man, Listen* (1957) further explained his observations on contemporary black life in the urban centers of America. Richard Wright's silent outrage against the prevailing conditions was an early, yet powerful catalyst of change. Future leaders like Al Raby, Ralph Metcalfe, and Jesse Jackson read his work carefully. It was a marked departure from the era of compliance.

The second great black migration from the rural South occurred after World War II. Between 1940 and 1950, the African American population increased from 277,731 to 492,265. It was a dramatic 5.4 percent gain. By 1970 the figures surpassed the million mark for the first time, at 162,620 or 32 percent of the entire city population. As blacks poured into formerly all-white neighborhoods, nervous real estate agents attempted to buck this trend by invoking the "restrictive covenant," a legal device inserted into many wills and deeds designed to prevent a residential dwelling from being sold to people of color. The covenants held until May 3, 1948, when the U.S. Supreme Court struck down this legal barrier to open housing.

Alarmed by the specter of economic deprivation in the black community and miles of slum housing on the South Side, the Chicago Housing Authority (CHA) took matters in hand and began demolishing the tenements to pave the way for the gleaming high-rise "projects" designed to end poverty and overcrowding. In theory, at least, the urban planners of the 1940s and 1950s believed they held the solution to a festering problem. There was no easy approach to housing conditions on the South Side. Many of the wooden buildings were constructed in the nineteenth century, and lacked running water and heat. They could not be repaired, so they had to be bulldozed. That much was true.

With the opening of the Ida B. Wells homes at 37th and Vincennes in 1941, and the 23 Cabrini buildings north of Chicago Avenue between Larrabee and Hudson in 1942, the 20-year period of urban renewal in the city began. One by one the black neighborhoods were transformed, almost overnight in some cases.

Between 1953 and 1968, the 2,000 unit Lake Meadows complex was constructed between 31st and 35th streets, followed by Stateway Gardens (1957) at 39th and Princeton, the Raymond Hilliard Homes for senior citizens at 22nd and State streets, and the Robert Taylor Homes, fronting the Dan Ryan Expressway. Their construction spelled the end of the blighted Federal Street slum. The 16-story high Taylor homes are the world's largest public housing facility, but they illustrate the glaring failure of urban renewal housing to address the social problems that accompanied the construction of high-rise housing complexes.

Though well-intentioned by 1940s standards, the CHA planners who designed the clean but sterile apartment units ultimately succeeded in rebuilding the old ghetto skyward. Within a few years the Taylor Homes, Cabrini Green, and Stateway Gardens became seedbeds of drugs, crime, and mayhem. The residents were crowded together in insecure, neglected buildings that became safe houses for junkies and pushers. The vision of Mayor Daley, Dwight Green and others did not extend much past the drawing boards and smoke-filled rooms of City Hall. The positioning of the Taylor Homes on the east side of the Expressway appeared to be little more than de facto segregation on the part of the politicians, who created a manmade barrier to separate the haves and have-nots. Similar plans to build housing projects in all-white neighborhoods were doomed to failure after it was shown that blacks occupied 84 percent of the 45,000 public housing units controlled by the CHA.

By the 1960s, Chicago was forced to come to grips with the Civil Rights movement, which had been in flower since the end of World War II, when thousands of black G.I.s returned to the U.S. from their posts overseas. They were in no mind to put up with segregated schools, black-only lunch counters, and the back of the bus. The battle began in Montgomery, Alabama, in 1955, when Rosa Parks refused to give up her seat on the bus. It reached Chicago a decade later when the Reverend Martin Luther King led 10,000 marchers from Buckingham Fountain to City Hall on July 26, 1965, to demand the ouster of Charles Swibel, whom they accused of using federal funds to build segregated public housing. At the center of the controversy was Chicago's embattled school superintendent, Benjamin C. Willis, who had been under fire since 1963 when he pushed through a plan to build mobile classrooms in over-crowded black districts. The NAACP accused Willis of promoting segregation. Late in 1963, black activists led by Al Raby and Alderman Ralph Metcalfe spearheaded an immensely successful boycott of the public school system. On October 22, 1963, exactly thirty days before John F. Kennedy was gunned down in Dallas, 224,770 of the 469,733 students enrolled in the public school system stayed home. Congressman Dawson endorsed this first boycott with reservations, but broke ranks with Raby and the NAACP when a second boycott was called in February, 1964. Dawson's philosophy was simplistic and old-fashioned: "We must play the game according to the rules. I always play it that way and I play with my team." The captain of the team, of course, sat on the fifth floor throne of City Hall. The anti-Willis crusade was the humble beginning of black political activism in the 1960s, a turbulent decade that brought profound social change.

In July 1965, comedian Dick Gregory led seventy anti-Willis marchers into Bridgeport, past the Daley residence at 3536 S. Lowe Avenue. "Chicago is the most ghettoized city in the country," complained King, who led an even bigger march into the all white neighborhoods of Gage Park, Cragin, Chicago Lawn, and South Deering in 1966. Sporadic rioting broke out on the West Side in 1965 and again a year later. Violence was triggered by the city's misguided decision to turn off the fire hydrants, which ghetto youngsters were likely to play under during the ninety-degree weather. These were the "long hot summers" of Chicago's all-too-recent history.

The West Side went up in flames following the assassination of Dr. Martin Luther King in Memphis, Tennessee on April 4, 1968. The arson and looting along Madison Street and Roosevelt Road enacted a heavy toll on the black community. One thousand people were left homeless and acres of one-and two-story buildings were reduced to rubble.

The Kerner Report laid the blame for the rioting on the city's doorstep. The city's school system was inadequate and beset by segregationist policy. The neighborhoods remained hopelessly divided along racial and economic lines, and the threat of renewed rioting hung in the air. By 1967, the Dawson machine was beginning to lose its grip on the voting public. That year two "independents" won seats in the City Council: A. A. "Sammy" Raynor in the Sixth Ward, and William Cousins in the Eighth. In each case, machine-backed candidates went down to defeat. After Dawson passed away in 1970, social worker Fred Hubbard bucked the organization and claimed the Second Ward alderman's seat. The old order, for all intents and purposes, was dead.

The 1980 census data showed a significant increase in the minority population. African Americans accounted for 39.8 percent of the city's ethnic makeup—up from the 32.7 percent registered in 1970. The evidence suggested that the older black communities like Grand Boulevard, Englewood, and West Lawndale, settled between 1920 and 1950, lost significant numbers of residents. A growing black middle class that had refused to linger in the crime-ridden neighborhoods, abandoned the core of the city in search of affordable housing in the outlying areas. Between 1960 and 1970 black home ownership increased nearly twofold from 36,000 to 74,000. The south and south west suburbs of Markham, Harvey, Phoenix, Dixmoor, and Maywood registered significant increases in their black populations during this time. (African Americans represent 6 percent of the suburban population base.)

While much of the original South Side Black Belt lay in ruins, or had been bulldozed years earlier to make way for high-rise housing projects, several black Chicago neighborhoods, notably Park Manor, West Chesterfield, Chatham, and the Jackson Park highlands, were rock-sold bastions of the middle class.

Chatham, a quiet, tree-lined "suburb within the city" is bounded by the Dan Ryan Expressway to the immediate west, and Cottage Grove Avenue on the east. The "bungalow-belt" neighborhood was once an ethnic melting pot of Swedes, Irish, and Germans. Now it is almost entirely black, and is the home of the esteemed author Dempsey J. Travis, former Illinois comptroller Roland Burris, and many other leaders from the black professional class. Pill Hill is a much smaller residential community to the south and east of Chatham. In the 1960s, many of the people that owned the two-story and split-level homes were wealthy white physicians, hence the nickname.

The loss of heavy industry and the abandonment of the once-thriving commercial strips in Englewood, Woodlawn, North Lawndale, and Austin have created a permanent displaced underclass. In order for these areas to be reclaimed from the drug gangs, pushers, and felons, it is first necessary for the business community to recommit its resources to the neighborhoods in the form of jobs and economic development. Until that time comes, entire communities within the city will continue to be a virtual no-man's land, unsafe for blacks and whites.

It matters little who controls the power in City Hall, which since the death of the elder Daley in 1976, has been a preoccupation of both races. In 1983 the black community scored its most significant political victory since Oscar DePriest's aldermanic election in 1915, when former congressman Harold Washington rode the tide of discontent into the mayor's chair. Washington, a product of the old Third Ward Democratic organization, spearheaded by his father Roy Washington, broke with the machine in 1977. The Washington "revolt" succeeded eventually in luring thousands of liberal thinking young whites, Hispanics from Pilsen and the near Northwest Side, and a unified black constituency into the "Rainbow Coalition," which relied heavily on religious and ethical symbolism to wrest control away from the white ethnics. Racial divisiveness underscored the campaign against Republican challenger Bernard Epton whose campaign literature tapped into the deepest fears of thousands of Poles, Germans, Lithuanians, and Irish on the Southwest and Northwest Side. They feared the "ghettoization" of their communities, and for their part, precinct workers were quick to exploit this anxiety on both primary and election day. "Epton—Before It's Too Late!" The terse, grim appeal to racial antipathy illustrates the caste system Chicago continued to operate

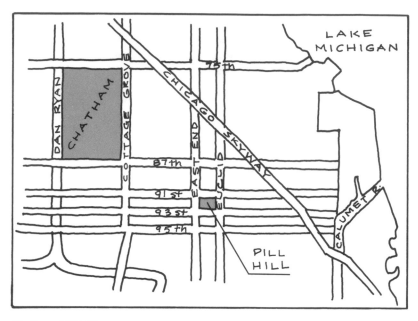

Chatham/Pill Hill

under. Nowhere in America is this fierce sense of community more prevalent than in Chicago. Commenting on this essential character of Chicago life, Connecticut writer Richard Conniff noted in the pages of *National Geographic* that "the neighborhoods are the city's strength and its weakness. . . . There is of course a flip side to the appeal of neighborhood intimacy. Every neighborhood enforces its own brand of conformity, and the old mold doesn't necessarily fit new arrivals." Though Chicago blacks have lived and worked in the community since the frontier days, they are still viewed suspiciously as the new, unwanted arrivals in a social order that until only recently saw fit to exclude them from sampling the rich harvest awaiting those who triumph within the system.

Ethnic Museum, Cultural & Resource Center, & Theater

DuSable Museum of African American History, *740 E. 56th Place, Chicago, (312) 947-0600.*   Named after Chicago's first permanent settler, the DuSable Museum in Washington Park explores the history, contributions, and culture of the African nations and people of African-American descent. Founded in 1961 by Charles and Margaret Burroughs, the unique collection of sculpture, masks, folk dolls, and jewelry was originally housed at 3806 S. Michigan Avenue, in the former headquarters of the Quincy Club, which served as a meeting place for African American railroad workers. In 1973 the DuSable Museum purchased a gray-stone building in Washington Park that once served as the South Side lockup for the Chicago Park District Police, an adjunct of the city police department until the two agencies were merged in 1959. The exhibits are shown on the first level, and they include a portrait gallery of prominent local and national African Americans, including Langston Hughes, Booker T. Washington, Robert S. Abbott, and Oscar DePriest. A wooden bas-relief mural carved by Robert Will Ames, completed in 1965 after six years of labor-intensive work, depicts forty episodic scenes and 225 identifiable figures who helped shape the African American experience from the time of the European slave trade up to the twentieth century. A separate room is devoted to the life and times of Harold Washington, including a display of 287 awards received by the late mayor between 1983 and 1987. A research library, auditorium, and gift shop are located on the grounds. During the year, the DuSable Museum sponsors an Arts and Crafts Promenade, African-American history courses, a "Know Your Heritage" bus tour of the city, African mask-making workshops, Family Day, an Annual Book Fair, and a series of summer concerts and festivals. For a calendar of events call the museum at (312) 947-0600. Membership in the DuSable Museum entitles individuals to certain benefits (depending on the program chosen). Yearly memberships are available for $15.00 for students and seniors up to a $1,000 "Annual Sustainer" donation. Hours: Monday through Friday, 9 A.M. to 5 P.M.; Saturday–Sunday, noon to 5 P.M. *Recommended.*

ETA Square Black Cultural Center, *7558 S. Chicago Avenue, Chicago, (312) 752-3955.* A black-owned performing arts center founded in 1971 by Harold Johnson, Abena Joan Brown, Al Johnson, and Archie Weston, Jr., to promote African-American drama, dance, and musical events under one roof. Six main stage productions are given on Thursday and Saturday nights at 8:00 P.M., between September and July. Such critically acclaimed dramatic works as *Stoops* and *Good Black* (both staged at ETA) have been nominated for Jeff Awards in the past. In the Spring of 1991, the theater sponsored the play *Survival,* a tribute to Winnie and Nelson Mandela and the struggle to end apartheid in South Africa. ETA also sponsors dramatic workshops for children six years and up, and theater classes for adults. The cost of the plays is $10 per person, Visa and Mastercard accepted.

Black Ensemble Theatre, *4520 N. Beacon Street, Chicago, (312) 769-4451.* A center for the performing arts founded by Jackie Taylor in 1976. In recent years audiences have delighted to the stage adaptation of *A Streetcar Named Desire, The Other Cinderella,* and *Muddy Waters: the Hootchy-Kootchie Man.* The theater was originally located on Wells Street in Old Town until 1986, when the company moved to its present location. Four plays are given each year, and are held at 8 P.M. on Friday and Saturday, and Sundays at 4 P.M. Tickets are $15 per person, Visa and Mastercard accepted.

Afro-American Genealogical & Historical Society (AAGHS). *Mailing Address: P.O. Box 377651, Chicago, IL 60637.* Meets the second Sunday of the month at 1:15 P.M. at the South Shore Cultural Center, 7059 South Shore Drive, Chicago. The AAGHS has 150 active members in Chicago, and an additional 600 on the mailing list who are tracing their family history through hands-on workshops, field trips to the Allen County Library in Fort Wayne, Indiana (the largest genealogical library in the nation), regular Sunday meetings, and an annual conference held the last Saturday in February at the South Shore Cultural Center. The group was organized in 1979, and has nine standing committees dedicated to archival work, computer research, publications, special events, and publicity. AAGHS publishes a newsletter four times a year, and sponsors a workshop in October, which teaches people family research methodology. Membership is $15 per year. Contact Tony Burroughs, president of the AAGHS at (312) 924-7172.

Annual Events and Celebrations

Bud Billiken Day Parade. A lavish, annual back-to-school parade kicking off from Oakwood Boulevard and King Drive, proceeding south on King to 55th Street in Washington Park, at 10:00 A.M., the second Saturday in August. The history of this parade dates back to 1929 when Robert Abbott, publisher of the *Chicago Defender,* decided to pay tribute to the newsboys who hawked his paper on the street corners. The employees of the *Defender* would walk with the youngsters from 35th Street to Washington Park, where everyone would participate in a day-long picnic. The selection of the king and queen by the newspaper staff, and the afternoon picnic are time-honored customs that are features of every Billiken parade. Abbott named his event after the ancient Chinese billiken doll, which according to legend is supposed to watch over little children. A "Buddy Billiken" doll stood on his desk for many years.

With more than 300 entries and sixty floats participating every year, Chicago's Bud Billiken Parade is the third largest parade in the country, following the tournament of Roses Parade in California on New Year's Day, and Macy's Thanksgiving Day Parade in Manhattan. The marching bands come all the way from Texas, Missouri, Nebraska, Kansas, and Iowa. For the politicians who regularly turn out for this event, it's only a short ride from City Hall. For additional information, call (312) 225-2400. For the best public transportation routes, call the CTA at (312) 836-7000. *Recommended.*

African Liberation Day. Parade, speeches, picnic, and entertainment held the last Saturday in May, and sponsored by the National Black United Front, Chicago Chapter. The three-mile parade, resplendent with floats, school bands, marchers and politicians, kicks off from Austin Avenue and Jackson Street, on the West Side at 10 A.M., and proceeds to Garfield Park for a day-long festival and ceremony marking the African independence movement, which took shape in Ghana during the 1950s. Under the leadership of Kwame Nkrumah, the people of Ghana threw off the last shackles of British colonialism in the early 1950s. This helped spark a broader-based independence movement that took shape in French Guinea and the Belgian Congo. As a result, the Organization of African Unity was organized in May, 1963, when thirty-one African heads of state convened a summit meeting to proclaim the fourth Saturday in May an international holiday. The first ALD was staged in the U.S. nine years later, on May 27, 1972. The event includes entertainment by the NAIWA Dance Corps, a Children's Choir, sales of African art, clothing, and jewelry, and speeches. For more information, call (312) 268-7500, ex. 154, or (312) 978-6766.

"African Festival of the Arts," *annual three-day street fair held on Harper Court, between 52nd and 53rd streets, in Hyde Park, during the Labor Day weekend.* Food booths, musical entertainment, story telling, crafts demonstrations, African puppet show for the children, and video displays. The festival revolves around a different theme every year. In 1990 the focus was on "Creativity and Survival." "A Window to Africa" highlighted the 1991 event, which is sponsored in part by the National Council of Artists, Chicagoland chapter. Hours: Labor

Day weekend, 11 A.M. to 6 P.M. For additional information, call (312) 955-7742.

"Ghana Fest," *(Original Name: "Ho Mowo"). A one-day ethnic folk festival held on the grounds of the DuSable Museum, 740 E. 56th Street, Chicago, the first Saturday in July.* Sponsored in part by the Mayor's Office of Special Events and the Ghana National Council of Metropolitan Chicago, which represents eleven different ethnic Ghanian groups in the city. The Republic of Ghana is a coastal nation facing the gulf of Guinea off the Atlantic Ocean, and is bordered by the Ivory Coast on the west, Burkina Faso on the northwest, and Togo, due east. Cultural life in this highly developed African republic is marked by a series of festivals and rites having to do with marriage, birth and death, and the harvest seasons. One such celebration occurs every August with the passing of the "lean season," and the return of the fish to the coastal waters. It is a time of great rejoicing and the giving of thanks to the Diety for gifts offered. This same spirit is preserved is Chicago's "Ghana Fest," held every year since 1984 on the South Side. Traditional African foods are served free of charge, and the folk music of West Africa is played by a local disc jockey. Merchandise vendors sell folk art. Dance troops entertain, and there are attractions for children. Hours: 11 A.M. to 8 P.M. Free admission. Call or write the Ghana National Council at 1414 E. 59th Street, Chicago, (312) 962-5546, or (312) 363-7916.

"Taste of Garfield," *a one-day outdoor street festival held on the grounds of the St. Barnabas Urban Center, 4241-4245 W. Washington Boulevard, Chicago, (312) 722-8333, the second or third Saturday in June.* Featuring live entertainment, including jazz music, the Marshall High School marching band, children's games, food booths, and an occasional appearance by the mayor of Chicago. The year 1991 was the fourth year of this festival. Admission: free. Hours: 11 A.M. to 6:30 P.M.

"ABLA Inner City Family Day," *Adams Park; Loomis & 15th streets, Chicago, (312) 738-0591.* Annual ethnic festival and community social gathering held the first Saturday in August on the park grounds. African dance troops perform. Food vendors, plenty of jazz music, blues, and pop sponsored by the ABLA Home Residents. Hours: 9 A.M. to 9 P.M. Free admission.

"Kwanzaa Summer Festival," *held the first Saturday in July at 95th and State streets, from 10 A.M. to 5 P.M. Sponsored by the Soweto Center of Chicago, 19 W. 103rd Street, Chicago.* Music entertainment, food, and children's activities. Free admission. Call (312) 264-1298.

"Blacklight Film Festival," *at the Film Center of the Art Institute, Columbus and Jackson, Chicago, (312) 443-3737.* Annual film festival presented each year since 1981 by the Film Center of the Art Institute, and featuring the work of leading contemporary black directors and producers including Spike Lee, Sijri Bakaba, and local independents, such as Ruby L. Oliver. Conceived and developed by Floyd Webb, the Blacklight Festival is a series of month-long events and workshops held every August. The center is closed on Mondays and Wednesdays. Individual film showings are $5 per person. Membership in the Film Center entitles you to a 40% discount on regular admission to programs; special previews to major new releases; a free subscription to the Film Center *Gazette;* free admission to the Tuesday night lecture series; and discounts to outlying Chicago theaters. Membership prices range from $35 to $75. Contact Robert Lueder at the Center for additional information.

Chicago Gospel Festival, *a two-day music extravaganza at Grant Park (Jackson Boulevard and Columbus Drive), the first or second weekend in June.* Unlike the larger, more chaotic city events, such as the Taste of Chicago, or the Jazz Festival, which annually lure upwards of 400,000 people, Chicago's Gospel Fest is a celebration of the spirit attended by church-going families. This means very few security problems for the often overextended Chicago Police Department. The Gospel Fest has been a "religious rite of summer" since 1985. Its roots run much deeper, however. Gospel music is derived from Pentecostal church worship services of the late 19th century and blues singing. The practice of "shouting" is directly related to African circle dances and "speaking in tongues." It became an art form popular with American blacks in the 1920s, and enjoyed a tremendous postwar popularity, due in no small measure to long-time Chicago resident Mahalia Jackson (1911–72), who toured internationally, appeared in films, and was broadcast around the world on TV and radio. The soaring tribute to the big-time gospel composers and singers, including Kenneth Morris, Marvin Yancey, H. W. Brewster, the Edwin Hawkins Singers, the Rev. A. C. Tindley, Sister Rosette Tharpe, New Life, and Mahalia Jackson, is performed on three stages: the Petrillo Bandshell, the Youth Stage, and the Chicago Gospel Stage from noon to 10:30 P.M. the first or second weekend in June. Admission is free. For a schedule of performers and times, call the Mayor's Office of Special Events at (312) 744-3315. The CTA will add extra busses along the South Side routes. For transit information call (312) 836-7000.

Chicago Blues Festival, *a three-day concert showcasing blues artists from Chicago and down south at Grant Park, (Jackson Boulevard and Columbus Drive), in mid-June (usually follows Gospel Fest by a week).* Though it is no longer exclusively an African-American art form, this secular folk music from the black rural south dates back to the post-Civil War period, and is a fusion of work songs, field hollers, minstrel show tunes, and mainstream white compositions. The blues were originally derived from southern black men, who tended the fields under the grueling mid-day sun in Georgia, the Carolinas, Texas, and Mississippi. The first reference to this form of music in a scored composition occurred in 1912 with the publication of W. C. Handy's *Memphis Blues*.

In the 1920s and 1930s Chicago played the greatest role in the development of the "urban blues" as we know it today, through the recordings of such renowned performers as Big Bill Broonzy, John Lee "Sonny Boy" Williamson, Tampa Red, and Memphis Minnie. After the second world war, a young generation of blues musicians came into their own, including Muddy Waters, Elmore James, Otis Spann, Howlin' Wolf (whose records, cassettes, and CD's are sold from a van every Saturday and Sunday at Maxwell and Halsted streets) and Little Walter Jacobs. In the 1950s, the recording studios of Chess Records at 2120 S. Michigan Avenue helped fuse a fledgling music art form known as "rhythm and blues" to mainstream pop. Leonard and Phil Chess opened their studio in 1947, with such blues artists as John Lee Hooker, Jimmy Rodgers, Howlin' Wolf, and Muddy Waters under contract. They added Chuck Berry, Bo Diddley, the Moonglows, Johnnie and Joe, the Tune Weavers, and the Monotones in the mid-1950s when the demand for black R & B music and sentimental "doo-wop" ballads expanded into the white neighborhoods. Allen Freed may have legitimized the new music while working as a disc jockey in Cleveland in 1952–53, but the birth of rock n'roll was foretold several years earlier when the Chicago blues performers stepped into the Michigan Avenue recording studios of Chess Records for the very first time.

The Grant Park Blues Fest exalts the famous Chicago sound that has become a music institution. The fest has been going strong since 1984, preserving these earlier traditions on four main stages: the Petrillo Music Shell (Jackson and Columbus Drive), the Front Porch (Jackson Boulevard and Columbus), the Crossroads Stage at (Jackson and Lake Shore Drive), and the rotunda at the tip of Navy Pier. Admission is always free, and the party continues until 10 or 10:30 P.M., Friday through Sunday. For a schedule of performers and times, call the Mayor's Office of Special Events at (312) 744-3315. *Recommended.*

Chicago Jazz Festival, *held in Grant Park the last weekend in August, and sponsored by the not-for-profit Jazz Institute of Chicago (JIC) and the Mayor's Office of Special Events.*   There was a time not so long ago, when Chicago was the jazz mecca of the Midwest; when dimly lit nightclubs, like the Happy Medium, the London House, the Blue Note, and a half-dozen smaller bistros near State and Randolph gave out a rich, vibrant sound. The legendary clubs have faded into memory—casualties of the social transformation wrought by the 1960s. Jazz lovers, take heart. The sprawling Grant Park festival has been growing in stature each year since its inception in 1979, and is broadcast coast-to-coast on National Public Radio (NPR), WBEZ, 91.5 FM in Chicago. An exciting array of local, national, and international acts are featured in the Petrillo Music Shell and the Jazz on Jackson Stage (Jackson and Lake Shore Drive) from noon till 10 P.M. through the festival. What you get is a mixture of traditional jazz, be-bop, swing, and Dixieland. This is probably the only major jazz festival in the U.S. that pays homage to the growing international flavor of the art form, which is disconcerting to some of the purists. One of the gripes expressed by members of the Association of Creative Musicians (AACM) is the inherent conservatism of Chicagoans when it comes to jazz music. Experimental and avant-garde performers have a hard time making their mark in hard-nosed, blue-collar Chicago. Their most receptive audiences are outside the mainstream, and very often found in Europe where a newcomer is able to catch a break. Innovation, if it is to be found in Chicago, very often comes from some of the smaller clubs around town, like the Bop-Shop at 1807 W. Division Street, and Jazz Showcase, at 636 S. Michigan Avenue. For Jazz Fest showtimes, call (312) 744-3370.

"Neighborhood Resident Blues Festival," *The first Friday, Saturday, and Sunday in August, at 100 N. Central Park, Chicago. Sponsored by the Fifth City Neighborhood Residents Association in conjunction with Habilitative Systems, Inc., at 417 S. Kimbark.* The Garfield Park Blues Fest is a community event that has been held every year since 1971. Local jazz performers are showcased on Saturday night. Pop singers and balladeers share the spotlight on Fridays. Food vendors. Clowns. Plenty of down-home Chicago music. Hours: 1 P.M. to 10 P.M., Friday through Sunday. Admission is free. Contact Minnie Dunlap at (312) 265-1902.

Silver Bullet Blues Fest. *A two-day music concert held at Lincoln, Belmont, and Ashland avenues, the second week in June.* Sponsored by the Lakeview Chamber of Commerce, and Coors Light Beer. Free admission. Plenty of blues music, beginning at 12:30 P.M. each day. Call: (312) 472-7171, for a schedule of performances.

Jazz Fest, *South Shore Cultural Center, 7059 South Shore Boulevard, Chicago, (312) 667-2707.* Two-day series of concerts and jazz workshops held on the grounds of the Cultural Center the first weekend in August. In 1974, Geraldine de Haas decided that in order for Chicago to expand its cultural horizons, it was first necessary to install an appreciation for the kind of music that used to be synonymous with the swinging South Side. The political sachems of the Daley administration were cool to the idea. Pork barrels and patronage were what really mattered in those days—but Geraldine was a patient woman. She bided her time until Mayor Jane Byrne came along and decided to spruce up the image of the city by sponsoring a myriad of festivals, weekend outings, and celebrations. Geraldine helped Jane spawn the immensely successful Grant Park Jazz Fest, which served to whet the public's appetite for more of the same. The South Shore Jazz Fest is sponsored by Jazz Unites, Inc., and other agencies. Since 1981 some of the biggest names in contemporary and traditional jazz including the Count Basie Orchestra, Ramsey Lewis, and the Ray Brown Trio have headlined the festival. Budgetary constraints make this one of the least publicized musical events in the city, but through word of mouth, and public service announcements, the South Shore Jazz Fest has drawn on the average of 15,000 people each of the last few years. Hours: noon to 2 P.M. for workshops. Concert: 2 P.M. to 8 P.M. Admission: free.

"Dance Africa," *sponsored by the Dance Center of Columbia College, 4730 N. Sheridan Road, Chicago.* A yearly festival of African-American choreography held in the college's 250-seat theater for one week in late September or early October. Following on the heels of the critically acclaimed "Present Vision/Past Voice: the African-American Tradition in American Modern Dance" in 1990, Columbia College has renewed its commitment to offering diversity within the program by presenting this seasonal pageant of African culture. Tickets are $12 per person. Visa and Mastercard accepted. For scheduled times, call the theater at (312) 271-7928.

Ebony Fashion Fair, annual traveling fashion show sponsored each year in May by Ebony Magazine in conjunction with the Chicago Area Club of the National Association of Negro Business and Professional Women's Clubs, Inc. Proceeds from this charitable event go toward scholarship programs and the African-American community. The fashion show is usually held at the Holiday Inn, O'Hare, in Rosemont, but the locations and prices are subject to change. Call (312) 322-9200.

"Walk of Elegance," an annual walk-a-thon to help support the DuSable Museum's operating expenses for tours, exhibitions, education and public programs. The day-long event begins at the DuSable Museum in Washington Park Payne Drive, the first Saturday in June, proceeds through the University of Chicago campus in Hyde Park, east to Lake Shore Drive, then west to 57th and Cornell, before ending at the finish line for a total distance of 16 kilometers. The fee is $12 for adults, $8 for youths, sixteen and under. Participants receive a tee-shirt, a raffle ticket for prizes, a "goodie bag" and a bagged lunch. To register, call (312) 947-0600.

"Festival of African Arts," *at the Beacon Street Gallery and Theatre, 4520 N. Beacon St., Chicago, (312) 561-3500.* A one-day celebration of African culture held the first week in June, and featuring arts and crafts, music, dance, fashion, and food.

Koco Fest, *annual one-day neighborhood festival held in mid-August between the 4700 and 4900 blocks of Drexel Boulevard on the South Side.* Proceeds from this event benefit the Kenwood-Oakland Community Organization. A potpourri of musical styles including jazz, blues, reggae, and rap keynote the event, but there are also food booths, merchandise sales, clowns, and a children's carnival. The famed Jesse White Tumblers usually put in an appearance. Free admission. Call (312) 548-7500.

Black History Month Events

February is "Black History Month" in Chicago, celebrating the heritage, art, music, customs, and achievements of African-Americans. Local theaters and museums feature an array of interesting events, including lectures, films, theatrical productions, ethnic dance, and gallery exhibitions, which are geared to a different theme every year.

"African Heritage Festival," *at the Field Museum of Natural History, Roosevelt Road and Lake Shore Drive, Chicago, (312) 922-9410.* The museum sponsors a month-long program of crafts demonstrations, music presentations, and children's hands-on workshops where skilled artisans will teach them the art of basket weaving and drum making. Story-telling sessions and a choral presentation by the greater Holy Temple Gospel Choir are regularly scheduled features in February. The Field Museum devotes one day a week in February to these special events. The fee for the workshop is $12 per child. Regular admission to the museum is $3 per person and $2 for students. Free on Thursdays. For additional information, contact Jesse Dimes in the museum's education department.

"Black Creativity," *at the Museum of Science and Industry, 57th Street and Lake Shore Drive, Chicago, (312) 684-1414, ex. 2436.* Held in the West Pavilion, the MSI exhibit revolves around a different cultural theme every year. In 1991 for example, visitors were treated to "Music! Music! Music!: An African-American Tradition." A juried art exhibit, featuring the works of African-American painters, sculptors, and photographers from around the country is a yearly custom. Lectures. Musical concerts. Dance ensembles. Admission to the exhibition is free with a museum ticket. The MSI charges $5 for adults, $4 for seniors, and $3 for children under twelve. Hours: Monday through Friday, 9:30 A.M. to 4 P.M.; Saturday and Sunday, 9:30 A.M. to 5:30 P.M.

Art Institute of Chicago Exhibition. *Michigan Avenue at Adams Street, Chicago, (312) 443-3680 (Museum Education Department)* In addition to an ongoing exhibit in the Gallery of African Art that features wood carvings, textiles and jewelry from Africa, the museum sponsors a different program every year during Black History Month. The public is invited to attend free lectures, workshops, and special showings, that pertain to black artistic endeavor and cultural history. The 1990 program was titled "Yourba: Nine Centuries of African Art and Thought." During the year, the education department sponsors various other African-American exhibitions in the museum. The "Gold of Africa" and "Senufo Woman" were two smaller showings on display during the spring and summer months of 1991. Museum hours: Monday, Wednesday, Thursday, Friday, 10:30 A.M. to 4:30 P.M.; Tuesday, 10:30 A.M. to 8:00 P.M.; Saturday, 10 A.M. to 5 P.M.; Sunday, noon to 5:00 P.M. Suggested donation: $6 for adults, $3 for seniors and students.

Chicago Public Library Cultural Center Exhibition, *78 E. Washington Street, Chicago.* The Chicago Department of Cultural Affairs presents a yearly ensemble of creative dance, musical performances, art exhibits, films, and lectures given by contemporary artists in the meeting rooms of the old library. Other activities are included in the calendar of events, which is drawn up several months in advance of the February showing. Admission is always free. For information about the itinerary, times and locations, please call the Department of Cultural Affairs at (312) 744-6630 during normal business hours.

Newberry Library Events, *60 W. Walton, Chicago, (312) 943-9090, ext. 457.* Free symposiums, lectures, and presentations pertaining to local black history and genealogy. The Newberry received a two-year project grant for its "Afro-American Family History Project," which concluded in 1991. The library assisted local scholars and genealogists who traced black family life in Chicago, through extensive archival, manuscript, and catalog material housed at the library. Each year the Newberry sponsors a program relating to Black History Month, though the focus will be different each time. A Lyceum series, with classes on black genealogy, is held twice a year, and is open to the public. The cost of these classes ranges from $50 to $60 per course, and can be booked by calling the library at the above number. The Newberry is a fine resource for local history, and is open Tuesday through Thursday, 10 A.M. to 6 P.M.; Friday and Saturday, 9 A.M. to 5 P.M.

Museum of Broadcast History events, *800 S. Wells, Chicago, (312) 987-1500.* Seminars, workshops, discussion on black ownership of radio and TV stations, and film documentaries about the history of the Civil Rights Movement are held throughout the month. Guest speakers, such as TV newsman Harry Porterfield, recount their experiences in Chicago broadcast journalism over the years. Contact Mark Veil, head of the education department, for a program of events (that varies from year to year). The museum is open from noon to 5 P.M. Wednesday, Thursday, Friday, and Sunday. Saturdays, 10 A.M. to 5 P.M. Admission is $3 for adults, $2 for students, and $1 for seniors and children under twelve.

Peace Museum exhibits, *430 W. Erie St., Chicago, (312) 440-1860.* The Peace Museum presents a different theme every year to mark Black History Month in Chicago. In 1990, the paintings and drawings of illustrator and journalist Franklin McMahon were featured in an exhibition titled "'An Artist's Notebook: Civil Rights, Selma to Chicago." In other years, the artwork of children living in the crime-ridden Cabrini-Green housing project have been displayed. The special exhibits will run the entire month of February, and sometimes longer. Admission: $3.50 for adults, $2 for students and senior citizens, members admitted free. Hours: Open seven days a week, noon to 5 P.M.; Thursday, noon to 8 P.M.

Chicago Historical Society exhibits, *Clark Street at North Avenue, Chicago, (312) 642-4600.* The CHS contributes much to our understanding of African-American, and Chicago history through special exhibits, lectures, and bus tours of the city conducted on a year-round basis. In 1991, the CHS hosted two exhibitions of note: "I Dream A World: Portraits of Black Women Who Changed America," a photographic study of 75 African-American women who helped fulfill the prophecy of essayist and author Langston Hughes (1902–67), who could only "dream a world where all will know sweet freedom's way," and "African American Passport," featured discussions and lectures given by visiting scholars, a dinner at the CHS, and related programs. Black History Month at the society is indeed a 365-day event, but in February it is likely that special concerts, films, and lectures will be listed on the program calendar. For more information, contact the education department at the museum. Hours: Monday through Saturday, 9:30 A.M. to 4:30 P.M.; Sunday, noon to 5 P.M. Suggested donation: $3 for adults, $2 for seniors. Mondays are free days.

Historical and Architectural Attractions

Kenwood Walking Tour. Two-hour tour of a landmark South Side neighborhood that is remarkably well preserved. Kenwood, described by many as a "suburb within the city," was founded by Dr. John Kennicott, a dentist of Scottish descent who settled here in 1856. The quiet, tree-lined streets were home to some of Chicago's most notable citizens, including Julius Rosenwald and the Gustavus Swift family. As the South Side underwent a profound racial transformation in the twentieth century, the northern portion of Kenwood became closely identified with the all-black Oakland community, while the southern end of the community forged a social, economic, and cultural link with neighboring Hyde Park and the University of Chicago. The Chicago Architectural Foundation sponsors four walking tours of Kenwood each year—in May, June, September, and October. Included on the tour are homes built by Frank Lloyd Wright, Alfred S. Altschuler, and Howard Van Doren Shaw. Tour guides provide historical interpretation and will answer questions. The tour begins at 1100 E. Hyde Park Boulevard (5100 S) and Greenwood Avenue (1100 E.) at the K.A.M. Isaiah Israel Congregation Temple. The cost is $5 per person, with no charge for CAF members. For more information, call the CAF offices at (312) 326-1393, or write to 1800 S. Prairie Avenue, Chicago, IL 60616.

Statue of the Black Doughboy, *35th Street and Dr. Martin Luther King Drive, Chicago.* The base of the memorial was erected in 1927, and is dedicated to black soldiers who gave their lives in World War I. The statue, designed by Leonard Crunelle was sculpted in memory of George Giles, a highly decorated World War I veteran. It was placed on top of the pedestal in 1936.

Ida Wells/Ferdinand Lee Barnett home, *3624 S. King Drive, Chicago.* Ferdinand Barnett, founder of the *Conservator,* the first black newspaper in Chicago, and his wife, social reformer Ida B. Wells, lived in this building from 1919 to 1930. In July, 1974, the Department of the Interior designated this site as a National Historical Landmark. Nearby, on King Drive, between 37th and 39th streets, stands the Ida B. Wells housing project.

Dr. Martin Luther King residence, *1550 S. Hamlin Avenue, Chicago.* In the summer of 1966, Dr. King established a temporary living quarters in this West Side apartment building while he fought for open housing and equal justice. As a result, the Leadership Council of Metropolitan Chicago was organized.

Jesse Binga home, *5922 South King Drive, Chicago.* Binga's amazing business success at a time when few black men prospered in the white man's North is partly explained by the lavish inheritance he received when his brother-in-law, John "Mushmouth" Johnson, passed away in 1907. Johnson was a swaggering gambler from St. Louis, who ran Chicago's South Side policy rackets for nearly twenty years, beginning in the 1880s. Johnson was the proprietor of the Frontenac Club, which catered to an exclusive white clientele that helped earn him an estimated $250,000 in illegal revenue, though he claimed to be down to his last penny shortly before his death. A year after Johnson passed away, Binga opened his bank at State and 35th streets. He was forced to close down in July 1930, bankrupting many depositors. Many people have blamed utilities czar Samuel Insull for Binga's misfortunes, but the Great Depression was already in full force, and it made no racial distinctions.

Binga's modest frame dwelling was bombed ten times by whites during the protracted period of racial troubles in 1918 and 1919.

Offices of the Chicago Defender, *2400 S. Michigan Avenue, Chicago.* Almost single handedly, Robert S. Abbott, the son of a slave butler, inspired the great northern black migration in the pages of his sometimes sensational, but always blunt and to the point, *Chicago Defender.* Under the guidance of Abbott's nephew, John Sengstacke, the *Defender* became one of two black papers to publish daily beginning in 1954. This modest stone building on the Near South Side houses the *Defender* editorial staff, and was designated an important "historical site in journalism" by the prestigious Sigma Delta Chi society on May 5, 1975.

Dining, and Shopping

Soul Food Restaurants

Army & Lou's, *422 E. 75th Street, Chicago, (312) 483-6550.* Serving up soul food at this location since 1945. The new owners Avis and Benjamin Piper have maintained the same high standards in their cuisine, but have tried to incorporate low-fat and low-cholesterol methods into a style of cooking that is no longer consistent with the eating habits of salad-eating, granola-munching, joggers. So you forget the diet for a day, that's all. Hours: Monday, 11 A.M. to 10 P.M.; Wednesday through Sunday, 9 A.M. to 10 P.M. Closed Tuesdays. Accepts credit cards.

Jackie's Place, *226 E. 71st Street, (312) 846-1487, and 425 E. 71st Street, Chicago, (312) 483-4095.* Specializing in short ribs of beef and other soul foods since 1968. Two locations. Jackie's I, at 226 E. 71st, is open from 8 A.M. to 10:30 P.M., Monday through Sunday. Jackie's II, down the street, never closes. No credit cards.

Nina's Restaurant, *5810 W. Madison Street, Chicago, (312) 921-5062.* Soul food. Daily luncheon specials. Hours: Tuesday through Saturday, 6 A.M. to 7 P.M. Closed Sunday and Monday. No credit cards.

Barbara's Restaurant, *422 E. 75th Street, Chicago, (312) 624-0087.* Soul food, including ham hocks, roast beef, chicken and fish. Hours: Monday through Saturday, 5 A.M. to 6 P.M., Sundays till 2 P.M. No credit cards.

Gina's Cafeteria, *4735 W. Chicago Avenue, Chicago, (312) 379-8010.* Be sure not to miss the daily $2.99 special, which includes many varieties of soul food. Five years at this location. Hours: Tuesday through Sunday, 8 A.M. to 8 P.M. Closed Mondays. No credit cards.

Richard's Jamaica Club & Restaurant, *303 E. 61st Street, Chicago, (312) 363-0471.* "Blue Monday" means chicken every week. Breakfast, lunch, supper, quick snacks. Free parking. Hours: Monday through Friday and Sunday, 9 A.M. to 2 A.M. Saturdays till 3 A.M. No credit cards.

Alexander's Restaurant, *3010 E. 79th Street, Chicago, (312) 768-6555.* The house specialties include prime rib and roast beef. Live jazz on Thursdays, beginning at 6:30 P.M. Music provided by the Jazz Masters in conjunction with Jazz Unites. According to the owners, the Jazz Masters are destined for greatness. Come and see the South Side's best kept secret. Alexander's has been a South Side institution for 51 years. Hours: Monday through Thursday, 11 A.M. to 11 P.M.; Fridays and Saturdays till 1 A.M.; Sunday: noon to 11 P.M. Credit cards accepted.

Hecky's Barbecue, *1902 Green Bay Road, Evanston, (708) 492-1182, and 412 Sheridan Road, Highwood, (708) 433-6180.* Chicago *Tribune* columnist Mike Royko is known to cook up a mean rack of ribs, but our award for spicy Chicago barbecue goes to the two Hecky's carry-out restaurants in Evanston and Highwood. The smell of cooking back ribs permeates the neighborhood, as anyone who lives or works near this part of Evanston will tell you. Smoked duck is the latest addition to the menu, which also includes fried seafoods, barbecued chicken, turkey, and links. Catering available. Hours: Tuesday and Wednesday, 11 A.M. to 10 P.M.; Friday and Saturday, 11 A.M. to midnight; Sunday, 12 P.M. to 8 P.M.; Monday, 4 P.M. to 10 P.M. *Recommended.*

African Restaurants

Ethio Cafe, *3462 N. Clark Street, Chicago, (312) 929-8300.* Authentic Ethiopian cuisine at modest prices. Live entertainment included on the weekends. Hours: Monday through Friday, 4:30 P.M. to 11 P.M.; Saturday and Sunday till 1 A.M. Credit cards accepted.

Moulibet, *3521 N. Clark Street, Chicago, (312) 929-9383.* Vegetarian and non-vegetarian Ethiopian food served in an amicable storefront location, with live entertainment on the weekends. Hours: Monday through Thursday, 5 P.M. to 10 P.M.; Friday and Saturday, 4 P.M. to 12 P.M.; Sunday, 4 P.M. to 9 P.M. Credit cards accepted.

Mama Desta's Red Sea Restaurant, *3218 N. Clark, Chicago, (312) 935-9561.* Fine Ethiopian foods, including chicken and lamb, beef and vegetarian dishes. Hours: Monday, 4:30 P.M. to 10:30 P.M.; Tuesday through Sunday, 11:30 A.M. to 11:30 P.M. Credit cards accepted.

Guide to the Local Jazz & Blues Clubs

(Note: For information about what's happening on the local jazz scene in Chicago, call the Jazz Institute Hotline at (312) 666-1881 for a prerecorded message, or stay tuned to WNUA, 95.5 FM, for frequent updates during the day.)

New Checkerboard Lounge *(Blues), 423 E. 43rd Street, Chicago, (312) 624-3240.* Some of the big-time rock performers like Mick Jagger and Eric Clapton who are heavily influenced by Chicago-style blues music (perfected to a high art on 43rd Street, otherwise known as "Muddy Waters Drive" during the blues "Renaissance") have been known to drop by to catch the hottest acts from the South and North Sides. Live music, Sunday through Friday, 9:30 P.M. to 1 A.M.; Saturday, 9:30 P.M. to 3 A.M. Cover charge on the weekend.

Buddy Guy's Legends *(Blues), 754 S. Wabash Avenue, Chicago (312) 427-1190.* This South Loop blues spot features the music of Buddy Guy (part-owner of the club), who teams up with the John Watkins Group, appearing nightly. Such international celebrities as Bill Wyman, the late Stevie Ray Vaughn, and Ron Wood have also performed here. Rock and R and B are featured occasionally. Open daily from 4 P.M. to 2 A.M.

B.L.U.E.S., *2519 N. Halsted Street, Chicago, (312) 528-1012.* Small-sized neighborhood blues club that is very popular with the out-of-town set, who elbow their way to the front just about every night. Only a block away from the Biograph Theater where John Dillinger met his demise in 1934. Live music, Sunday through Thursday, 9 P.M. to 2 A.M.; Friday, 8:30 P.M. to 2 A.M.; Saturday, 8:30 P.M. to 3 A.M. Cover charge varies.

B.L.U.E.S. Etcetera, *1124 W. Belmont Avenue, Chicago (312) 525-8989.* Spawned by B.L.U.E.S., but the parking is easier and there is greater room to roam, unlike the Halsted Street location. The club features a number of out-of-town acts, and special performances are given by musicians from B.L.U.E.S. Live music, Sunday through Friday, 9 P.M. to 2 A.M.; Saturday, 9 P.M. to 3 A.M. There is a modest cover charge. B.L.U.E.S. Etc. sponsors an annual four-hour "Blues Cruise" on Lake Michigan, on board the MV *Chicago,* which includes food and music from 7 P.M. to 11 P.M., the third Saturday in July. Tickets are $22 at B.L.U.E.S. Etc., and are available through all Ticketron outlets. Call (312) 559-1212.

Rosa's Lounge *(Blues), 3420 W. Armitage, Chicago, (312) 342-0452.* Rosa's calls itself the "friendliest blues club" in Chicago, and has done much to promote local blues artists over the years. Located in Logan Square, and maintained by Tony Manguilo and his mother Rosa who tends bar, the club features something different every night. Club hours: Sunday through Friday, 8 P.M. to 2 A.M.; Saturday, 8 P.M. to 3 A.M. There is no cover charge on Sunday, Wednesday, Thursday, and Monday. Free parking next door.

Blue Chicago, *937 S. State Street, Chicago, (312) 642-6261, and Blue Chicago on Clark, 536 N. Clark Street, Chicago, (312) 661-0100.* The two locations feature a potpourri of blues styles, but tends to favor such female blueswomen as Gloria Shannon, Dietra Farr, and Katherine Davis. Excellent sound system, very spacious. Hours: Monday through Friday, 9 P.M. to 2 A.M.; Saturday, 9 P.M. to 3 A.M. Cover charge ranges from $3 or $4 during the week to $5 or $6 on the weekends.

Brady's Liquors and Lounge *(Blues), 525 W. 47th Street, Chicago, (312) 536-6326.* A favorite of South Siders, particularly grad students from the University of Chicago, who show up for the live performances on Thursday and Sunday nights.

The Bop Shop Jazz Club, *1807 W. Division Street, Chicago, (312) 235-3232.* The place for contemporary jazz, Chicago style. Unpretentious. The look and feel of this Wicker Park club is authentic, so much so that the club sponsors an annual Nelson Algren celebration. Algren lived and worked nearby. Shows start at 10 P.M.

The Jazz Showcase, *636 S. Michigan Avenue, Chicago, (312) 427-4300.* Joe Segal's "non-smoking" Jazz Showcase in the Blackstone Hotel pays homage to all who have gone before: Charlie "the Bird" Parker, Duke Ellington, and Dizzy Gillespie. It's a downtown kind of place that has been around since 1947, so expect to pay a hefty cover charge, typically $12 per person. Hours: Tuesday, Wednesday, Thursday, 8 P.M. and 10 P.M.; Friday and Saturday, 9 P.M. and 11 P.M. Sunday matinees at 4 P.M. Sunday evening, 8 P.M. and 10 P.M.

The Green Mill, *4802 N. Broadway (at Lawrence), Chicago, (312) 878-5552.* In the days of Prohibition, this was a real gangland hangout run by the late Henry van Horne. His son Rudy went on to become a stand-up comic and latter day vaudevillian. Rudy once sat on Ruth Etting's knee, and performed a nifty tap dance for one of Al Capone's boys way back when. Things are a little more sedate today. The gangsters have been replaced by local jazz impresarios like the Green Mill All-Stars and Ed Peterson, who perform in a 1940s setting. The acclaimed "Uptown Poetry Slam" hosted by Marc Smith in mid-July breaks the routine. Hours: Sunday through Friday, noon to 4 A.M.; Saturday, noon to 5 A.M. Free parking at Lawrence & Magnolia.

Pop's For Champagne *(Jazz), 2934 N. Sheffield, Chicago, (312) 427-1000.* Desire a romantic interlude, at a definitely upscale jazz club in the Clybourn corridor? This is definitely the place for a rendezvous. The wine bar features 100 champagnes, and twelve by the glass. A "jazz brunch" is featured on Sundays from 10:30 A.M. to 2 P.M. The champagne and all that jazz are pricey, so beware. Music on Sunday and Monday, Wednesday and Thursday, 8 P.M. to midnight; Friday and Saturday, 9 P.M. to 1 A.M.

Wise Fool's Pub *(Blues), 2270 N. Lincoln Avenue, Chicago, (312) 929-1510.* Down-to-earth blues club that has held up well over the years, by featuring a mix of big time jazz, blues, and pop performers. Music Monday through Friday, 9:30 P.M. to 2 A.M.; Saturday, 9:30 P.M. to 3 A.M.; Sunday, 5 P.M. to 9 P.M. and 9:30 P.M. to 2 A.M.

Andy's *(Jazz), 11 E. Hubbard Street, Chicago, (312) 642-6805.* The informal approach to jazz works best at Andy's, one of the oldest clubs of its kind in Chicago. Andy's features the music of the Chicago Jazz Band, the Rhythmmakers and Swingtet, and the only noontime jazz in the city. Music: Monday, 5 P.M. to 8:30 P.M.; Tuesday through Thursday, noon to 2:30 P.M. and 5 P.M. to 8:30 P.M.; Friday, noon to 2:30 P.M. and 5 P.M. to 12:30 A.M.; Saturday, 9 P.M. to 1 A.M. Closed on Sunday.

The Bulls Jazz Nightclub, *1916 N. Lincoln Park West, Chicago, (312) 337-3000.* Basement bar and nightclub featuring local contemporary jazz musicians. The best time to go is during the week, when there are no lines. It has been jumping since way back in 1963, due in no small measure to the fine acoustics. Music: Sunday through Thursday, 9:30 P.M. to 2:30 A.M.; Friday, 9:30 P.M. to 3 A.M.; Saturday, 9:30 P.M. to 4 A.M. Cover charge during the week is $3 and $6 on Friday and Saturday.

Oz *(Jazz), 2917 N. Sheffield, Chicago, (312) 975-8100.* Contemporary jazz fusion in a cozy storefront surrounding. Very popular with the upscale Lincoln Park crowd. Shows are staged Thursday and Friday nights, 9:30 P.M. to 1:30 A.M.; Saturday, 10 P.M. to 2:30 A.M. Cover charge: $2 on Thursday, $4 on Friday and Saturday.

Cairo *(Jazz & Rock), 720 N. Wells, Chicago, (312) 266-6620.* A jazz club with a disc jockey and noisy disco located in the lower level. The restaurant and the piano jazz are located upstairs. Considered to be one of the "hip" places to see. Hours: Tuesday through Saturday, 6 P.M. until early morning.

George's *(Jazz and Blues), 230 W. Kinzie, Chicago, (312) 644-2290.* Supper club and showy art deco lounge that features R & B singers, jazz performers and other lyrical artists Tuesday through Sunday, from 8 P.M. to midnight.

Lilly's *(Blues), 2513 N. Lincoln Avenue, Chicago, (312) 525-2422.* Intimate piano and acoustic blues club in a cafe atmosphere. The place is a personal favorite of a number of veteran blues performers including Jimmy Rogers and Big Moose Walker. Music: Wednesday through Saturday, 9 P.M. to 2 A.M.; Saturday and Sunday, 8:30 P.M. to 5 A.M. No cover charge on Wednesday & Thursday.

The Backroom *(Jazz), 1007 N. Rush Street, Chicago, (312) 751-2433.* A former Rush Street hotspot that used to be a horse barn (believe it or not) still reverberates with the sound of jazz, even though the neighborhood isn't quite the adult playground it used to be. Music: Sunday through Friday, 9 P.M. to 2 A.M.; Saturday, 9 A.M. to 3 A.M. Cover charge every night.

The Cotton Club *(Jazz and Latin rhythms), 1710 S. Michigan Avenue, Chicago, (312) 341-9787.* Maybe one day the owners of the Cotton Club will be able to take credit for the rebirth and development of South Michigan Avenue, which once crawled with jetsetters, society swells, and the ne'er-do-wells of the old Levee eager to partake of the gin spirits of Colosimo's nightclub on Wabash. Colosimo's, and the horn players who carried on there, are ghostly memories now, amid the ruins of decaying warehouses and abandoned courtyard flats. The Cotton Club, with its eclectic variety of Dixieland jazz and down home blues, is in vogue these days in less-than-elegant surroundings.

The Other Place *(Jazz), 7600 S. King Drive, Chicago, (312) 874-5476.* Popular South Side spot that disdains the cover charge, but attempts to make up the difference with higher drink prices when the big out-of-town acts perform.

Kingston Mines *(Blues), 2548 N. Halsted, Chicago, (312) 477-4646.* One of the oldest established clubs in the city, that promotes itself as Chicago's "Blues Center." Live blues, and two bands, seven days a week. Hours: Sunday and Tuesday through Friday, 8:30 P.M. to 4 A.M.; Monday, 8 P.M. to 4 A.M.; Saturday, 8:30 P.M. to 5 A.M.

Dick's Last Resort *(Jazz), 435 E. Illinois Street, Chicago, (312) 836-7870.* If you enjoy unstructured Dixieland music, Dick's is the place to go. Food and drink are served. Music: 8 P.M. until closing. Other hours: Sunday through Thursday, 11 A.M. to 2:30 A.M.; Wednesday through Saturday, 11 A.M. to 4 A.M.; Saturday, 11 A.M. to 5 A.M. No cover charge.

Europia *(Jazz, Rock, and Blues), 2838 N. Lincoln Avenue, Chicago, (312) 528-5339.* Disc jockeys spin dance music Tuesday–Saturday. Live jazz and blues every Thursday, Friday, and Saturday. Open bar on Tuesday from 9 P.M. to midnight. Five-dollar cover charge on Thursday, Friday, and Sunday.

African-American Video

African-American Images, *9204 S. Commercial Avenue, Chicago, IL 60617, (312) 375-9682. Ordering number: 1-800-552-1991.* This Chicago-based mail-order firm sells a full line of documentary videos pertaining to the African-American experience in the U.S., from the historical and sociological standpoint. A free catalog of titles is available by calling the office phone number during regular business hours.

Chicago Public Library, *Dr. Martin Luther King Branch, 3636 S. King Drive, Chicago, (312) 225-7543.* This CPL branch loans out a number of historically important Hollywood movies that either portray blacks in prominent roles, or deal with African-American themes.

Afro-Am Distributing Co., *819 S. Wabash Avenue, Suite 610, Chicago, IL 60605. (312) 922-1147.* Mail-order firm that sells documentaries and educational films of importance to the black community. Some notable Hollywood films, such as *Sounder* and the *Learning Tree* are listed in a catalog that will be sent free by calling the above-listed phone number.

Chicago's Largest Selection of Jazz and Blues CDs & Tapes

Jazz Record Mart, *11 W. Grand Avenue, Chicago, (312) 222-1467.* Located just a few blocks away from where the legendary Clark Street jazz hot spots of the 1920s, '30s, '40s, and '50s once stood—the Hi-Note, the Liberty Inn, The Ship, and the Victory Club—the Jazz Record Mart on Grand Avenue caters to the serious connoisseur of jazz music, offering the largest inventory of jazz and blues CDs and cassettes in the Midwest. The mart publishes an annual "Rhythm and News" catalog that is sent to subscribers all around the country, listing current inventory by record label, and news of the local jazz scene. If you happen to be in town for the Chicago Jazz Festival, a sidetrip to the Record Mart, located at the State-Grand Subway stop, should definitely be included in your itinerary. Hours: Monday through Saturday, 10 A.M. to 8 P.M.; Sunday, noon to 5 P.M. Credit cards accepted. *Recommended.*

Art Galleries

Les Primitifs Gallery, *706 N. Wells Street, Chicago, (312) 787-9440.* West and North African ceremonial figurative sculpture, graphic works, masks, drums, beads, jewelry, and regional furniture. Two years at this location. Hours: Tuesday through Saturday, 9:30 A.M. to 5:30 P.M. Closed Sunday; open Monday by appointment. Credit cards accepted.

Nicole Gallery, *734 N. Wells Street, Chicago, (312) 787-7716.* Artwork produced by craftsmen from Zimbabwe, Haiti, and the U.S. The paintings were done by American and Haitian artists; the sculpture comes from Zimbabwe. Hours: Tuesday through Saturday, 10:30 A.M. to 5 P.M.; Sunday and Monday by appointment. Credit cards accepted.

Isobel Neal Gallery, *200 W. Superior Street, Chicago, (312) 944-1570.* Contemporary paintings, sculpture, three-dimensional construction, and prints done by African-American artists. Hours: Wednesday through Saturday, 11 A.M. to 6 P.M.; other times by appointment. Credit cards accepted.

Woodshop Art Gallery, *441 E. 75th Street, Chicago, (312) 994-6666.* Largest retail dealer of African-American art in the city. Free admission. Hours: Monday through Friday, 9 A.M. to 6 P.M.; Saturday, 10 A.M. to 3 P.M. Closed Sunday.

Gift Shops and Books

Window to Africa, *5210 S. Harper, Chicago, (312) 955-7742, and 842 Custer Avenue, Evanston, (708) 475-6696.* Traditional and contemporary African paintings, sculptures, beads, jewelry, and textiles for sale. Hours: Monday through Friday, noon to 7 P.M.; Saturday, 10 A.M. to 7 P.M.; Sunday, noon to 5 P.M. The Evanston location is closed on Sunday and Monday. Credit cards accepted.

African-American Book Center, *7524 S. Cottage Grove Avenue, Chicago, (312) 651-0700.* Full line of fiction and nonfiction titles pertaining to African American and contemporary African themes. No CDs or tapes. Hours: Monday through Friday, 10 A.M. to 6 P.M.; Saturdays, 10 A.M. to 5 P.M. Credit cards accepted.

Night Clubs

Wild Hare and Singing Armadillo Frog Sanctuary, *3530 N. Clark Street, Chicago, (312) 327-4273.* Live reggae music everyday at this busy North Side nightclub and bar. Hours: Sunday through Friday, 9 P.M. to 2 A.M.; Saturday till 3 A.M.

Equator Club, *4715 N. Broadway, Chicago, (312) 728-2411.*
Bar and nightclub featuring Afro-pop, Caribbean, disco, and calypso
music played by a disc jockey. Two-dollar cover during the week, $5 on
Friday and Saturday. Hours: Wednesday through Friday; Sunday, 9:30
P.M. to 2 A.M.; Saturday till 3 A.M.

New Regal Theatre, *1645 E. 79th Street, Chicago.* Big name
jazz, blues, and gospel performers booked on a regular basis. WGCI radio
sponsors a talent showcase each year, and a limited number of stage plays
and musicals are also included during the year. This is an experience that
harkens back to the days of old vaudeville. Special dinner theater pack-
ages available. Ticket prices will vary depending on the event, but can be
purchased through Ticketmaster outlets or at the New Regal box office
between the hours of 11 A.M. and 7 P.M., Tuesday through Friday, and
Saturdays from 10 A.M. to 4 P.M. Closed on Sunday and Monday except
for specially scheduled events. To charge tickets by phone, call (312)
559-1212. Visa and Mastercard accepted. For a recorded message listing
upcoming events, call (312) 721-9230.

— Ethnic Recipe —

Northern Style Mississippi Ribs

Ingredients:
   1 tablespoon of French Dijon mustard
   1 tablespoon of honey
   1 tablespoon of brown sugar
   1 teaspoon of paprika
   1/2 teaspoon of onion powder
   1 tablespoon of lemon juice
   1 teaspoon of Accent
   1/4 cup of cooking sherry

Directions:
   Mix the above ingredients in a pan, cook and stir for twenty minutes
until the sauce starts to bubble. Let the sauce simmer for ten minutes
before marinating the ribs. The night before the ribs are to be served,
marinate them in one-quarter cup of red wine vinegar, sprinkle a touch of
seasoned salt and a dash of ground pepper. Precook the ribs at 350 degrees
for 25 to 30 minutes.

Chinese Chicago

═══════ History and Settlement ═══════

Eight Chinese laundrymen lived and worked in Chicago the year before the Great Fire of 1871. Their names are lost to history; swept away in conflagration that reduced the city to ashes and sorely tested the "I Will" spirit of Chicago. Historian Paul Siu identified "Opium Dong," one of the eight who sold his grocery store to T.C. Moy, who arrived from San Francisco in 1878. Because so little is known about Opium Dong, T.C. Moy enjoys the distinction of being the first permanent Chinese settler in Chicago. He lived in a wooden shanty on the teeming West Side, but moved to Clark Street, north of the Chicago River a few months later.

Life was good in Chicago, Moy reported in glowing terms to his relatives in Hong Kong. There were no discriminatory head taxes or contract labor, and the virulent racism of local whites who competed for scarce jobs during the building of the Transcontinental Railroad was greatly diminished in Chicago. By 1878 Moy had convinced sixty friends and relatives to embark on the perilous journey to Chicago. "They never said to me that the Chinese have got the perfection of crimes of 4,000 years," Moy recalled years later. "They never asked me whether or not I ate rats and snakes. The Chicagoans found us a peculiar people, to be sure, but they liked to mix with us. I was destined not to return to my fatherland, I thought." Even today, the Moy family continues to influence the social and cultural life of Chinatown.

They came slowly, at first. The Exclusion Act signed into law by the President in May, 1882, stemmed the tide of Chinese immigration for the next twenty or so years. In 1890, 500 Chinese huddled together in dingy hovels along South Clark Street—the squalid vice district know as the Custom House Place Levee. Dr. Wu Ting-Fang, a community organizer and a man of profound insights, realized that if his people were to escape the lowest rung of the social order and prosper in Chicago, it was necessary for the immigrants to disperse across the city. Ting-Fang devised an ingenious strategy. His people would bridge the cultural differences by opening Chinese restaurants that catered to the American public. The first "chop suey" house, *King Joy Lo,* was located at Dearborn and Randolph. Curious Chicagoans flocked to the restaurant to sample traditional Cantonese dishes. It was a first for the city.

Typical Chinese restaurants of this period featured orchestras and public dancing. But the immigrants arriving from the Port of Canton (the only one open to foreign powers after 1840) were peasant farmers. Few of them were able to make good use if their skills in the large urban centers of the U.S. Instead, most became laundrymen, especially after 1869, when the transcontinental railroad was completed, and thousands of contract workers found themselves unemployed. The laundries and restaurants were a peculiarity of the Chinese immigration, since there was a scarcity of laundries and even fewer restaurants in the homeland during this period. By 1900 there were 1,179 Chinese living in Chicago. Most came from the Sai-Ya district near Canton. According to the Lakeside Annual Directory for 1900, 239 of the 255 Chinese who were surveyed were employed as laundrymen. No doubt it was dirty, unpleasant work and a reflection of fierce anti-Chinese biases that denied these people a legitimate share of the American dream.

Ethnic prejudice was a factor in the 1905 uprooting of the immigrants from their homes in "Old Chinatown," in the Custom House Levee, to the modern day location at 22nd and Wentworth on the South Side. The vice lords who ruled the South Loop from the time of the Chicago Fire until 1905 were a source of continuing embarrassment to the downtown businessmen. The tippling rooms, panel houses, and wine rooms existed in the shadow of the majestic loop office buildings for years. In 1905 the state's attorney, backed by various civic agencies, drove them south to 22nd and Wabash. At the same time, no provisions were made for the Chinese, who were made to feel equally unwelcome. The anti-Chinese hysteria that had spread eastward in the three decades following the completion of the transcontinental railroad infected the Custom House Place landlords, who raised their rents to exorbitant levels. With no other recourse, the Chinese followed the criminal gangs and vice lords southward to 22nd and Wentworth—the fringe of Chicago's notorious Levee district.

The Chinese in Chicago, 1870–1960

Year	Population
1870	1
1880	250
1890	567
1900	1,179
1910	1,778
1920	2,353
1930	2,757
1940	2,013
1950	3,334
1960	5,082

The evil specter of racial prejudice made assimilation into the American culture exceedingly difficult, despite the Chinese demonstrated capacity for hard work and perseverance. The 22nd Street district on the near South Side was a "badlands." Rents were generally cheap, but police protection was minimal. Open lawlessness and vice in its lowest forms tested the spirits of these hearty immigrants, banished as they were by the city fathers.

It was not so surprising that this unsavory environment fostered criminality within the community. The early 1900s gave rise to the secret societies or "Tongs," which numbered twelve by 1912. Some of these early Tong gangs did much good during the early years, providing the community with mutual assistance programs, cultural identity, and a small, but certainly viable political lobby. In 1910 Dr. Sun Yet Sen visited Chicago, where he was greeted by a delegation of several hundred Chinese. He imparted to them the idea of organizing a "revolutionary" society in the city. A year later a branch of the Chinese Nationalistic League was formed. The Chicago chapter, a branch of a nationwide movement, was aimed at bringing down the Manchu Dynasty. But as the years passed, members of this secret society concerned themselves more with the advancement of economic issues and working conditions.

Similar to the aims of the Nationalistic League was the Mon Sang Association, organized in 1918 to fight inadequate wages and excessive working hours. In the first decade of the twentieth century Chinese restaurant workers toiled an average of fourteen hours a day. Poor wages denied many of the immigrant men the opportunity to send for their wives and family members stranded in China. The Mon Sangs addressed this grievance, providing members a forum for public debate, music clubs, reading rooms, classes for instruction in Chinese and English, and health insurance programs. The Mon Sangs looked past religious, social, and family issues to become the largest, most influential organization in the community.

The most serious problems facing Chinatown's leaders were the criminal activities of two Tong gangs: the Hip-Sings and the On-Leongs, existing for the purpose of protecting the lucrative gambling rackets and opium trade within the neighborhood. Gambling was a popular diversion for the immigrants, notably lotteries (called tze-fa), fan-tan, and tinkou. Two types of gambling houses sprung up within the community. One was the establishment given over entirely to games of chance, the other was a commercial business, with back rooms reserved for wagering. Gambling reached the height of its popularity in New Chinatown before the Depression. By 1938 there were only eight gambling dens left in the neighborhood. Declining economic conditions forced many to close their doors. For many years, though, the Hip-Sings and On-Leongs fought a series of protracted gang wars to resolve territorial issues and spheres of influence. The Hip-Sings were composed of members from "Old Chinatown," at Harrison and Clark. The much larger On-Leong gang had its roots near 22nd and Wentworth. Differences were finally resolved through the careful mediation of Chin Kung Fong. Today the On-Leong Merchant's Association, and the Hip Sing engage in much more peaceful endeavors, as they work toward the betterment of the community.

The absence of family life, due to the exclusion laws, no doubt contributed to the crime problem. In 1910 there were 1,713 Chinese men living in Chicago, but only 65 women. This situation began to change after 1943 when the Exclusion Act was repealed by Congress. Non-quota status was given to wives of the Chinese citizens in 1946, which permitted them to stream into the U.S. without government interference. Through the 1940s, Chinatown continued to serve as the focal point of community life in Chicago. This began to change, especially after the 1949 Revolution in China which brought to Chicago a new class of immigrants, the urban professional. These new arrivals were for the most part Mandarin, and they had little in common with the Cantonese who first settled Chicago. Separated by language differences and cultural links to the homeland, the Mandarin Chinese dispersed across the city and into the Western suburbs. The presence of hospitals and universities on the North Side, in particular, led to a "clustering" of Chinese along Clark Street, Broadway, and other major thoroughfares near the lakefront.

The "New" Chinatown community extending between Sheridan Road and Broadway along Argyle Avenue on the city's North Side is symbolic of the changing realities of postwar immigration. When the Federal Detention Center was erected in the South Loop in 1970, the displaced Hip Sing Association was forced to seek new headquarters. Under the guidance of noted restaurateur Jimmy Wong, the North Side Chinatown was founded. But to a majority of Chicagoans, the traditional Chinatown will always be the Wentworth Avenue corridor.

In many ways it is a hermetically sealed environment. There are residents here who do not speak a word of English. Many of them have lived in the community for fifty years but rarely venture past the street signs marked with Chinese characters. These first-generation Chinese from Taiwan, Hong Kong, and the People's Republic remain relatively unassimilated. It is estimated that 9,000 people live within a narrow ten block radius. The expanding Chinatown has had its problems in recent years acquiring the land necessary to relieve the residential clog. The Santa Fe Company rejected the community's bid for the abandoned property north of Cermak Road—much of it comprised the old Levee before being turned into rail yards. At one point, city planners envisioned a multipurpose sports stadium on the site, but that, too, was cancelled.

Today Chinatown remains very much as it was fifty to sixty years ago; a slice of the Old World in the shadows of urban Chicago. You know you are there when you cross under the imposing Chinatown Gate at the corner of South Wentworth Avenue and Cermak. The tile-ornamented structure is the brainchild of George Cheung, restaurateur and civic promoter who conceived the idea in 1971. Cheung led the campaign to raise $70,000 in city and private funds to build an arch that embodied ancient Chinese customs. Cheung envisioned a more contemporary motif, but architect Peter Fung decided to go with a more traditional approach. A number of the decorative tiles were shipped from Taiwan in 1973, but not nearly as many as originally planned, which led to some last-minute difficulties, since native craftsmen were not available to complete the project. Work continued right up to the moment of dedication in November, 1975. The decorative panels on the pagoda contain messages of peace, harmony, and the spirit of cooperation between people—echoed in the words if Dr. Sun Yat-sen, who proclaimed that "the world is for all," and Chiang Kai-shek's admonition that mankind should respect "Propriety, Justice, Integrity, and Conscientiousness."

Annual Events and Celebrations

Chinatown Events (South Side)

Chinatown New Year Parade and Lion Dance. If you happen to be dining in one of the many fine Cantonese restaurants in Chinatown during the day of the big New Year Parade (which is always held the Sunday after New Year's Day in February), do not be too surprised to see a ferocious looking man-lion decked out in black and red sweatpants and a papier-mâché head seasoned with herbs and the blood of a rooster, come bursting through the front door. It is customary for the lion (costumed members of the Chicago Lion Dancers who perform at the Chinese Community Center, 250 W. 22nd Place), to accept gifts of food and money from the house as a way of fending off evil spirits in the coming year. This is but one of many traditions that are carefully maintained in Chinatown, which remains a tightly woven, highly insulated community, despite the presence of so many out-of-town tourists and local sightseers who crowd into the restaurants and shops near 22nd and Wentworth. During the new year celebration, the local restaurants begin serving special seasonal banquets to patrons, many of whom are second- and third-generation Chinese who have left the neighborhood, but are lured back for sentimental reasons. The annual parade begins at the corner of 24th Place and Wentworth Avenue, and ends at Cermak Road and Princeton Avenue. Because the date of the Chinese New Year changes every year, it is necessary to check with the local Chamber of Commerce before February. Call (312) 326-5320. *Recommended.*

Chinatown Summer Fair, a showcase of Asian food, art, and dance, held every year on Wentworth Avenue the last Sunday in July, or the first Sunday in August. The main stage between 24th Street and 24th Place features Chinese, Japanese, Korean, and Philippine dance troupes. Chinese artists display their paintings and etchings, while vendors hawk traditional items such as lanterns, Indian silk scarves, and assorted Asian foods. A farmer's market begins at 9 A.M. Children's activities include a carnival in the main parking lot with puppeteers, clowns, and animals from the Lincoln Park Mobile Petting Zoo. This event lures upwards of 70,000 people, so it is advisable to take public transportation, if possible. The Summer Fair was originally conceived and developed by local restaurateur and noted long-distance runner George J. Cheung. It is now jointly sponsored by the Chinatown Chamber of Commerce, the Merchant's Association, and the American Legion Post. Call the Chinese Community Center at (312) 225-6198 for dates and times. Free admission.

Double-Ten Parade, held the first Sunday in October, marking the overthrow of the Manchu dynasty by Sun Yat-Sen's Kuomintang (Nationalistic Party) in 1911. Lion dancers, marching groups, and music. The parade travels down Wentworth Avenue from 24th Place to Cermak and Princeton. The Double-Ten Parade observed its eighteenth anniversary in 1991. For information, please call the Chinese Community Center at (312) 225-6198.

Chinatown Moon Festival, in the community parking lot at Cermak and Wentworth Avenue the second week in July. This is not quite the same ethnic festival that it once was years ago. The event has been taken over by a local promoter who sells tickets to carnival rides and a kiddie midway set up for four days in the refurbished Chinatown Parking lot. The proceeds of the four-day event benefit the Chinese Dragon Athletic Association, a youth sports league. Call (312) 326-5320.

Olga Huncke Scholarship Dinner, at alternating restaurants in Chinatown on a Saturday night in mid- or late May. At a time when there was considerable discrimination directed against the Chinese immigrant population, the deeds of an American educator assigned to the Chinatown community are remembered today in the form of scholarships awarded to deserving students who best exemplify the spirit and dedication of Olga Huncke, who taught kindergarten for many years at the John C. Haines Elementary School at 247 W. 23rd Place. For the generations of Chinese-Americans who passed through the Chicago Public School System, Olga Huncke was their first encounter with Western-style education. The year 1992 marks the twentieth anniversary dinner, which includes a scholarship presentation to the recipients (typically five to ten students each year), dinner, and musical entertainment. Tickets are $20 per person, and the dinner is always open to the public. Interested parties should contact Eunice Wong at 2263 S. Wentworth Avenue, Chicago, or call (312) 842-2820 for the date and location.

New Chinatown (North Side) Events

Chinese New Year on Argyle. The Chinese New year begins with the second new moon of winter, which means that the date of the festive celebration will vary from year to year. The new year generally falls between the second and third weeks in February, with lavish parades on both the North and South sides. The New Chinatown parade, with a traditional lion dance and fireworks display, begins at Broadway, proceeds down Argyle and ends at Sheridan Road. In 1991, there was a special reason to celebrate. The new $100,000 pagoda, which drapes the Argyle Street CTA elevated stop was officially dedicated. The pagoda symbolizes peace, unity, and prosperity for the area. The AASBA is confident that it will help establish Argyle Street as the leading purveyor of Oriental food in the Midwest. Depending on the schedule of events within the Chinese-American community each year, the North Side parade will usually follow the South Side festivities. But this is not always the case. It's best to call Charlie Soo, Director of the Asian-American Small Business Association, 5023 N. Broadway, Chicago, for dates and times: (312) 728-1030.

Argyle Fest, a one- or two-day Asian-American street festival, held on the last Sunday in August between Broadway and Sheridan Road. Argyle Fest is a coordinated venture of the Chinese Mutual Aid Association, the Vietnamese Association of Illinois, the new Chinatown Chinese Council, and the Asian-American Small Business Association. This ethnic fair, featuring food vendors from the forty local restaurants, clowns, arts and crafts, Asian and American music, dancers, and children's events, has been held annually since 1985, and lures 15,000 people to the neighborhood. Free admission. For additional information, please call David Wu, or the Chinese Mutual Aid Association at (312) 784-2900. *Recommended.*

Hong Kong Film Festival, at the School of the Art Institute, Columbus Drive and Jackson Boulevard, Chicago, (312) 443-3737 for a recorded message, or (312) 443-3733 for general information. Until Bruce Lee arrived, the Southeast Asian film industry was an unknown commodity in the West. But in the 1970s, Lee and dozens of imitators popularized the martial arts genre. The low budget "chop and slash" action films gave way to a new, more sophisticated style of moviemaking. The School of the Art Institute sponsors the annual Hong Kong Film Festival as a part of its ongoing commitment to bringing the world a little closer to Chicago's doorstep through cinema. Students of the visual arts are afforded a chance to preview the films of some of the Orient's biggest stars, including Jackie Chan, Michael Hui, and Chow Yun-fatt.

South Side Chinatown:
===== The Far East at Our Back Door =====

Chicago's Chinatown is a major tourist attraction that has come a long way from its humble beginnings in the early 1900s. Covering eight square blocks of land that was once hemmed in by railroad yards and expressway barriers, the future of the community seems assured, due to the steady influx of new immigrants each year from Taiwan and mainland China, and to the new Chinatown Square retail and commercial mall at Archer Avenue and Wentworth (the site of the old Santa Fe property). The rapid population growth between 1970 and 1980 (in 1970 there were 14,077 Chinese compared to 29,000 a decade later) was spurred by the U.S. government's decision to relax immigration requirements following the normalization of relations with the People's Republic of China.

Many of the older residents are buying homes in nearby Bridgeport, and in the developing residential neighborhood taking shape in the abandoned railyards to the immediate north. Chinatown Square, opening in early 1992, will add 130 new townhouses to the area, a number of mid-rise apartments, and condominiums, which for the time being should alleviate much of the critical housing shortage. Retailers are excited by the prospects of a 100,000 square foot Asian trade center, scheduled to be built within the next several years. For the tourist, an Oriental garden and colorful festival square designed by Harry Weese & Associates promises to be an aesthetic delight amid the frantic hustle of Asian commerce.

Whatever preconceived notions a person may have about the Chinese way of life are quickly overcome after touring the neighborhood and watching the people as they go about their daily business. Observe, if you will, senior citizens caring for their grandchildren. Listen to the colorful stories told by Helen Wong Jean, the executive director of the Chinese American Civic Council, and a recognized authority on the history of the Chinatown settlement in Chicago. Helen is in her eighties, but during the heyday of Vaudeville, she used to dance the Charleston at the Palace in New York.

Visitors to Chinatown encounter a fascinating collage of ethnic sights, sounds, and smells. Whole cooked chickens and ducks hand in the windows of the groceries and delicatessens. At 22nd Place and Wentworth on a busy Saturday afternoon, Italian produce wholesalers unload their goods on the street, while Chinese shoppers sift through the wooden packing crates searching for only the freshest vegetables and fruit to take home for the evening meal. The old world customs of Europe and the Orient have endured the thrust of technology, urbanization, and the unfortunate by-product of modern times: sophistication.

The grocery stores and gift shops are stacked to the ceilings with exotic foreign spices, herbs, wind chimes, books, Oriental teakwood furniture, artwork, cooking utensils, porcelain tea sets, Chinese fabrics, and of course, the usual tourist kitsch from Hong Kong and Japan. The overcrowded stores bursting to the seams with merchandise arranged haphazardly and seemingly without purpose are the most successful, by neighborhood standards.

The temple-like On Leong Building, ar 2216 S. Wentworth Avenue, anchors the commercial district of Chinatown. Its reception hall represents the one and only indigenous Chinese shrine in the Midwest. In years past, Chinatown was almost exclusively a bachelor community, and many of the single men and who came to the U.S. to earn their livelihood rented apartment quarters on the second floor of this historic building. There has been some talk in recent years about converting the On Leong building into a Chinese-American museum, but so far it is only in the discussion stage.

The Chinatown branch of the Chicago Public Library in the new Galleria on the south end of Wentworth is another fascinating place to visit. Chinese language books and cassettes account for nearly half of its total circulation. The Chinatown branch is the largest circulating library in the city. Albany Park, which serves a predominantly Korean and Jewish clientele on the far North Side ranks second in the total number of circulating books. The people you see in the reading room are not simply reading newspapers for pleasure. They are digesting the stories and vicariously experiencing the outside world through the printed word. There is a high premium attached to education in the Asian cultures. Nowhere is this more evident than at the St. Therese Elementary School and Catholic Mission at 247 W. 23rd Street, which is built in the Chinese architectural style. The facility operates on an austere budget, but consistently produces one of the highest levels of education in the city. The elaborate sanctuary of the St. Therese Catholic Mission at 218 W. Alexander (about 100 feet off Wentworth) was originally an Italian parish when it was constructed in 1904. The adjacent Chinese garden manse and "Moongate" reflect the predominantly Asian culture of the neighborhood since that time. According to Chinese folklore, the Moongate wards off evil spirits.

It is the restaurants, however, representing the four regional styles of Cantonese cooking, that draw the largest share of tourists to the neighborhood. The Eastern Region (1) especially in the provinces of Kiangsu and Chekiang is best known for its redcooking method, which uses dark soy sauce simmered by low heat. Seafood and meat dishes sprinkled with a generous amount of vegetable and fresh bamboo shoots are characteristic of this region. The Northern Style dishes (2), coming from the Hopei, Honan, and Shantung Provinces, are lighter and milder. Scallions, leeks, and garlic are the preferred seasonings. In the Southern Region (3), stir-frying and blanching are the most popular cooking methods. Dishes braised in dark soy sauce and roasted for hot or cold plates are the standard fare in Canton and the surrounding areas. And finally, the Western Region (4), dominated by the Szechuan and Hunan provinces, offer up the hottest, most spicy dishes. Oil, mixed with hot spices, garlic, and scallions, seal in the taste of the ingredients.

The Wentworth Avenue Chinatown also remains the city's only real source for Dim Sum—the traditional Chinese Tea Brunch—which can be appreciated by the casual gourmet only if he comes with an empty stomach and an open mind.

Chinatown Dining and Shopping Guide

Restaurants

Emperor's Choice, *2238 S. Wentworth, Chicago, (312) 225-8800.* Seafood and poultry, especially Peking Duck (which you should order a day in advance) are the preferred menu choices at this modestly styled eatery housed in a former antiques store. You'll dine amid the emperors . . . whose likenesses are reproduced in paintings on the wall. Hours: 11:45 A.M. to 1 A.M. daily. Credit cards accepted.

Chiam, *2323 S. Wentworth, Chicago, (312) 225-6336.* Serving Dim sum daily from 10 A.M. to 2:30 P.M., for about $10 a person. One of Chinatown's best known restaurants, it is a favorite of many of the neighborhood people. Private banquet rooms and cocktail lounge. Dim sum served from 10 A.M.–2:30 P.M. daily. Free parking available. Hours: Monday through Thursday, 11 A.M. to midnight; Friday through Sunday, 11 A.M. to 2 A.M. Credit cards accepted. *Recommended.*

Chee King, *216 W. 22nd Place, Chicago, (312) 842-7777.* Specializing in seafood, but also offering the full gamut of Chinese cooking ranging from hot Szechuan and Hunan to the milder dishes of Canton and casseroles at this modest storefront restaurant. Peking duck is usually available at a moment's notice. Hours: Sunday through Thursday, 11:30 A.M. to 10 P.M.; Friday and Saturday, till 11 P.M. Dim sum served daily from 11 A.M. Complete carryout service. Credit cards accepted.

Hong Min, *221 W. Cermak Road, Chicago, (312) 842-5026.* A modest storefront restaurant specializing in Canton and Mandarin foods, especially seafood, and beef dishes. Most of the items on the menu are exceptional, and the dim sum is served Monday through Friday, 10 A.M.–3 P.M. and Saturdays and Sundays till four. Regular hours: 10 A.M. to 2 A.M. Credit cards accepted.

Sixty-Five, *2409 S. Wentworth, Chicago, (312) 842-6500.* Reasonably priced seafood restaurant that is always crowded. The reason is the outstanding food, which is always served in generous portions. Whether you have it steamed or stir-fried, you won't be disappointed. Family-style dinners are included on the menu. Hours: 11 A.M. to midnight daily. Credit cards accepted.

Three Happiness, *2130 S. Wentworth, Chicago, (312) 791-1228, and 209 W. Cermak, Chicago, (312) 842-1964 for carryout.* A large, spacious eatery that quickly fills to capacity when the dim sum carts roll out of the kitchen during the mid-day. You'll want to sample the steamed dumplings, a rich assortment of cold meats, and some very fine Chinese pastries. Dim sum is served between the hours of 10 A.M. to 2 P.M. The regular menu items are only fair, by comparison. Credit cards accepted.

Mandar-Inn Restaurant, *2249 S. Wentworth, Chicago, (312) 842-4014.* A neighborhood institution that serves the four main styles of Chinese cooking: Mandarin, Cantonese, Hunan, and Szechuan. Hours: Tuesday through Thursday, 11:30 A.M. to 10 P.M.; Friday–Saturday, 11:30 A.M. to 11:30 P.M.; Sunday, 2 P.M. to 10 P.M.

Royal Pacific Restaurant, *2217 S. Wentworth, Chicago, (312) 842-4444.* Specializing in tropical drinks and Cantonese dishes. A large spacious restaurant on two stories. The second-floor window seating offers a fine view of Wentworth Avenue and the imposing On Leong Merchant's Building. No dim sum. Hours: Monday through Thursday, 2 P.M. to 1 A.M. Friday and Saturday, noon to 2 A.M.; Sunday, noon to 1 A.M. Credit cards accepted. *Recommended.*

Gum Luck Restaurant, *2412 S. Wentworth, Chicago, (312) 225-7060.* Cantonese style, and American cooking, but no dim sum. In case you wondered, *gum luck* means "happiness" in Chinese. Hours: Monday through Friday, 11 A.M. to 10 P.M.; Saturday and Sunday till 11 P.M. Credit cards accepted.

Jade East Restaurant, *218 W. Cermak Road, Chicago, (312) 326-4224.* Authentic Cantonese cuisine. Live crab, snails, and clam. Dim sum served at noon. Carry-out service. Hours: daily, noon to midnight.

Lee's Canton Cafe, *2300-02 S. Wentworth, Chicago, (312) 225-4838, or 4861.* Cantonese and Szechuan cuisine. Dim sum served daily at 11 A.M. to 2 P.M. The prices are reasonable, but the dinner menu items will cost more in the evening. Hours: Monday through Friday, 11 A.M. to 11 P.M.; weekends till midnight. Credit cards accepted.

Haylemon Restaurant, *2201 S. Wentworth Ave., Chicago, (312) 225-0891 or (312) 225-0892.* Serving a wide selection of Cantonese and American dinners. Dim sum, consisting of thirty different items, is served by cart till 2 P.M., every day. Daily luncheon specials. Bar service. Carry-out. Hours: Monday through Thursday, 9 A.M. to 11 P.M.; Friday and Saturday till midnight. Free parking. Credit cards accepted.

Cantonesia, *204 W. Cermak Road, Chicago, (312) 225-0100.* Cantonese, and Szechuan food. Dim sum is served on Saturday and Sunday between 11 A.M. and 2 P.M. Full bar service, business luncheons, and banquet rooms available for up to 100 people. Hours: Monday through Friday, 11 A.M. to midnight. Till two on Saturday and Sunday. Credit cards accepted. Free parking in the rear of the building.

Moon Palace Mandarin Restaurant, *2206 S. Wentworth, Chicago, (312) 225-4081.* Hot and spicy food and poultry and pork dishes are the specialty here. Full cocktail service, banquet rooms, and carry-out, but no dim sum. Hours: Sunday through Wednesday, 11 A.M. to 9:30 P.M.; Friday and Saturday, 11 A.M. to 11 P.M. Closed on Thursday. Credit cards accepted.

Wing Wah Restaurant, *208 W. Cermak Road, Chicago, (312) 225-4611, or (312) 225-2817.* This restaurant is the old Lung Fung, but under a new name and at a new location. Wing Wah specializes in Cantonese and Mandarin food, and is always crowded. For that reason host Paul Lam only serves dim sum during the off-peak hours.

New Lung Fung Restaurant, *2200 S. Wentworth, Chicago, (312) 225-5050.* Rice and noodle dishes, seafood, soups and a variety of home cooked meals. For dim sum, try the Three Happiness across the street, because the New Lung Fung does not serve it. Hours: Monday through Thursday, 11 A.M. to 10 P.M.; Friday through Sunday till 11 P.M. Credit cards accepted.

The Junk, *2143 S. Archer Avenue, Chicago, (312) 326-3311.* Located in the "suburbs of Chinatown" an appropriate description supplied by owner George Cheung. It was Cheung who spearheaded the drive to construct the colorful Chinatown Gateway arch, which opened in

1975, and spans Wentworth Avenue at Cermak Road. The civic-minded Cheung was born and raised in Chicago, and is the cofounder of the Junk Running Club, headquartered in his popular restaurant and bar across the street from the Chinatown Square shopping mall and commercial center, scheduled to open in July, 1992. The Cheungs have been in business for nineteen years, serving the usual Chinese standbys with such exotic names as "Shanghai Sally," "Captain's Delight," and the "Coolie Caper." The atmosphere is pleasing, and a trip to the "suburbs" is highly recommended the next time you visit Chinatown. Full cocktail service. Hours: Monday, Wednesday and Thursday, 4 P.M. to 11 P.M.; Friday and Saturday till 1 A.M.; Sunday till midnight. Credit cards accepted.

King Wah Restaurant, *2225 S. Wentworth, Chicago, (312) 842-1404.* Since 1962, the Lee Family has made frequent trips to Hong Kong and Taiwan in order to keep up to date with the latest techniques in ethnic Chinese cooking. The result: some excellent Cantonese and Mandarin menu items, including the chef's special, spicy chicken and shrimp. The Marco Polo steak and tea-smoked duck are also recommended. One of the more upscale restaurants on the street. Hours: Sunday through Thursday 11 A.M. to 10 P.M.; Friday, Saturday, and holidays, 11 A.M. to 11 P.M. Credit cards accepted.

Evergreen, *2411 S. Wentworth, Chicago, (312) 225-8898.* Szechuan, Hunan, and Cantonese cooking. This is one of the newer Chinatown restaurants, located near the Galleria on the south end of Wentworth Avenue. Hours: Sunday through Thursday, 11:30 A.M. to 11:30 P.M.; Friday and Saturday, 11:30 A.M. to midnight. Credit cards accepted.

South Side Chinatown Shopping Guide
Books and Video

Roxy Book and Gallery Co., *215 W. 23rd Street, Chicago, (312) 225-6683.* Chinese and English books. Giftware, herbal medicines, figurines, Chinese-language newspapers and dictionaries. Wall paintings and artwork are available for purchase. The China Tours & Travel Co., specializing in international and domestic travel, is located in the same building. Phone: (312) 567-9100. Hours: Monday through Friday, 9:30 A.M. to 6 P.M.; Saturday, 10 A.M. to 2 P.M.; Closed Sunday. Credit cards accepted.

Bang Bang Video & Audio, *2337 S. Wentworth, Chicago, (312) 326-5770.* Chinese movies from Hong Kong available for sale or rental. Magazines, newspapers, and audio cassettes are also stocked. Hours: Monday through Saturday, 9 A.M. to midnight. Credit cards accepted.

Bakeries

Happy Garden Bakery, *2358 S. Wentworth, Chicago, (312) 225-2730, and 227 W. Cermak, Chicago, (312) 842-7556.* Fresh Chinese and French pastries, some gooey and sweet, can be eaten at a leisurely pace inside the store or carried out. Hours: open every day from 8 A.M. to 7 P.M.

Keefer Bakery, Inc., *249 W. Cermak Road, Chicago, (312) 326-2289.* Try the Red Bean Lotus Cake, or the Red Bean Puff for something delicious and totally out of the ordinary. Keefer has been at this location for fifteen years. Hours: open every day except Wednesday from 8 A.M. to 7 P.M.; Wednesdays, 8 A.M. to 6 P.M. *Recommended.*

Gifts, Souvenirs, and Jewelry

Dong Kee Company, *2252 S. Wentworth, Chicago, (312) 225-6340.* Large, prosperous gift shop that sells a variety of Oriental foods, cooking utensils, wind chimes, tea, almond cookies, and dishware. Hours: Monday through Thursday, 9 A.M. to 9 P.M.; Friday, 9 A.M. to 11 P.M.; Saturday, 9 A.M. to 10 P.M.; Sunday, 9 A.M. to 9 P.M.

Woks 'n' Things, *2234 S. Wentworth, Chicago, (312) 842-0787.* One of the leading suppliers of Oriental cookware in the Midwest. Choose from a large selection of woks and the cookbooks that explain how to use them. Electronic appliances, hardware, and other related items are also found in the store. Hours: Monday through Friday, 9 A.M. to 6 P.M.; Saturday, 9 A.M. to 7 P.M.; till 6 P.M. on Sunday.

China Arts and Gifts, *235 W. Cermak, Chicago, (312) 225-7261.* Quaint, old-fashioned store selling fine bone porcelain figurines, tea sets, silk mats, jewelry, and paper fans. It's too bad the counter help was so unresponsive when it came to telling us about the quality and the prices of the merchandise in the store. It must have something to do with the old Oriental proverb about talking to strangers. Hours: daily, 10 A.M. to 5 P.M. Credit cards accepted.

Pacific Imports, *241 W. Cermak Road, Chicago, (312) 808-0456.* Elegant teakwood furniture, hand-crafted porcelain figurines, tea sets, masks, and some import items from Japan. Wholesale and retail. Hours: daily, 10 A.M. to 7 P.M. Credit cards accepted.

Chinatown Fashion, *2214 S. Wentworth, Chicago, (312) 225-0022.* This is more a souvenir shop catering to the impulse buying habits of tourists than a full-line clothing store, though some women's fashions and accessories are sold on the premises. Oriental bric-a-brac, decorative masks, "Suzy Wong" dresses, tee-shirts, dolls, fans, and fortune cookies clutter the store. Hours: daily, 10 A.M. to 10 P.M. Credit cards accepted.

Mandar-Inn Gifts, *2319 S. Wentworth, Chicago, (312) 326-5082.* Porcelain floor vases, wall hangings, teakwood furniture, and tapestries. Popular with the tourists, and no longer owned by the Mandar-Inn Restaurant. Hours: Sunday through Thursday, 10:30 A.M. to 7 P.M.; Friday and Saturday, 10:30 A.M. to 8 P.M.

Dor Fook, *2410 S. Wentworth, Chicago, (312) 326-1941.* Jeweler and goldsmith who caters more to the neighborhood people than the tourist trade. Birthday, anniversary, and wedding plaques embossed on red velvet. Red is the traditional color of happiness in China. Hours: open every day from 10:30 A.M. to 6 P.M.

Oriental Boutique, *2262 S. Wentworth, Chicago, (312) 842-3798.* China, jade, and Oriental gifts from Taiwan. Kung-Fu supplies, slippers, and pajamas. Porcelain figurines. Hours: daily from 11 A.M. to 7 P.M.

Tea, Ginseng, & Herbs

Ten Ren Tea & Ginseng Co. of Chicago, Ltd., *2247 S. Wentworth, Chicago, (312) 842-1171.* The Ten Ren Co. of Taipei, Taiwan, owns and operates thirty-six chain stores and five factories world wide that manufacture and sell ginseng—the "king of herbs." For generations, ginseng has long been regarded as a restorative elixir with a high concentration of effective nutrients. Ten Ren grows cultivated ginseng in a 120-acre plantation in Wisconsin, which is considered the ideal geographic location in North America today. Wisconsin Ginseng Co., Inc., a subsidiary of the parent company, harvests 500,000 pounds each year, much of it winding up in domestic markets such as this one. People come from all over the Midwest and the Great Plains states to purchase from among fifteen high grade teas and ginseng at this branch location. There are always one or two samples available to taste. Hours: daily from 9:30 A.M. to 9 P.M.

Sun Sun Tong: *Chinese Herb, Ginseng, Gifts, & Food Co., 2260 S. Wentworth, Chicago, (312) 842-6398.* Chinese herbs, ginseng, and nutritional health foods. Wholesale, retail, and mail order. Tea sets, vases, and figurines round out the gift line. Margaret Lau, the resident herbalist, is available to answer your questions about the healing powers of ginseng. Hours: daily from 10 A.M. to 7 P.M. Credit cards accepted.

Bark Lee Tong: *Ginseng, Tea & Herbs Company, 229 W. Cermak Road, Chicago, (312) 225-1988.* A thousand different herbs, tea, and Chinese pharmaceuticals sold by Andy Hoi-Csiu Chan, owner of this family-run business that has been a fixture in the Chinatown community for thirty-five years. Andy is also an artist in residence. He serves as president of the Chinese Artist's Association of North America, and is an art advisor to the People's Republic of China. In the basement underneath his herb store, Andy Chan teaches painting, conducts photography workshops, and hosts poetry readings for the Chinese-American community. Chinese art supplies, including rice paper, water colors, and brushes are available for purchase. For information about the workshops, poetry readings, and other on-going creative activities within the Chinatown neighborhood, call Andy Chan at (312) 225-1988. Store hours: daily 9 A.M. to 7 P.M. No credit cards. *Recommended.*

Ethnic Grocery

Tai Wah Grocery, *2226 S. Wentworth, Chicago, (312) 326-4120.* Barbecued hogs and ducks hang seductively in the window. Inside you'll find some exotic Asian foods that you may want to try if you're in an adventurous frame of mind. Dried octopus, barracuda, and anchovy are sold in clear plastic bags. That way, you can see just what it is you're getting yourself into. To wash this down, you may wish to sample imported sugar cane juice, sold in pop-top cans.

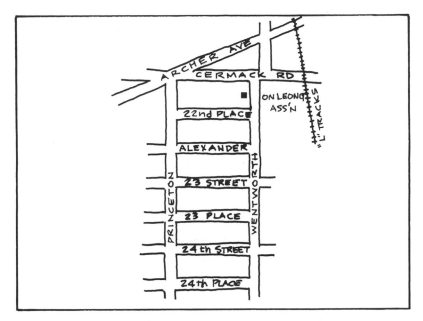

Chinatown (South Side)

Chicago Seafood Market, *2245 S. Wentworth, Chicago, (312) 842-4361.* Fresh fish. Live shellfish in the tank. Imported Chinese foods and candies.

Wing Chan Bar-B-Q, *211 W. Alexander Street, Chicago, (312) 791-9389.* The best spot in Chinatown for barbecued pork, chicken, and duck "to go."

Getting to Chinatown

By car: If you are driving from the south, exit the Dan Ryan Expressway (I-94) at the 22nd Street-Canalport turnoff. From the north, exit the Dan Ryan Expressway at 18th Street. From the Chicago Loop, drive south on Michigan Avenue to 22nd Street (Cermak Road), and turn right. Proceed west on Cermak for five blocks. There is a public parking lot at Wentworth and Cermak, on the right-hand side of the street. Many of the Chinatown restaurant owners will discount your parking if you show them a valid ticket.

By public transportation: Lake-Dan Ryan train: from the Loop, board the southbound elevated at the Lake Street or Wabash stations.

Service runs every five to ten minutes all day and evening. Between 6 A.M. and 7 P.M. only the "B" train will stop at the CERMAK-CHINATOWN exit. All other times, the "A" and "B" train makes all stops.

Wentworth Bus #24: daily service every ten to fifteen minutes, day and evening. Operates until midnight. Begins at Clark and Randolph in the Chicago Loop, operating via Clark, Cermak, and Wentworth. A fifteen-minute ride from downtown.

Archer Bus #62: service every five to ten minutes all day and evening. Twenty-four-hour service. Express service (limited stops) Monday through Saturday, daytime. Board downtown on State Street starting at Marina City. Fifteen-minute trip from the Chicago Loop. Get off at the Archer/Cermak stop and walk one block east..

Wallace-Racine #44: service every twelve to fifteen minutes weekdays (only) from downtown, everyday from the far south side to Chinatown until midnight. Board on State Street downtown, a fifteen-minute trip.

Cermak #21: service every ten to fifteen minutes 5 A.M. to midnight. Operates between McCormick Place and 54th Avenue. Douglas train terminal.

For additional information about public transportation to Chinatown, call 1-800-872-7000 from the suburbs, or 836-7000 in Chicago.

A Chinatown Recipe For Tea Preparation

A tea pot, tea boat, tea pan, tea cups, tea leaves and boiling water are necessary ingredients for classic Chinese tea.

1. Scald the tea equipment. With the pot boiled, the flavor is improved.

2. Fill the tea pot half full. Oolong, Wu Yi, and To Kuan Yin tea are recommended by the Ten Ren Tea and Ginsing Co., of Chinatown.

3. Fill the tea pot with boiling water until the water overflows the brim.

4. Within fifteen seconds, empty the water from the teapot. Empty the water from the tea boat into the pan. This will loosen up the tea leaves, enabling the flavor to be released gradually.

5. Fill the pot with boiling water and cover it immediately. Allow the contents in the teapot to be steeped for one minute.

6. Pour boiling water over the pot until the tea boat is half filled.

7. Clean and warm the tea cups one at a time by quickly rolling them in the tea boat against the handle of the tea pot. After it is hot, line them up against the edge of the tea pan.

8. After steeping for one minute, lift the teapot out of the tea boat, and rub the bottom of the pot in circles against the edge of the tea boat in a manner that makes a pleasant sound so as to get the dripping water off.

9. Pour the tea by moving the teapot back and forth over the tea cups which have been previously lined up until each cup is evenly blended and one cup is not stronger than the other.

10. Serve the hot tea. Fine tea should be sipped slowly to fully appreciate the fine taste and aroma.

11. Repeat steeping the tea from step five, adding fifteen seconds for each additional steeping. This may be repeated as many as six times. Note: To make the best tea, don't oversteep the tea leaves.

General Guidelines:

1. Water temperature: Unfermented green leaves, Long-Ching (dragon well) tea, 70° C. Slightly fermented teas such as green teas and Jasmine tea: 80° C. Semi-fermented teas such as Oolong and Ti-kuan-yin tea, 85°-90° C. Completely fermented teas such as black tea and Pu-Erh tea, 95°-100° C.

2. Quality of tea leaves: In general, three grams (or two teaspoons) of tea leaves are used for brewing 150 cc of tea in a cup with a lid, while half a pot of leaves are used if a miniature tea pot is used. Steep until the desired concentration is obtained. If a cup with a lid is used, brew about 2-$\frac{1}{2}$ to 3 minutes. Longer time is required for a second steeping.

Asian Chicago

History and Settlement

Although they account for only 3 percent of the Chicago metropolitan population, the combined Asian communities are the fastest growing ethnic group in the region. The Asian population increased 70 percent between 1980 and 1988, with Filipinos (44,317), Indians (28,847) and Chinese (24,351) accounting for more than half the total. The 1980 census counted 24,351 Koreans, 18,432 Japanese, 6,287 Vietnamese, and 3,265 Thais to round out the totals. There are Asian pockets in Cook, Du Page, and Will County, but the greater number of Asian Americans reside in nine North Side wards: the 39th, 40th, 42nd, 43rd, 44th, 46th, 48th, 49th, and 50th.

With the loosening of immigration restrictions, and continuing political strife in Southeast Asia, thousands of Koreans, Filipinos, Thais, Vietnamese, and Cambodians swelled the 1980 figures which placed their collective number at 166,000. These trends are consistent with recent patterns of immigration across the U.S. Language barriers, cultural differences, climatic changes, and housing and employment discrimination are obstacles to progress—barriers that are quickly being broken down through hard work, self-reliance, and a penchant for resourcefulness that has turned one economically depressed crime-ridden Chicago neighborhood into a major wholesale center of Southeast Asian commerce.

Before 1980, Argyle and Broadway was a neglected corner of Uptown, a faded, blowsy neighborhood overrun by street people, substance abusers, and an economically displaced underclass victimized by the system. Today Uptown is on the rebound, given new life by Vietnamese businessmen who opened grocery stores and restaurants alongside the Chinese merchants, who sought to expand the boundaries of the South Side Chinatown to the far North Side. Argyle and Broadway, the "Little Hanoi" of Chicago, is an ethnic success story that draws on values the Asian cultures hold in equally high esteem: honor, a sense of obligation to the family and society at large, and a profound respect for education. Much attention has been focused on the achievements of Asian children in the U.S. school systems, and their parents in the white collar sectors of the economy. According to the most recent census data, Asian Americans are more likely than white, Hispanic, or black Americans to hold down professional jobs. Asians have often been stereotyped as "model minorities." Their high-profile academic and business achievements have brought mixed blessings. On the one hand, American educators marvel at this work ethic. (A 1986 survey commissioned by the U.S. Department of Education found that half of all Asian American high school sophomores spend five hours per week on homework assignments. Contrast this to whites, who spend a third of that time on homework, and a quarter of the time for blacks, yet community leaders are quick to point out that these success stories often ignore the economic hardships that many refugees encounter when they make the transition from rural to urban life. Foreign-born Asian Americans are also more likely to hold down the lowest-paying jobs on the bottom rungs of the employment ladder: domestic, manual laborer, or busboy.)

One should not, however, generalize when speaking about Chicago's multinational Asian population. Each is unique, and each group would bristle at the thought of being pigeon-holed into one category. Philippine history, for example, is marked by both Hispanic and other Western influences. Within China alone there are more than a hundred nationalities. There are four regional dialects in Thailand, where Buddhism is the prevailing religion. The Vietnamese are also predominantly Buddhist, but there is an overlay of Western influence that lingers from the French colonial period.

The Asian people have not yet influenced the political process in Chicago. This failure to close ranks in order to achieve a common purpose has retarded progress in the public sector. In 1983, however, the Asian American Coalition was founded. It is an umbrella group formed to close the cultural and political gulf separating the Asian nationalities.

The late Mayor Harold Washington helped open the door to Asians, who have forced Illinois politicians to re-evaluate their policy toward ethnic groups.

Ken Moy, a Chinese American attorney is the highest ranking politician to occupy an office in the tricounty area. Moy has been a member of the Du Page County Board since 1984. In 1990 for the first time, an Indian American attorney named Ahmed Patel was slated to run for a Cook County judgeship on the Democratic ticket.

Even though the Asian American population is still not considered large enough to be a crucial swing vote in statewide elections, nearly every major office holder now has an Asian liaison officer on staff. The politicians no longer take for granted their quiet presence and past silence concerning issues of importance. In 1987, North Side community leaders set up voting registration booths along the 1200 block of Argyle Street with hopes of registering the 10,000-strong Asian vote. Two years later, Mayor Eugene Sawyer proposed the formation of a Commission on Asian American Affairs.

Cook County pols turn out in full force for the annual Lunar New Year Banquet, a cross-cultural social function for the dozen or so Asian ethnic groups scattered across the city. It is testimony to the growing political awareness and voting strength of a segment of the population that will become the trend-setters of the twenty-first century and beyond.

Filipinos

Since the nineteenth century, the designation of "Filipino" has been applied to the Christianized Malays who populate the islands constituting the Philippine archipelago. During the period of the Spanish conquest, the term Filipino was loosely applied to persons of Spanish descent born in the Philippines. The Spanish presence officially ended on June 12, 1898, when General Emilio Aguinaldo proclaimed the first Philippine Republic and proudly unfurled the state flag for the first time. However, the Treaty of Paris, signed on December 10, 1898, ended the Spanish-American War, but ceded the entire island nation to the United States in return for a payment of $20 million. Philippine insurgents fiercely resisted American military and civilian rule for the next forty years. The struggle to establish home rule was resolved by the passage of the Tydings-McDuffie Bill in 1934, which guaranteed Philippine independence by 1946. The Republic was formally established that year, coinciding with the anniversary of the American Declaration of Independence on July 4.

The first Filipino settlers arrived in North America in 1765, via the Spanish galleons. They settled in what is now New Orleans. Filipino immigration into Chicago picked up after World War I. St. Mary's in downtown Chicago was the first parish in the city to welcome the new Asian arrivals.

At St. Mary's, the Christmas tradition of the homeland is kept alive in the *Simbanggabi* (Night Mass), which is part of a nine-day celebration that makes the Philippine Yuletide season the longest in the world. Simbanggabi dates back more than 300 years, when the Spanish introduced Catholicism to the Philippines. Up until the mid-eighteenth century, the Philippine Christmas was a two-day festival, including the December 24 "Vespera." Philippine history tells us about a parish priest who was overwhelmed by the piety of a certain group of farmers in a Bulacan town, who prayed on their knees around a "siga"—or bonfire—for nine straight days. The priest asked for official sanctions from Rome to adopt this "psalamat" as a part of the Christmas observance. The papal grant was awarded and the other unique Filipino Christmas tradition—the Simbanggabi Mass (commencing on December 16, and continuing up to the first Sunday of the New Year)—followed. The nine-day holiday has served as a powerful unifying force in the Philippines, known as "the bastion of Christianity in the Far East," but divided by political and cultural ideology. The Simbanggabi in Chicago is tailored to the specific requirements of American life, but is a nostalgic reminder of family and homeland.

The Filipino community in Chicago was given formal direction in 1937 when Francisco M. Elizalde, the resident commissioner of the Philippines in the United States, sent his assistant, Francisco Varona, to Chicago for the purpose of organizing a central committee to represent Filipino immigrants in all matters of social and political concern. Varona succeeded in convincing the numerous social clubs scattered across the city to form a Council of Clubs, which evolved into the National Filipino American Council of Chicago. In 1953, this umbrella group, representing thirty-four regional provisional groups, was incorporated as a nonprofit organization. The Dr. Jose Rizal Memorial Fund was created for the purpose of purchasing or renting a community center. The dream became a reality on May 7, 1966, when the first FACC building was dedicated at 1139 W. Webster Street on the North Side by Mrs. Estela Sulit, Consul General of the Philippines in Chicago. Four years later the Filipino American Political Association was organized as the political arm of the FACC, with Roberto D. Roque, an attorney and prominent community leader, elected charter president. Under the direction of Roque, the first Philippine Week celebration with a lavish downtown parade and special exhibits at the

Museum of Science and Industry was held during the week of June 12–19, 1970. It is now a yearly tradition, in which thousands of Filipino Americans pause to reaffirm their appreciation and affection for the national heritage.

A steady tide of Filipinos arrived in Chicago in the 1960s, when changes in immigration laws encouraged many professional people with medical and technical skills to emigrate. They found employment in hospitals, medical clinics, and extended health care facilities.

Their economic status and familiarity with the English language has made the process of acculturation relatively easy. Though they are a close-knit community, the Filipinos are widely dispersed across the North and Northwest sides. Many can be found in Edgewater and Uptown, which is close to the Howard-Englewood-Jackson elevated line—the best mode of transportation to the hospitals and medical clinics that dot the lakefront.

Community life continues to revolve around the representative organizations of the FACC, now headquartered at the Jose Rizal Memorial Center, at 1332 W. Irving Park Road on the North Side. The yellow and blue brick building was originally constructed for the Orphei Singing Club, a Swedish choral and fraternal society. But with the changing patterns of immigration, the few remaining Orphei members were forced to disband the club and sell the property to the Filipino community in 1974. Such are the ethnic realities of Chicago. Neighborhoods are nothing more than temporary harbors in a sprawling urban center, the only defining quality of which is change.

Indian

There was a time during the 1960s when Chicago's growing population from the Indian subcontinent considered the city to be only a temporary residence while they acquired their education at American universities or advanced their careers with American firms and gained a perspective on Western culture.

Like the earlier European groups, the Indian people soon discovered that there was no going back. In every respect they had assimilated into the cultural mainstream and had planted roots in Chicago that were not easily severed. India, the world's largest democracy, is home to 850 million people. It has sent more of its sons and daughters to New York and Chicago than to any other American cities. Only in recent years, however, has there emerged a readily identifiable Indo-Pakistani community. It is located along the congested Devon Avenue commercial strip between Western and California avenues in West Ridge—formerly an all-Jewish neighborhood.

The genesis of this bustling retail district dates back only about twenty years—to 1971—when a Hong Kong-based Indian firm named the Sun Palace decided to sell some items from its product line in the Harrison Hotel. The overwhelming response encouraged these entrepreneurs to open a branch outlet on Devon Avenue, adjacent to an existing Indian import store. Since that time, an exotic collection of vegetarian and nonvegetarian restaurants, sari shops, Indo-Pakistani video rental stores, and import groceries catering to the tastes of Chicago's 70,000-strong Indian community has slowly squeezed out the string of Jewish businesses that were fixtures in this community for years. In the last few years, a tiny but steadily growing Assyrian and Arabic presence on Devon Avenue between Oakley and Western shows signs of significantly altering the ethnic composition of West Ridge. Devon Avenue, designated the "Gandhi Marg" by the City Council remains one of Chicago's most frequently overlooked ethnic treasures.

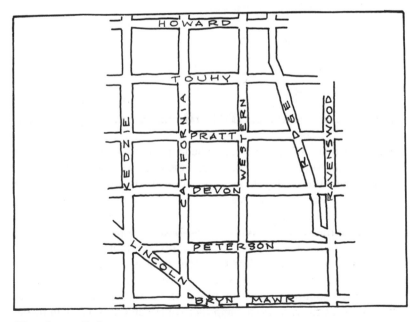

West Rogers Park

The religious and cultural heritage of this apolitical group is scattered across Cook County, but in South Suburban Lemont, the Hindu Temple of Greater Chicago has become the most important religious shrine for adherents of that faith. The large white temple, covering nearly twenty acres of land, was sanctified in October, 1987, and is dedicated to Rama, an important Hindu deity representing the human body. According to Hindu legend, Rama was the heir to the kingdom of Ayodhya. He is the central figure of the Sanskrit epic poem the *Ramayana,* which tells of a plot hatched by his enemies to banish him from his rightful place on the throne. Rama spent the next fourteen years living in exile with his wife Sita, his half-brother Laksmana, and the monkey general Hanuman, who helped the deity rescue Sita from Ravana, the demon-king of Lanka (now Sri Lanka). Rama is worshipped as the seventh incarnation of Vishnu, and his image, and those of his attending figures, are located in the *mahamandapum,* or main prayer hall, in the Lemont shrine. Other Hindu deities, including Sri Venkataeshwaram, Bhoo Devi, Krishna, Radha, and Sri Ganesh are located in two side halls. Construction of this impressive building began in 1984 and cost $4 million, of which $1.4 million came in the form of bank loans.

Chicago's Sikh population, though comparatively small at 3,000, has its own religious society of *gurdwara* in Palatine, and the World Sikh Organization is located in Schaumburg.

Koreans

A handful of Koreans turned up on U.S. shores as early as 1903, but local exclusionary laws prevented a mass immigration until 1965, when the door to the West opened ever so slowly. The next year, 2,000 Koreans who preceded the exodus of boat people from Laos, Cambodia, and Thailand, pooled their savings and came to America. Nearly two-thirds of these people were college-educated professionals, seeking acceptance and economic gain within the capitalist system. By 1973, the number of foreign-born Koreans had increased substantially to more than ten times the 1966 figure.

For the Koreans who arrived in the late 1960s, the adjustment to American life was arduous. There were language and serious cultural barriers to overcome, and compromises to be made with the traditional values Koreans held sacred. Since 1962, the Korean American Association of Chicago has served as a community outreach agency, bridging the cultural gap between East and West. The president of the KAAOC is the unofficial mayor of "Koreatown" and a powerful voice at City Hall and at the Mayor's Advisory Council on Asian-American Affairs. Despite working out of a cramped, windowless office at 5941 N. Lincoln Avenue, there is fierce competition among local leaders for this unsalaried position come election time. It was no different in 1991, when the two contestants took off the kid gloves to engage in some mud-slinging that was extraordinary, even by Chicago's shifty electoral standards. Hak Soo Jin, owner of a jewelry store, spent upwards of $75,000 to challenge the incumbent president Hyo Hyun Byun. Both candidates were permitted to *buy* the loyalty of the Korean voters by signing them up for membership in the association. Amid charges of vote-stealing, duplicity, and double-dipping by paid members of the electorate, the frenetic campaign came to an end on June 16, 1991, but not before one of Byun's men slugged it out in a parking lot in suburban Lincolnwood with candidate Jin following the election. Young Whan Kim emerged from the fray in a neck brace; Jin sported a plaster cast on his punching arm. The story made the front page of the *Chicago Korea Times,* which prompted Jin to run an advertisement

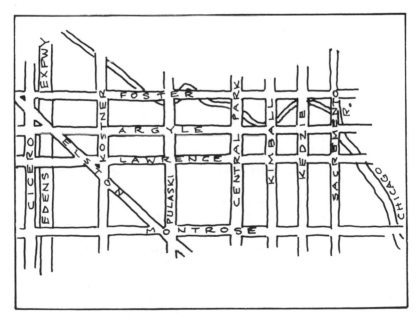

Albany Park ("Seoul" of Chicago)

in the paper, apologizing for the incident. The city had not witnessed an election with this kind of intensity in many a year. When all the votes were counted, Hak Soo Jin, despite his unfavorable publicity surrounding the boxing match with Vice President Kim, emerged the victor by a scant 295 votes. Byun, a 62-year-old former radiologist, filed a court challenge—and won a temporary restraining order. He cited innumerable voting irregularities. Chicago-style politics, which is the normal way of doing business in "clout city," had seemingly come home to roost in the Korean community, which numbers 150,000 people in the six-county area, according to 1990 census figures.

The Koreans have demonstrated entrepreneurial skills. They are a resourceful people, unafraid of putting in the long hours and painful sacrifice that accompany the harvest. The borders of Chicago's Korea-town were first defined in the early 1970s, when the immigrants began buying commercial property in Albany Park, from Foster and Pulaski on the north, Montrose on the south, and the north branch of the Chicago River.

The Koreans inherited a community beginning to experience the first signs of urban decay, empty storefronts, escalating crime, and a blaze of neon signs on Lawrence Avenue beckoning lonely men to spend their money in a score of corner adult bookstores and peep shows. In the late 1970s, the Koreans opened dry cleaning stores, groceries, martial arts emporiums, and gift shops, all of which restored stability along the commercial strip between Kedzie and Elston. The Korean Businessman's Association has worked very hard to promote the Asian ethnic flair of Albany park while local churches and the Korean Services Agency labored quietly behind the scenes, sponsoring family counseling programs, language translation, and day-care centers for the children of working parents. One such program is the Employment Service for Indo-Chinese refugees, which places not only Koreans, but Vietnamese, Cambodians, Laotians, the Hmong, and Chinese into good-paying jobs in service industries and the white-collar sector.

A high point in the revitalization of Albany Park was reached several years ago with the opening of the Moo-Goong Terrace, a seventy-five unit senior citizen complex at Kedzie and Lawrence. It was built in partnership with the federal housing and urban development department.

There is a flip side to the American dream that immigrant groups since the time of the Irish potato famine know all to well—the decay that is overtaking the corridors of the inner city, although that is the place that offers the only hope of advancement for these groups. The Koreans, like others who have gone before, are often steered to these high-crime areas by well-meaning business contacts who understand that the lowest rents can be found here. Opportunity sometimes exacts a terrible price, however. In recent years Asian and Arabic shopkeepers have been victimized by thieves and ghetto gunmen. In addition, Asian businesspeople have encountered a backlash from the African-American community over alleged double standards.

The problem, which is not unique to Chicago, (Mayor David Dinkins had to intervene between Korean grocery store owners and black residents in Manhattan) crystallized in the Far South Side community of Roseland on Michigan Avenue. Blacks complain that the Korean American merchants there are insensitive to consumer needs and that they suspiciously view each customer as a potential threat. Picket lines were set up outside Korean business locations and a widespread consumer boycott was threatened by frustrated residents in the summer of 1990. Blacks complained to Alderman Robert Shaw of the Ninth Ward that the Koreans were absentee landlords who took their money out of the neighborhood and failed to provide employment to local residents. Store owners replied that Roseland was a dangerous place in which to run a business. Shoplifting, burglary, and vandalism were chronic problems—which contributed to escalating insurance rates and many sleepless nights. The impassioned Shaw was accused of fanning the seeds of discontent with his black constituents by reading from a prepared statement with the headlines "Let's Take Control Of Our Community!" Meetings were set up between the Commission on Human Relations and the two feuding factions. Both sides indicated a willingness to resolve the difficulties. It will take time, but a spirit of cooperation will emerge from this painful period of social adjustment. Rivalries between ethnic and racial groups in Chicago are as old and historic as the city itself. The conflict in Roseland is but a new page in a painfully familiar story.

Japanese

Immigrants from the rural farming districts of Japan arrived in the United States in the late nineteenth century, but few made it as far as Chicago. Kamenosuke Nishi, who lived in San Francisco prior to the 1893 World's Fair, was among the first Japanese residents of Chicago. He made a fortune for himself operating a gift shop at the corner of Cottage Grove Avenue and 27th Street. It wasn't until the middle years of World War II that the Japanese community in Chicago took shape. Beginning in 1942, a steady stream of former internment camp inmates established temporary residence in Chicago's "Little Tokyo" near Clark and Division. The proliferation of Japanese Americans, who had become refugees in their own country, were lured to the city by the abundance of light manufacturing, clerical, and wartime jobs. The city provided steady employment until the cessation of hostilities and the lifting of wartime restrictions that barred the Japanese from returning to their West Coast homes.

In 1945, a number of Chicago's "Nisei" (second-generation Japanese) who were concerned about the well-being of the former internees, organized the "Tei Ju Sha," or Japanese American Service Committee, for the purpose of locating affordable housing and jobs in the private sector. The JASC was assisted in this endeavor by the United Way, the Community Trust, the Catholic Church, and the American Friends. The JASC marked its forty-fifth year of service to the community with an anniversary celebration at the Heiwa Terrace building on June 23, 1991.

Before Pearl Harbor, there were only 390 people of Japanese ancestry living in the city. Most were students living in Hyde Park-Kenwood dormitories and attending classes at the University of Chicago. By 1950 the Japanese-American population stabilized at 10,829. These numbers increased only slightly in the next three decades, due in no small measure to improving economic conditions in postwar Japan. The history of the Japanese settlement in Chicago is characterized by rapid assimilation and social mobility. The anti-Japanese phobia of the West Coast was never a factor in Chicago. Jobs were plentiful and the prejudicial attitudes of employers and landlords were minimalized.

Buddhism teaches interdependence. Western cultures teach rugged individualism, and the virtues of the "self-made man." The success of the Japanese in the face of historic racial discrimination reflects the tenets of Buddhism: respect for the family and the educator, hard work, and pride in achievement. There is a high premium placed on success, and conversely, shame awaits those who do not produce.

The Japanese community in Old Town is dispersed now, having given way to commercial and residential development in the 1960s and 1970s. Sandburg Village occupies a site formerly inhabited by many ethnic Japanese. All that remains of "Little Tokyo" is the Midwest Buddhist Temple, designed by Hideaki Arao, and opened at Menomonee and Hudson avenues in 1972. Religious and cultural life evolve around the North Side house of worship, even as more and more Japanese make their way into the suburbs. As presently constituted, the Japanese are still one of the smallest ethnic groups in the suburban sprawl, but they have moved from the inner-city neighborhoods for much the same reasons as the Europeans: to ensure that their children will profit from better schools and drug-free environments. What this ultimately means is a shift away from the activities revolving around church and temple, though the Futabakai

Japanese Day School in Niles continues to instill Asian culture in the third and fourth generations.

Vietnamese

Bewildered, alone, and afraid, thousands of Vietnamese, Cambodians, and Laotians who had been forced into refugee camps along the Thai border, or cast adrift in the raging current of the South China Sea, found a new home in America in the weeks and months following the U.S. pullout from Saigon in 1975. The Vietnamese who were fortunate to escape their homeland following the collapse of the Thieu regime, faced additional perils on the open sea from marauding Thai "river pirates" in search of precious gold "taels"—finely crafted wafers accepted as payment for a safe passage to Malaysia. Those who were able to smuggle their families out of Vietnam with a few of the valuable ingots in their possession sewed the wafers into the linings of their coats for safekeeping. The Thai pirates knew about the manufacture of gold wafers, weighing about 1.2 troy ounces, and systematically attacked refugee boats on the high seas. The passengers would be forced to strip before the boat was plundered and burned. Very often the refugees would be shot to death, or simply tossed overboard.

Still, over 130,000 Vietnamese managed to escape their war-torn lands, but they often found themselves inpoverished by the time they arrived in the U.S., where immigration officials herded them into resettlement camps. Life in the camps was a lonely ordeal, but a small price to pay for freedom. Fort Chaffee, Arkansas, was the last refugee camp to close in December, 1975. For those who were left, the time had come to adjust to the rigors of American life. Chicago took in 2,000 Vietnamese in those first few months. That number has since tripled.

Finding a job in a recession-wracked economy proved to be the toughest challenge. Many highly skilled clerical workers who had served the pro-Western Thieu government were forced to accept menial jobs in the service economy.

The Vietnamese are the newest immigrant group to seek their fortunes in Chicago. Seventeen years after the great upheaval, the close-knit community has made tremendous strides. The Argyle-Broadway-Sheridan Road neighborhood is a busy, thriving retail corridor, where hard work and self-reliance carry a great weight. It is an old story with a new twist when sixty-five year old refugees eagerly sign up for English classes at nearby Truman College. You have to start over somewhere.

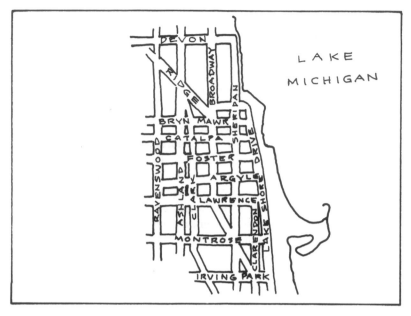

Argyle-Broadway-Sheridan Road (New Chinatown)

Annual Events and Celebrations
Multi-Ethnic

Asian American Coalition of Chicago, Annual Lunar New Year Celebration. Organized for the purpose of fostering greater political, social, and economic cooperation between the diverse cultures, the AACC is comprised of fourteen different ethnic groups representing Chicago's South and Southeast Asian communities. A banquet has been held in February each year since 1984, revolving around a different theme each time. In 1991, the AACC slogan was "Together We Can." The location will vary from year to year, depending on the preferences of the particular committee responsible for planning the event. During the last three years, the Lunar New Year Celebration has been held at the Hyatt Regency O'Hare, New Grand Ballroom, 9300 W. Bryn Mawr Avenue, Rosemont. Between 1,000 and 1,700 people have attended each year for the past eight years. Since the banquet rotates among the fourteen representative groups in the coalition, it is likely that the location may change in the future. Dinner, guest speakers, and musical entertainment are included for the price of $35 per person. The AACC does not have a central office, so interested parties are encouraged to call Irene Cuatoping who handles publicity at (312) 630-6882.

Japanese

Japanese Summer Festival (Natsu Matsuri), *1151 W. Leland Avenue, Chicago.* A two-day fund raising event sponsored by the Midwest Buddhist Temple, and held the Saturday and Sunday before the fourth of July weekend. The Summer Festival has been going strong since 1945, featuring judo, aikido, kendo, and karate demonstrations; Japanese classical and folk dancing; flower arrangements, ceramics, and bonsai miniature plants. Plenty of Japanese food available on the grounds, including sushi, barbecued chicken teriyaki, and yakisoba. Hours: Saturday, 11 A.M. to 9 P.M.; Sunday, 11 A.M. to 7 P.M. Admission: $2 per person. For additional information, contact the Midwest Buddhist Temple at 435 W. Menomonee, Chicago, or call (312) 334-4661. During the year the Temple conducts religious services, which are open to the public every Sunday at 11 A.M. following the 9:30 meditation classes. The Buddhist Temple also sponsors Japanese language classes for adults at 1151 W. Leland, Chicago. Summer classes last seven weeks, and the tuition fee is $90 per person. Call (312) 334-4661 for information.

Obon Odori Festival, *held on the grounds of the Midwest Buddhist Temple at 435 W. Menomonee, Chicago, (312) 943-7801.* Also known as the Festival of Lanterns, because the cho-ching (paper lanterns) decorate the parking lot of the Buddhist Temple where the traditional folk dancing is enjoyed by the spectators. Japanese music, and kimono-clad dancers. Obon means a bowl or tray with which one serves guests, expressing hospitality and sincere welcome. It is in this spirit that the Obon Odori Festival is sponsored each year. Held the second Saturday evening in July before the customary Obon religious service (Hatsu-bon) the following morning at 10 A.M., which honors the loved ones who have passed away during the previous year. Admission is free to the public. Hours: 8 P.M. to 10 P.M.

Annual Ginza Holiday, three-day festival of Japanese culture, martial arts, demonstrations by the Waza master craftsmen from Japan, classical and folk dancing, Buddhist Taiko (drum) group, prize drawing, and ethnic cuisine held on the grounds of the Midwest Buddhist Temple the second weekend in August for the past thirty-six years. The event is named after the Ginza, a busy and colorful shopping center and street in the heart of Tokyo. Three hundred years ago, this area was a marshy swamp, inhabited by wild ducks. In 1873, housing construction began on this site. The Ginza became the first street in Japan with brick houses and pavement. Free admission to the festival. Hours: Friday, 6:30 P.M. to 9 P.M.; Saturday, 11:30 A.M. to 8:30 P.M.; Sunday, 11:30 A.M. to 7:30 P.M. Please call (312) 943-7801 for additional details.

Japanese Cultural Center, *1016 W. Belmont Ave., Chicago, (312) 525-3141.* Year-long activities include classes and lectures in zen meditation, karate, Japanese cooking and language. Office hours: Monday through Friday, 10 A.M. to 7 P.M.; classes till 9 P.M.

Filipino

— Philippine Week Events —

Philippine Independence Parade. The Commonwealth of the Philippines was established in 1935 in an attempt to pave the way for political and economic independence from the U.S., which had been autonomous in the region since 1898. The Japanese occupation and World War II delayed this process until July 4, 1946, when the Republic of the Philippines was established, with Manuel Roxas installed as the first president. However, the lavish Chicago parade featuring twenty floats and three to four marching bands commemorates the political separation from Spain, which occurred on June 12, 1898. The first Chicago Independence Day parade was staged June 12, 1970, but did not become a yearly event until 1980. Festivities begin at 12 P.M., along the Dearborn Street parade route between Wacker Drive and Van Buren. The parade is co-sponsored by the local fraternal organizations within the Philippine Week Committee. A ceremony marking Philippine independence is held in the Daley Civic Center during the noon hour on the day before the actual parade, as a part of the city's "Under the Picasso" ongoing program of entertainment. Short speeches by local dignitaries and a Health-o-Rama are featured. For additional information please call Mr. Roberto D. Roque at (312) 342-0059, or (312) 744-0833.

Open House *at the Rizal Memorial Center, 1332 W. Irving Park Road, Chicago, (312) 281-1210.* In 1974, the Filipino American Council of Chicago (FACC) purchased the former home of the

Swedish Orphei Singers, and converted the facility into a social club, dinner theater, and cultural center, which features Filipino entertainment and food that is available to the public on Friday evenings. During Philippine Week, the Rizal Center sponsors a one-day open house, featuring exhibits and mementos from the Filipino Historical Society. Admission is free, but there is a nominal charge for food and beverages. For additional information, call Thelma Bascos at (312) 965-2874.

Sunday picnic at Labagh Woods Forest Preserve *(Cicero and Foster, Chicago).* Food, music, and games held the Sunday following the big downtown parade. Hours: 10 A.M. to 7 P.M. Free admission. Call (312) 965-2874 for details.

Community Ball, *at the Hyatt Regency O'Hare Hotel, 9300 Bryn Mawr Avenue, Rosemont.* Cocktails, dinner, musical entertainment, and speeches marking Philippine independence. Held at 7:30 P.M. the Saturday evening following the parade. Tickets: $35 per person. Call (312) 965-2874.

Korean

Korean Fest (Kyng-Ro-Jan Chi: The Day to Respect and Honor Elders), *at Margate Park, 4921 N. Marine Drive, Chicago.* Korean-style entertainment, with food booths, merchandise sales, contests, and music brought to you by the Korean-American Senior Center, 4750 N. Sheridan Road, Chicago, IL 60640. The event is held the second Saturday in July, between the hours of 10 A.M. and 6 P.M. Admission is free. For additional information, contact Joshua Pang, director of the Senior Center at (312) 878-8617, or the Mayor's Office of Special Events at (312) 744-3370.

Korea Day (Chu Shunk), *at Gomper's Park, 4224 W. Foster, Chicago.* Held the second or third Sunday in September in alternating even-numbered years. Food booths, folk dancing, and music, sponsored by the Korean Association of Chicago, 5941 N. Lincoln Avenue, Chicago. For the date and time, call (312) 878-1900. Free admission to the event.

Bultasa Buddhist Temple of Chicago, *4358 W. Montrose, Chicago, (312) 286-1551.* One of five Korean Buddhist temples in the Chicagoland area. This one is unique however, because it features the lovely "1000 Buddha Temple Altar," believed to be the only one of its kind in the Midwest. The monks in residence are happy to lead visitors on a guided tour of this facility, which until four years ago still housed residential apartments upstairs. The temple is open from 6 A.M. to 9:30 P.M. To arrange a tour by phone, or for information about the zen meditation group which meets regularly on Monday and Thursday evening at 7 P.M., please call Ron Kidd at (312) 327-1695.

Vietnamese

Vietnamese Catholic Community Fair and Dance, *St. Thomas of Canterbury Church, 4827 N. Kenmore Ave., Chicago, (312) 784-1932.* Ethnic folk fair includes food, games, and entertainment in the parish hall the Saturday following the Lunar New Year in February. A dance is held the night before, at 8 P.M. Tickets are $7 per person. Hours: 10 A.M. to 9 P.M..

New Year Celebration, *at the Vietnamese Buddhist Temple, 4429 N. Damen Ave., Chicago.* Day-long activities planned the Saturday of New Year, from 9:30 A.M. to 9 P.M. Regular services are held at 7 A.M., Monday through Saturday, and at noon on Sunday. To arrange a guided tour of the temple, call the Reverend Quang Tam at (312) 275-6859.

Indian

India Independence Day Parade, marking the formal political separation of India from the British Empire, achieved on August 15, 1947, after years of nonviolent struggle led by Mohandas K. Gandhi and supporters of the India National Congress. The Chicago parade is held the Saturday closest to August 15, on Michigan Avenue between Wacker Drive and Van Buren. The Federation of India Association, an umbrella group representing twenty different fraternal organizations in the city, sponsors the annual pageant, which includes a noontime rally featuring dance troops, speakers, and musical bands in the Daley Center Plaza the day of the parade. The decorated floats depict the regional customs of India, revolving around a different theme each year. In alternating years, there may be a second Independence Day Parade held on Michigan Avenue the Sunday afternoon preceding the holiday. At other times, the sponsors of this much smaller parade may join forces with the Federation of India Association for one large extravaganza. For dates, and times, call the Mayor's Office of Special Events Hotline at (312) 744-3370, or 744-3315.

Taste of India Festival, *at Chino Park, Illinois Boulevard and Evanston Street, Hoffman Estates.* A one-day arts and crafts bazaar held the first Sunday in September, with food supplied by some of the more notable Indian restaurants around town. Cultural entertainment. Music. Games for children. Free admission. Hours: 11 A.M. to 8 P.M. Call Mr. Anil Pillai at (708) 674-7694 for information. This event was launched in 1991 by the Federation of India Association.

Federation Banquet, held at alternating sites in metro-Chicago or in the suburbs the second week in May. Dinner and drinks. Testimonial speeches by the Indian Consul General, or elected officials from Cook County. Musical entertainment. An annual event for the Indian community for the past eleven years. Tickets are $50 per person, subject to change. Call Mr. Anil Pillai at (708) 674-7694 for information.

Republic Day Celebration at the Dawes School, *440 Dodge Avenue, Evanston, (708) 492-7951.* Each year on January 26 (or the weekend closest to this date), the Federation of Indian Association commemorates the founding of the Indian Republic with food, guest speakers, and cultural activities. The event is free to the public. Call (708) 674-7694 for details.

Hindu Temple of Greater Chicago, *12 S. 701 Lemont Road, Lemont, (708) 972-0300.* Located high atop a hill on a wooded thirty-acre lot in Du Page County, the majestic Hindu Temple is open for a guided tour each day from 9 A.M. to 9 P.M. Sunday afternoon, however, is the preferred time to explore the religious customs and traditions of Southern Asia. On the last Saturday in July, the temple hosts an annual Great Lakes Hindu Youth Conference, featuring lectures, a cultural program, outdoor activities, and group discussions. Call ahead for times and date. Admission to the shrine is always free, but donations are accepted.

Thai

Thai Food and Cultural Festival, *at the Siam Square Restaurant, 622 Davis Street, Evanston, (708) 475-0860.* A month-long festival held in June, featuring Thai gourmet foods prepared in the courtyard, and served by waitresses dressed in traditional ethnic clothing.

Original mural artistry is on display, and Thai classical dance is performed at designated times. Reservations recommended. Free parking at the Sherman/Grove Garage. Hours: Monday through Thursday, 11 A.M. to 10 P.M.; Friday and Saturday, 11 A.M. to 10:30 P.M.; Sunday, 4 P.M. to 9 P.M.

Thai Buddhist Temple (Wat Dhummram), *7059 W. 75th Street, Bridgeview, (708) 594-8100.* For fifty years, the Thai Buddhist Temple has served the religious needs of Chicago's Asian community. Guided tours of the building are generally held on Thursdays and Sundays at 6:30 P.M. and 9:30 P.M., or by special arrangement. To schedule a special tour, call Sangiam Suebplai at the above number.

Pan-Asian Shopping and Dining Guide
Korean
— Shopping Guide —

Seoul Books and Records, *3450 W. Peterson, Chicago, (312) 463-7756.* Korean magazines, books, newspapers, cassettes, and records. A limited selection of cookbooks in the English language. Hours: Monday through Saturday, 10 A.M. to 6 P.M.; Sundays, noon to 6 P.M.

Korean Books, *5810 N. Lincoln Avenue, Chicago, (312) 463-7755.* Wall-to-wall Korean books, magazines, newspapers, and audio cassettes and tapes, side by side with Japan Books and Records. Hours: Monday through Saturday, 10 A.M. to 8 P.M.; Sunday, noon to 6 P.M.

Asiana Video, *3312 W. Lawrence Avenue, Chicago, (312) 539-3566.* Recent film releases and television programs from South Korea are available for rental only. Hours: Monday through Saturday, 10 A.M. to 8 P.M. Closed Sunday.

Hundai Video, *3513 W. Lawrence, Chicago, (312) 588-8737.* Hundreds of imported Chinese and Korean movies available for rental or purchase. Hours: Monday through Saturday, 10 A.M. to 9:30 P.M.; Sunday, noon to 8 P.M. No credit cards.

Hokyong Market, *3519 W. Lawrence, Chicago, (312) 267-2746.* Southeast Asian herbs and ginseng root sold for medicinal purposes. Groceries. Korean newspapers. Hours: open every day from 10 A.M. to 7 P.M. Credit cards accepted.

First Gift Store, *3550 W. Lawrence, Chicago, (312) 463-3533.* Gift items, clothing, and imports from Korea and the Orient. Video rental of Korean language films at the back of the store. Hours: open every day from 10 A.M. to 9 P.M. Credit cards accepted.

Arirang Super Market, *4017 W. Lawrence, Chicago, (312) 777-2400.* A grocery store that sells Korean foods only. Hours: open every day from 9 A.M. to 8 P.M. No credit cards.

First Gifts, *3550 W. Lawrence, Chicago, (312) 463-3533.* Gift items, Korean handicrafts, wind chimes, video cassettes, plates, floor vases, and clothing items. Hours: open every day from 10 A.M. to 9 P.M. No credit cards.

Dae Han Korean Food and Housewares, *3547-53 W. Lawrence, Chicago, (312) 463-1311.* A grocery, delicatessen, and bakery all rolled into one. The store stocks Korean-language CDs, audio cassettes, and newspapers. Hours: open every day from 9 A.M. to 9 P.M. Credit cards accepted.

Word of Life Books, *3523-A W. Lawrence, Chicago, (312) 736-2288, or 1-800-654-5124.* A neat, and well organized store that stocks Korean religious books and gift items. Drinking mugs, children's books (some in English), and audio cassettes. Hours: Monday through Friday, 10 A.M. to 7 P.M.; Saturday, 10 A.M. to 6:30 P.M. Credit cards accepted.

Modern Gift, *3432 W. Lawrence, Chicago, (312) 588-6055.* Pharmacy, cosmetics, and general merchandise distributor. Hours: Monday through Saturday, 10 A.M. to 8 P.M.

Asiana Jewelry & Handicraft, *3312 W. Lawrence, Chicago, (312) 539-2886.* Imports from Korea and Japan. Figurines, wind chimes, religious items, telephones, plates, and toys. More of a tourist trap than anything else. Hours: open everyday from 10 A.M. to 8 P.M.

Asian Treasures, Inc./Dong Bo Plaza, *3239 W. Lawrence, Chicago, (312) 463-2662.* Large import house featuring an assortment of gift items, toys, clothing, shoes, and cassettes from Korea and Europe. Think of it as the "Korean Walgreen's." Hours: Monday through Saturday, 10:30 A.M. to 8 P.M.; Sunday, 11 A.M. to 6 P.M. Credit cards accepted.

Master Cookware Corp., *3212-1/2 W. Lawrence, Chicago, (312) 588-3232.* A large selection of woks and Asian cooking utensils. Tea sets, teak wood chests, and electric appliances. Hours: Monday through Friday, 10 A.M. to 8 P.M.; Saturday, 10 A.M. to 7 P.M. Closed Sunday. Credit cards accepted.

Joong Ang Food Market, *3318 W. Lawrence, Chicago, (312) 539-7733.* Small Korean grocery store stocking frozen foods, import items, candy, and newspapers. Hours: Monday through Saturday, 9 A.M. to 9 P.M. Closed Sunday. No credit cards.

— Restaurants —

Bando Korean Restaurant, *2200 W. Lawrence, Chicago, (312) 728-7400.* An indoor waterfall, and a barbecue grill at every table enhances the pleasing decor, regarded by many as the best Korean restaurant in town. Entrees are reasonably prices at $7–$10 a person, and they include seven to eight side dishes per person. Chicken, pork, beef, and short ribs are the house specialties. Hours: from 11 A.M. to 11 P.M. Credit cards accepted. *Recommended.*

Yung Bin Kwan, *7011 N. Western Avenue, Chicago, (312) 338-1545.* Elegant decor, and an exotic menu await the diner. There's more to this menu than the usual kim chee dishes that Westerners equate with the Korean diet, so it is best to let the waitress help you select from the wide variety of items. Slightly upscale decor and prices. Hours: 11 A.M. to 11 P.M. Credit cards accepted.

Shilla, *5930 N. Lincoln, Chicago, (312) 275-5930.* Any one of the eight private banquet rooms captures the essence of the Orient, if you care to reserve a private party in elegantly appointed surroundings. Japanese and Korean dishes, including barbecued short ribs, sashimi, and shrimp tempura are the house specialties. Hours: from 11:30 A.M. to 10:30 P.M. Credit cards accepted.

Chun Soo Chang, *3534 W. Lawrence, Chicago, (312) 539-2444.* Four of the tables in the restaurant are equipped with gas grills, so you can cook your own pot of seafood, or pork and beef dish, depending on your tastes. No poultry dishes, but there is plenty to choose from on the menu. Like many of the Korean stores and restaurants up and down Lawrence Avenue, the servers and counter help speak faltering English. Credit cards accepted. Hours: Thursday through Tuesday, 10 A.M. to 10 P.M.

Korean Restaurant, *2659 W. Lawrence, Chicago, (312) 878-2095.* Open around the clock, in case you desire a late-night kim chee feast. The decor is not fancy, but an extensive menu, including an array of noodle dishes, marinated and grilled beef, and spare ribs make up for lost ambience.

Gin Go Gae, *5433 N. Lincoln, Chicago, (312) 334-3895.* An established North Side Korean restaurant with an impressive assortment of side dishes. You may want to try the octopus in hot red sauce for something out of the ordinary. Hours: daily from 10:30 A.M. to 10:30 P.M. Credit cards accepted.

Japanese

— Shopping Guide —

Japan Books and Records, *3450 W. Peterson Avenue, Chicago, (312) 463-7755.* Located in the same building with Seoul Books and Records. Specializing in Japanese paperback books, magazines and audio. Hours: Monday through Saturday, 10 A.M. to 6 P.M. Sundays, noon to 6 P.M.

Asahiye Bookstores, U.S.A., Inc., *2318 S. Elmhurst Road, Mt. Prospect, (708) 228-9851.* Located in the Colony Square Shopping Center at Oakton and Elmhurst Road, adjacent to several other Japanese businesses. This is a full-line Japanese magazine and book store, with a limited number of English-Japanese language instruction manuals. No audio or video equipment. Hours: Tuesday through Saturday, 10 A.M. to 8 P.M.; Sunday, 10 A.M. to 6 P.M. Closed on Monday. Credit cards accepted.

Scholars Bookstore, *1379 W. 53rd Street, Chicago, (312) 288-6565.* Chinese-Japanese book store and full-line computer supplier. The store also sells Chinese and Japanese audio tapes. Hours: Monday through Thursday, 11 A.M. to 7 P.M.; Friday and Saturday, 11 A.M. to 8 P.M.; Sunday, noon to 5 P.M.

Kiyo's Oriental Gift Store, *2831 N. Clark, Chicago, (312) 935-0619.* Japanese gift items ranging from inexpensive "kitsch" up to fine porcelains, jewelry, and shoji screens. Try on the kimonos for size. Kiyo's has been at this location for twenty years. Hours: Monday through

Friday, 10:30 A.M. to 9 P.M.; Saturday, 10:30 A.M. to 6 P.M.; Sunday, 11 A.M. to 6 P.M. Credit cards accepted.

J. Toguri Mercantile Co., *851 W. Belmont (near Clark), Chicago, (312) 929-3500.* Japanese imports, including magazines, books, records, tapes, and household items such as tableware, lacquerware, and china (some of it actually coming from China). Hours: Monday through Saturday, 10 A.M. to 6 P.M.; closed Sunday. Credit cards accepted.

Aiko's Art Material Import Co., *3347 N. Clark, Chicago, (312) 404-5600.* Chicago's leading supplier of Japanese art materials and handmade papers used for printmaking, bookbinding, screens, and book restoration. Japanese greeting cards, artwork, ceramics, and artist's tools are available for purchase. Hours: Tuesday through Saturday, 10 A.M. to 5 P.M. No credit cards.

Star Market, *3349 N. Clark, Chicago, (312) 472-0599.* One of the original ethnic Japanese groceries to open in Chicago. In business now for nearly forty years. Fresh fish, produce, and other perishables. Canned and frozen foods. Hours: Monday through Saturday, 9 A.M. to 7 P.M.; Sunday, 10 A.M. to 3 P.M. No credit cards.

York's Super Food Market, *3240 N. Clark, Chicago, (312) 477-0802.* Helen Fukuda and her family have owned this small Japanese grocery for thirty years. Fresh fish and imported foods from Japan. Cookbooks and a small line of gifts. Hours: Monday through Friday, 11:30 A.M. to 7 P.M.; Saturday, 10:30 A.M. to 7 P.M. No credit cards.

Tokyo Video of Chicago, *2616 N. Halsted, Chicago, (312) 528-3592.* Hundreds of Japanese language films and television documentaries for children and adults are available for rental or sale. Hours: Monday through Saturday, 1 P.M. to 8 P.M.; Sunday, noon to 6 P.M.

— Restaurants —

Benkay Restaurant, *320 N. Dearborn, Chicago, (312) 744-1900.* Located in the Hotel Nikko, next to Marina City and overlooking the Chicago River. The Japanese-style foods are good but expensive, so you better take along the credit cards. Hours: open for breakfast during the week from 7 A.M. to 10 A.M.; lunch, 11:30 A.M. to 2 P.M.; dinner 5:30 P.M. to 10 P.M.

Honda, *540 N. Wells, Chicago, (312) 923-1010.* A spacious, but well-managed Japanese restaurant located on several stories. Visit the "kushi" bar and select from a variety of meats, vegetables, and skewered fish. Hours: lunch served from 11:30 A.M. to 2:00 P.M., Monday through Friday; dinner from 5:30 P.M. to 10 P.M.; open until 11 P.M. on Friday, and 10 P.M. on Sunday. Credit cards accepted. *Recommended.*

Hatsuhana, *160 E. Ontario, Chicago, (312) 280-8287.* Thirty different varieties of sushi to choose from. If you can't decide among them, or need help, consult the chart provided near the bar. The house specialty includes teriyaki, tempura, and sashimi. This is one of the more popular Japanese restaurants in the city. Hours: lunch served 11:45 A.M. to 2 P.M., Monday through Saturday; dinner 5:30 P.M. to 10 P.M. Closed on Sunday. Pricey and upscale. Credit cards accepted.

Kuni's, *511 Main Street, Evanston, (708) 328-2004.* This world-famous sushi bar presided over by master chef Yuji Kunii has pleased area residents for over twenty-four years. House specialties include beef, chicken, teriyaki, tempura, and softshell crab. Hours: lunch from 11:30 A.M. to 2 P.M., Monday, and Wednesday through Saturday. Dinner served from 5 P.M. to 10 P.M., Monday, and Wednesday through Sunday. Closed on Tuesday. Credit cards accepted.

Midori, *3310 W. Bryn Mawr Avenue, Chicago, (312) 267-9733.* Japanese restaurants tend to be among the most expensive Asian cuisines. Midori is the exception, with the lunch and dinner menu ranging in price from $4.50 to $10.95. All dinners include salad, soup, rice, tea, and fresh fruits. Hours: open Monday through Saturday, 11:30 A.M. to 11 P.M.; Sundays, 4 P.M. to to 10 P.M. Credit cards accepted.

Kiyo's Japanese Restaurant, *2827 N. Clark, Chicago, (312) 935-0474.* Fine Japanese cuisine served in a quaint "teahouse" setting, with the food prepared tableside. Hours: Tuesday through Thursday, 5 P.M. to 10 P.M.; Friday, 5 P.M. to 10:30 P.M.; Saturday, 4 P.M. to 10:30 P.M.; Sunday, noon to 4 P.M. Credit cards accepted.

Restaurant Suntory, *13 E. Huron, Chicago, (312) 664-3344.* Much like the Italian Village, Restaurant Suntory combines three elegantly appointed dining areas under one roof. The sushi bar is one of the most extensive in the city in terms of variety. Hours: lunch served Monday–Friday, 11:30 A.M. to 2 P.M.; dinner from 5 P.M. to 10 P.M.; Saturdays, 5:30 P.M. to 9:30 P.M.; Sundays, 5 P.M. to 9:30 P.M. Credit cards accepted.

Tokyo Marina, *5058 N. Clark, Chicago, (312) 878-2900.* Seafood, soups, and casseroles are the preferred menu items, and the sushi is generally fresh. A selection of Chinese entrees are also included on the menu. Hours: open every day from 11:30 A.M. to 11 P.M. Credit cards accepted.

Sai Cafe, *2010 N. Sheffield, Chicago, (312) 472-8080.* The place to go for sushi. The chefs can do wonders with a cutting knife and are a delight to behold as they carve up raw but tender pieces of fish before your eyes. Hours: Monday through Thursday, 4:30 P.M. to 11 P.M.; Friday and Saturday, 4:30 P.M. to midnight; Sunday, 3:30 P.M. to 10 P.M. Credit cards accepted.

Thai

— Shopping Guide —

Thai Grocery, *5014 N. Broadway, Chicago, (312) 561-5345.* A Thai delicatessen and grocery that stocks sausages, fresh meats and poultry, prepared foods, fish, and exotic Asian ice cream. Hours: Monday through Saturday, 9 A.M. to 7 P.M. No credit cards.

Thailand Plaza, *4821 N. Broadway, Chicago, (312) 561-5345.* Full-service grocery and newsstand selling videos, newspapers, cassettes, cookbooks, and Asian food. Hours: Monday through Saturday, 9:30 A.M. to 7 P.M.

Thai Imports, *108 W. Chicago, Chicago, (312) 642-1270.* Fine imported artwork and antiques direct from Thailand. Chau Warin and his family plan regularly scheduled visits to the remote villages of Thailand, where they locate and bring back to Chicago traditional and functional pieces, including porcelains, wood carvings, ceramics and textiles. Mr. Warin regularly participates and exhibits at local art fairs. Hours: Monday through Friday, 10 A.M. to 7 P.M.; Saturday, 10 A.M. to 6 P.M.; Sunday, 1 P.M. to 5 P.M. Credit cards accepted.

— Restaurants —

Arun's Restaurant, *4156 N. Kedzie Ave., Chicago, (312) 539-1909.* Small, but delightful surroundings enhance the food, which ranges from mild to highly spiced. The pork satay, chicken curry, and tom yum goong are recommended. Hours: Tuesday through Sunday, 5 P.M. to 10 P.M. Closed Monday. Credit cards accepted.

Rim Klong, *2203 N. Clybourn Ave., Chicago, (312) 883-0434.* Located in the trendy, and oh so upscale "Clybourn Corridor," which until the arrival of the Yuppie rehabbers was just another inner city neighborhood on the slide. You wouldn't expect to find a Thai restaurant here, but then again, maybe you would, given the eclectic tastes of the local residents. The food is only mildly seasoned, so you won't be shedding any unnecessary tears. Ginger beef, Singha shrimp, and the crab and shrimp sausage are all worth a try. Hours: Monday through Thursday, 11:30 A.M. to 10 P.M.; Friday and Saturday, 4:30 P.M. to 11 P.M.; till 10 P.M. on Sunday. Credit cards accepted.

Cozy Thai, *4834 N. Damen Ave., Chicago, (312) 334-7300.* Here it is, for all you hot-and-spicy food lovers: sizzling Thai fare served in a pleasing, if not modest, storefront location. Entrees include pad ped catfish, whole fried red snapper, and pork satay. Hours: luncheon served from 11 A.M. to 3 P.M., Monday through Friday, and dinner from 5 P.M. to 10 P.M. Credit cards accepted.

P.S. Bangkok, *3345 N. Clark, Chicago, (312) 871-7777.* The food is heavily seasoned with curry and red peppers, as you might expect; but the extensive menu allows the patron to experiment with a variety of Thai dishes. The oil paintings on the wall depict traditional Thai scenes. Hours: Sunday and Monday, and Wednesday and Thursday, 11:30 A.M. to 10 P.M.; Friday and Saturday until 11:30 P.M. Credit cards accepted.

Siam Cafe, *4712 N. Sheridan Road, Chicago, (312) 769-6602.* An inexpensive Thai restaurant located in Uptown. Be sure to order the fried greens with oyster sauce, considered to be the best in the city. Other specialties include pork satay (barbecued ribs), chili chicken, and cuttlefish. Hours: Monday and Wednesday through Sunday, 11:30 A.M. to 9 P.M. Credit cards accepted.

Thai Town, *3201 N. Clark, Chicago, (312) 528-2755.* Clark Street is home to more than the usual share of Asian restaurants. Thai Town, with its varied and extensive menu selections, pleasing decor, and prompt personal service is among the best on the Near North. Not to be missed from among the more unusual dinner selections is the beef dad deu (strips of honey-glazed beef). Hours: Sunday through Thursday, noon to 10 P.M.; Friday and Saturday, noon to 11 P.M. Credit cards accepted.

Siam Square, *622 Davis Street, Evanston, (708) 475-0860.* The annual Thai Festival in June is definitely worth a trip to Evanston. (See annual events.) Otherwise, the seafood menu items are served in pleasant surroundings in the lush garden patio. Musical entertainment on the weekends. Hours: Monday through Thursday, 11 A.M. to 10 P.M.; Friday and Saturday, 11 A.M. to 10:30 P.M.; Sunday, 4 P.M. to 9 P.M. Credit cards accepted.

Thai Touch, *3200 W. Lawrence, Chicago, (312) 539-5700.* An "outstanding" Thai restaurant. The Chicago *Sun-Times* voted Thai Touch one of the twelve best Chicago restaurants in 1989. Hours: Tuesday through Thursday, noon to 9 P.M.; Friday and Saturday, noon to 10 P.M.; Sunday, noon to 9 P.M. Credit cards accepted.

Bangkok Village, *1123 N. State St., Chicago, (312) 943-4966 and 22 E. Chicago, #122, Naperville, (708) 369-4510.* A moderately priced, but elegantly appointed Thai restaurant located in the Rush Street district. Choose from a selection of highly seasoned curry dishes including panang, Thai royal chicken, or tasty duck. Rice dishes, poultry, and meat entrees round out the menu. Carry-out service. Discounted self-parking at Cedar and State. Hours: Sunday through Thursday, 11 A.M. to 11 P.M.; Friday and Saturday, 11 A.M. to 2 A.M. Credit cards accepted.

Filipino

— Shopping Guide —

Philhouse Market, *5845 N. Clark St., Chicago, (312) 784-1176.* Tucked into a steadily growing colony of Asians who inhabit the Swedish Andersonville and Edgewater communities, the spacious Philhouse Market is a full-line grocery store and fresh produce exchange that also sells roast pork on the weekends. Wall posters, books, records and tapes are available for purchase. Hours: Monday through Saturday, 8:30 A.M. to 8:30 P.M.; Sundays, 8:30 A.M. to 7:30 P.M. Credit cards accepted.

Philippine Grocery and Gift Shop, *5750 N. California, Chicago, (312) 334-4628.* Imported foods from the Philippines, newspapers, and a limited selection of gift items. Filipino movies on tape available for rental. Hours: Monday through Saturday, 9 A.M. to 8 P.M.; Sunday, 9 A.M. to 6 P.M. Checks, but no credit cards.

Villamar Food Mart and Gifts, *5949 W. Fullerton, Chicago, (312) 637-1686* Imported foods from the Philippines and a line of gift items. Hours: Monday through Friday, 10 A.M. to 8 P.M.; Saturday, 10 A.M. to 6 P.M.; Sunday, 10 A.M. to 6 P.M. No credit cards.

3R's Food Market, *5200 W. Grand, Chicago, (312) 745-1701, and 2714 W. Montrose, Chicago, (312) 539-4714.* Stocking plenty of Filipino food items at both locations. Credit cards accepted. Hours: Monday through Friday, 8:30 A.M. to 8:00 P.M.; Saturday and Sunday till 7:30 P.M.

Feliz Cakes, *3056 N. Lincoln, Chicago, (312) 549-4188.* Bakery and cafe, specializing in Filipino barbecue foods, pastries, and meat cakes. Various American and European foods served also. Hours: Tuesday through Saturday, 10 A.M. to 8 P.M.; Sunday, 10 A.M. to 4 P.M. No credit cards.

DeLeon's Oriental Store, *3143 W. Irving Park Road, Chicago, (312) 539-2178.* Filipino movies (many current titles with subtitles) are carried in stock, and are available for purchase or rental. Hours: Monday through Saturday, 9:30 A.M. to 7:30 P.M.; Sunday, 11 A.M. to 4 P.M. No credit cards.

— Restaurants —

Fiesta Manila Restaurant and Bakeshop, *3146 W. Montrose, Chicago, (312) 604-8227.* The owner plans eventually to expand his bakeshop, but for now the focus is on nontraditional Philippine food, which is prepared in a variety of interesting ways to please every palate. The flavoring ranges from sweet to sour, and from bitter to salty. Filipino food bridges the gap between East and West, and should not be confused with Chinese cooking, according to the owner. Coconut milk is mixed with egg plant, squash and other vegetables. Fiesta Manila has been at this location for a little over a year. The food is reasonable, especially during the week between 11:30 A.M. and 3 P.M., when the $3.50 lunch is served. Other hours: Monday through Saturday, 11:30 A.M. to 8 P.M.; Sunday, 11:30 A.M. to 4 P.M..

Little Quiapo Restaurant, *4423 N. Clark, Chicago, (312) 271-5441.* Small, homey little restaurant located on the North Side. Hours: Monday through Friday, noon to 9 P.M.; Saturday and Sunday, 11 A.M. to 9:30 P.M. Credit cards accepted.

Ihaw-Ihaw, *5945 W. Fullerton, Chicago, (312) 889-0100.* A storefront restaurant that recently underwent a significant remodeling. The food is generally good, and the portions served are surprisingly generous. The house specialty is also one of the national dishes of the Philippines—kare-kare—which consists of oxtails and honeycomb tripe cooked in a peanut sauce with eggplant, green beans, and assorted vegetables. Hours: Sunday through Thursday, 4 P.M. to 10 P.M.; Friday and Saturday, 4 P.M. to 2 A.M. Credit cards accepted.

Manila/Manila, *3401 N. Western Avenue, Chicago, (312) 327-0000.* American influences are still very strong in the Philippines. Country music has enjoyed a revival in this corner of the world. Hank Williams. Blue grass. Hillbilly twang. It's all here at Manila/Manila, a country and western Filipino restaurant in Chicago with a house band that plays the top tunes Wednesday through Sunday from 8:30 P.M. to 1 A.M. Pull up a chair. Order a bottle of San Miguel (the native Filipino beer) and give a listen . . . buckaroo! No cover, but a two-drink minimum. Other hours: Monday and Tuesday, 11 A.M. to 10 P.M.; Thursday 11 A.M. to 11 P.M.; Friday and Saturday till 2 A.M. Seafood buffet on Friday and Saturday, from 6:30 P.M. to 9:30 P.M.

Indian/Pakistani

— Shopping Guide —

Kamdar Plaza, *2646 W. Devon, Chicago, (312) 338-8100.* Grocery and retail store all in one. In the food section, select from a variety of Indian spices, sweets, canned, and bulk foods. The other side of the store features saris and other imported clothing items. Hours: Wednesday through Monday, 11 A.M. to 8 P.M. Credit cards accepted.

Patel Brother, *2610 W. Devon, Chicago, (312) 262-7777.* A pioneer retailer in Indian and Pakistani groceries. The store also sells cookware, "thalis" (dinnerware), appliances, fresh produce, mango pulp, ground flour for making Indian bread, rice, Ceylon tea, and vegetarian and nonvegetarian foods. The aromatic fragrance of Indian spice hangs in the air. Hours: daily from 10 A.M. to 8 P.M.

Thomsun Traders, *6408 N. Rockwell, Chicago, (312) 508-0119.* Charles and John Varghese have operated this tiny little grocery store since 1982, which ranks them as one of the longest continuing businesses in Chicago's "India Town." Charles is a community organizer who is involved in Democratic politics at the grassroots level, and is somewhat of an authority on the Indian settlement in Chicago. He knows all of the neighborhood people who come in to rent Indian movies, purchase their groceries, and share the latest political gossip. Hours: daily from 11 A.M. to 8 P.M.

Zabiha Meat Market, *2907 W. Devon, Chicago, (312) 274-6700, and 2502 W. Devon, Chicago, (312) 743-1200.* Middle Eastern. Among the many Indian businesses on Devon Avenue, this one serves the needs of West Town's growing Assyrian and Iranian population. Exotic spices, frozen goat meat, rice, and some Indian and Pakistani foods are sold at both locations. Hours: 9 A.M. to 9 P.M. daily.

Jainson International Corporation, *2514 W. Devon, Chicago, (312) 262-8787.* Importer of Indian spices, bagged rice from Karachi, Pakistan, flour for making Indian "chappati" bread, canned foods, and audio cassettes. No credit cards. Hours: daily except Tuesday, from 11 A.M. to 8 P.M.

Sunilco International, *2551 W. Devon, Chicago, (312) 761-7044.* Fine imported gifts from India. Vases, brass candlesticks, figurines, goblets, men's and women's clothing, and decorative items. Credit cards accepted. Hours: daily except Tuesday, from noon to 8 P.M.

I.S.P. (India Sari Palace), *2536 W. Devon, Chicago, (312) 338-2127.* The Sari material is sold by the yard, and is available in an incredible array of colors and patterns. I.S.P., Devon Avenue's original sari shop, also sells imported gift items, luggage, handbags, CDs, and Indian video movies. Hours: Wednesday through Monday, 11 A.M. to 8 P.M. Closed Tuesday.

Sari Sapne, *2623 W. Devon, Chicago, (312) 338-SARI.* Their phone number tells it all. For exclusive Indian and Japanese Saris, this is the place to go. Hours: Open every day except Tuesday, from 11 A.M. to 8 P.M. Credit cards accepted.

Jai Hind Plaza and Meena Jewelers, Inc., *2658 W. Devon, Chicago, (312) 973-3400.* Two stores in one. The jewelry store is an exclusive importer of 22K gold jewelry, video cassettes, and newspapers. In the adjacent Jai Hind Plaza, you'll find cookware, fresh produce, and groceries. Don't forget to sample the tasty dessert "Kulfi" which is similar to ice cream in its consistency. During the week, Meena Jewelers is open from 5 to 9 P.M.; Jai Hind Plaza is open from 10 A.M. to 9 P.M. Credit cards accepted.

Zaveri Jewelers, Inc., *2603 W. Devon, Chicago, (312) 764-8185.* Imported gold items from London and India. Hours: open daily except Tuesday, from 11 A.M. to 8 P.M. Credit cards accepted.

Video Palace, *2315 W. Devon, Chicago, (312) 262-3990.* Indian and Pakistani movies available for sale or rental. Same-day conversion and film transfer. The store also sells a line of electronic appliances. Hours: Monday, 11 A.M. to 8 P.M.; Wednesday through Sunday, 11 A.M. to 8 P.M..

V.I.P. Video Vision, *2325 W. Devon, Chicago, (312) 465-3344.* The latest American, Indian, and Pakistani movies available for rental or sale. VCR repair service. CDs, and records. Hours: Daily, 11:30 A.M. to 8 P.M..

— Restaurants —

Bukhara, *2 E. Ontario, Chicago, (312) 943-0188.* The restaurant features cooking from India's Northwest Frontier, and may not be quite what you expect from this part of the world. Cloth bibs are provided by the waiters, since all foods are eaten with the fingers. The house specialties include shimla mirch, Khyber tikka, and sikandari raan. Hours: buffet-style lunch served from 11:30 A.M. to 2:30 P.M., Monday through Friday; from noon till 3 P.M., Saturday and Sunday; dinner from 5:30 P.M. to 10 P.M. Sunday through Thursday; Friday and Saturday till 11 P.M. Credit cards accepted. Reduced rate parking across the street.

Klay Oven, *414 N. Orleans, Chicago, (312) 527-3999.* Plush surroundings, an extensive menu, and attentive wait help ready to explain Indian cuisine make the Klay Oven one of the top-notch Indian restaurants in the city. Owner Pari Gujral stocks a large wine cellar and has made great strides toward having this become one of the top ethnic restaurants in the city. Hours: lunch served from 11:30 A.M. to 2:30 P.M., Monday through Saturday; dinner from 5:30 P.M. to 10:30 P.M., Monday through Thursday; 5:30 P.M. to 11:30 P.M., Friday and Saturday. Closed Sunday. Credit cards accepted. *Recommended.*

Raj Darbar, *2350 N. Clark, Chicago, (312) 348-1010.* Chicago's newest Indian restaurant serves an all-you-can-eat lunch buffet every

Friday, Saturday, and Sunday from 11:30 A.M. to 2:30 P.M. for only $6.95. Northern Indian cuisine. Reduced parking available. Hours: Tuesday through Friday, 11 A.M. to 3 A.M.; Saturday, noon to 3 A.M. Closed on Sunday. Credit cards accepted.

Standard India, *917 W. Belmont, Chicago, (312) 929-1123.* A vegetarian/non-vegetarian restaurant. Buffet lunch on the weekends from noon to 3 P.M. Vegetarian buffets served on Tuesdays and Thursdays at 5 P.M. Other hours: 5 P.M. to 11 P.M., Monday–Friday; Saturday–Sunday, noon to 11 P.M. Credit cards accepted.

Bombay Palace, *50 E. Walton, Chicago, (312) 664-9323.* A restaurant that reflects the wide diversity of Indian cooking. A five-course appetizer plate is a good way to start. Then choose from a selection that includes Tondoori, cooked in a clay oven, or the Gosht patiala, which is a mild lamb curry spiced with ginger, onion, and garlic. The dessert selection is exceptional. Hours: buffet lunch served from Monday through Friday, from 11:30 A.M. to 2:30 P.M.; Saturday and Sunday, lunch till 3 P.M. Dinner served Sunday through Thursday from 5:30 P.M. to 10 P.M.; Friday and Saturday, till 11 P.M. Credit cards accepted.

Himalaya India Restaurant, *6410 N. Rockwell, Chicago, (312) 761-5757.* Master chef Tikka Ram Sharma earned the kudos of Chicago's restaurant critics when he prepared sumptuous entrees for the Bombay Palace, Moti Mahal, and the Viceroy of India Restaurant for more than thirty years. Now he has opened his own place down the street from the Viceroy, and through word of mouth and a little help from the local media, Sharma hopes to make a similar impact. Buffet lunch for $4.95 served from 11:30 A.M. to 3:30 P.M.; Dinner, 5 P.M. to 10 P.M. Open seven days a week. Reduced parking in the lot across the street. *Recommended.*

Viceroy of India Restaurant, *2516 W. Devon, Chicago (312) 743-4100.* An institution for many years, owned by Shashi and Surinder Jain who decided to move back to Devon Avenue after operating in Villa Park for a while. The food is reliable, and any one of the three chef's specials are recommended for the culinary novice unfamiliar with Indian cooking. Vegetarian/non-vegetarian. A daily buffet which includes tandoori chicken, goat meat, and masala dosa (an Indian crepe) is served between noon and 3:30 P.M. every day, for only $5.95. Other hours: Monday through Friday and Sunday, noon to 10 P.M.; Saturday, noon to 11:00 P.M. Credit cards accepted.

Natraj Restaurant, *2240 W. Devon, Chicago, (312) 274-1300.* Southern Indian cuisine, and the meeting place for the Krishna Yoga Foundation on Sundays. Buffet dinners are served from 6 P.M. to 9:30 P.M. on Thursday. Other hours: Monday through Friday, 4:30 P.M. to 10 P.M.; Saturday, 11:30 A.M. to 10 P.M.; Sunday, 11:30 A.M. to 10 P.M.

Art Galleries/Asian

Cathay Gallery, *620 N. Michigan Avenue, Chicago, (312) 951-1048.* A fine collection of Chinese museum-quality antiques, dating from the Neolithic period up to 1900 is included in the collection, which may be viewed between the hours of 10 A.M. and 5 P.M.; Monday through Friday, or by special appointment. Porcelain, ivory, jade, carvings, and snuff bottles round out the collection.

Decoro, *224 E. Ontario, Chicago, (312) 943-4847.* Located near the Museum of Contemporary Art. The collection includes an interesting variety of antique Japanese kimonos and mingei art, Korean bandaji chests, and traditional Chinese rugs, chairs, and cabinets. Hours. Monday through Wednesday, and Friday and Saturday, 11 A.M. to 6 P.M.; Thursdays, noon to 8 P.M.

East West Contemporary Art, *311 W. Superior, Chicago, Suite 310, (312) 664-8003.* The oil paintings of contemporary artists from mainland China who now work in the U.S. are available for viewing and purchase. This spacious gallery recently moved from the Merchandise Mart, and is open Tuesday through Saturday from 11 A.M. to 5 P.M., and Thursdays until 7 P.M. Other hours by appointment.

Saito Oriental Antiques, *645 N. Michigan, Chicago, (312) 642-4366.* Fourth floor at Michigan Avenue and Erie Street. Museum-quality antiques, bronzes, porcelain and lacquerware from the Shang and Ching Dynasties. Korean art and Japanese screens, ukiyo-e prints, and ivory carvings. Two years at this location. Hours: Monday through Friday, 10:30 A.M. to 5:30 P.M.; Saturday, 11 A.M. to 4 P.M. No credit cards.

Asian House of Chicago, *159 W. Kinzie, Chicago, (312) 527-4848.* Wholesale and retail works of art and antiques from the Orient. Included in the collection are finely crafted porcelain vases, Byobu screens, ornate rosewood furniture, Thai bronzes and tapestries, fishbowls, hand carved jade, and lamps. Located east of the Merchandise Mart. Hours: Monday through Saturday, 10 A.M. to 6 P.M..

Tobai International, *21 W. Elm, Chicago, (312) 482-8566.* Original Japanese watercolors, antique paintings and decorative chests from Korea, hand-painted porcelains, selected pieces of artwork from China, Japanese Tansu, and lighting fixtures. Credit cards accepted. Hours: Monday through Friday, 10 A.M. to 7 P.M.; Saturday, 10 A.M. to 6 P.M.; Sunday, noon to 5 P.M.

══ Argyle Street: Getting Things Done ══

A Chinese proverb teaches us that "a journey of a thousand miles begins with one step." Charlie Soo, the "unofficial mayor" of Argyle Street, and the director of the Asian America Small Business Association of Chicago (AASBA) is a great believer in the wisdom of the ancients. His enthusiasm and buoyant optimism in the face of considerable adversity has gone a long way toward reversing the downward slide of this Edgewater/Uptown neighborhood. In 1978, when Soo and other members of the AASBA began considering the ways and means of revitalizing the commercial strip, they encountered the usual resistance and apathy from local shopkeepers, city bureaucrats, and weary residents who had abandoned hope for their community. Since 1972, when the last remnants of the old Chinatown at Clark and Van Buren were bulldozed in order to make way for the new state detention center, Jimmy Wong and leaders of the Hip Sing organization envisioned the formation of a "New Chinatown" on the far North Side. Wong purchased several buildings near Sheridan and Argyle, and things appeared to be on proper course. But within a few years optimism gave way to despair. Storefronts stood empty. Street gangs accosted pedestrians. The sidewalks were littered with broken glass and debris, and within a two-block stretch along Argyle the police counted thirty-six taverns and liquor stores. According to Charlie Soo, the area was "a mess."

In other words, the situation was hopeless, but not impossible. To lure new business and retail traffic to the area, it was necessary to ensure the public's safety. Soo convinced the Chicago Transit Authority to clean up the dank, filthy Argyle Street elevated stop, which was covered with graffiti and garbage and smelled of urine. The CTA responded by installing a new platform, two heated windbreaker shelters, a $250,000 lighting system, and an Oriental ticket booth inside the station was a part of their

"Adopt-a-Station" program which was supported in part by a $10,000 donation from the neighboring AON Corporation. The inside of the station was painted a bright green and red. (Chicago artist Kathleen Eaton, whose work focuses on architectural spaces in Chicago and on the unexpected solitude and human activities that often accompany such urban spaces, completed an oil painting of the Argyle Station for the Hollister Corporation, which in turn produced 18,000 posters for worldwide distribution.) The colorful Oriental pagoda-style roof, constructed at a cost of $100,000, is the first of its kind in the world, according to Soo. "People will know what is here now," he promises.

A free parking lot was opened at Broadway and Winnemac for the convenience of weekend shoppers and tourists. During the mayoral administrations of Jane Byrne and Harold Washington, new curbs and sidewalks were added. Street crime, which was a chronic problem for many years, was curbed when Commander William Antonick, of the 20th Police District, assigned a foot patrolman to cover the area.

The past decade has witnessed remarkable growth, as the vacancy rate along Argyle Street fell to zero. A steady influx of ethnic Chinese and Vietnamese refugees in the middle to late 1970s spurred the remarkable the growth of the community. The economic initiative undertaken in the late 1970s has generated over $30 million in private investments in buildings, stores, and other commercial establishments. While much of Uptown remains squalid, business has never been better on Argyle Street. Today there are over fifteen ethnic restaurants, twelve Oriental grocery stores, and a number of gift and variety emporiums catering to local residents, out-of-town shoppers, and an increasing number of tourists who are eager to experience another slice of Southeast Asia.

Argyle Street Restaurants

Ba Le European and Oriental Gourmet and Sandwich Shop,
5108-20 N. Broadway, Chicago, (312) 561-4424. Elegant French pastries and croissants are sold in the bakery. Gourmet sandwiches and soups can be eaten on the premises or carried out. The menu items are inexpensive and very tasty, reflecting the fusion of two divergent cultures which clashed during a pivotal moment in the world history—French and Vietnamese. Hours: daily, 7 A.M. to 11 P.M. No credit cards.

Le Bistro Restaurant and Cocktail Lounge, *5004 N. Sheridan Road, Chicago, (312) 784-6000.* Oriental and French cuisine priced moderately. Stylish, understated elegance. The house specialties include

sauteed crab (Cua Rang Muoi), Vietnamese Pancakes (Banh Xeo) and marinated sliced beef with lemon grass and sesame oil (Thit Nuong Banh Hoi). A selection of finely cut steaks are also available for the less adventurous diner. Hours: Tuesday through Sunday, 10 A.M. to 10 P.M. Closed Monday. Credit cards accepted.

Nha Trang, *1007 Argyle, Chicago, (312) 989-0712.*   Vietnamese and Chinese cooking. Chicken, seafood, and Vietnamese steamed rice noodles dishes are the house specialties. You may want to try some of the more unusual menu items, including Ca Chien Cary (spicy catfish, with curry and coconut sauce) or the Muc Xao Ot Xa (cuttle fish stir-fried with lemon grass and chili) if you enjoy sea food with an exotic flavoring. Hours: daily from 10 A.M. to 9:30 P.M. Credit cards accepted.

Sun Wa Bar B-Q, *1132-34 W. Argyle, Chicago, (312) 769-1254 or (312) 334-8860.*   Located in what used to be a Japanese restaurant, the Eric Cheng, owner of this modest establishment moved here from New York several years ago. Standard Chinese food served, with a mixture of barbecue dishes including, pig, duck, and chicken. Carry-out service available in the front. Hours: daily from 11 A.M. to 8 P.M. Credit cards accepted.

MeKong Restaurant, *4953 N. Broadway, Chicago, (312) 271-0206.*   Vietnamese food served by the new owners who bought this restaurant in 1988. Formerly located on State Street. Buffet all-you-can-eat luncheon served from 11 A.M. to 2:30 P.M., Monday through Friday. Other hours: Sunday through Thursday, 10 A.M. to 10 P.M.; Friday and Saturday, 10 A.M. to 11 P.M.; Wednesday, 4 P.M. to 10 P.M. Carry-out service. Credit cards accepted.

Phoenix Company, *1133 W. Argyle, Chicago, (312) 878-5833.* The roasting chickens hanging in the window are there to stimulate your appetite. Inside you can select from a variety of duck and pork dishes, with a selection of puto, taho, and fresh noodle plates. Dim sum is also available during the midday. Hours: Tuesday through Sunday, 10 A.M. to 7 P.M.

Yum Yum Cafe, *1113 W. Argyle, Chicago, (312) 728-0283.* Catonese and Szechuen cuisine prepared by their in-house chef direct from Hong Kong. Two separate dining rooms that don't seem to be too busy on Saturdays. This restaurant recently underwent an expansion. Hours: daily, 9 A.M. to 10 P.M. Credit cards accepted.

Pho Hung, *1063 W. Argyle, Chicago, (312) 769-1499.* Busy family restaurant serving lunch, dinner, and carry-out. Chinese and Vietnamese cuisine. A favorite meeting place for the neighborhood people. Hours: daily 8 A.M. to 7:30 P.M. No credit cards.

Pho Xe Lua (The Train), *1021 W. Argyle, Chicago, (312) 275-7512.* By the looks of things, this restaurant is appropriately named. The "Train" is just as busy and congested as Argyle Street on a Saturday morning, when the residents come out to do their shopping. The house specialties include a variety of beef and chicken dishes, and rice noodle soup. Hours: Monday through Friday, 9 A.M. to 8 P.M.; Saturday and Sunday, 8 A.M. to 9 P.M. No credit cards.

Nhu Hoa Cafe, *1020 W. Argyle, Chicago, (312) 878-0618.* Di ne on Vietnamese and Laotian food in an elegant surrounding, and watch big screen color television at the same time. The restaurant is owned by the same family that also runs the Tiem Vang A Chau jewelry store across the street at 1019 Argyle. Luncheon specials are served from 11:30 A.M. to 3 P.M. Other hours: Tuesday through Friday, 10 A.M. to 10 P.M.; Saturday and Sunday, 9:30 A.M. to 10:30 P.M. Closed Monday. Credit cards accepted.

Hau Giang Restaurant, *1104-06 W. Argyle, Chicago, (312) 275-8691.* Fine Vietnamese cuisine and cocktails. Dine in or carry out. Hours: Sunday through Thursday, 9 A.M. to 10 P.M.; Friday and Saturday, 9 A.M. to 11 P.M. No credit cards.

Furama Restaurant, Inc., *4936 N. Broadway, Chicago, (312) 271-1161.* Spacious two-story Chinese restaurant that was an automotive repair garage in its former life. With a little imagination, you might be able to visualize lube jobs and ball joint repairs as you dine on your dim sum, which is served from 9:30 A.M. to 4 P.M. every day. Credit cards accepted.

Lac Vien Restaurant, *1129 Argyle, Chicago, (312) 275-1112.* "Thumbs up" for this Vietnamese restaurant, according to the local restaurant critics. Reasonable prices, a cheap luncheon special (typically $3.59), and good service are the reasons. This is also the place to go for chicken livers in pig's tripe. Hours: daily from 9 A.M. to 10 P.M. Credit cards accepted.

Tin Lung, *4949 N. Broadway, Chicago, (312) 271-8999.* A favorite lunchtime spot for the employees of AON Corporation (Combined Insurance) down the street. The name of the restaurant, which is humorous to many Westerners who are somehow reminded of the implications of cigarette smoking, serves Chinese food at reasonable prices in a less-than-luxurious decor. Hours: open every day from 11 A.M. to 8 P.M.

Pasteur, *4759 N. Sheridan Road, Chicago, (312) 271-6673.* One of the hottest, up-and-coming Vietnamese restaurants in the city. It's usually "S.R.O," even on the week nights, so be prepared to wait. The prices are moderate, and the food is usually outstanding. The cuttle fish, which is sold in some of the groceries and delis on Argyle Street, is recommended. Hours: lunch serves from noon to 2:30 P.M., Tuesday through Sunday; dinner from 5 P.M. to 10 P.M. Credit cards accepted. *Recommended.*

Argyle Street Gift Shops, Video Rental, Jewelry, and Book Stores

Tiem Vang A Chau (Asian Jewelers), *1019 W. Argyle, Chicago, (312) 878-0083.* Exclusive jade and gold jewelry imported from Hong Kong by owner Julie Hoa, whose family runs the Nhu Hoa Restaurant across the street. The store will buy scrap gold. Watch and jewelry repair on the premises. Hours: Tuesday through Sunday, 11 A.M. to 6 P.M.

Saigon Boutique and Jewelry, *4956 N. Sheridan Road, Chicago, (312) 561-2388.* Clothing fashion and footwear for men and women. Jewelry, perfume, and gift items from Southeast Asia. Hours: 10 A.M. to 7 P.M., seven days a week. Credit cards accepted.

Kim San Jewelry Sale and Gift Shop, *1008 W. Argyle, Chicago, (312) 878-5666.* Toys, jewelry, Chinese shell art, and ceiling fans. Hours: daily, 10 A.M. to 7 P.M. No credit cards.

Superior Gift Shop, *1004-6 W. Argyle, Chicago, (312) 271-0253.* Importer and wholesaler of merchandise from the Orient. Floor vases, silk plants, wind chimes, and fine porcelain. A large selection of movies direct from Hong Kong are available for rental. Hours: daily from 9 A.M. to to 7 P.M.

Le Dung Cosmetics and Gifts, *1028 W. Argyle St., Chicago, (312) 989-7850.* Southeast Asian imported items including furniture, jewelry, Laotian flutes, decorations, cosmetics, jade, and porcelain figurines. Most of the decorative artwork is done by Vietnamese artists

living in the U.S. Five years at this location. Hours: open daily 10 A.M.
to 7 P.M.

Kinh Do Wholesale & Retail, *1066 W. Argyle St., Chicago,
(312) 784-4388.* Decorative inlay, and painted wall hangings of Vietnamese and Chinese motif. Electronic appliances, clocks, silk plants, film
videos, and gift items are also stocked. Hours: Monday and Wednesday
through Sunday, 10 A.M. to 7 P.M.

World Journal & Bookstore, *1126 W. Argyle, (312) 728-7633,
and in Chinatown (South Side) at 2235 S. Wentworth, Chicago,
(312) 842-8080.* Chinese language books, magazines, greeting cards,
audio tapes, newspapers, and gift items. Hours: daily 10 A.M. to 6 P.M.
Credit cards accepted.

Tan Thanh Books & Gift Co., *1135 W. Argyle, Chicago, (312)
275-8687.* Specializing in a wide assortment of jade, figurines, wind
chimes, audio cassettes, Chinese magazines and newspapers. Hours:
daily, from 10 A.M. to 6 P.M. Credit cards accepted.

Pailin Video & Gifts, *1114 W. Argyle, Chicago, (312) 275-7754.*
A Cambodian-owned business, specializing in the rental and sale of
Southeast Asian movies. Porcelain figurines, audio cassettes, watches,
jewelry, and other gift items included in the inventory. Hours: daily 10
A.M. to 7 P.M., but open at noon on Tuesday. No credit cards.

Hoang Kim, Inc., *1025 W. Argyle, Chicago, (312) 271-3132.*
Fine Vietnamese jewelry, custom design. A specialist in diamonds and
gemstones. Wax carving and casting, faceting and polishing of jade.
Jewelry appraisals. Hours: open daily from 10 A.M. to 6 P.M.

Kim Huot, Inc., *1107 A W. Argyle, Chicago, (312) 769-6190.*
Gold items, gifts, children's dolls, fine silks, shoes, perfumes, and bed-
spreads. Chaotic, but interesting. Hours: open daily from 9:30 A.M. to 6
P.M. Credit cards accepted.

Argyle Street Bakeries

Double Happiness Bakery and Restaurant, *1061 W. Argyle,
Chicago, (312) 334-3735.* Chinese bakery located in the front, with
snack tables in the rear in case you desire to indulge your sweet tooth.
Hours: daily, 8:30 A.M. to 7 P.M.

New Chinatwon Bakery and Coffee Shop, *1019-1/2 W. Argyle, Chicago, (312) 784-1700.* Opened in November, 1990. Chinese and Vietnamese bakery items, with an adjacent dining area. No credit cards. Hours: Monday and Wednesday through Sunday, 8:30 A.M. to 7 P.M. Closed on Tuesday.

New Hong Kong Bakery, *1050-52 W. Argyle, Chicago, (312) 878-3226.* Oven-fresh bakery products, and all kinds of Chinese and American pastries. Everything is baked on the premises. Hours: daily, 9 A.M. to 7 P.M.

Argyle Street Grocery and Food Import Stores

Thai Grocery, Inc., *5014 N. Broadway, Chicago, (312) 561-5345.* Importer, wholesaler, and distributor of Southeast Asian foods, spices, and teas. A delicatessen in the rear of the store sells hot pork ribs and seafood. Hours: daily, 9 A.M. to 7 P.M. Checks, but no credit cards.

Hoa Nam Grocery, Inc., *1101-3 W. Argyle, Chicago, (312) 275-9157.* You'll discover that many of the Asian shopkeepers in the New Chinatown do little in the way of display advertising. Merchandise is stacked high to the ceilings, and often arranged in a haphazard manner. Because stores like Hoa Nam cater to a regular neighborhood clientele that buys its groceries here every week, it is not necessary to lure new business off the street with special sales, come-ons, or gimmicks. The goods are moderately priced, and the store is always congested. Hours: daily, 11 A.M. to 8 P.M.

Viet Hoa Plaza, Inc., *1051 W. Argyle St., Chicago, (312) 334-1028.* The owners of the Viet Hoa Plaza, on the other hand, just completed a $30,000 renovation of their building. With or without the new exterior, this Cambodian-Vietnamese marketplace will no doubt continue to lure Asian shoppers from all over the Midwest. Offering a wide variety of Southeast Asian foods that appeal to every taste, including canned goods, seasonings, live crabs, and bakery items, Viet Hoa is one of the busiest stores on the street. Free parking. Hours: daily, 9 A.M. to 7:30 P.M.

Trung Viet Co., Inc., *4940-4942 N. Sheridan Road, Chicago, (312) 561-0042.* Ethnic Chinese grocery that services the local restaurant trade. Frozen foods, Chinese herbs, bulk rice, meats, and fish.

Hours: Monday and Wednesday through Sunday, 9 A.M. to 8 P.M. Closed Tuesday. No credit cards.

Wah Leung Co., *4926 N. Broadway, Chicago, (312) 271-4922.* A restaurant upstairs seats 800 people. The cluttered downstairs grocery sells an assortment of bulk foods and vegetables, canned goods, and an incredible hodgepodge of goods. Wah Leung also rents Asian movies on cassette in the rear. Hours: Tuesday through Sunday, 9 A.M. to 7 P.M. Closed Monday.

Mien Hoa Market, Inc., *1108-1110 W. Argyle, Chicago, (312) 334-8393.* Grocery, delicatessen items, and candies. Hours: daily, 9 A.M. to 7 P.M.

Mya Market, *1100 W. Argyle, Chicago, (312) 878-7126.* Formerly a drug store. Now it's a full-line Asian grocery store. Things change fast on Argyle Street. Hours: daily, 11 A.M. to 7 P.M.

Asian Broadcasting
WSBC, 1240 AM

Filipino Programming, Wednesday evenings, 8 P.M. to 9 P.M.

Thai Programming, Thursday evenings, 8 P.M. to 9 P.M.

"Sangeeta," Indo-Pakistani Programming, Thursday evenings, 9 P.M. to 10 P.M.

"Kala Academy," Indo-Pakistani Programming, Sunday evenings at 9 P.M.

chapter fourteen

Hispanic Chicago

History and Settlement

The future of Chicago and the direction it will be taking by the year 2000 and beyond will be heavily influenced by the burgeoning Hispanic population now occupying the neighborhoods on the West Side and Northwest Side—parts of the city formerly occupied by immigrants from Eastern Europe. By the year 2000 it is expected that one in every four Chicagoans will be of Hispanic descent: Mexican, Puerto Rican, Cuban, and other Latin and South American nationalities. Today there are four predominantly Hispanic wards in Chicago—the 22nd and 25th, representing the Southwest Side Mexican "barrio" communities of Pilsen and the Little Village, and the 26th and 31st Wards, encompassing West Town and the Humboldt Park neighborhoods, where the majority of Puerto Ricans now reside. Until very recently these wards were controlled by the "old guard" white ethnic aldermen like Vito Marzullo, Thomas Keane, and the "regulars" who formed the axle of the seemingly invincible Daley Machine of the 1950s and 1960s. Little attention was paid to the Hispanic voting constituency, which then was perceived to be indifferent to city politics and at odds within itself. Though all the divergent Hispanic groups share a common language, cultural, political, and socioeconomic differences among them have created a wide gulf, which translate into political inertia at City Hall and in the State House in Springfield. So while there is a Hispanic (or, some prefer, Latino) community in Chicago, they have often failed to unite to achieve political parity. In this regard there is little sense of community among the Hispanic groups.

Many of the Mexicans, for example, who have been a factor in Chicago life for generations, consider themselves culturally distinct from other Latino groups; their traditions and customs more closely paralleling the experiences of the white ethnics who once populated their neighborhoods. The Mexicans, for the most part, comprise the blue-collar, laboring classes, while at the other end of the economic spectrum the Cubans generally are white-collar professionals who came to Chicago as political refugees following the Castro revolution of 1959. They identify more closely with the political right and are more likely to vote for those conservative candidates who would support military intervention to topple Cuba's Communist regime. A University of Florida poll conducted in 1991 indicated that 57% of Cuban-Americans would favor some form of overt military action against Fidel Castro.

Puerto Ricans, who are second in number to the Mexicans in Chicago, are U.S. citizens by birth, but rank below blacks on the economic scale. They are less concerned with immigration and repatriation issues than the Mexicans or Cubans, and are more likely to be assimilated into the mainstream Anglo culture. The Hispanic population in Chicago stands at 545,852, according to 1990 census figures. There were 352,560 Mexicans, 119,866 Puerto Ricans, 10,044 Cubans, and a scattering of Guatemalans, Colombians, Ecuadorians, Peruvians, Spanish, Hondurans, Chileans, El Salvadorans, and fewer Panamanians, Dominicans, and Argentineans.

Despite a cumulative population of 422,063 Hispanics in the Metro-Suburban area in 1980, the community was represented only marginally by a Democratic Cook County Commissioner (Irene Hernandez) and a University of Illinois trustee (Arturo Velazquez, Jr.). Velazquez was emblematic of a new breed of Hispanic politician who was no longer content to play by the old guard's rules—in this case, crusty old Vito Marzullo, alderman of the Twenty-Fifth Ward since 1953. Marzullo, who was a product of the Italian quarter, never missed a chance to speak his peace. Concerning well-meaning reformers and liberals like Velazquez, Vito had this to say: "You give them ten dollars and they couldn't get your dog out of the pound!" Marzullo's campaign rhetoric must have counted for something with his Mexican constituency. Velazquez garnered only forty-one percent of the vote in 1983.

In 1980, *Illinois Issues* published an article titled "Mañana Will Be Better: Spanish American Politics in Chicago." The authors predicted great strides within the Hispanic community in the coming decade. It might have come to pass in 1981 when 29-year-old Rudy Lozano organized community support to battle the machine regulars. Lozano, a labor organizer, failed in his aldermanic runoff by the narrowest of margins: seventeen votes. The popular and charismatic leader accused his opponents of purging Hispanic names from the poll sheets before the election. Lozano enjoyed the support of Mayor Harold Washington in his bid to unseat incumbent Alderman Frank Stemberk. It never came to pass. Lozano was murdered on June 8, 1983, allegedly by a youthful gang member named Gregory Escobar. The tragedy underscored the larger inabilities of the community to coalesce to achieve mutually advantageous goals. Even though Hispanics succeeded in electing Juan Soliz, Jesus Garcia, and Luis Gutierrez to the Council in the 1980s, the larger goals remain unfulfilled, indicating that "mañana" has not yet come.

Mexicans

There are more Mexicans in Chicago than any other Hispanic group; 352,560 according to the 1990 census data. In the span of ten years (1970–80), the Mexican population nearly tripled. As escalating poverty, joblessness, and a sinking peso shattered the Mexican economy, thousands of Mexicans from the interior and the border regions made their way to Chicago in the 1950s and 1960s. The American dream was a powerful motivator for many of these people to abandon their families and friends for the promise of better paying jobs in the industrial north. The tide of immigration began much earlier, when 206 railroad workers were recruited for duty by Chicago firms at the turn of the century. By 1920, 1,200 Mexican workers, most of them railroad section hands, lived in close proximity to the industrial basin near the Chicago River, South Chicago, Back of the Yards, and farther south, near the steel yards. In 1927 the Catholic Archdiocese, under the direction of George Cardinal Mundelein, designated the first Spanish-speaking parish, St. Francis of Assisi, at 12th Street and Newberry Avenue. By this time the Mexican population of Chicago had grown to nearly 26,000.

The coming of World War II marked the next major influx of Mexicans into Chicago. The international "bracero" contract labor agreements, signed in 1942 and 1943, allowed for the temporary entry of migrant farm laborers to fulfill manpower shortages in the Southwest brought on by the war. In the Midwest the labor drain was particularly acute as the factories and industrial plants geared up to meet wartime quotas. The large railroad consortiums, including the Chicago, Burlington and Quincy, the Chicago, Minneapolis, St. Paul and Pacific, and Chicago, Rock Island, and

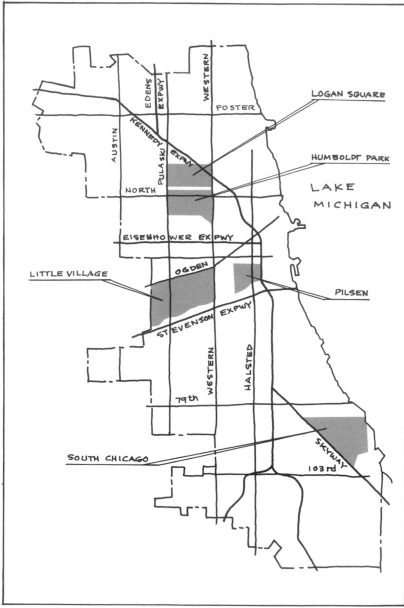

Hispanic Neighborhoods

Pacific lines took advantage of the bracero laws to hire 15,344 Mexicans between 1943 and 1945. Mexican braceros (workers) poured into New City, Back of the Yards, and the Lower West Side communities of Pilsen and South Lawndale (now called "Pueblo Pequeño" or Little Village), and the adjacent "Heart of Chicago" neighborhood. Bordered by 17th Street on the north, the city limits on the west, and the South Branch of the Chicago River on the south and east, Mexicans slowly displaced the Bohemians and Poles of Pilsen in the 1950s. South Lawndale, once called "Cesca California" by the Czechs who lived there, was dubbed the "Little Village" by Mexicans, who have given this immigrant neighborhood a decided south-of-the-border flavor. Every year on September 16, the residents of the Little Village celebrate Mexican Independence Day with a large, colorful parade that winds its way down 26th Street from Kedzie to Cicero.

Pilsen and the Little Village continue to serve as the most important port of entry in Chicago for newly enfranchised Mexicans. Grocery stores, restaurants, and newsstands along the commercial strip of 18th and 26th Streets cater more to the Spanish-speaking residents than to the small tourist trade that may visit this community in the course of a year. The numbers tell the real story. Between 1960 and 1980, the Mexican population exploded from just 6,972 to 83,385. A decade later, the census taker noted a large Mexican presence in Du Page doubled from 17,302 to 34,567. It is estimated that a full 90 percent are Mexican. The new immigrants from south of the border are bypassing the large metro areas in favor of the manufacturing and service jobs that have followed the great inner city exodus into the suburbs. Half of all Hispanics now residing in the western suburbs are here illegally. They are the *indocumentados*— who become the unwitting tool of factory owners who exploit the system for economic gain.

In the 1950s, amid the postwar prosperity of the Eisenhower years, the Mexican-American community in the U.S. experienced the first major backlash against undocumented workers that resulted in the "Operation Wetback" roundup of thousands of Mexicans who were returned to their native land. With stricter immigration laws enacted by the government, fewer Mexicans came to Chicago.

Meanwhile in Chicago, Mexican community leaders banded together in an effort to advance their social and political status in the face of the crackdown. The Catholic church took up the cause of the *indocumentados* in the Summer of 1982, when federal immigration officials detained over 2,000 Mexicans in a military hangar at O'Hare Airport. Father Fred Brandstrader of the Providence of God Roman Catholic church, (7171 W. 18th Street), organized his fellow priests from the six parishes serving the Pilsen community to protest the actions of the government. Father Brandstrader presided over one of the largest Mexican parishes in the city; one that had shed its Lithuanian character by the 1960s, when many of the older residents had either moved out of the neighborhood or had died away. The march he organized in 1982 was symbolic of the strong ties forged between the church and the community.

Over the years, other agencies have helped. A $100,000 grant from the Office of Inter-American Affairs resulted in the formation of the Mexican Civic Committee in 1943, then later in 1950, the Mexican American Council. A Mexican Social Center opened in 1945, and was dedicated to the memory of Manuel Perez, who had won the Congressional Medal of Honor during World War II. These coordinated efforts showed that cooperation was not only desirable, but fruitful. Years later in 1977, this community spirit was again felt among members of the Pilsen Neighbors Community. They won a major victory over city bureaucrats who had attempted to bus Mexican-American children out of the district against the wishes of the parents. The Board of Education desired to bolster sagging enrollments across the city, but the plan was opposed by Teresa Fraga and others within the Pilsen neighborhood, who called for the construction of their own school. They fought hard over this issue for nearly four years, until the city decided to build them a new facility at 2150 S. Laflin Street. The discordant voices of 1,000 community residents were heard outside the offices of the Board of Education the day of the vote, until the members caved into the tremendous political pressure and agreed to build the spacious Benito Juarez High School, which was designed by a Mexican architect named Ramirez Vazquez. Juarez, which offers bilingual instruction, is the crown jewel of Pilsen, which has the highest density Hispanic community in Chicago.

Because Pilsen and the Little Village were overcrowded, and much of the housing old and dilapidated, many Mexican-Americans who had accumulated a savings left the neighborhood and moved to the suburbs. Cicero, Aurora, Joliet, Waukegan, Melrose Park, and West Chicago absorbed much of the city overflow in the 1970s and 1980s. In Aurora alone, there are at least 30,000 Hispanics, comprising 3.8% of the residential population. This trend is likely to continue into the next decade as Mexican-Americans continue to make economic strides. Those who remain behind have valiantly banded together to fight off the scourge of drugs, gangs, and crime. The Latin American Job Center, begun in 1972, was formed to train workers for higher paying, skilled union jobs, and to assist small contractors desiring to do business in the community. On September 10, 1984, solidarity became evident in Pilsen, when 1,200 residents marched in support of the church's efforts to establish the Pilsen

Catholic Youth Center, aimed at taking youngsters off the streets to give them religious instruction and provide them with a wholesome place in which to meet socially.

For Chicago's Mexican community, it has been a hard climb. But now at last, the time of "prosperidad" seems to be at hand. The number of independently owned businesses continues to grow—there were about 5,000 of them, according to 1987 census figures. Thanks to minority set-aside programs that provide assistance to Hispanics seeking to break into the markets, immigrants who would have otherwise ended up in factories can now share in the entrepreneurial spirit that has been the lifeblood of the city. Of course most of these businesses are of the storefront variety and are confined to the Hispanic neighborhoods, but if history teaches us anything, it is that small deals and big dreams sometimes point the way toward a brighter future.

Puerto Ricans

Puerto Ricans are a young immigrant group, though one can hardly call the Puerto Ricans immigrants, since the three islands were ceded to the U.S. on December 10, 1898 by terms of the Treaty of Paris ending the Spanish-American War. Puerto Rico was granted commonwealth status on July 25, 1952.

In 1980, the average age in the Puerto Rican community was only 21. A full 59% of the population was under the age of 25. These numbers suggest—and the reality of their urban existence bears out—the point that they are among the poorest of Chicago's ethnics, suffering from chronic unemployment, low per capita income, and a high drop-out rate as reflected in the 1982 graduating class at Roberto Clemente High School. Of the 855 eligible seniors, 55.7% of the Hispanic students dropped out before commencement.

Assimilation into the Anglo culture has been difficult ever since the first great exodus from the island began after World War II. Like the Mexican farm workers who crossed into Texas and the American Southwest in the early years of the century, the Puerto Rican immigrants were also agrarian farmers who harvested coffee, sugar cane, bananas, pineapples and rice on small uncompromising plots of land. By the 1950s, the Puerto Ricans began supplanting the Italians, Poles, and Ukrainians in the ethnically diverse West Town community on the lower part of Milwaukee Avenue. This process of displacement of older European groups was hastened by the construction of the Kennedy Expressway in the later

1950s. In 1960 there were 32,371 Puerto Ricans counted in the census, but a full 10,000 of them lived in Spanish-speaking West Town. In the next twenty years, the growth of the community was explosive. While West Town continued to serve as a port of entry for new arrivals, other Puerto Ricans who had lived in Chicago for a few years pushed farther north into Humboldt Park, which, until its incorporation into Chicago, in 1869, was far removed from the bustle of downtown Chicago, and was inhabited for the most part by ethnic Germans. The Puerto Ricans who tried to carve out a better life along the spacious Logan and Humboldt Boulevards typically worked on factory assembly lines, in fancy Loop hotels and restaurants, and in various manufacturing concerns. Relief from the drudgery of menial labor could be found through social and fraternal societies like "Los Caballeros de San Juan" (Knights of San Juan), organized in 1954 to foster a sense of well-being within the Spanish community. Los Caballeros also filled a larger need in that they were able to assist their members in finding decent housing outside of the ramshackle tenements of West Town and in locating better-paying jobs. The organization began in the Woodlawn community, but quickly reformed into twelve "concilios" (councils) in Chicago. Beginning in 1956 and continuing through 1965, the fraternal society sponsored an annual El Dia de San Juan (St. John's Day) which included a banquet and a dance. After 1965 this event became known as La Parada Puertorriqueña (The Puerto Rican Parade), which took into account all of the Puerto Rican societies and promoted a sense of sorely needed community pride.

This occurred at a time when jobs were increasingly harder to find, and when conditions in the "barrio" were nearly intolerable. Job discrimination and an unresponsive city administration contributed to a feeling of growing despair that culminated in the first Puerto Rican riot in U.S. history on June 12, 1966, when 21-year-old Arcelis Cruz was shot and killed on Division Street by police officers during the annual parade. For the next two days and nights the West Town streets became an armed battleground that left sixteen people injured and fifty buildings damaged. And then, after another eleven years had passed, violence flared anew when two more Puerto Ricans were shot down by police. Out of this turmoil came the realization by city officials of the special needs of the Puerto Rican community. The Spanish-speaking Coalition for Jobs drew attention to discriminatory practices against Latinos and sought to address the broader problems that cut across both the dominant Hispanic cultures. In 1975 the Latino Institute, bringing the different Hispanic organizations together under one roof, was founded with a two-year grant of $70,000 from the Community Fund of Chicago. Sensitive to the divided loyalties of the community leaders, the Institute was headquartered downtown at 105 S. LaSalle Street. To build a facility in West Town or in Pilsen would seem to favor one group at the expense of the other.

In 1981 Mayor Jane Byrne, recognizing the growing political influence of Chicago's Puerto Ricans, appointed Jose Martinez interim alderman of the Thirty-First Ward, which extended from West Town into Humboldt Park. Edward Nedza, the only white Democratic ward committeeman to slate Hispanics before 1986, selected Joseph Berrios as the party's standard-bearer for the Ninth District seat in 1982. Berrios was reelected in 1984. Interestingly, Nedza was ousted as a state senator in the 1986 Democratic primary by another Hispanic—Miguel del Valle. In turn, Del Valle was named chairman of the Mayor's Advisory Commission on Latino Affairs in 1983.

The Puerto Rican community of Chicago looks forward to a brighter day when it might consolidate these modest political achievements to formulate a new social order, which will hopefully close the economic chasm preventing them from harvesting the fruits of prosperity.

Cubans

Before 1960, the Cuban community in Chicago was virtually nonexistent. On March 17, 1958, one of the epochs of political history in the Western Hemisphere began when Fidel Castro, a former lawyer, engaged in guerrilla activities and announced his intentions to lead a general revolt against the entrenched regime of Fulgencio Batista. In 1955, after several years of military rule, Batista had restored constitutional rule and granted amnesty to political prisoners. Castro and his supporters stormed into Havana on January 1, 1959, and drove Batista into permanent exile. With him went thousands of political refugees, many of them skilled workers from the professional classes who were lucky to escape with only the shirts on their backs. Some 20,000 Cuban exiles poured into Chicago. They were provided relocation assistance by the Catholic Charities of Chicago, and were generally warmly received, not only because they were fervent anticommunists during the height of the Cold War, but also because the Cubans brought with them skills that would benefit American society.

Their assimilation into American culture was far easier than the Mexicans and Puerto Ricans for these same reasons. Published statistics in 1979 showed that 45% of Cuban Americans in Cook County owned their homes, compared with only 35.8% of other Hispanic groups. An employment survey, conducted by the U.S. Immigration and Naturalization Service in the late 1970s, still showed that 10% of Cubans in the work force were professional or technical, while 7.7% were employed in the white-collar sector as clerical and office personnel. This survey was commissioned at a time when a number of working-class Cubans, unable to speak English and less prepared for the challenges of the marketplace, began appearing in the U.S. This "second wave" of immigrants left Cuba for purely economic reasons and, unlike the 1960 refugees, were far less likely to resettle on the island even if the hated Castro government were to be toppled.

Unlike the Puerto Ricans and Mexicans who are concentrated in their "barrio" neighborhoods, the Cubans are widely dispersed across the North and Northwest Sides of Chicago. The refugee immigrants, determined to locate in inexpensive housing near the Spanish-speaking neighborhoods (but not caught up in the barrio itself), tended to settle between the north branch of the Chicago River and Lake Michigan. In 1980 the largest concentration of Cubans was in the Logan Square neighborhood (1,590), and the Far North Side Edgewater community, with 1,441 residents. Their desire to live among the white ethnics no doubt contributed to some rancorous feelings and heightened mistrust that has characterized the relationship between Cubans and the rest of the Hispanic community. According to sociologist Ruth Horowitz, in her 1983 study of Chicago's Mexican population, it is the community culture, *chicanismo,* that allows other Hispanics to proclaim that "those people are like us and those others are not."

But there is no denying that the Cubans have overcome tremendous adversity and have prospered in the Anglo culture. Thirty-five percent of the Cubans residing in the Chicago metropolitan area have migrated to the suburbs, far and away the highest percentage of any Hispanic group.

However the economic success of the 1960 arrivals belies the problems encountered by the 1980 Mariel boatlift refugees, exported to U.S. shores by Fidel Castro, who relaxed immigration policies to permit only malcontents and criminals to leave the island. Until 1984, these people were not eligible for immigrant status under U.S. laws. Following the Mariel boatlift, the Castro government held fast to its longstanding policy of permitting only men over 45, and women 40 or over to visit relatives in the U.S. There are indications that these restrictions may be softened in the 1990s, however.

The Cuban community today reflects a peculiar dichotomy in that it is both settled and transient. To build a sense of unity with other Hispanics remains an unfulfilled goal.

Ethnic Museum

The Mexican Fine Arts Center Museum, *1852 W. 19th Street, Chicago, (312) 738-1503.*   In recognition of the historic settlement of the Pilsen community by thousands of Mexican immigrants, the Chicago Park District in January, 1986, signed an agreement to convert the Harrison Park Boat Craft Shop into a permanent home for the Mexican Fine Arts Center Museum, which was founded five years earlier in September, 1982. The renovation phase began in August, 1986, with the festive grand opening taking place on March 27, 1987. A newly remodeled west wing was unveiled on June 8, 1990. It is the first Mexican Museum of its kind in the Midwest, and since its founding, it has achieved most if not all of its stated objectives. Those are: (1) to sponsor special events and exhibits that reflect the rich cultural diversity of the Mexican visual and performing arts; (2) to develop a significant permanent collection of Mexican art; (3) to encourage local Mexican artists to achieve excellence; and (4) to offer regularly scheduled educational programs. The Mexican Fine Arts Center Museum has held 18 exhibits in the main gallery between 1987 and 1990, and has welcomed over 600 groups and 75,000 visitors during that time. The museum houses a permanent collection of prints, photographs, folk art pieces, and selected works of such noted artists as David Alfaro Siqueiros and Jose Clemente Orozco (both famous for their wall-sized public murals depicting pivotal events from Mexican history and culture), Alfredo Zalce, Jose Guadalupe Posada, and Rufino Tamayo. A gift shop, small auditorium, main gallery, and courtyard gallery are located in the building. Hours: Tuesday through Sunday, 10 A.M. to 5 P.M. Closed on Mondays. Free admission. *Recommended.*

Theater Company

Latino Chicago Theatre Company: The "Firehouse," *1625 N. Damen Avenue, Chicago, (312) 486-5120.*   A 12-year-old theater company showcasing the work of American playwrights of Hispanic descent. Plays are shown year round (most are in English, but from time to time a few may be presented in Spanish) at the Firehouse, a tiny North Side theater than seats 90. In 1990, a television documentary focusing on the "Puffin Project," a collaboration between Mexico and the Latino Chicago Theatre Company during the International Theatre Festival of Chicago was aired on PBS. Plays, musical performances, poetry readings, and dance are presented year round. Showtime: Thursday, Friday, and Saturday at 8:00 P.M.; Sunday, 7:00 P.M. Tickets can be purchased at the box office up to fifteen minutes before curtain. All seats are $10. No credit cards.

Annual Events and Celebrations
Multi-Ethnic

Summer Latin Music Festival (Festival de Musica Latina). A series of eight musical concerts at participating city parks throughout the summer months. Concerts ranging from the polyrhythmic and exciting salsa, to the brass sounds of the mariachis, and various other Latin music styles are showcased at the Chicago Park District's annual Summer Latin Music Festival which runs from the fourth of July through the end of August. Headlining the 1991 concert at Dvorak Park, 1119 W. Cullterton, was longtime favorite Tony Gomez and his Latin Orchestra. For dates, locations and additional information about the Concerts in the Park series, call the Chicago Park District at (312) 294-2320. Free admission.

Hispanic Festival, *at the Museum of Science and Industry, 57th and Lake Shore Drive, Chicago.* A 17-day ethnic folk fair highlighting the cultural heritage of the Hispanic peoples in music, classical, and folk dance, theater and a juried art exhibition presented in the museum's West Pavilion. The special programs are held in conjunction with National Hispanic Month activities in Chicago, held each year from September 15 through October 16. The museum brings in musical performers and guest speakers from Spanish-speaking countries, including Guatemala, Cuba, Bolivia, Panama, Spain, and Mexico. In 1991 a special traveling exhibition, "Spain/U.S.A. Hall of Fame," focusing on the individuals from the Hispanic community who have made the greatest impact on communications, aviation, and technology, made its national debut at the Museum of Science and Industry. The festival runs from late September through mid-October. There is no additional charge for admission to the exhibitions and performances after the standard entrance fee has been paid. The museum fees are as follows: Adults 13-64, $5; senior citizens, $4; children 5-12, $2; children under 5, free.

Hispanic Heritage Month: "Celebracion" *at the Field Museum, Roosevelt Road and Lake Shore Drive, Chicago.* Week-long activities and exhibits at the museum include music, art, and performances by local Latin American talent. The exhibits deal with themes relating to the ancient cultures of Latin America. The demonstrations, workshops, lectures, and performances are for the most part aimed at school groups, but the public is invited to view the special exhibits, which are on display during the third week of September. Admission is free. For a calendar of events and times, please call the Education Department of the Field Museum at (312) 922-9410, ext. 204 or 351.

Pan-American Festival, *at Arvey Field on the south end of Grant Park, across from the Field Museum of Natural History, the last weekend in July.*   Two days of music, food and fun from south of the border. Musical headliners from the Dominican Republic, Puerto Rico, Mexico, and Central America make this one of Chicago's liveliest, best-attended ethnic festivals. The 1991 lineup included Alejandra Guzman, Banda Blanca, Tito Nieves, Tropical Panama, and Gilberto Santa Rosa. The year marks the eighth year of the Pan American Festival, sponsored by Cardenas and Fernandez Associates. Admission: $7.00 in advance if purchased through Ticketron or other local outlets; otherwise $10 for adults, $5.00 for children. Hours: noon through 11:00 P.M. Call: (312) 944-7272 for additional information, or Ticketmaster at (312) 559-1212. *Recommended.*

Festival of Latin Music, *sponsored by the Old Town School of Folk Music, 909 W. Armitage, Chicago.*   Featured musical performers from all over Latin America, Puerto Rico, Mexico, and South America have made this one of Chicago's premier musical festivals. The renowned Old Town School of Folk Music has sponsored numerous concerts and special performances presented by artists from all over the world in recent years. But the Latin Music Festival is by far one of the most successful and popular events that the school has sponsored, so much so that the concerts have been moved to The Vic at 3145 N. Sheffield in order to accommodate the overflow crowds who come to see such acclaimed performers as Flaco Jiminez, Guayaneca, and Los Kjarkas—described by executive director Jim Hirsch as the "greatest Andean group in the world." The festival runs during the first two Saturdays in October. Tickets are $13 to $15 per person, and can be purchased through a credit card or by cash at the Old Town School of Folk Music or by calling (312) 525-7793.

International Latino Film Festival. A series of award-winning feature-length films from Latin America that are shown on ten different nights beginning the last week in September and ending in the first week of October. The movies are shown at three locations around the city: Facets Multimedia, 1517 W. Fullerton, (312) 431-1330; the Three Penny

Cinema, 2424 N. Lincoln Avenue, (312) 935-5744; and Roberto Clemente High School Auditorium, 1147 N. Western Avenue, (312) 292-5000. It is advisable to purchase opening night tickets in advance, but there is generally no problem securing walk-up seating on any night afterward. Prices per performance: $6 for adults; students and senior citizens, $4. For dates and show times, please call Facets, the Three Penny Cinema, or the event coordinator, Pepe Valdez, at the Chicago Latino Cinema, c/o Columbia College, 600 S. Michigan, Chicago, IL 60605, (312) 431-1330.

Viva Chicago! A two-day Latin Music festival in Grant Park, the weekend following Labor Day. Latin music is more popular than ever, evidenced by the throngs of people who flock to the Petrillo Bandshell and the "Day Stage" at Jackson Boulevard and Lake Shore Drive each year since 1989 to catch the hottest acts, be it pop singer Gloria Estefan, Los Angeles rockers Los Lobos, percussionist Mongo Santamaria, salsa stars Ruben Blades and Eddie Santiago, or balladeer Beatrize Adriana. There's something here to suit everyone's musical tastes, ranging from mambo to meringue. Virtually every Latin musical style is represented at Viva Chicago! which seems destined to rival the Grant Park Jazz Fest as the premier event of summer. Attendance at the 1990 concert series topped out at 75,000 on Sunday. Sponsored by the Mayor's Office of Special Events. Hours: Saturday and Sunday, noon until 10 P.M. Free admission. Vendors sell Mexican, Puerto Rican, Caribbean, and South American food and beverages in the park. Call (312) 744-3315 for additional details.

Central American Independence Day Parade, *first Saturday in September following Labor Day.* In 1989, when this colorful pageant first began, the theme revolved around Guatemalan independence. Now it is a cross-cultural event honoring all of the Central American nations. The parade travels along Michigan Avenue from Wacker Drive to Van Buren. For additional information call (312) 744-3315.

Mexican

Annual Independence Day Parade (Downtown), marking Mexico's political separation from Spain, an event that occurred in 1820 when Guerrero and Agustin de Iturbide negotiated a status quo independence with the colonial government following a protracted and violent struggle that first took shape in 1810. An insurrection led by Miguel Hidalgo y Costilla was brutally suppressed. Jose Maria Morelos y Pavon's military campaign against the Spanish in 1814 met with similar failure. But in 1823, Mexico was declared a republic, and a federal constitution patterned after the United States Constitution was adopted a year later. Chicago's big downtown parade is scheduled on the Saturday closest to September 15. Each year, over 130 floats, bands, marching groups, and even the Chicago Police Department's much heralded Emerald Society Band takes part in this extravaganza. The parade route (down Michigan Avenue from Wacker Drive to Van Buren) is annually witnessed by 250,000 spectators proudly waving Mexican flags. Many of them sport huge sombreros and brightly colored folk costumes. The parade is organized by the Mexican Civic Society, and it kicks off at 1:30 P.M. Call the Chicago Office of Tourism at (312) 280-5740 for additional information.

Independence Day Parade (Little Village), a festive neighborhood celebration that winds its way down 26th Street between Kedzie Avenue and Cicero in the heart of Chicago's Little Village, home to thousands of Mexican-Americans. It is a rollicking good time, with floats, marching bands, costumed matadors, dancers, men on horseback, and of course, the "Miss Little Village" parade queen. The Grand Marshal of the 1991 parade was Illinois governor Jim Edgar, who was eager to cultivate the good will of Chicago's sizable Mexican community during his first year in office. The event is sponsored by the Little Village Chamber of Commerce, and is held on the Sunday afternoon following the downtown parade, or September 16. For dates and time, call (312) 521-5387.

Fiesta en la Villita (Little Village Festival). Four days of music, carnival rides, live performances of Mexican folk and contemporary, music, and food booths beginning on the Thursday before the Independence Day Parade in September. Location: 26th Street and Albany, in the Little Village Mall. Hours: early afternoon until 11 P.M. Free admission. For information, call the Little Village Chamber of Commerce at (312) 521-5387.

Fiesta del Sol. Four day street fair on Blue Island Avenue between 18th Street (on the north) and Cermak Road (on the south), the first week in August. The festival, one of the largest in the city and sponsored by the Pilsen Neighbors Association, began as a block party in 1973 to celebrate the Board of Education's decision to build Benito Juarez High School. Since that time, Fiesta del Sol has become one of the most important social events in the Mexican community. The proceeds of the event benefit the Pilsen YMCA, the various neighborhood parishes, and El Hogar del Niños (a daycare center). More than 500,000 people attended in 1990, and it stands to reason that these numbers will only increase in the coming years. There are carnival rides, an arts and crafts promenade, free medical exams for children, local jazz and rock artists and well-known performers like Elsa Garcia, a Texas-based singer, Suzy Gonzalez, and Antonio de Jesus, who are flown in especially for the occasion. The savory Mexican food, including tostadas, gorditas, and the famous enchiladas prepared by Jovita Andrade and other past and present Pilsenites are a mainstay of the festival. Free admission. On-street parking available near the festival. Hours: Thursday, 5 P.M. to 10 P.M.; Friday, 5 P.M. to midnight; Sunday noon to midnight. Free admission. For additional information, contact the Pilsen Neighbors at 2007 S. Blue Island Avenue, Chicago, or call (312) 666-2663.

Viva Mexico! *Hawthorne Park Racetrack, 35th Street and Laramie, Cicero.* Two-day street fair and folk festival in mid-July that has attracted upwards of 100,000 people each year since its inception in 1986. The reason: festival promoters book some of the top musical acts from Mexico each year, who are well known to the Hispanic residents of Pilsen and Little Village communities. Twenty food vendors dispense Mexican burritos, enchiladas, chimichangas, and hot salsa. There is a carnival midway and games for youngsters. Admission: $10 for adults, $5 for children. Sponsored by Cardenas and Fernandez Associates and participating advertisers. They can be reached at (312) 944-7272.

Viva Aztlan Street Festival, *at the Casa Aztlan, 1831 S. Racine, Chicago, (312) 666-5508.* One-day outdoor street festival at Casa Aztlan, a multi-service community and cultural center, which was founded as the Howell Neighborhood House eighty years ago when Pilsen was a port of entry for thousands of Eastern Europeans. Through its various youth, family services, and education divisions, Casa Aztlan promotes self-determination within the Mexican community it now serves. The street fair is held the third Saturday in July from noon to 8:00 P.M.

Religious Observances

The Way of the Cross (Via Crucis), *Providence of God Church, 717 W. 18th Street, Chicago, (312) 226-2929.* Religion is a powerful, unifying force in Hispanic life; deeply rooted in mysticism, spirituality, and centuries-old traditions that succeeding waves of immigrants have carried with them into the northern cities of the U.S. On Good Friday, hundreds of worshippers from the eight Catholic parishes that serve the Pilsen community participate in the stirring dramatization of the Passion Play in the basement of the Providence of God Church, and a reenactment of the walk to "Calvary" (in this case, Harrison Park). The members of the cast are dressed in costume, and a mounted Roman centurion clears 18th Street so that the actors portraying Christ, the Virgin Mary, and the twelve Apostles, may proceed past hundreds of onlookers to Harrison Park. The Way of the Cross is a powerful affirmation of faith and a custom that dates back to antiquity. It was brought to Mexico by the conquering Spanish armies hundreds of years ago, and is recreated each year in the small ranches and rural villages high in the mountains. "Via Crucis" begins at 8 A.M. on Good Friday at the Providence of God Church, 18th and Union. (where, by the way, Pope John Paul conducted an open-air mass in 1979), and it concludes at St. Adalbert's Church, 1650 W. 17th Street, at 2 P.M. *Recommended.*

Day of Our Lady of Guadalupe, *Providence of God Roman Catholic Church, 717 W. 18th Street, Chicago, (312) 226-2929.* About 450 years ago, the Blessed Virgin appeared before a poor Mexican peasant named Juan Diego. She ordered the man to go before the bishop of Mexico City and to tell him to build a church in her honor. When the bishop twice refused, the Virgin again appeared, and caused roses to grow out of the rocks in the hills. The disbelieving bishop refused a third time. The image of the Virgin then appeared on Juan Diego's apron. Legend or miracle, call it what you will, but it remains the most important religious feast day in Mexico, and for that matter, in Chicago's Pilsen community as well. At the Providence of God Church, where so many Lithuanian parishioners once worshipped, the Pilsen community attends an evening mass conducted in Spanish by a visiting priest from Mexico. A mariachi band with three guitars, two violins, and a trumpet accompany the choir in the *magnanitas,* a hymn that speaks of faith, devotion, and hope. When the service has ended, Mexican pastries are served in the church basement. The evening service is conducted in December. Please call the church for the date and time.

Puerto Rican

Puerto Rican Day Parade, *Michigan Avenue, from Wacker Drive to Van Buren, the second Saturday in June.* There is no special significance attached to the date of the Puerto Rican community's gala event. It just happened to fit into the city of Chicago's prearranged schedule of cultural events, and has remained a yearly tradition since

1966. It's all about being Puerto Rican, and the heartfelt pride that goes with it. There is no political message or solemn anniversary to be commemorated, just a lively Caribbean salsa beat, an army of baton twirlers, the Roberto Clemente High School Marching band, beauty queens, 150 floats, and a score of dignitaries, which in 1991 included Chicago's treasurer Miriam Santos, who appeared with the grand marshal, Mayor Richard M. Daley. The parade and the accompanying festival held in Humboldt Park are sponsored each year by the Puerto Rican Parade Committee, which was losing money every year until Daniel Ramos took over in 1985 and reversed this pattern. A second Puerto Rican parade, more political in nature than this one, proceeds down North Avenue on the same day before winding up at Humboldt Park for the special festivities (see entry below). For information and dates, call the Puerto Rican Parade Committee at (312) 292-1414.

Fiestas Patronales Puertorriqueñas, *Humboldt Park, 1400 N. California Avenue, Chicago.*   A six-day outdoor festival marking Puerto Rican Week activities in Chicago, which coincides with the two major city parades. Over sixty food vendors dispense such Puerto Rican delicacies as codfish fritter, stew of pig's ears, and boiled green bananas. A midway carnival entertains the children, while older people relax under the shade playing bingo with their friends. Caribbean music performed by noted salsa musicians fills the air. Vendors from seventy-eight Puerto Rican cities exhibit their crafts, ranging from sculptured glass and pottery to leather work. Regardless of the weather, which usually tops out at a sultry ninety degrees, there's something here for everyone, evidenced by the 50,000 to 100,000 people who show up each year. Free admission. During the week, the celebration continues from 4 P.M. to 11 P.M.; weekends, from noon to midnight. Sponsored by the Puerto Rican Parade Committee, 1237 N. California, Chicago, (312) 292-1414.

Puerto Rican Parade Committee, Beauty Queen Pageant. It is quite an honor to be crowned "Queen for a Day," and the competition among the sixteen finalists hoping to represent Chicago's 120,000-strong Puerto Rican community on parade day is quite intense. Many of the contestants who vie for the coveted "satin sash" which guarantees them a $2,000 scholarship, a white sable coat, and round-trip tickets to Puerto Rico, are Americans unfamiliar with their own Hispanic heritage. Very often the grueling competition is a "baptism by fire." The girls are required to spend long hours studying their history, language, native dance, and folk traditions, while developing the necessary poise and charm to win the hearts of the judges. The annual pageant (and dinner, if the event is scheduled for a hotel ballroom) is held the last Saturday in May at the Chicago Theatre, 175 N. State Street, or the grand ballroom of one of the big downtown hotels. In addition to the coronation of the queen, big-name performers like Danny Rivera and Lourdes Robles—major celebrities in Puerto Rico—are flown in to entertain the audience. Ticket prices range from $10 to $50, and can be purchased through the Puerto Rican Parade Committee by calling (312) 292-1414.

Spanish

American-Spanish Dance Festival, presented by Ensemble Español, the premier Spanish dance company in the U.S. to have "in residence" status at a university—in this case Northeastern Illinois University, 5500 N. St. Louis Avenue, Chicago. The ensemble has presented thousands of performances throughout the U.S. in its brief fourteen-year history. Founded in 1976 by "Dama" Libby Komaiko Fleming (a Chicagoan of Russian-Lithuanian descent who performed in Jose Greco's company), the Ensemble promotes cultural pluralism at the community, state, national, and international levels, and collectively through the two-week American Spanish Dance Festival held each year in July on the Northeastern campus. Seminars, college credit classes, films and workshops highlighting all aspects of flamenco, classic, and folkloric dance are presented each day for two weeks in the summer. You can register for the day-time non-credit program for $175.00. Single classes are $18 each. Performances are given Tuesday through Thursday at 8 P.M.; Friday and Saturday at 8 P.M.; and Sundays at 3 P.M. Spanish films are shown on Monday evenings at 7 P.M. Contact Ensemble Español at (312) 583-4050, ext. 3015

Art Galleries

DeGraaf Fine Art, *9 E. Superior, Chicago, (312) 951-5180.* Paintings, sculpture, and folk art from Mexico, the Caribbean, and South America. The representative work of Alejandro Romero, and Fernando Ramos are previewed. Hours: Tuesday through Friday, 10 A.M. to 5:30 P.M. No credit cards.

Phyllis Kind, *313 W. Superior, Chicago, (312) 642-6302.* Special exhibitions during the year of European, Soviet, and Hispanic painters. Represents artists Martin Ramirez and Luis Jiminez. Hours: Tuesday through Saturday, 10 A.M. to 5:30 P.M.; Thursdays till 8 P.M.

Gallerie Thomas R. Monahan, *301 W. Superior, Chicago, (312) 266-7530.* Contemporary European art, with special emphasis on a Latin-American artist's colony in Paris that in recent years has produced some of the finest paintings in the surrealistic genre. This group of influential artists includes Carlos Aresti and Mario Murua of Chile, Eduardo Zamora and Heriberto Cogollo of Colombia, and Roberto Matta, an avante-garde painter considered by many to be the founder of surrealism. The Monahan gallery has a collection of the artist's work dating back to the 1930s. Hours: September through May, 10:30 A.M. to 6 P.M., Tuesday through Friday; Saturdays till 5 P.M. During the summer months the gallery is open by appointment only. Credit cards accepted.

A Guide to Hispanic Restaurants in Chicago

Spanish

Cafe Ba-Ba-Reeba, *2024 N. Halsted, Chicago, (312) 935-5000.* The pleasant decor and ambience of this restaurant make it a real favorite of Chicagoans who wait in line each night for seating. This is more than just a tapas (Spanish for "little dishes," or appetizers that should be shared) bar. The menu is substantial, ranging from the regional specialties of Spain such as grilled squid, paella, baked goat cheese, tuna cannelloni, and desert delicacies like bananas with caramel sauce and flan. Hours: Luncheon served Tuesday through Friday, 11:30 A.M. to 2:30 P.M.; Saturday till four; dinner, Monday through Thursday, 5:30 P.M. to 11 P.M.; Friday till midnight; Saturday, 5 P.M. to midnight; Sunday till 10:30 P.M. Credit cards accepted.

Emilio's Tapas Bar Restaurant, *4100 W. Roosevelt Road, Hillside, (708) 547-7177.* A pleasing taste of old Spain brought to you by Emilio Gervilla, who earned critical acclaim when he was a chef at Cafe Ba-Ba Reeba. The menu lists eighteen different tapas dishes with a complement of daily specials. Begin with the cold appetizers before moving on to the main entrees. Intimate, cozy, and highly recommended. Hours: Monday through Thursday, 11:30 A.M. to 10 P.M.; Friday, 5 P.M. to 11 P.M.; Saturday and Sunday till 10 P.M. Credit cards accepted.

Meson Sabika, *1025 Aurora Avenue, Naperville, (708) 983-3000.* Located in a quaint, old fashioned mansion in Naperville that was built in 1847. In Spanish the name means "house on the hill." And indeed, the three chandeliered dining rooms are as pretty as a postcard. Emilio Gervilla opened at this location in 1990. The menu is nearly identical to his place in Hillside, which is the sister restaurant. Hours: Sunday through Thursday, 11:30 A.M. to 11 P.M.; Friday and Saturday, 5 P.M. to 11 P.M. Credit cards accepted.

La Paella, *2920 N. Clark, Chicago, (312) 528-0757.* Items from the tapas menu (your best value) are served from Tuesday through Thursday and again on Sunday (all you can eat for $16). If you're planning a quiet, romantic dinner in a quaint Spanish setting, La Paella, which incidentally is also the "dish of Spain" is a good choice. Hours: dinner, Tuesday through Saturday, 5:30 P.M. to 10:30 P.M.; Sunday, 5 P.M. to 9 P.M. Credit cards accepted.

Tania's, *2659 N. Milwaukee, Chicago, (312) 235-7120.* Spanish and Cuban cuisine, with seafood as the house specialty. Be sure to try some of the gourmet Cuban food, like ropa vieja (shredded beef in tomato sauce) and lechon asado (roast pork). Latin dancing and music till 4 A.M. Lambada, merengue. Hours: open every day from 11 A.M. to 4 A.M. Valet parking. Credit cards accepted.

Caribbean

Caribbean Delight, *7303 N. Damen, Chicago, (312) 743-2900.* Jamaican food at its best, though the service can be somewhat slow at times. Spice steak, curried goat, and jerk chicken are some of the house specialties. Hours: Tuesday through Thursday, 5 P.M. to 10 P.M.; Friday and Saturday till 11:30 P.M.; Sunday 4:30 P.M. to 9:30 P.M. No credit cards.

Blue Mountain Cafe, *3517 N. Clark, Chicago, (312) 248-1111.* Clark Street contains an incredible melange of ethnic restaurants to tempt even the most discriminating palate. The Blue Mountain Cafe, featuring fine Jamaican cuisine, is yet another example. The restaurant features an all-you-can-eat vegetarian buffet for $6.95 on Tuesdays and Thursdays. Hours: Tuesday through Thursday, 5 P.M. to 11 P.M.; Friday, 5 P.M. to midnight; Saturday 2 P.M. to midnight; Sunday, 2 P.M. to 11 P.M. Credit cards accepted.

Mexican

Su Casa, *49 E. Ontario, Chicago, (312) 943-4041.* A long-time Chicago favorite that seems to improve with age. The food is still a bargain, despite its location in one of the priciest neighborhoods in town. The standard Mexican dishes; shrimp chimichanga, enchiladas, and chicken fajita are recommended. Hours: Monday through Thursday, 11:30 A.M. to 11 P.M.; Fridays till midnight; Saturday, noon to midnight. Closed on Sunday. Credit cards accepted.

Frontera Grill, *445 N. Clark, Chicago, (312) 661-1434.* For people who really know their Mexican food. This North Side eatery is owned by Rick and Deann Groen Bayless, authors of a cookbook listing recipes for dozens of regional dishes from the "Heart of Mexico." Hours: luncheon served from 11:30 A.M. to 2:30 P.M., Tuesday through Friday; Saturday brunch 10:30 A.M. to 2:30 P.M.; dinner, Tuesday through Thursday, 5:20 P.M. to 10 P.M.; and till 11 P.M. on Friday and Saturday. Closed Sunday and Monday. Credit cards accepted. *Recommended.*

Mestizo Fonda Mexicana, *311 W. Superior, Chicago, (312) 787-4160.* Musical entertainment on the week nights provides a pleasing backdrop as you sample the regional cuisine of Mexico in a subdued setting in the River North area. The fiesta dinner is particularly good, with a variety of roasted meats, and so is the *mojo de ajo* (shrimp). Hours: 11 A.M. to midnight. Closed Sunday. Credit cards accepted.

Lindo Mexico, *2642 N. Lincoln, Chicago, (312) 871-4832.* Festive atmosphere, new menu items, and reasonable prices complement the existing charm of this restaurant. Recommended dishes include garlic sauteed shrimp or boneless chicken served with toasted ancho chilis, lime, and cilantro. Hours: Sunday through Thursday, 11 A.M. to 2 A.M.; Friday and Saturday till 4 A.M. Credit cards accepted.

Las Palmas, *1773 W. Howard, Chicago, (312) 262-7446.* Fine Mexican cuisine at reasonable prices. Live entertainment Wednesday through Saturday. Hours: Monday through Thursday, 11 A.M. to midnight; Friday through Saturday till 1 A.M.; Sunday noon to midnight. Credit cards accepted.

Topolobampo, *445 N. Clark, Chicago, (312) 661-1434,* Adjacent to the Frontera Grill, and named for a Pacific Coast town, Rick Bayless's latest creation comes highly recommended. The Mexican dishes, as prepared by Rick and Deann are original and savory. Hours: Tuesday through Thursday, 5:30 P.M. to 10 P.M.; Friday and Saturday, 5:30 P.M. to 11 P.M.; closed Sunday and Monday. Credit cards accepted.

Los Panchos, *901 W. Armitage, Chicago, (312) 871-2232.* Homemade authentic Mexican dishes prepared with the family touch. Casual but surprisingly elegant dining. Hours: Sunday through Thursday, 11 A.M. to midnight; Friday and Saturday, 11 A.M. to 2 A.M. Credit cards accepted.

Concordia Restaurant and Nightclub, *3801 W. 26th, Chicago, (312) 521-4095.* Mexican cuisine with a special emphasis on sea food and parrillada. The small dance floor can get very crowded on the weekends, when the live entertainment appears. For a quiet Mexican lunch at very reasonable prices, it's best to stop by on a Saturday afternoon, when the waiters have little else to do but to gaze out at the street traffic. Hours: 9 A.M. to 2 A.M. every day except Tuesday.

La Fonda Del Recuerdo, *3756 W. 26th Street, Chicago, (312) 521-8444.* Cafe-style restaurant and banquet hall. Mexican cuisine. Hours: daily from 7 A.M. to 3 A.M. No credit cards.

Peruvian

La Llama, *2666 N. Halsted, Chicago, (312) 327-7756.* Angel Asturrizaga and his wife Nelly lovingly attend to every detail in this charming South American hacienda, featuring a variety of seasoned meat dishes, seafood, and homemade tamales. Hours: daily, 5 P.M. to 11 P.M. Credit cards accepted.

Rinconcito Sudamericano, *1954 W. Armitage, Chicago, (312) 489-3126.* A storefront location that serves hearty portions of seafood and shellfish to beef, veal, and lamb. If you order a dinner for two, you'll be able to experience the full spectrum of Peruvian cooking. Hours: Tuesday through Thursday, 1 P.M. to 10 P.M.; Friday and Saturday, noon to 10:30 P.M.; Sunday, till 9:30 P.M. Credit cards accepted.

Guatemalan

El Tinajon, *4638 N. Western, Chicago, (312) 878-5862.* Serving both Mexican and Guatemalan dishes in a tiny, storefront location. The prices are low, typically $4.50 to $11 per person, and the variety of menu items are bound to please. Hours: Sunday and Monday and Wednesday and Thursday, 11 A.M. to 10 P.M.; Friday and Saturday till 11:00 P.M. Credit cards accepted.

Argentine

El Criollo, *1706 W. Fullerton, Chicago, (312) 549-3373.* A unique blend of South American food served up by Margarita Porto, an immigrant from Buenos Aires. The parrilladas (an assortment of beef, meats, and sweetbreads) are recommended. Hours: Monday, 4 P.M. to 10 P.M.; Tuesday through Thursday, noon to 10 P.M.; weekends till 11:30 P.M. Credit cards accepted.

Casa España, *3137 W. Logan Boulevard, Chicago, (312) 772-0441.* Spanish, Argentine, Mexican, and Cuban entrees served at this neighborhood restaurant in the Humboldt Park community. The Spanish tapas and seafood menu items are recommended. Live music after 8 P.M. on Fridays and Saturdays. Other hours: Monday through Friday, 11 A.M. to 11 P.M.; Saturday and Sunday, 3 P.M. to 2 A.M. Credit cards accepted.

Cuban

Little Havana, *3006 N. Sheffield, Chicago, (312) 929-3370.* Located in a tiny, but certainly recognizable, Cuban neighborhood, Little Havana specializes in sumptuous seafood dishes as well as the standard black beans and yucca. From Friday through Sunday, a guitar player entertains in the evening. Hours: Tuesday through Friday, 11 A.M. to 10 P.M.; till midnight on Saturday and Sunday. Closed Monday. Credit cards accepted.

La Lechonera, *2529 N. Milwaukee, Chicago, (312) 772-6266.* Cuban and South American entrees. Musicians entertain from 9 P.M. to 1 A.M. on Saturdays. Other hours: Monday through Friday, noon to 10 P.M.; Saturdays till 2 A.M.; Sundays till 10:00 P.M. Credit cards accepted.

Ambassador Cafe, *3605 N. Ashland, Chicago, (312) 404-8770.* At first glance, you wouldn't think that a restaurant with the unlikely name of Ambassador Cafe is a preferred choice for gourmet Cuban cuisine. Actually, the name was inherited from the previous owners, but Omelio Rodriguez decided to retain the moniker when he took over in 1990. The restaurant is small, but the menu items are very savory. Cuban sandwiches, a variety of seafood items, and meat entrees are included on the menu. You should also sample a "mamey" milkshake, made from South American fruits. Hours: Monday through Saturday, 10 A.M. to 9 P.M. Closed on Sunday

Restaurant and Nightclub

Casa España, *3137 W. Logan Boulevard, Chicago, (312) 772-0441.* Piano and guitar players entertain on Friday, Saturday, and Sunday evenings. Hours: daily from 11 A.M. to 11 P.M. Credit cards accepted.

Mestizo Fonda Mexicana, *311 W. Superior, Chicago, (312) 787-4160.* Large spacious room features a dance floor in the middle and plenty of Latin music supplied by visiting orchestras and bands on Friday and Saturdays, 9 P.M. to 1 A.M., and Sunday from 6:30 P.M. to 10:30 P.M. Other hours: Monday through Friday, 11 A.M. to 10:30 P.M.; Saturday till 1 A.M., and Sunday till 9:30 P.M.

Decima Musa, *1901 S. Loomis, Chicago, (312) 243-1556.* A cozy Pilsen restaurant with occasional entertainment on the weekends. There are definite language barriers to be overcome if you are not fluent in Spanish. Hours: Tuesday through Sunday, 11 A.M. to midnight. Closed on Monday. Credit cards accepted.

Rio's Casa Iberia, *4611 N. Kedzie, Chicago, (312) 588-7800.* Latin jazz music and other entertainments are scheduled for most evenings. Thursday is always "Tango Night" at this pleasant restaurant and show lounge. Hours: open Monday through Saturday from 5 P.M. to 2 A.M. Closed on Sunday.

Pilsen: The Color of a
═══ Great Historic Neighborhood ═══

Chicago, for all of its individual might and "I Will" entrepreneurial spirit, is no more than the sum total of its parts; a delicate weave of interlocking communities separated by culture, ideology, and the tide of history. Neighborhoods become half-way houses, receiving the poor, the hungry, and the uprooted masses in search of a better way. Pilsen is the most often referred to as the "Port of Entry," and with good reason. The Irish and the Germans arrived first, and soon provided a steady and dependable work force for the brickyards and small manufacturing concerns that sprang up along the south branch of the Chicago

River. After the 1871 fire, displaced Bohemians from other parts of the city and from Europe began pouring into the neighborhood, which had miraculously escaped the conflagration. The Bohemians were joined by Lithuanians, Poles, Slovenians, and Italians within a few short years.

The Bohemians shaped the direction of the community for seventy years. Their historic presence can still be felt on 18th Street, if only in the architecture. Like dinosaur bones unearthed from a long forgotten age, these wonderful old stone buildings are a last testament to Chicago's "age of empire." With a little imagination, it is possible to visualize the Czech craftsmen applying the final touches to the elaborate cornices and mansard roofs of the remarkably well-preserved nineteenth century storefronts and two-flats that loom over 18th Street west of Halsted. Pilsen has endured the profound changes that altered the character of the South Side since the 1920s. Massive construction of public housing units, the corresponding deterioration of neighborhoods, and the exodus of industry exacted a heavy toll on much of the surrounding neighborhoods, until all that remains, really, are Pilsen and sections of Bridgeport to stand as testa-

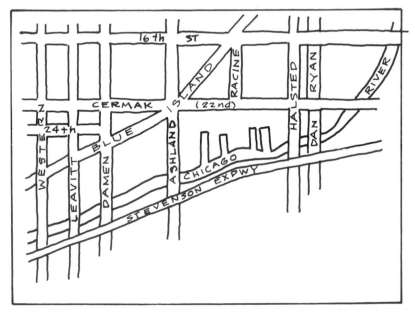

Pilsen and Little Tuscany

ments to the currents of history. The churches of Pilsen are cathedrals of hope for the individual who is trapped in the industrial corridor of a tough city. St. Procopius, at 18th and Allport, was designed in 1883 by Paul Huber for the Czechs. St. Adalbert's at 17th and Paulina is done in an enduring beaux arts style with clock towers and pink Corinthian columns. The church that has withstood the test of time once served the Polish community of Pilsen. The Providence of God Church at 18th and Union was Lithuanian. Today it is almost entirely Mexican.

Pilsen continues to be a "stopping-off point," a temporary way station before the rich harvest. With ingenuity, thriftiness, gritty determination, and a little luck, many of the Mexican residents who arrived here from the central highlands in the 1950s have already moved farther south to the slightly more upscale "Little Village," or to western and northern suburbs such as Waukegan. Those who remain behind channel their efforts toward community improvement. Amid the specter of abandoned factories and vacated manufacturing plants that once provided an important source of continuing employment for the European immigrants, there are hopeful signs of economic turnaround (The old Schoenhofen Brewery at 18th and Canalport is a good example. It is boarded up now, even though the building has been placed on the National Historic Register) A flourishing artists' colony centered near 18th and Halsted provides an important, emerging outlet for creative expression on the Southwest Side. It was founded by John Podmajersky in the 1960s, after he failed in his efforts to sell a renovated tavern. Instead, the second generation Pilsen native converted the building into a studio loft and within a few short years he was joined by other working artists, writers, and photographers who established residence between 18th and 19th streets. Each year in October the "Pilsen East Artists" sponsor an open house in the 700-block of West 18th Street, and the 800-block of West 19th Street, in which the public is invited to attend a special showing of the artists' work.

The Pilsen Neighbors Community Council combines the resources of numerous neighborhood organizations. It seeks to promote the collective good through voter registration drives, the construction of a new field house and gymnastic center at Harrison Park, and the "New Homes For Chicago" program. (The housing program was launched by Mayor Richard M. Daley to provide affordable housing for community residents.) Founded in the 1950s, when the neighborhood was still essentially Eastern European in its character, Pilsen Neighbors is the only community-based organization in the city to be funded under the terms of the "New Homes For Chicago" program. The Pilsen Neighbors Community Council is a powerful voice of hope within the inner city.

On September 7, 1989, the Rudy Lozano branch of the Chicago Public Library was officially dedicated at 1805 S. Loomis Street after years of bureaucratic footdragging and delay. The results were certainly worth the wait. The graceful lines of the new library feature a pre-Columbian terra cotta design inside and out, and a twenty-five-foot-high glass dome skylight arching over a Royal Fan palm tree. Named in honor of the Twenty-Second Ward community activist who was gunned down by a reputed gang member in June, 1983, the building houses the largest Spanish-language collection in the city's library system, including books, newspapers, magazines, and audio-visual cassettes.

As you stroll 18th Street, the blare of Latin music can be heard from inside the Victorian buildings. From the second floor windows, young children and old men gaze down at the passing street traffic. In the hot days of summer, few people can afford air conditioning. As you walk past the family-owned "taquerias" (grocery stores), department stores, and corner taverns advertising "cerveza fria" (cold beer) on a warm afternoon, your appetite is whetted for another helping of Mexican food. Street vendors are there to oblige, selling floury Mexican pastries from pushcarts. The walk-up windows dispense tacos and hot corn on the cob, spiced with lemon and hot pepper. You linger for only a moment, and then continue on to preview raw, creative expressionism at its finest.

Twenty hand-painted wall murals depicting historical, cultural, religious, and political themes are scattered throughout Pilsen. They include the murals at 1305 W. 18th Street; the 16th Street viaduct (near Blue Island); Casa Aztlan at 18th and Racine, where portraits of Mexican and Latin leaders adorn the exterior wall; Miller and 18th; and, finally, another artistic motif at 18th and Blue Island. The murals came into being during the 1960s and 1970s and were executed by such artists as Ray Patian and Aurelio Diaz.

A Marxist-Leninist book store near Ashland Avenue and 18th Street is a gentle reminder of the political discontent that has simmered beneath the surface of this community for several years. In this regard, the Mexican community of Pilsen carries on the historic traditions of dissent that began with the Bohemian socialists in July, 1877. During the tense days of the nationwide railroad strike, they had rioted for better wages and a shortened work week at the 16th and Halsted viaducts.

Getting There: The CTA Congress-Douglas line stops at 18th Street in Pilsen. Busses run along Cermak (#21 begins at Lake Shore Drive and 21st Street), and 18th Street (#18, begins at Michigan and 18th). By car, exit the southbound lanes of the Dan Ryan Expressway at 18th Street and proceed west.

Bienvenidos a Little Village:
══ The "Suburbs" of Pilsen ══

At first glance, the old South Lawndale neighborhood seems like an unlikely place to resurrect the American dream of home ownership, two chickens in every pot, and a shiny new Ford in the garage. Because as you will observe in your walking tour, the ominous looking Metropolitan Corrections Center at 26th and California stands opposite the festive gateway arch that leads into the "Pueblo Pequeño" (Little Village). The solemnity of the jail, its barbed wire walls and imposing guard towers offer an unsettling, yet conspicuous contrast to the inner vitality of 26th Street—The "Calle Mexico"—the shopping, restaurant, and nightclub area between the Little Village Mall at Albany, and the Chicago Central Industrial Park further west at Kostner Avenue.

The Little Village began filling up with Mexicans in the 1950s. Most had migrated from nearby Pilsen, and in all likelihood would have continued to move farther westward into Cicero and Berwyn if not for the prevailing social attitudes toward minorities in those two suburbs. Making the best of a tough situation, the Mexican community has prospered in its Southwest Side surroundings. Property values continue to rise, and the storefronts along 26th Street are nearly at full occupancy. Old-fashioned inner city retailers like Goldblatt's and Three Sisters continue to serve a predominately Hispanic clientele. In other neighborhoods, these kinds of stores are boarded up, burned out and deserted shells—grim reminders that the economic well-being of some neighborhoods has been sapped by the influx of gangs, crime, and poverty. But in the Little Village, Goldblatt's, a respected name in Chicago retailing for generations, seems to be making a go of it.

The merchants, supported by an enthusiastic Chamber of Commerce and Community Council, promote the stability and togetherness of the Little Village, reflected in the colorful wall murals—far less political than the outdoor artwork of Pilsen—which are located at the Bank of Chicago, 26th and Homan; 25th and St. Louis; 25th and Pulaski at the Second Federal Savings; and in back of the Los Camales Restaurant at 26th and Kedzie, opposite McDonald's. The "Broken Wall Mural," as it is called, was painted by the Marshall Savage Boys and Girls Club. The message of faith is poignant in its simplicity: "Beyond the walls of doubt there is a great reward that can only be reached through faith in God." The most visible landmark in the community is the welcome arch next to the Little Village Mall at Albany and 26th. The pink-colored gateway, which in some ways is reminiscent of the Chinatown arch, was financed by local subscription and private donation. The formal dedication ceremony took place on April 30, 1990. A year later on April 11, 1991, the President of Mexico, Carlos Salinas de Gortari, inaugurated the clock before 2,000 well wishers and city officials including Mayor Richard M. Daley during a state visit. As a symbol of good will between the two respective nations, this stretch of 26th Street was rechristened the "Calle Mexico."

The storefronts are well-maintained family businesses, due in part to a city and federal Facade Rebate Program, which provides financial and technical assistance to the owners and tenants of buildings that have street-level commercial space. The improvements listed under the rebate program are intended to promote and revitalize Chicago's neighborhood commercial retail areas, which have suffered a slow decline since the advent of the large suburban shopping malls. The independent merchants of 26th Street sell wearing apparel, books and records, and imported grocery items from Mexico. The owners of these establishments often find themselves in friendly competition with street-corner hustlers hawking sharply discounted music cassettes from Mexico, fresh fruit, and tee-shirts. copies of *El Mañana,* as well as *La Raza*—the largest circulating Hispanic newspaper in the city—can be purchased in the stores or in the corner boxes. *La Raza* and the seven Spanish-language community papers provide the only link to the distant culture of Mexico, valiantly preserved here in the Little Village.

In many respects the neighborhood mirrors Chinatown in its expansive economic growth, but it is much less touristy. You will not find the proliferation of gift shops selling inexpensive souvenir paraphernalia and gadgets, however restaurants and Mexican nightclubs may abound. In fact, you'll find two, three, maybe even four restaurants, ranging from fast food to quasi elegant, on every block. The difference is in the clientele. Since the Little Village is an undiscovered treasure, the owners cater, for the most part, to the neighborhood residents. That may all change if and when the plans for the Plaza de Mexico, a $30 million shopping mall, go through. The idea for a 351,000 square foot plaza was put forward by the Matanky Realty Company on Halsted Street. The developers encountered a storm of protest in 1990 from the 600 businessmen and businesswomen, who fear that the long-term consequences of such a mall would destroy their livelihood and the viability of the community. Young boys selling wholesale cassettes on the street is one thing. A well publicized real estate development costing millions of dollars is something else again. The Chicago Central Industrial Park continues to occupy the site until the matter can be resolved one way or the other.

With or without the addition of the first "Mexican Theme Mall" in the Midwest, the future of the Little Village seems assured for the time being.

Even though the number of votes cast during a typical city election is the smallest, percentagewise, in the city, that phenomenon is partly explainable by the large population of young children and adolescents who now reside in the Twenty-Second Ward. Once they come of age, they alone will determine the destiny of this blue-collar Chicago neighborhood that was once known as "Ceska California" in the days when Anton Cermak greeted his Bohemian neighbors on the street. Will the next generation of Mexicans choose to remain behind and preserve the indigenous Hispanic culture, or will this Little Village be absorbed into the whole, its boundaries virtually indistinguishable from its tragically blighted neighbor, North Lawndale? Only time, and the unpredictable patterns of neighborhood settlement can provide a clue.

Shopping Guide

The Little Village is a bustling commercial district extending for several miles down 26th Street. Begin your walking tour at the Little Village Mall at Albany and 26th Street, and proceed west. The best time to experience the "south-of-the-border" flavor of the community is to preview it on a Saturday afternoon, when the local residents shop the flea markets and go about their daily business. Space limitations prevent us from listing all of the retail stores and restaurants on the strip. We have included only a sample of the most interesting ones here.

Bakeries

Panaderia Bakery, *3117 W. 26th Street, Chicago, (312) 254-0006.* An unusual self-service bakery located in the Little Village Mall. Select from an assortment of Mexican Pastries, bismarcks, and donuts, which are arranged along the walls. The metal serving trays are available at the counter. Hours: daily, from 5 A.M. to 10 P.M.

El Nopal Mexican Bakery, *3648 W. 26th, Chicago, (312) 762-9204, and 1844 S. Blue Island, Chicago, (312) 226-9861.* Fancy puff-dough pastries, wedding cakes, and sweet rolls. Two locations in the Little Village and Pilsen. Hours: daily from 10 A.M. to 5 P.M.

Coral Bakery, *3807 W. 26th, Chicago, (312) 762-4132.* Cookies, pound cakes, sliced and buttered bread, and tarts for every occasion. Hours: Monday through Friday, 5 A.M. to 9 P.M.; Saturday, 5 A.M. to 7:30 P.M.; Sunday, 7 A.M. to 7:30 P.M.

El Charrito, *3424 W. 26th, Chicago, (312) 522-8121.* Mexican cookies, fancy pastries and cakes. Hours: Monday through Saturday, 5 A.M. to 10 P.M.; Sunday till 8 P.M.

Grocery

Supermercados "La Justicia," *3644 W. 26th, Chicago, (312) 277-6148 and 3435 W. 26th, Chicago, (312) 521-1593.* T wo friendly neighborhood grocery stores owned by Ruby, Julio and Sergio Martinez. Imported food items from Mexico, fresh produce, canned goods, Spanish-language magazines and newspapers. Hours: daily from 7 A.M. to 10 P.M.

Armando's Finer Foods, *2627 S. Kedzie, Chicago, (312) 927-6688.* Mexican supermarket with a full line of imported foods, bakery items, meats, produce, and magazines. Hours: Monday through Friday, 8 A.M. to 10 P.M.; Saturday and Sunday, 7 A.M. to 10 P.M.

Books, CD's, and Videos

Rolo's Video, *3800 W. 26th Street, Chicago, (312) 277-2362.* Rolando G. De La Vega rents Spanish language and standard English titles every day from 11 A.M. to 10 P.M.

Libreria Giron, *3527 W. 26th Street, Chicago, (312) 521-5651.* Spanish-language books and magazines, CD's, cassettes, greeting cards, and newspapers. Hours: daily, 10 A.M. to 8 P.M.

Video Mexico, *4204 W. North Avenue, Chicago, (312) 384-7758.* Not exactly in the Little Village, but this Northwest Side location stocks thousands of Spanish-language films from Mexico that are available for rental only. There are some American films dubbed in Spanish. Hours: daily from 10 A.M. to 10 P.M.

Video Latino, *3511 W. Armitage, Chicago, (312) 276-0373.* A full line of rental movies from Spain, Mexico, Puerto Rico, and South America. Hours: Monday through Friday, 11 A.M. to 10 P.M.; Saturday and Sunday, 10 A.M. to 11 P.M.

Native American
Chicago

══════ History and Settlement ══════

Twenty-five thousand Native Americans, representing forty different tribes
from across the country (but mostly drawn from the Chippewa, Winnebago, Sioux, Potawatomi, and Ottawa tribes) struggle to make ends meet
in the congested Uptown neighborhood of Chicago. Prior to 1950, there
were only 775 American Indians living in Chicago, according to available
census figures. As a result of a Congressional federal relocation program
that began in the early 1950s, the figures increased steadily. The U.S.
government encouraged American Indians to abandon tribal reservations
in order to gain valuable work skills and begin a new and hopefully more
productive life in the large urban corridors of Chicago and Los Angeles—
the two main relocation centers selected by the Bureau of Indian Affairs.
Today Chicago ranks third behind San Francisco and Los Angeles among
the large cities in the reported number of Native American residents.

The misguided "termination/relocation" program, aimed at "getting the
government out of the Indian business" and breaking up long-standing
reservations, reached its heyday between 1951 and 1972. In 1972
the program officially ended. However, the "general allotment" policy

failed in its stated goals. Very often the jobs awaiting the American Indian in the designated city were nonexistent, and the prospects for enrolling in an accredited vocational school exceedingly slim. Receiving little more than a pat on the pack, a wallet sized I.D. card that categorized him as an "enrolled" member of a tribe, a one-way bus ticket, and $45 in spending money, the displaced Native American very often found himself suddenly abandoned and alone in Chicago. For Stephen Horman, an American Eskimo who came to Chicago in 1969, the only indoctrination he received was a CTA route map of the city, and fifteen minutes of agency time.

Life in this rugged urban frontier has been an endless series of compromises between doing what is right and living from day to day. Unemployed parents stare out or their tenement windows unhappily as their children spend endless hours feeding quarters into the video arcade machines on Wilson Avenue, while groups of men huddle together underneath the Jackson Park elevated line in order to keep the swirling March winds that whip off the lake from searing their skin. Alcohol abuse. Poverty. Lines at the unemployment office. These all-too-familiar images of despair have acutely affected the Native American population of Chicago in many profound ways.

Amid the deprivation of Uptown there are hopeful signs that the proud Indian heritage has not been sacrificed. The American Indian Center, founded in 1953 at 411 N. La Salle, but eventually relocated to a converted Masonic Hall at 1630 W. Wilson, has sponsored many worthwhile cultural events over the year to benefit their senior citizen, youth, and social services program. The Center continued the important mission of the Indian Council Fire, a social services agency that existed from 1923 through World War II. It differed in one major respect: the American Indian Center was created specifically for the purpose of meeting the needs of the relocation Indians arriving in Chicago for the first time. The presence of the American Indian Center is a major reason why the Native American population remains anchored to Uptown. In a similar vein, the All-Nations Assembly of God Church at 1126 W. Granville began its ministry in April 1981, and has served the Chicagoland Native American community as a part of approximately 160 worship centers across the U.S. The ministry communicates the gospel to every tribe represented in the city and has sponsored training seminars, family-oriented social events, and counseling centers.

Incorporated on May 17, 1974, the Native American Educational Services (NAES) College at 2838 W. Peterson Avenue, offers an academic program leading to a B.A. degree in community services for persons employed in American Indian programs and agencies. Affiliated with Antioch University, NAES College emphasizes the cultural and historic traditions of the tribal and Indian communities, and teaches the requisite skills to begin professional work. In this sense, the Native American is made to feel that he or she is an important part of the social milieu of Chicago, rather than strangers in their own land.

Ethnic Museums

Mitchell Indian Museum, *on the campus of Kendall College, 2408 Orrington Avenue, Evanston, (708) 866-1395.* As a small boy, John Mitchell was fascinated by the history and culture of the Indian tribes of the Great Lakes and the Plains. His uncle served as an Indian agent in Oklahoma, and when John came to visit him one year, he was presented with several genuine Indian artifacts, which were to form the basis of a collection that was to grow to more than 2,000 pieces. John Mitchell was a successful businessman who was president of his own realty company and a trustee of Kendall College. When he retired in 1977, the extensive collection of Indian art and artifacts was turned over to the school, so that the whole community could benefit from his gift through ongoing exhibits, workshops, lecture, and an archive library. Betty Mitchell provided a generous endowment which enabled the college to turn her husband's vision into reality. The collection of items is maintained by curator Jane Edwards, and it illustrates Native American life through pottery, basketry, clothing, textiles, bead and quillwork, from four cultural areas: the Plains, Western Great Lakes, the Pueblo, and the Navajo. A children's table invites youngsters to experience history and folklore through the sense of touch, sight, and smell. Youngsters can build their own teepee, grind corn, or spin wool just as the Indians did.

A permanent collection of items dating back to 6000 B.C. right up to the twentieth century await the visitor to the Mitchell Indian Museum, one of the newest cultural attractions in the city. Hours: Monday through Friday, 9 A.M. to 4 P.M.; Sundays, 1 P.M. to 4 P.M. Closed in August. Donations are accepted, and memberships are available. To become a "Friend of the Mitchell Indian Museum," please designate from one of five categories: $25 (individual/family), $50 (donor), $100 (contributor), $500 (patron), or $1,000 (benefactor). Contributions are always tax deductible. *Recommended.*

Schingoethe Center For Native American Cultures, *Dunham, Hall, Aurora University, Aurora, IL 60506, (708) 844-5402.* Herbert Schingoethe shared John Mitchell's interest in Native American folklore. For much of his life he collected arrowheads and pottery, much of it unearthed from Kane and Du Page County farms. In 1960 Schingoethe began to manage ranches in Southwest Colorado, a job that afforded him the opportunity to roam through antique shops, Indian trading posts, and pawnshops. The collection grew until it numbered more than 3,000 objects. As a strong supporter of Aurora University, Schingoethe bequeathed much of his collection to the school. Dunham Hall, named in honor of his wife Martha's family, houses the collection of Southwest, Plains, Woodlands, Arctic, and Northwest Coast Indian artifacts in a 1,500 square feet area within the main gallery. The gallery was inaugurated in the fall of 1990, and is open to the public on Monday and Tuesday, and Thursday and Friday from 10 A.M. to 4 P.M.; and Sundays from 1 P.M. to 4 P.M.

Woodlands Native American Museum, *16860 S. Oak Park Avenue, Tinley Park, (708) 614-0334.* A small, little-known museum run by members of the Potawatomi Tribe, who were indigenous to the Northern Illinois region when the first of the French *voyageurs* surveyed the area in the seventeenth century. The museum is open Monday through Saturday, 9:30 A.M. to 6:30 P.M.; Sunday, noon to 5:30 P.M. Admission: Adults, $1.75; seniors age 60 and older, $1.00; children, 50 cents.

Webber Resource Center at the Field Museum of Natural History, *Main Floor, Roosevelt Road and Lake Shore Drive, Chicago, (312) 922-9410.* A reading room and center for Native American lore since 1987. The resource center also stocks videos, which are available for viewing. All in all, the museum's permanent collection of Indian costumes, artwork, hand-tools and weaponry fills seven halls. Hours: daily from 9 A.M. to 5 P.M., except Thanksgiving, Christmas, and New Years. Admission: $3 for adults, $2 for children. Free on Thursday.

The Logan Museum, *Beloit College, 700 College Street, Beloit, Wisconsin (608) 365-3391.* The museum houses a large and impressive collection of Indian artifacts and historical items. Hours: Friday through Sunday, noon to 5:00 P.M. Donations accepted.

The Winnebago Public Indian Museum, *3889 River Road, Wisconsin Dells, Wisconsin, (608) 254-2268.* A collection of Indian artifacts assembled by one family over the course of several generations. Avoid the touristy gift shops that sell fake Indian goods. You can buy beautiful Indian-made baskets at this location. Hours: Friday through Sunday, 9 A.M. to 5 P.M. Admission: adults, $2.00; children, $1.00.

Where to Purchase Indian Artwork, Books, and Giftware

Gifts

The American Indian Gift Store, *1758 W. Wilson Avenue, Chicago, (312) 769-1170.*   An American-Indian owned business specializing in authentic fine arts and crafts, including colorful and intricate beadwork from the plains tribes, handwoven rugs from the Southwest, Indian stationery and notecards, paintings, prints, and sand paintings by Native American artists, Indian records and tapes, bone carvings by Stanley Hill, Kachina dolls, and hand-signed Indian pottery. The store also does some custom-made work and repairs Indian jewelry. Hours: Monday through Wednesday, and Friday, noon to 6 P.M.; Thursday, noon to 9 P.M.; Saturday, 10 A.M. to 6 P.M.

Gall: Southwest Silver and Jewelry Co., *9014 W. 31st Street, Brookfield, (708) 387-0460.*   Southwestern and Native American jewelry items, rugs, and pottery. Hours: Monday through Saturday, 9 A.M. to 5 P.M. Credit cards accepted.

Art Galleries

Native American Art Gallery, *810 Dempster Street, Evanston, (708) 864-0400.*   Owner Mary L. Dwyer personally selects items for her collection during an annual buying expedition to the Southwest. Mary has lived among the Hopi, the Zuni, and the Blackfeet, and has gleaned an understanding of tribal customs and spirituality. She is able to pass on this appreciation of the Indian way to her customers as they shop for contemporary and antique Indian art, including pottery, baskets, rugs, drums, and lithographs (both original and limited editions). Hours: Tuesday through Saturday, 10 A.M. to 6 P.M.; Thursday, 10 A.M. to 8 P.M.; Sunday, noon to 5:00 P.M.

American West, *2110 N. Halsted, Chicago, (312) 871-0400.* Contemporary Southwestern art includes Native American lithographs, original oils, and some antique etchings dating back to 1875, basketry and beadwork. In business since 1979. Hours: Tuesday through Friday, noon to 6 P.M.; Saturday, 11 A.M. to 6 P.M. Credit cards accepted.

Southwest Trading Company, *211 W. Main Street, St. Charles, (708) 584-5107.* A gallery of Indian art from the Plains states and the Southwest. Water color, acrylics, basketry, pottery, weavings, and a collection of sand art from the Navajo. Hours: Monday and Tuesday, Thursday and Friday, 10 A.M. to 5:30 P.M.; Sunday, noon to 5:00 P.M. Credit cards accepted.

Southwest Expressions, *1459 W. Webster Place, Chicago, (312) 525-2626.* A different kind of Chicago art gallery specializing in contemporary Native American and Southwestern art. All media covered; including oils, basketry, lithographs, and pottery. Hours: Monday through Thursday, 11 A.M. to 6 P.M.; open until 8 P.M. Friday and Saturday and until 5 P.M. Sunday. Credit cards accepted.

Bookstore

NAES College Book Store, *2828 W. Peterson Avenue, Chicago, (312) 761-5000.* Chicago's only full-line Native American bookstore features paperbacks and children's books dealing with historical and contemporary aspects of Indian life in the U.S., contemporary fiction, poetry, and art. The bookstore serves the student body that is enrolled in the four-year liberal arts program, but is also open to the public Monday through Friday from noon to 7 P.M. Credit cards accepted.

Special Places

The Totem Pole (Kwanusila), in Lincoln Park east of Lake Shore Drive at Addison. During one of his forays to the Canadian Pacific Northwest in 1926, James L. Kraft, the founder of Kraft Foods, Inc., purchased a hand-carved totem pole with tribal symbols, family crests and mythological depictions created by the Northwest Coast Indians. Kraft donated the artifact, which dated back to the turn of the century, to the Chicago Park District for the enjoyment of the city's school children. The pole remained in its familiar location until 1985, when concern arose over the physical deterioration caused by Chicago's changing climates and air pollution. The original pole was taken down and returned to Canada that year. A wooden replica was carved by Tony Hunt and paid for by J.L.

Kraft. It has been chemically treated to withstand the elements and now stands in the same spot fronting Lake Shore Drive.

A Signal of Peace **statue,** located in Lincoln Park north of the Diversey Harbor entrance. The statue depicts a mounted Sioux Indian giving the traditional gesture of peace. Sculpted by Cyrus Edwin Dallin (1861-1944), *A Signal of Peace* was on display at the 1893 World's Fair. It was rescued from oblivion and donated to Chicago by Judge Lambert Tree, who incidentally lent his name to the Police Department's medal of valor.

The Bowman and the Spearman Statues, adjoining the Grant park entrance at Michigan Avenue and Congress Parkway. The towering Indian warriors silhouetted against the Chicago sunset provide a poignant, historical image of a distant time and place. Sadly, few if any Chicagoans pay much attention to these statues. They are taken very much for granted, except by a handful of out-of-town tourists, who are struck by their simple, yet majestic posture. They are the creation of renowned sculptor Ivan Mestovic (1883-1962) who was commissioned by the B.F. Ferguson Monument Fund to pay homage to the Native American. Erected in 1928, the Indians guard the entrance way to Grant Park, and were originally located on both sides of a stairway that was replaced in the 1940s in order to permit automobile traffic to flow through.

The Alarm, the first permanent monument to the Indians to be erected on Chicago Park District land was dedicated in Lincoln Park, east of present-day Lake Shore Drive (3000 North) on May 17, 1884. The bronze sculpture is the work of John J. Boyle (1851-1917), and it shows a man and a woman belonging to the Ottawa tribe. *The Alarm* was commissioned in 1880 by Martin Ryerson, a lumber magnate and commercial trader who worked with the Ottawa people early in his career. Ryerson was concerned that the artist present his figures only in the most favorable light, thus avoiding the usual prejudices against Indians common in those times.

NAES College, *2828 W. Peterson, Chicago.* The Native American Educational Services, Inc., is the only accredited institution of higher learning in the Chicago area specifically designed to provide a quality educational environment and job skills tailored to the need of the Native American resident. NAES offers a selection of courses in tribal languages, and at the Chicago campus, courses are taught in Menominee, Navajo, Lakota, and Ojibwe. Additional campuses are located on the Fort Peck Reservation, Poplar, Montana; Keshena, Wisconsin; and

Minneapolis, Minnesota. The student body is comparatively small in relation to other liberal arts colleges in the area. Between 1975 and 1988, 108 students were enrolled in the degree program. Thirty-five graduated. But NAES is not a conventional college. Most of the students are older, with the average age being 36.3. As a rule, the Native American student is usually the first member of his family to attend college, and therefore must balance the responsibilities toward the family and earning a livelihood with the burdens of higher education.

Annual Events

American Indian Center Annual Powwow, a three-day Native American festival held every year since 1953 during the second or third weekend in November at alternating locations, most recently the University of Illinois at Chicago, UIC Pavilion, 1150 W. Harrison Street. Since 1953 the American Indian Center has staged its annual powwow, which is regarded as a "unification ceremony," to promote the heritage and cultural diversity of the thirty to sixty tribes represented each year. Members of each tribe will don the ceremonial headgear and costumes unique to their region before performing native dances. The corn dance, for example, salutes the fall harvest, while the snake dance is performed in long lines. The fest also includes an arts and crafts promenade, displays of tribal clothing, vendors selling Native American foods such as corn soup, fried bread jams, Sioux blueberry pudding, and tacos. All proceeds from the event go toward the American Indian Center to help meet their yearly operating expenses. The "Grand Entry" procession begins on Friday night at 7 P.M.; Saturday at 1 P.M. and Sunday at noon. Admission is $6 for adults, and $3 for children, ages 6 to twelve. For dates and times call (312) 275-5871. *Recommended.*

Native American Arts and Crafts Festival, *1630 W. Wilson Avenue, Chicago, (312) 275-5871.* Each year since 1969, the American Indian Center has showcased the work of Native American artisans during a two-day exhibition in mid-May, which also features a dance exhibition, art gallery, and Indian foods in the gymnasium. The proceeds of this event benefit the many worthwhile programs of the American Indian Center, including youth and social services, and senior citizens' activities. Admission is free, but small donations are requested. Hours: Saturday, 10 A.M. to 10 P.M., and Sunday, 10 A.M. to 4 P.M.

Multi-Ethnic Festivals

Chicago Ethnic Fair. Three-day street fair, carnival, and crafts show held each year on the 5100 block of Western Avenue on the South Side during the first weekend in August. Neither rain nor the staggering humidity of August have deterred the promoters of this wide-ranging event celebrating Polish, Lithuanian, African-American, Croatian, and Irish culture from taking place as scheduled. The fair emphasizes the public services available to all Chicagoans, but it also features ethnic dance troops, specialty foods, and boutiques selling hand-made arts and crafts from the representative ethnic groups in attendance. For the children there is a petting zoo, carnival rides, and a magic show. Senior citizens may wish to play a game of bingo or take advantage of free medical testing and immunization shots available to all ages. Also on hand will be the Veteran's Administration to provide free health care to vets. The event is sponsored by the Chicago Ethnic Fair, Inc., a not-for-profit agency in cooperation with the City of Chicago. Hours: early afternoon until 11:30 P.M. Friday through Sunday. Free admission. Call (312) 585-6085.

Suburban Ethnic Fair. The Northwest Cultural Council sponsored its very first folk fair on the grounds of the Square D Company, at Roselle Road and Euclid in suburban Palatine on August 4, 1991. The family event is aimed primarily at providing a unique cultural and ethnic program for Northwest suburbanites who would not otherwise make the long drive into Chicago. The festival promotes ethnic music and dance, including Japanese Fujima and Spanish Flamenco. Also included in the afternoon's events are storytelling, gourmet ethnic foods, photography exhibits, and a giant raffle. The Cultural Council has established galleries in a number of large corporations, including Square D, Zurich-American Insurance, and the NBD Bank of Arlington Heights. Hours: 1 P.M. to 5 P.M. Times and location of subject to change. Call (708) 382-6922.

Chicago International Art Exposition, held at Donnelley International Hall, McCormick Place, 411 E. 23rd Street and the Lakefront, beginning the second weekend in May and continuing for five days, featuring the work of artists and craftsmen from around the world. The Art Expo is a premier cultural event that has been sponsored every year since 1979 by John Wilson's Lakeside Group. The show affords Chicagoans a rare opportunity to browse (and buy) the work of some of the world's most celebrated painters and sculptors of this generation, including Andy Warhol, Willem de Kooning, Claus Oldenburg, Ed Paschke, and the controversial Robert Maplethorpe. Hours: Friday through Monday, noon to 8 P.M., Tuesday, noon to 6 P.M. Admission: $12. Students and senior citizens, $7. A two-day ticket is available for $20; a five-day pass, for $45. Shuttle busses running approximately every twenty minutes are available on Michigan Avenue. Call the Lakeside Group at (312) 787-6858 for information about special exhibits.

Chicago International Film Festival. The festival has gained considerable stature in the last few years by attracting the big name directors and performers like Sophia Loren and Lina Wertmuller who introduce their work to enthusiastic Chicago audiences. The International Film Festival runs for approximately two weeks in mid-October, with over 100 different titles from around the world shown at the Music Box Theatre, 3733 N. Southport, (312) 871-6604; and the Fine Arts, 410 S. Michigan, (312) 939-3700. Festival promoters attempt to book the best (and sometimes the not-so-best) feature films, independent studies, documentaries, animation, and 3-D from the U.S., Europe, South America, Africa, and Asia. During the year, the Film Festival sponsors a grab bag of events, including a Summer Benefit in August with a wine and beer reception to follow, and various special screening at the city's art houses. Tickets to individual films shown during the festival run from anywhere from $6 to $10. For a schedule of events, check the local newspapers, or call (312) 644-FILM for a recorded message. *Recommended.*

European-American Festival *at Wicker Park, 1500 N. Damen, Chicago.* The European-American Association was organized early in 1991 to provide special assistance to newly arrived immigrants in the form of language instruction, educational support and job placement. The association sponsored its first day-long ethnic festival at Wicker Park on September 1, 1991, featuring food and musical entertainment representing the German, Italian, Polish, Lithuanian, Ukrainian, Yugoslav, Czech, and Romanian cultures. In addition to the many gourmet international foods available for purchase, visitors may also feast on standard U.S. and Mexican dishes from the various vendors in attendance. The European-American festival runs from noon to 10 P.M. on or about September 1, and is supported by the City of Chicago and the Mayor's Office of Special Events, and by local advertisers. The gala event promises to become one of Chicago's premier ethnic festivals in years to come. Free admission. For more information, call John Herman at (312) 324-5868, or write to the European-American Association at 2827 W. Division Street, Chicago.

Holiday Folk Fair, *Mecca Convention Center, 500 W. Kilbourn Avenue, Milwaukee, Wisconsin.* Third weekend in November. An international village and marketplace, featuring ethnic food, handicrafts, dance, costumes, and entertainment. This fair has been going strong since 1943. Admission is $7.00; $5.50 for children 6–12. Call 1-800-231-0903.

Chicago Humanities Festival. One day exploration through words, music, and art of the "alternative" cultures in Chicago. Readings by internationally known authors, lectures, and musical concerts. Held the second Sunday in November at various locations including the Art Institute, The Chicago Public Library Cultural Center, The Field Museum, and Orchestra Hall. Times and individual admission prices vary. Presented by the Illinois Humanities Council. Please call (312) 939-5212 for details.

Some Useful Phone Numbers and Addresses in Chicago

Activities and Events

City of Chicago, Office of Tourism	(312) 280-5740
Chicago Visitor Information Center at the "Here's Chicago" video exhibit at the Water Tower, 163 E. Pearson	1-800-ITS CHGO
Chicago Convention and Tourism Bureau	(312) 567-8500
Illinois Bureau of Tourism	(312) 793-2094
Illinois Information Center, 310 S. Michigan Ave.	1-800-223-0121
*Mayor's Office of Special Events	
(General Information)	(312) 744-3315
(24-Hour Hotline)	(312) 744-3370
Film and Entertainment	(312) 744-6415
Chicago Fine Arts Hotline	(312) 346-3278
Chicago Art Dealer's Association	(312) 649-0065
Chicago Music Alliance (classical concerts and opera)	(312) 987-9296

Concert Line (popular music concerts)	(312) 666-6667
Jazz Hotline	(312) 427-3300
Dance Hotline	(312) 419-8383
Curtain Call (24-hour theater schedule)	(312) 977-1755
ArchiCenter (Architectural Tours)	(312) 782-1776
Chicago Park District (Information)	(312) 294-2200

*Note: During the summer months in Chicago, there are musical concerts, art shows, folk festivals and street fairs held every weekend. The Special Events Hotline will keep you informed about what is going on around town.

Tickets

Ticketron	(312) 902-1919
	1-800-843-1558
	(312) 842-5387
Ticketmaster	(312) 559-1212

Hot Tix, 24 S. State Street, Chicago. (Discounted half-price tickets for the day of the performance can be purchased Mondays, noon to 6 P.M.; Tuesday through Friday, 10 A.M. to 6 P.M.; Saturday, 10 A.M. to 5 P.M. Cash only.)

Lodging

Hotel/Motel Association of Illinois	(312) 236-3473
Hot Rooms (discount hotel reservations)	(312) 468-7666

Getting Around

American United Cab	(312) 248-7600
Checker and Yellow Cab	(312) 829-4222
Flash Cab	(312) 561-1444
Amtrak	(312) 558-1075
	1-800 USA-RAIL

Greyhound/Trailways Bus Line	(312) 693-2474
	(312) 781-2900
Chicago Transit Authority (CTA) Information	(312) 836-7000
Regional Transit Authority (RTA) (Suburban and Outlying)	(312) 836-7000
Illinois Department of Transportation (IDOT)	DOT-INFO
METRA (Regional Commuter Rail System)	(312) 322-6777
Continental Bus Airport Service	(312) 454-7800
O'Hare International Airport	(312) 686-2200
Midway Airport (South Side)	(312) 767-0500

Car Rental

Downtown Locations

Avis:	214 N. Clark St.	(312) 782-6825
	430 S. Clark	(312) 922-7155
	401 E. Erie	(312) 482-8030
Hertz:	540 N. Michigan (Marriott Hotel)	(312) 329-0036
	200 N. Columbus Dr. (Fairmont Hotel)	(312) 861-9473
	9 W. Kinzie	(312) 372-7600
National:	203 N. LaSalle	(312) 236-2581

Chicago O'Hare Airport

Avis	(312) 694-5600
Hertz	(312) 686-7272
National	(312) 694-4640

Chicago Midway Airport

Avis	(312) 471-4495
Hertz	(312) 735-7272
National	(312) 471-3450

Tour Chicago

CTA Culture Busses: Here's a way to preview the city's major attractions without breaking your wallet. The Chicago Transit Authority provides special Culture Busses, operated on Sundays and holidays from May through September, which will take you on a special 75- to 90-minute guided tour of the neighborhoods. Choose from among three routes: the North Side, West Side, and South Side for $2.50 per person ($1.25 for children ages 7 to 12, and free for youngsters 7 and under), which allows you unlimited rides on all three routes for the entire day. The busses depart from in front of the Art Institute at Michigan Avenue and Adams Street every thirty minutes or so. For information call: (312) 836-7000, or from the suburbs, 1-800-972-7000. Here's what you will see:

Culture Bus North: Departs from the Art Institute every thirty minutes beginning at 10:55 A.M., and continuing all day until 4:55 P.M. The bus makes fifteen stops along the Gold Coast, including the Lincoln Park Zoo, the John Hancock Center, the Old Town Neighborhood, and the Chicago Historical Society.

Culture Bus South: Leaves the Art Institute every thirty minutes beginning at 10:30 A.M., up to 5 P.M. You'll see twelve points of interest on Chicago's South Side, including the Museum of Natural History, the Museum of Science and Industry, the DuSable Museum of African-American History, the Wentworth Avenue Chinatown, and the nearby Prairie Avenue Historic District where many of Chicago's most prominent socialites and LaSalle Street financial wizards resided in the nineteenth century.

Culture Bus West: Departs the Art Institute every half-hour beginning at 10:45 A.M., and continuing until 4:15 P.M. The tour covers the Near West, and Northwest Side. You'll see Greektown and Chicago's original Polish settlement near Milwaukee Avenue and the Kennedy Expressway (including the Polish Museum of America), and the Museum of Broadcast Communications.

Gray Line Sightseeing Tours, *500 S. Michigan Avenue, (312) 346-9506.* Comfortable air-conditioned busses depart from 33 E. Monroe Street every day at 9:30 A.M. and 1:30 P.M., with scheduled pickup at the major downtown hotels. Check with your concierge or doorman to find out the exact times. The standard three-hour tour includes visits to the lakefront, the Gold Coast and the South Side. The tours are conducted by multilingual guides.

American Sightseeing/Chicago. Two- or four-hour bus tours of the city with a knowledgeable guide on board to explain the many cultural attractions. The bus stops at several locations, including the Museum of Science and Industry and Michigan Avenue. Tours depart daily at 10 A.M. and 2 P.M. from the Congress Hotel, 530 S. Michigan. Price: adults, $13 to $20; children 5 to 14, half-fare. Call (312) 427-3100.

Wendella Sightseeing Boats. One-and-a-half-hour tour of the Lake Michigan shoreline and the Chicago River, embarks from the foot of the Wrigley Building at the northwest corner of the Michigan Avenue Bridge and the Chicago River every day at 10 A.M., 11:30 A.M., 1:15 P.M., 3 P.M., and 7:30 P.M. Additional weekend departures at 4:30 P.M. The cost is $8 for adults, and $4 for children. Through September 2 only. Call (312) 337-1446 for information.

Spirit of Chicago **Lakefront Cruises.** Tour the majestic Chicago lakefront and be entertained by a musical entertainment revue featuring the renowned *Spirit of Chicago* waiters and waitresses. Expert narration. Freshly prepared buffets. The boat departs from the south side of Navy Pier, Grand Avenue and the Lake, Monday through Saturday, noon to 2 P.M. Tickets for these day-time cruises are $14.68 to $29.35. Dinner-dance cruises are scheduled for Sunday through Wednesday, 7 P.M. to 1 A.M., June through August. The cost is $22.55 to $45 per person. Call (312) 836-7888.

Untouchable Tours: Chicago's Original Gangster Tours. The Chicago Office of Tourism bristles at the very mention of Al Capone and the city's lusty gangland past, but the Roaring Twenties legacy lives on. The Untouchable Tours takes you through some of the neighborhoods and back alleys where Prohibition mayhem occurred. The guided tour passes through Little Italy on Taylor Street, where you'll get to see "Deadman's Tree"; the old Maxwell Street ghetto; and up Milwaukee Avenue, where Machine-Gun Jack McGurn was mowed down in a bowling alley on February 14, 1936, the seventh anniversary of the St. Valentine's Day Massacre. Daytime tours begin at 10 A.M. at the Water Tower, Michigan and Pearson. The cost is $19 per person, credit cards accepted. Dinner-tour packages that include a 1920s floor show at Tommy Gun's Garage, 1239 S. State, are held on Friday evenings at

6:00 P.M.; Saturdays, 5:00 P.M; Sundays, 4:00 P.M. The cost is $47 per person. Call (312) 881-1195 for additional information.

Let It Be Known Historical Black Chicago Tour. A tour of the historic African-American neighborhoods and historic sites. Included in the tour is an ethnic lunch and visit to the DuSable Museum, and a black trivia quiz. There are other tours included on the schedule. The city bus tour departs every Saturday at 10 A.M. and 3 P.M. The price is $28 per person. For additional information please call (312) 326-6716 or write to Let It Be Known Cultural Tours, 639 E. 92nd Street, Chicago.

Chicago Jewish Historical Society Bus Tours. Throughout the summer months, the Chicago Jewish Historical Society sponsors a series of day-long bus tours on Sundays to significant locations in the city pertaining to the early Jewish settlement of the community. The "Chicago Jewish Roots" guided tour explores the history of Maxwell Street, Lawndale, Humboldt Park, Logan Square, Albany Park, and the Rogers Park neighborhoods. A "Summer Safari" to Northwest Indiana winds its way through Hammond, Michigan City, and Gary, and makes periodic stops at some of the local synagogues. An excursion through the "Southern Suburbs" takes you through Homewood, Olympia Fields, and Flossmoor. The history of the Jewish movement in Chicago and its surrounding suburbs is discussed by local experts, including the retired University of Illinois professor, Dr. Irving Cutler. The cost of these tours ranges from $14 to $34 for adult members, and $7 to $29 for children. Advance reservations are always necessary. Please call (312) 663-5634 for information.

Help

Travelers and Immigrants Aid, 2732 N. Kedzie   (312) 489-7303

The Consulates

Austria, 400 N. Michigan   (312) 222-1515

Belgium, 333 N. Michigan   (312) 263-6624

Great Britain, 33 N. Dearborn	(312) 346-1810
Canada, 310 S. Michigan	(312) 427-1031
Denmark, 875 N. Michigan	(312) 787-8780
Dominican Republic, 3228 W. North Avenue	(312) 772-6363
France, 737 N. Michigan	(312) 787-5359
Germany, 104 S. Michigan	(312) 263-0850
Greece, 168 N. Michigan	(312) 372-5356
India, 150 N. Michigan	(312) 781-6280
Ireland, 400 N. Michigan	(312) 337-1868
Israel, 111 E. Wacker Drive	(312) 565-3300
Italy, 500 N. Michigan	(312) 467-1550
Japan, 737 N. Michigan	(312) 280-0400
Korea, 500 N. Michigan	(312) 822-9485
Luxembourg, 180 N. LaSalle	(312) 726-0354
Mexico, 300 N. Michigan	(312) 726-3942
Netherlands, 303 E. Wacker Drive	(312) 856-0110
People's Republic of China, 104 S. Michigan	(312) 346-0287
	(312) 346-0288
Peru, 180 N. Michigan	(312) 853-6171
	(312) 782-1599
Philippines, 30 N. Michigan	(312) 332-6458
Poland, 1530 N. Lake Shore Drive	(312) 337-8166
	(312) 642-4102
Commonwealth of Puerto Rico, 233 N. Michigan	(312) 565-0910
Spain, 180 N. Michigan	(312) 782-4588
Sweden, 150 N. Michigan	(312) 781-6262
Switzerland, 737 N. Michigan	(312) 915-0061
Thailand, 35 E. Wacker Drive	(312) 236-2447

Suggested Reading

The following books, essays, and unpublished research papers deal with important aspects of Chicago's neighborhood settlements, and are recommended reading for anyone interested in researching the ethnic history of the city. All of the books are available in the Chicago Public Library's Social Science and History Collection.

Beijbom, Ulf. *Swedes In Chicago: A Demographic & Social Study of the 1846–1880 Immigration.* Stockholm: Laromedelsforlagen, 1971.

Bicha, Karel B. "The Survival of the Village in Urban America: A Note On Czech Immigrants in Chicago To 1914." International Migration reports, vol. 1, Spring 1974, (pp. 72–74).

Fremon, David K. *Chicago Politics Ward By Ward.* Bloomington & Indianapolis: Indiana University Press, 1988.

Heimovics, Rachel Baron. *Chicago Jewish Sourcebook.* Chicago: Follett Publishing Co., 1981.

Hellenism In Chicago. Chicago: United Hellenic American Congress, 1982.

Hispanics In Chicago. The Chicago Reporter and the Center For Community Research and Assistance of the Community Renewal Society, 1985.

Holli, Melvin, and d'A. Jones, Peter. *Ethnic Chicago.* Grand Rapids: William B. Eerdmans Publishers, 1977.

Hofmeister, Rudolf A. *The Germans of Chicago.* Chicago: University of Illinois Press, 1976.

Horowitz, Ruth. *Honor & The American Dream: Culture and Identity In A Chicano Community.* New Brunswick, N.J.: Rutgers University Press, 1983.

Lane, Kerstin B. "Andersonville: A Swedish American Neighborhood Landmark." Unpublished paper.

McCaffrey, Lawrence J., and Fanning, Charles, and Funchion, Michael, and Skerrett, Ellen. *The Irish In Chicago.* Urbana & Chicago: University of Illinois Press, 1987.

Mayer, Harold, and Wade, Richard. *Chicago: Growth of a Metropolis.* Chicago: University of Chicago Press, 1969.

Nelli, Humbert. *Italians In Chicago: 1880–1930.* New York: Oxford University Press, 1970.

Olson, Anita. "North Park: A Study In Community." Covenant Archives & Historical Society, North Park College. Unpublished paper.

Pacyga, Dominic A., and Skerrett, Ellen. *Chicago: A City of Neighborhoods.* Chicago: Loyola University Press, 1986.

Padilla, Felix. *Puerto Rican.* Notre Dame: University of Notre Dame Press, 1987.

Poles of Chicago, 1837–1937. Chicago: Polish Pageant, 1937.

Ropka, Gerald. *The Evolving Residential Patterns of the Mexican, Puerto Rican, & Cuban Population of Chicago.* New York: Arno Press, 1980.

Scamon, Robert A. *Back of the Yards: The Making of a Local Democracy.* Chicago: University of Chicago Press, 1986.

Spear, Allan H. *Black Chicago: The Making of A Negro Ghetto, 1890–1920.* Chicago: University of Chicago Press, 1967.

Strauss, Terry, ed. *Indians of the Chicago Area.* Chicago: NAES College Press, 1990.

Wilson, Margaret Gibbons. "Concentration and Dispersal of the Chinese Population of Chicago, 1870–Present." University of Chicago: Unpublished M.A. thesis, 1969.

Other Books By Richard Lindberg

Stuck On The Sox (1978)

Who's On Third? The Chicago White Sox Story (1983)

The Macmillan White Sox Encyclopedia (1984)

Chicago Ragtime: Another Look at Chicago, 1880–1920 (1985)

To Serve and Collect: Chicago Politics and Police Corruption from the Lager Beer Riot to the Summerdale Scandal (1991)

TRAVEL AND CULTURE BOOKS

"World at Its Best" Travel Series
Britain, France, Germany, Hawaii,
Holland, Hong Kong, Italy, Spain,
Switzerland, London, New York, Paris,
Washington, D.C.

Passport's Travel Guides and References
IHT Guides to Business Travel in Asia &
Europe
New York on $1,000 a Day (Before
Lunch)
London on £1,000 a Day (Before Tea)
Mystery Reader's Walking Guides:
London, England, and New York
Chicago's Best-Kept Secrets
London's Best-Kept Secrets
New York's Best-Kept Secrets
Everything Japanese
Japan Today!
Japan at Night
Japan Made Easy
Discovering Cultural Japan
Living in Mexico
The Hispanic Way
Guide to Ethnic Chicago
Guide to Ethnic London
Guide to Ethnic New York
Passport's Trip Planner & Travel Diary
Chinese Etiquette and Ethics in Business
Korean Etiquette and Ethics in Business
Japanese Etiquette and Ethics in Business
How to Do Business with the Japanese
Japanese Cultural Encounters
The Japanese

Passport's Regional Guides of France
Auvergne, Provence, Loire Valley,
Dordogne, Languedoc, Brittany, South
West France, Normandy & North West
France, Paris, Rhône Valley & Savoy;
France for the Gourmet Traveler

Passport's Regional Guides of Indonesia
New Guinea, Java, Borneo, Bali, East of
Bali, Sumatra, Spice Islands,
Underwater Indonesia, Sulawesi

Up-Close Guides
Paris, London, Manhattan

Passport's "Ticket To..." Series
Italy, Germany, France, Spain

**Passport's Guides: Asia, Africa, Latin
America, Europe**
Japan, Korea, Malaysia, Singapore, Bali,
Burma, Australia, New Zealand, Egypt,
Kenya, Philippines, Portugal, Moscow,
Leningrad, The Georgian Republic,
Mexico

Passport's China Guides
All China; Beijing; Fujian; Guilin,
Canton & Guangdong; Hangzhou &
Zhejiang; Hong Kong; Macau; Nanjing
& Jiangsu; Shanghai; The Silk Road;
Taiwan; Tibet; Xi'an; The Yangzi
River; Yunnan

Passport's India Guides
All India; Bombay and Goa; Dehli, Agra
and Jaipur; Burma; Pakistan;
Kathmandu; Bhutan; Museums of
India; Hill Stations of India

Passport's Thai Guides
Bangkok, Phuket, Chiang Mai, Koh Sumi

On Your Own Series
Brazil, Israel

"Everything Under the Sun" Series
Spain, Barcelona, Toledo, Seville,
Marbella, Cordoba, Granada, Madrid,
Salamanca, Palma de Majorca

Passport's Travel Paks
Britain, France, Italy, Germany, Spain

Exploring Rural Europe Series
England & Wales; France; Greece;
Ireland; Italy; Spain; Austria;
Germany; Scotland

Nagel's Encyclopedia Guides
35 volumes on countries and regions
ranging from Albania to the U.S.S.R.

Passport Maps
Europe; Britain; France; Italy; Holland;
Belgium & Luxembourg; Scandinavia;
Spain & Portugal; Switzerland; Austria
& the Alps

Christmas in Series
France, Mexico, Spain, Germany, Italy

PASSPORT BOOKS
a division of *NTC Publishing Group*
Lincolnwood, Illinois USA